THE WAR LOVERS

THE WAR LOVERS

ROOSEVELT, LODGE, HEARST, AND THE RUSH TO EMPIRE, 1898

EVAN THOMAS

LITTLE, BROWN AND COMPANY
NEW YORK   BOSTON   LONDON

Little, Brown and Company
Hachette Book Group
237 Park Avenue, New York, NY 10017
www.hachettebookgroup.com

First Edition: April 2010

Little, Brown and Company is a division of Hachette Book Group, Inc. The Little, Brown name and logo are trademarks of Hachette Book Group, Inc.

Maps by George W. Ward

Library of Congress Cataloging-in-Publication Data
Thomas, Evan.
    The war lovers : Roosevelt, Lodge, Hearst, and the rush to empire, 1898 / Evan Thomas. — 1st ed.
        p. cm.
    Includes bibliographical references and index.
    ISBN 978-0-316-00409-1
    1. Spanish-American War, 1898 — Causes.   2. United States — Territorial expansion.   3. United States — Politics and government — 1897–1901.   4. Business and politics — United States — History — 19th century.   5. Press and politics — United States — History — 19th century.   6. Roosevelt, Theodore, 1858–1919.   7. Lodge, Henry Cabot, 1850–1924.   8. Hearst, William Randolph, 1863–1951.   9. McKinley, William, 1843–1901.   10. Reed, Thomas B. (Thomas Brackett), 1839–1902.   I. Title.
    E721.T47 2010
    973.8'91 — dc22   2009043616

10 9 8 7 6 5 4 3 2 1

RRD-IN

Printed in the United States of America

To Stephen G. Smith, my friend and a great editor

Contents

CONTENTS

THE WAR
LOVERS

Introduction

April 23, 1950. Beverly Hills, California.

HIS HANDS SHOOK with palsy, and his body was wasting away. A few days shy of his eighty-seventh birthday, William Randolph Hearst had little more than a year to live. He had given up San Simeon, his castle in the California hills, and moved with two dozen servants to a three-story Spanish-style house in Beverly Hills set amid eight acres of gardens and palm trees. Hearst still loved to buy things, and at night he pored over catalogues of art objects and antiques. In between placing orders for Baroque statuary or fifty Arabian horses, he would send cables to his editors in the Hearst empire, dictating what they should print.[1]

Hearst had never been the smooth, ruthless megalomaniac portrayed by Orson Welles in *Citizen Kane*. His charm was quirky, and he could be softhearted to his employees. His papers still had the power to stir people, though they were now seen as overly strident and obsessed with the communist threat. Lately, however, he had been stricken with feelings of remorse, even self-doubt, and he now ordered a cable sent to all Hearst editors:

THE CHIEF INSTRUCTS NOT, REPEAT NOT, TO PRESS
THE CAMPAIGN AGAINST COMMUNISM ANY FURTHER.
HE WISHES THE CAMPAIGN HELD BACK FOR A WHILE,

William Randolph Hearst (Library of Congress)

PARTICULARLY THE EDITORIALS. HE FEELS WE HAVE
BEEN PRESSING THE FIGHT TOO HARD FOR TOO LONG
AND MIGHT BE AROUSING WAR HYSTERIA.[2]

Using newspapers to create war hysteria was a subject Hearst
knew something about.

July 1, 1898. Outside Santiago, Cuba.

The thirty-five-year-old newspaper editor and publisher liked to
think that the War Against Spain was *his* war—that he had created it. This was an exaggeration, though not entirely. For more
than two years William Randolph Hearst had campaigned for

an American invasion to liberate the Cuban people from Spanish rule. Not much concerned with proof, his paper, the New York *Journal*, had blamed the sinking of the American battleship USS *Maine* on a Spanish plot. When war was declared, Hearst had devoted the full resources of the *Journal* to covering the American invasion of Cuba. He had dispatched more than a score of reporters, chartered a fleet of a dozen ships, and transported a printing press, a hot-air balloon, and the first motion-picture camera ever to film a war. And, too restless to sit back in New York, he had come to Cuba to see the battle firsthand, arriving in yachting clothes and accompanied by a pair of showgirls.[3]

Gangly and bug-eyed, Hearst was almost painfully shy and stiff in public. But he was ecstatic about his work, which he described as "the journalism that acts."[4] He gloried in headlines that were bigger, louder, lustier. Dressed in the evening clothes he'd worn to the theater, he would sweep into the *Journal*'s newsroom after midnight, ordering up stories that would shock, entertain, and remind readers of the long reach of W. R. Hearst.

On the day of the decisive battle, he went ashore before dawn. He put on a scarlet red tie (matching his scarlet hatband), tucked a pistol in his belt, then mounted a mule and headed with his entourage for the front lines.[5]

Not far from Hearst, waiting impatiently on a Cuban hillside teeming with troops, Theodore Roosevelt prepared himself for what he would call his "crowded hour."[6] It was a day he would always regard as the finest of his life.

Roosevelt was "pure act," according to his friend Henry Adams.[7] Roosevelt liked to boast that he was "fit as a bull moose," though at age thirty-nine his muscles were beginning to run to fat.[8] He had abandoned a position as assistant secretary of the

Theodore Roosevelt (Library of Congress)

navy to seek combat as a cavalry officer. When he had joined the army in May, the odds were greater that he would die of tropical fever than become a war hero. At the time his friends feared that he was delusional. His wife and eldest son had been seriously ill but, as Roosevelt would later confess, he would have deserted his wife's deathbed to go into battle.[9] He wanted to become a legend, and he made sure to keep newsmen nearby to tell the tale, including a reporter from Hearst's paper, even though he personally disdained Hearst.

On this hot July morning he took his blue polka-dot handkerchief and tied it to his felt cowboy hat, so it could shield his neck from the sun—but with the effect that the bandana streamed out behind him. (Like Hearst, Roosevelt was a dandy.) As he

Henry Cabot Lodge (Library of Congress)

rode forth on his horse, Little Texas, toward the Spanish-held ridgeline known as the San Juan Heights, the kerchief made Roosevelt a target, yet he did not dwell on mortal danger; he wished to be seen leading the charge.[10]

In Washington, D.C., on that warm July day Roosevelt's best friend and chief political adviser, Henry Cabot Lodge, waited anxiously for news of the battle. In a room in the southwest corner of the White House, President William McKinley and top officials of the Navy and War Departments studied maps plotting troop movements and waited for messages coming in by telegraph or a new contraption, the telephone.[11] Senator Lodge of Massachusetts was a familiar figure at the White House. He was the president's closest national security and foreign policy adviser from Capitol Hill. More than anyone, he was responsible for America's sudden (if somewhat accidental) emergence as an expansionist power.

Several times during the day the senator rode by carriage from his mansion on Massachusetts Avenue to the White House War Room to check for any word from the front. Natty, thin, haughty, the forty-eight-year-old Lodge could be a forbidding figure—a cold snob in the view of many of his colleagues. Among his intimates, only his friend Theodore regarded him as sensitive and warm, full of "big boyish" enthusiasm.[12] Lodge had stage-managed Roosevelt's career, and the two men shared a love of what Roosevelt called "Americanism"—a faith in the national spirit, which both men took to be brave, adventurous, warlike. But Lodge had opposed Roosevelt's decision to join the Rough Riders, and on this morning, as Washington awaited word of the attack on the Spanish fortifications, Lodge was seized with a mixture of excitement and dread. He revealed no feelings behind his severe Brahmin mask, confiding his fears ("almost unbearable") only in letters to his mother and his friend Roosevelt.[13]

Down Pennsylvania Avenue from the White House, in his book-lined rooms on the fourth floor of the old Shoreham Hotel, Thomas Brackett Reed was quietly brooding. A vast man, nearly three hundred pounds of smooth flesh, the fifty-eight-year-old Reed was known as "the Czar." His serene countenance was sometimes compared to Buddha's, though his wit could be vicious. When a congressman, quoting Henry Clay, announced that he would "rather be right than be President," Reed replied, "Well, the gentleman will never be either."[14] As Speaker of the

Thomas Brackett Reed (Library of Congress)

House, he was regarded as the second most powerful man in the nation and an obvious candidate for the presidency. He joked about the talk of his securing the Republican nomination in 1896. "They could do worse," he said with his dry Maine drawl, "and probably will."[15] When McKinley won the post, Reed had been severely disappointed.

Reed's campaign advisers had been Theodore Roosevelt and Henry Cabot Lodge. The three men shared a contempt for machine politics and mushy reformers (called "mugwumps" or "goo-goos"). The trio was highly literate, bound by a love of poetry and history, and, in their individual ways, romantic. They routinely delighted in each other in their extensive correspondence. But their friendship had fallen apart over the fundamental question of America's future. Lodge and Roosevelt believed that America had to expand and seize new territories or lose its vital frontier spirit. Speaker Reed was wary of such talk; he distrusted the temptations of war and conquest.

Reed's reticence about America's manifest destiny made him a man out of his time in 1898. When he tried unsuccessfully to block America's intervention in Cuba as well as the annexation of Hawaii and the Philippines, he was marginalized and ultimately cast aside. In late June he was absent from Congress, reportedly because he was ill, though sick at heart is more like it. In July, as Congress entered its last week before summer recess, Reed pretended to be carefree with the occasional reporter who still sought him out, but he was bitter over what he saw as a betrayal of America's founding principles.

As evening fell on July 1, William James watched the moon rise over Mount Marcy, in the faraway Adirondack Mountains of upstate New York. He had been worrying about the progress of the war he had come to oppose, but he tried not to dwell on it. "I have felt extraordinarily well," he wrote his wife, Alice. He had gone to the mountains seeking relief from the insomnia, backaches, indigestion, and "nerves" that routinely plagued him. James's neurotic symptoms were not unusual for men of his time and class. The late 1890s were robust years—the "Gay Nineties"—a time of flag-waving boosterism about America's national identity, bolstered by a Darwinian faith in the Anglo-Saxon "race." Still, many in the Ivy League precincts suffered from ennui and worried about their manliness. James, like his former student at Harvard, Theodore Roosevelt, sought refuge and meaning by exploring the frontier. But while he admired men like Roosevelt who thrust themselves into the arena, James's

William James (Houghton Library, Harvard University)

own explorations were more often of the mind. He sought to understand why men fought—and what was worth fighting for.

At fifty-six, Professor James of Harvard was known as the nation's leading philosopher and psychologist. He well understood the appeal of war. During the Civil War he had seen the Union soldiers marching off sure of glory, and when the War on Spain was declared in late April 1898, James had—for a brief moment—wondered whether war would have a regenerating effect on the American soul.

He knew better. He understood that war, while sometimes necessary and unavoidable, could be a bitch goddess, a seductress of young men and old fools, particularly the kind who had never experienced her savage embrace. James praised (and envied) the courage men showed in battle, and he saw war lust as natural to the human condition. But he believed this was a drive to be understood but resisted, or at least channeled toward higher callings. When Roosevelt was hailed everywhere as a war hero, James wrote in a letter published in a Boston newspaper that Roosevelt "is still mentally in the *Sturm und Drang* period of early adolescence."[16] James had a vivid, pungent way of putting things; he feared, for instance, that by embracing a policy of foreign conquest, America was "puking up" her cherished principles of self-determination.[17] In his writings and teachings, he became a kind of Greek chorus on the American stage, warning against the temptations of hubris. But in the summer of 1898, he was a voice crying in the wilderness.

The Spanish-American War is little remembered now. But more than the Civil War or World War II, it was a harbinger, if not the model, of modern American wars. It has some eerie parallels to the invasion of Iraq, another "war of choice" not immediately vital to the national security but ostensibly waged for broader and sometimes shifting humanitarian reasons. Just as the threat of weapons of mass destruction turned out to be bogus in Iraq, the sinking of the *Maine* — the pretext for intervention — was caused not by a Spanish plot but rather almost certainly by a shipboard accident. The War Against Spain began as a "splendid little war," as diplomat John Hay wrote Roosevelt after the Spanish were defeated in Cuba, but the conflict turned dangerous and ugly after the liberation of the Philippines from Spain. The United States plunged into a counterinsurgency that cost over four thousand American lives between 1898 and 1902, roughly the same death toll the nation suffered in Iraq between 2003 and 2009. To extract intelligence from the rebels, American soldiers pioneered the torture known as waterboarding—one of several inhumane American practices used against Filipinos.[18]

Scholars have described the Spanish-American War variously as a blow for empire; as an act of economic aggression; as a bid for post–Civil War reconciliation; as the expression of gender insecurity; and as a kind of national psychic outburst. To different degrees, all of those forces came into play. But what interests me is the human dynamic—the eternal pull of war on men. I have chosen to tell the story through five central figures—three hawks and two doves—a media mogul, two war-loving national politicians, a lawmaker who tried to stop them, and a public intellectual who sought to understand and explain it all.

My narrative spans the years of America's war fever from 1895 to 1899. But I pick up the story of man's love for war a half century earlier, with the fantasies of a rich boy in a house on a hill, and I end it on Omaha Beach on D-day, June 6, 1944. As in any book, there must be a conclusion, but the story is never ending.

1

Dreaming of Father

"Are me a soldier laddie too?"

NEAR THE TOP of Beacon Hill in Boston—John Winthrop's shining "city on a hill"—down the block from Charles Bulfinch's gold-domed statehouse, is 31 Beacon Street, the house where Henry Cabot Lodge grew up. "The sunny street that holds the sifted few," in the description of Oliver Wendell Holmes, Sr., Beacon Street runs along the south slope, overlooking the Boston Common. Number 31 is a graceful redbrick mansion known as a "swell front" for its bay windows. Inside, on a rainy day in 1860, one would find a butler, a footman, a valet, a cook, a second cook, a housemaid, a parlor maid, and a ladies' maid, possibly Mr. and Mrs. Lodge, and, in the library, "wander[ing]," as he later described himself, their only son, ten-year-old Henry Cabot.[1] Within the light, high-ceilinged rooms was practiced a discreet form of ancestor worship. In the "world of Boston," by which he meant upper-class Boston, "everybody knew everybody else and all about everybody else's family. Most people were related...," wrote Lodge in his memoir, *Early Days*, the first chapter of which is entitled "Heredity."[2]

Cabot (never Henry) was a frail boy and, though he tried, never very adept at games, he recalled. He was more at home

15

Lodge at about age ten (Courtesy of the Massachusetts Historical Society)

among the books collected by his father and grandfather, reading tales of chivalry and derring-do. His father was his guide. "He was a lover of [Sir Walter] Scott, and in my tenth year I read all the Waverly Novels from beginning to end," Lodge wrote. Pulling volumes from the high shelves, the youngster entered the world of the hunter-warrior, both make-believe and real— Scott's *Ivanhoe*, Cervantes' *Don Quixote*, Macauley's histories, the *Odyssey* and the *Iliad*. He read the Bible, too, but more for the histories, "full of fighting and of battle, murder and sudden death," than for religion.[3]

Beacon Street was an oasis of gentility in a city seething with poor newcomers. The shaded north side of Beacon Hill, where the freed Negro slaves lived, was sometimes called "Nigger Hill" or "Mount Whoredom," for its prostitutes.[4] The mass migration of poor Irish to Boston after the potato famines of the 1840s was regarded as a threat—economic, political, physical—to the sifted few. Class warfare erupted on a regular basis in the form of snowball fights. On the frozen Common, surging up from the overflowing slums in the South and North Ends, young Irish toughs and blackguards—"whom we called 'muckers,'" related Lodge—would charge the swells who lived on Beacon Hill. Young gentlemen in wool mufflers and Eton collars would fire icy projectiles, then engage in hand-to-hand combat against bigger, more brutish boys (at least they looked that way) in thin shabby coats. Insults were exchanged, but never conversation.[5]

Henry Adams, another young Brahmin who ventured out against the muckers, recalled a "grisly terror called Conky Daniels" who came armed "with a club and a hideous reputation." In his memoir, *The Education of Henry Adams,* he recalled the viciousness of the battles: "A stone may be put in a snowball, and in the dark, a stick or a slungshot...is as effective as a knife." One stone struck Henry Lee Higginson, known to his schoolmates as "Bully Higg," later a rich banker who donated to Harvard its playing fields. On the Common that day, Adams reported, Higginson was "led off the field bleeding in a rather ghastly manner." In the daytime the rich boys from the Hill had home-ground advantage: they could stockpile frozen ice balls and carry them from their houses in picnic baskets. But as dusk fell the Irish toughs generally carried the field, the rich boys "dwindling in numbers and disappearing," recalled Adams.[6] In his memoir Lodge described the battles as "Homeric" and "savage." One can imagine the ten-year-old Lodge, a slip of a boy with a pointy chin, dressed in his mittens by his nanny, desperately trying to find the courage not to run from the muckers. But writing in 1912, when he was sixty-two, he was all brio. He conceded defeat in those class-struggle snowball fights "owing purely to superior numbers, as I have always religiously believed."[7]

A month before Lodge's eleventh birthday real war broke out. The great conflict that would divide the nation and in many ways shape young Lodge was initially greeted with mixed emotions by the denizens of Beacon Hill. In the 1850s the wealthy merchants of Boston sympathized with the Southern planters who sold them cotton. (When a few young radicals broke off from the Somerset Club to form the Union Club, the Somerset members made jokes about the "Sambo Club.")[8] But Fort Sumter and war fever soon changed upper-class hearts and minds. As patriotism and dreams of glory swept away mercantile and brotherly bonds, even Ralph Waldo Emerson, heretofore a Christian pacifist, announced, "Sometimes gun powder smells good."[9] Lodge's father had always stood above mere commerce; he had long been a "Free Soiler" and had once bought a slave in order to set him free.[10] At 31 Beacon Street the Union cause was sacred.

Lodge loved his father as "the kindest and most generous of men," who never spoke a harsh word, except to correct his only son when he displayed "either physical or moral timidity." Most of all Cabot admired his father's courage. Writing in reverent, almost mystical tones, he recalled witnessing his father scuffle with two muggers, one armed with a knife, one winter's night "as we were going to the theatre, at a dark place on the Common": "I can see the shine of the distant gas light on the new-fallen snow, the sudden collision of the two men with my father, then one of them on his back in the white drift with something glittering in his hand. Then we were walking quietly along again, and I have no recollection of either fright or excitement. My faith in my father was too great to admit such emotion."[11]

Lodge proudly wrote that with the coming of the Civil War, his father hoped to ride at the head of a cavalry regiment "which he wished to raise himself." But the senior Lodge missed his chance at glory. His son blamed old age (his father had just turned forty) and a weak knee caused by a riding injury, but one senses his deep disappointment—and then his shock when, "in September 1862, my father, worn out and broken down nervously by too much work, too many cares, and too many responsibilities, died suddenly."[12]

Lodge was left alone at 31 Beacon Street with his sister and his mother, Anna, a strong-willed, demanding woman who would be a central force in his life until she died in 1900 at age seventy-nine. The war remained a constant presence; "it overshadowed everything," Lodge recalled. He attended the funeral of a soldier killed in the war, the older brother of a schoolmate, and never forgot the sight of the young body clad in Union blue stretched out in the casket. In the parlor of 31 Beacon Street he listened as a young cousin of his mother—Oliver Wendell Holmes, Jr.—described his experiences at the front, the horror and glory of charging enemy lines, of getting shot (three times in Holmes's case).[13]

On May 28, 1863, Lodge witnessed one of Boston's proudest moments. A favorite son of the Brahmin class, Robert Gould Shaw, was leading the first African American regiment, the four hundred men of the Massachusetts Fifty-fourth, through the city. The black men were hooted at by some and at one point attacked by Irish toughs who threw stones and started fistfights. But most of the thousands of Bostonians lining the streets on that bright May morning were moved by the sight of proud black men marching to battle so that their brothers might be set free. A few in the crowds tossed flowers at the slender, blond young man at their head. Riding his charger, Colonel Shaw led the long column up Beacon Street. Shaw's family lived at 44 Beacon Street, a few doors down from the Lodge mansion. When his column — flags flying, drums beating — reached number 44, Shaw stopped his horse. Looking up at his family, he raised his sword, the terrible swift sword of God's truth, to his lips. Then he rode on, past the gaping young Lodge, who never forgot.[14]

As the soldiers marched off to war and not all returned, Lodge indulged in reveries of bravery and heroism. He wanted to enlist as a drummer boy, a suggestion that was "not taken in either a favorable or even a serious spirit by my family." Drifting off to sleep at night, he "imagined desperate assaults and gallant exploits, from which I always escaped alive and glorious."[15]

For Theodore Roosevelt, eight years younger than Lodge, war was at first a game of dress-up. Little Theodore, or "Teedie," as he was called, was a lifelong fop, and at the age of four he fancied the brightly colored uniforms of the Zouaves, a Union regiment that went off to war in turbans and red pantaloons (until smokeless gunpowder cleared the air of the battlefield and made soldiers wish to dress as inconspicuously as possible). Little Teedie insisted on being outfitted in a tiny Zouaves uniform and asked, "Are me a soldier laddie too?"[16]

There is a photograph of a scene that made as profound an impression on young Roosevelt as Colonel Shaw's march up Beacon Hill made on the young Lodge. Taken on April 24, 1865, the day Lincoln's body was carried through the streets of New York, the photo shows the slain president's cortege making its way into Union Square past a large mansion on the left. The house, one of the grandest in New York at the time, belonged to Theodore Roosevelt's wealthy grandfather, Cornelius. In a window on the

Theodore and Elliott Roosevelt, the two small heads in the window on the second story of their grandfather's house on Union Square, watch Lincoln's funeral procession. (Theodore Roosevelt Collection, Houghton Library, Harvard University)

second floor, two small boys peer out. One is Theodore, age six and a half, the other is his brother Elliott, five. The president's coffin is followed by the Invalid Brigade, a column of veterans who had lost limbs in the war. Little Edith Carow was visiting the Roosevelts that day, and she recalled that she had been overcome with grief at the sight of the grievously wounded men.

She had begun to cry. Irritated, young Theodore had shoved his future wife, who was not yet four, into a back room.[17]

Theodore was fascinated by the maimed veterans. All his life he would venerate "the empty sleeve," the mark of a man who had sacrificed a limb in battle. When he had asthma attacks, his mother wrote his older sister that little Theodore would "dress up in rags to imitate a soldier" whose uniform had been shredded in battle.[18]

When the Civil War came, Roosevelt's father, Theodore Senior, was only twenty-nine years old. Like many of his social class among the New York Knickerbockers, he bought an exemption from the draft, hiring two substitutes for three hundred dollars each. According to his daughters, he was deferring to the wishes of his Southern-born wife, Mittie, whose family was fighting for Dixie. "Mother was very frail, and felt it would kill her for him to fight against her brothers," recalled the eldest Roosevelt daughter, Anna (known as "Bamie," or "Bye").[19] In later years it became conventional wisdom among the Roosevelt women — Bamie; her younger sister, Corinne; and Roosevelt's eldest daughter, Alice — that Roosevelt was deeply affected by the sense of shame, unacknowledged and perhaps inadmissible, that he felt about his father ducking a soldier's duty in the Civil War. "He felt he had to explain it always, about the father he admired so hugely," said one of TR's nieces in an oral history. "He subconsciously felt that it was a spot on his father that had to be erased by him."[20]

At the time, Theodore Senior felt guilty about hiring a substitute. "He always afterward felt that he had done a very great wrong in not having put every feeling aside and joined the fighting forces," said one of his daughters. He spent most of the first two years of the war away from home, helping soldiers get medical attention and stay in touch with their families, and, when they died, bringing their bodies home. Roosevelt Senior possessed what he called a "troublesome conscience."[21] He was a "muscular Christian" who believed that he had a duty to do good, to use his wealth and position to aid the less fortunate. He helped create the Children's Aid Society and the Newsboys' Lodging House (where he spent every Sunday night with the often poor and familyless boys), as well as a hospital, the American Museum of Natural History, and, with John Pierpont Morgan, the Metropolitan Museum of Art.

One of his closest colleagues in the New York charitable world was a young woman named Josephine Shaw Lowell. Many years later, when Mrs. Lowell was known as the "City's Saint" for her good works, she tried to act as a social conscience to Governor, then President, Theodore Roosevelt. He dutifully wrote her to say that he hoped to live up to his father's example of civic duty, but he seems to have regarded her as a bit of a nag.[22] As a boy, however, he saw her differently—as a gravely handsome young widow dressed in black, telling in her gently thrilling voice tales of martyrdom in war.

"Effie," as she was called, was the daughter of wealthy Boston Brahmins who had become transcendentalists, believers in a utopia of virtue. She was still a teenage girl, though a very precocious one, when the Civil War broke out, and the struggle enthralled her. She hoped that sacrifice for such a noble cause, the freeing of the slaves, would purify the country. Deciding that she would make a good soldier, she wrote in her diary, "for I am not an atom afraid of death and the enthusiasm of the moment would be sublime." To her family, sacrifice for goodness' sake was sublime. Her parents had been overjoyed when their sunny, golden-haired son, Robert Gould Shaw, was chosen to lead the

Union army's first black regiment. A staunch foe of slavery, he took the commission despite the still strong prejudice against blacks in polite Boston society because he felt it would be cowardly not to.

Effie had been on the balcony when her older brother—whom she called Rob—stopped his horse to kiss his sword before 44 Beacon Street, a few doors from the Lodge mansion where young Cabot had stood wide-eyed at the window. Missing her brother, she wrote him that she wished he could sustain a small wound so he could come home. "I am much obliged to you, for wishing me a wound," he wrote back, amused. "Is there any other little favor, I could do for you?" In July 1863 Colonel Shaw was ordered to attack a Confederate redoubt, Fort Wagner, on the South Carolina coast. Leading the charge under heavy fire, he was killed as he mounted the parapet. The Confederate commander was quoted as saying that he would have given Shaw a proper military burial had he fought with white troops, but as it was, he would bury him in a common grave (he was later misquoted as saying "with his niggers"). Shaw's father, Frank, resisted efforts to recover the body from its mass grave with his son's black soldiers. Years later the poet Robert Lowell would write:

> Shaw's father wanted no monument
> except the ditch, where his son's body was thrown
> and lost with his 'niggers.'[23]

At nineteen, Effie had married another doomed hero, Charles Russell Lowell, her teenage sweetheart who became one of the Union's most celebrated cavalry commanders. Lowell had thirteen horses shot out from under him without sustaining a scratch.

Finally wounded at the Battle of Cedar Creek in October 1864, he had insisted on mounting his horse for one last, fatal charge.

The widow Lowell dressed in black and began mailing friends copies of *Harvard Memorial Biographies*, detailing how her brother and husband had died. For a short time she was depressed and made her bedroom into a campsite shrine, with her blanket on the floor and pictures of her dead husband everywhere. Then she transformed private grief into public duty. Dressed in her widow's weeds — she wore black for the rest of her life — Effie plunged into social work, often working side by side with Theodore Roosevelt, Sr., in the effort to help Union soldiers and then, after the war, to keep New York's charities from being exploited by the city's political machine. Thus, during and after the war she came to be a regular visitor in the Roosevelt home. She was shy and slight, with light hair and blue eyes; her distinguishing feature was her voice — "low, vibrant, and enormously compelling," according to her husband's biographer, Carol Bundy. It is likely that little Teedie first heard of the legends of Robert Gould Shaw and Charles Russell Lowell from their grieving and fiercely proud sister and widow.[24]

Teedie, who was small and sickly, prone to gasping asthma attacks, worshipped his warm and civic-minded father. His attempts to banish a sissyish self-image and win his father's respect were epic, including daily weightlifting and climbing the Matterhorn before he turned fifteen. As a fourteen-year-old, in 1873 he wrote his father describing a boxing match he had fought with his cousin John Elliott while visiting Germany:

After some striking and warding, I got Johnie into a corner, when he sprung out. We each warded off a right hand blow and brought in a left hander. His took effect behind my ear, and for

a minute I saw stars and reeled back to the centre of the room,
while Johnie had his nose and upper lip mashed together and
been driven back against the door. I was so weak however that I
was driven across the room, simply warding off blows, but then
I almost disabled his left arm, and drove him back to the middle,
where some sharp boxing occurred. I got in one on his forehead
which raised a bump, but my eye was made black and blue.[25]

And so on, the blacker and bluer the better. "If you offered rewards for bloody noses you would spend a fortune on me alone," Theodore Junior proudly wrote his father.[26] On his European tour, Roosevelt was fascinated by dueling German students, especially one known as Herr Nasehorn (Sir Rhinoceros) because the tip of his nose had been sliced off in a duel and sewn on again. The physical training was matched with the intellectual: Roosevelt memorized Longfellow's *Saga of Olaf* and read and reread the *Nibelungenlied*, reveling in the prowess of Norse gods and men whom Roosevelt regarded, in some misty way, as his Viking forebears.[27]

In 1878, in the winter of Theodore's sophomore year at Harvard, his father died. The cause was metastatic colon cancer, but in Roosevelt's mind his father had been fatally weakened by a foray into the treacherous world of politics. A would-be reformer, Theodore Senior was appointed by President Rutherford B. Hayes to clean up the corrupt Customs House of New York, but he was thwarted and publicly embarrassed by the machine of Roscoe "Boss" Conkling and made to appear a naive pawn in a game played by political professionals. A swaggering womanizer, Conkling made clear that regular politicians were manly, while gentlemen reformers were not, a message not lost on the younger Roosevelt.[28]

Teddy Roosevelt at Harvard (Theodore Roosevelt Collection, Houghton Library, Harvard University)

Rushing home from college, Roosevelt arrived too late to say good-bye to his father, who died screaming in agony from a stomach tumor. In February Roosevelt wrote his Harvard friend Hal Minot, "It is almost impossible to realize I shall never see Father again; these last few days seem like a hideous dream."[29]

By that summer a tormented Roosevelt struggled with his conviction that he would never live up to the example of his father's moral and physical strength—while burning with a less conscious desire to outdo him. The family believed that Theodore Senior had been weakened by an overly ambitious hiking expedition six months before he died. The summer of 1878 found his nineteen-year-old son furiously riding his horse and rowing his little boat about Long Island Sound, complaining of attacks of cholera morbus (his family's melodramatic term for nervous diarrhea) but relentlessly pushing himself.

Roosevelt had named the rowboat the *Edith*, after Edith Carow, an attractive, bookish, quietly formidable friend of his sisters—the playmate little Teedie had stuffed in the back room when Lincoln's cortege passed by. He found her "very pretty," he wrote his sister Bamie, "when she dresses well and don't frizzle her hair," and he began courting her, taking her rowing and sailing every day. Then, in late August, meeting alone in the "summer house" of Tranquility, the estate his family rented in Oyster Bay, a quiet hamlet on the verdant north shore of Long Island, the two quarreled and broke up. In a highly agitated state, Roosevelt nearly rode his horse to death, and when a neighbor's dog barked at him, he took out a pistol and shot it.[30]

He returned to Harvard in September full of determination to honor his father. "For the next two years, my duty is clear—to study well and live like a brave Christian gentleman," he wrote in his diary. But he was soon distracted by the pleasures of club life. At the top of Harvard's social hierarchy, in which students were ranked with some precision, stood the Porcellian Club, an organization of some twenty members who dined and drank together (the latter prodigiously). Bruising some feelings and showing a sense of expediency that would have raised his father's eyebrow, he accepted membership in one club, the A.D., then renounced it to join the Porcellian.[31] Roosevelt was not an obvious choice for the "P.C." Well-born boys were supposed to be "chill and genteel," as his clubmate Owen Wister put it; they affected "a cult of indifference."[32] Roosevelt was far too enthusiastic.

"Of course I spend a good deal of my spare time up in the Porcellian Club, which is great fun," Roosevelt proudly wrote his sister Corinne in early November, a month after joining. "I am going to cut Sunday School today, for the second time this year."[33] Though as a somewhat priggish freshman Roosevelt had disdained the college swells, he became one. "Please send my silk hat *at once*," he instructed his mother in a letter written on Porcellian stationery. "Why has it not come before?"[34]

In October, just as he was joining the Porcellian, he began courting Alice Lee, a prize girl—sunny, flirtatious, athletic, golden haired, a princess with a pert upturned nose. She shared bloodlines with most of upper-crust Boston (a distant cousin was Henry Cabot Lodge).[35] Roosevelt was an ardent suitor who may have seemed a little overwhelming to a seventeen-year-old girl. He pressed; she drew back, though never so far that he gave up. Finally, in the winter of 1880, as Roosevelt neared graduation, she accepted his hand. By April he was crowing about "my sweet, laughing, teasing little queen," though he confided to his cousin John (the same "Johnie" he had battered in the boxing ring), "The little witch led me a dance before she surrendered, I can tell you." He was so worried about rivals that he sent off to Europe for dueling pistols.[36]

In the years after the Civil War, gentlemen generally did not seek public office. Governments, particularly in municipalities run by political machines like New York's Tammany Hall, were considered corrupt (which they were) and degrading. Roosevelt was warned, he wrote in his autobiography, that politics were "low," the province of "saloon-keepers, horse-car conductors, and the like."[37] But a few earnest patricians like Roosevelt's father were expected to do their duty and offer proposals for reform, even if no one expected much good to come of them. In 1881, at the age of twenty-two, Roosevelt accepted the Republican nomination for the New York State Assembly. "Too true! Too true! I have become a 'political hack,'" he wrote a wellborn friend.[38] He was being uncharacteristically arch. He had a deep purpose, half recognized—to stand up to the pols who had defeated his father and, possibly, to succeed where his father had failed.

Ever a fancy dresser, Roosevelt made the mistake of appearing on the Assembly floor wearing a purple satin waistcoat and speaking a society drawl. Mocked as a "Jane Dandy" and "Oscar Wilde," Roosevelt did not flinch.[39] Hearing of a plan to humiliate the new "dude" by tossing him in a blanket, he marched up to "Big John" McManus, an ex-prizefighter and Tammany lieutenant, and hissed, "By God, if you try anything like that, I'll kick you, I'll bite you, I'll kick you in the balls. I'll do anything to you—you'd better leave me alone." McManus did.[40]

2

The Noble Hacks

"Black care rarely sits behind a rider whose pace is fast enough."

OOSEVELT AND LODGE, nine years apart at Harvard, had
met, casually and briefly, in the rooms of the Porcellian
Club on the days of commencements and football games.[1]
Both were scholars—Roosevelt had written a naval history of
the War of 1812, while Lodge was one of the first three PhDs
awarded at Harvard, in "Anglo Saxon" history—and both had
taken the road less traveled as gentlemen politicians. Lodge was,
in his way, as tough-minded as Roosevelt. As a Massachusetts
state legislator, he had shrugged off the mockery of less well-
born politicians, learned to ask for Irish votes, and made peace
with interest groups like the liquor lobby. He was known as "the
Dude of Nahant" (the site of Lodge's summer home, just north
of Boston), but according to the New York *Tribune*, "[he] is
the gentleman and scholar in politics without the guilelessness
and squeamishness of the said gentleman and scholar."[2] Like
Roosevelt, Lodge was chosen to attend the 1884 Republican
National Convention to be held in Chicago in June. That April
he wrote his mother, "I hate political conventions & political
fights & yet these last are the most important part of politics."[3]

In mid-May Roosevelt invited Lodge to his home in New York

to discuss their shared interest in reform—that is, reform within the realm of real-world politics. Lodge arrived at Roosevelt's house at 6 West Fifty-seventh Street to find a depressing scene. With fourteen-foot-high ceilings and heavy Victorian furniture, the house was grand, but gloomy and barren. Packing crates lay about. Roosevelt explained that the house was "breaking up," being prepared for sale. He did not say much, if anything, about the tragedy that had befallen him three months earlier, on a foggy winter's day in February.

Roosevelt had been on the floor of the Assembly when word reached him that he had become the father of a baby girl named Alice. Then came a second telegram: his young wife was very sick—and so was his mother. Roosevelt took the long, agonizing train ride down the Hudson, arriving near midnight. His mother succumbed to typhoid at 3:00 a.m.; his wife died in his arms early the next afternoon. "The light has gone out of my life," Roosevelt wrote in his diary before returning to Albany to plunge back into political work.[4]

Deprived of his family, Roosevelt seems to have virtually adopted Lodge, almost on the spot.[5] They were kindred spirits, fellow gentlemen adventurers in a rough sport. Roosevelt was lonely and though he would never admit it, needy; he seems to have instantly recognized Lodge as the big brother, adviser, and father figure he longed for. Salutations of "Dear Mr. Lodge" quickly became "my dear Lodge," then "old fellow," and by the time the two men arrived in Chicago on May 31, they were joined in resolve to take on the machine—without showing the characteristic timidity of gentlemen reformers.[6]

The press made fun of them. The "rather dudish Roosevelt" and the "properly English" Lodge "applauded with the tips of their fingers, held immediately in front of their noses," wrote one reporter, exaggerating for effect. At first their voices were barely heard—Lodge's "rasping" Brahmin accent, Roosevelt "shaking with the effort" to shout above the roar.[7] Nevertheless, the two were far from impotent. Playing the role of upstart reformers, they managed to unseat the party regulars' choice for convention chairman—a "spoilsman" named Powell Clayton—and replace him with John R. Lynch, an honorable congressman from Mississippi. Reconstruction was not quite dead yet, and Lodge was true to his father on the emancipation of the black race; Lynch was a black man. But, inevitably, the reformers were crushed. Tom Platt, the "boss" of Albany (and later TR's nemesis), was handing out "boodle"—bundles of cash—to delegates to win their votes for James G. Blaine, the magnetic, boozy, corrupt "Plumed Knight" of the GOP.[8]

The aftermath of the convention was a moment of truth for Lodge and Roosevelt, a test that sealed their friendship. A "boodler" like Blaine—oozing false sincerity—was too much for most gentlemen reformers to stomach. Young Roosevelt had come to Chicago on a private railway car with his father's friend, George William Curtis, a white-whiskered champion of civil service reform.[9] A righteous gentleman like Curtis would have nothing to do with a slippery character like Blaine. Rather than soil themselves, the "goo-goos"—the good government goody-goodies—abandoned the party and sat out the election or cast their votes for the Democratic nominee, Grover Cleveland. But not Lodge and Roosevelt.

In the days and weeks after the 1884 convention, it seemed to Lodge and Roosevelt that they had only each other to trust and confide in. On a warm night in June the two young men sat on the porch of Lodge's house in Nahant, staring out to sea. The next morning Roosevelt told reporters: "I intend to vote for the Republican presidential ticket. While at Chicago, I told Mr. Lodge that such was my intention.... A man cannot act both without and within the party; he can do either, but he cannot possibly do both." Democracy had spoken, they argued, and Blaine had won the votes of the delegates. Besides, Lodge wanted to run for Congress, and if he crossed the party regulars, he was finished. Realism had trumped idealism.

Lodge would pay a heavy social price for his decision. In proper Boston, childhood friends cut him off; older couples crossed Beacon Street to avoid him. He was chin up, but wounded. Boston society saw Lodge not only as a hack but as having led young Roosevelt astray. Typical was the remark overheard by their Porcellian brother Owen Wister. As a bored young clerk blearily calculating interest in a bank vault, Wister heard the boss of the bank, Henry Lee, telling his cousin George Lee of his disappointment in Roosevelt (in the tiny world of upper-crust Boston, George Lee was the father of Theodore's recently deceased wife) and his contempt for Lodge. "As for Cabot Lodge, nobody's surprised by *him*," hissed Henry to his cousin. "But you can tell that young whippersnapper in New York from me that his independence was the only thing in him we cared for; and if he has gone back on that, we don't care to hear anything more about him." As Wister heard the two codgers grumble, it seemed that Lodge, in the mind of Old Boston at any rate, had become Roosevelt's "evil genius."[10] Finally elected to Congress in 1886 (after defeat in 1884), Lodge ran into William Endicott, son of an old Boston family, who was living in Washington, and Endicott reminded him that he was expected to dinner the next day. Lodge's voice was choking with emotion when he replied, "It is very kind of your father and mother to ask us to dinner. People in Boston would not do that."[11]

Roosevelt had seemed to waver for a moment after Blaine was

nominated, but he was able to jokingly write Lodge, "Most of my friends seem surprised to find that I have not developed hoofs and horns."[12] Then the widower headed west to hunt big game. "Black care," he wrote, "rarely sits behind a rider whose pace is fast enough."[13]

Roosevelt was Lodge's best friend—and in some real way, his only one. Lodge seemed to most of his colleagues to embody Brahmin coldness and snobbery. As a congressman in the 1880s he had been nicknamed "Lah-di-dah Lodge." Stiff, thin, his tailored coats tightly buttoned, he was no backslapper; his hand, if extended, was quickly withdrawn. His grating, high-pitched voice was once compared to the "tearing of a bed sheet." As a campaign orator he was "the worst stump speaker on this planet," according to the senior senator from Massachusetts, George Hoar.[14] Lodge was perceived to be so chilly that at the 1884 Republican convention delegates had turned their collars up as he approached and pretended to shiver.[15]

Lodge lived in a mansion on Massachusetts Avenue in Washington with a stable of horses and a well-stocked and much-loved library to which he would retreat after dinner. He was not quite as rich as he seemed: riding the boom of modern technology, he overinvested in a new company called General Electric and was caught out in the Panic of 1893; thereafter he lived largely on contributions from his mother.[16] Descendant of Boston shipping magnates, she was rich enough.

A family friend, Sturgis Bigelow, captured some of Lodge's rather machinelike aura of superiority in notes he jotted as Lodge took his seat on a speaking platform at a campaign event in Massachusetts: "Cabot looked tall. A point in his favor. Slender. Legs very straight. Looked in good form & self-possessed.... Forehead

Lodge by John Singer Sargent (National Portrait Gallery, Smithsonian Institution / Art Resource, NY)

an inch bigger each way than any other man's on the platform.... Head, in profile, very large above the line of the ears....[He] subsided into a chair, cocked up his leg & began to swing his foot....He swung that foot for an hour and twenty minutes, without missing a stroke, except when he changed legs."[17]

Lodge was a figure perhaps too easy to caricature. Tough and principled, he was also sensitive, though that sensitivity was well hidden from most men. Roosevelt was not blind to Lodge's forbidding public persona. Once, Lodge spluttered that he couldn't understand why newspaper writers "persist in calling me cold, and reserved, and a Brahmin." Roosevelt replied, "I can tell you Cabot—it's because you are."[18] But Roosevelt recognized the sweeter, boyish side to Lodge, in part perhaps because it suited his own emotional needs. "Dear old Cabot stayed here till Thursday," Roosevelt wrote his sister Bamie on June 14, 1888. "He was the same delightful, big boyish personage as ever."[19]

Lodge, in turn, was devoted to Roosevelt. He wasn't given to gushing, but when toward the end of his life he collected their correspondence, he declared that after the 1884 Republican convention, Roosevelt "was my closest friend, personally, politically, and in every other way, and occupied toward me a relation that no other man has ever occupied or will occupy."[20] In his private letters to his mother he complained of being "depressed" whenever his friend was absent for a time, and of "miss[ing] Theodore beyond expression."[21] It was a relationship of extraordinary intimacy, given the stoicism of the age and the supposed uptightness of upper-class Wasps.*

Roosevelt was far more approachable than his friend Cabot. But even he, as he flashed his teeth and brayed with laughter, could exude a slight condescension. Both men could not help but feel a moral superiority rooted in class. Lodge was a Boston Brahmin, Roosevelt a New York Knickerbocker. They did not like the term "aristocrat"—that was for British snobs—but at some level they believed they lived and thought on a higher plane than the grasping nouveaus of the Gilded Age or the flood of immigrants arriving daily at Ellis Island. Indeed, they perceived—as

---

* Lodge's other best friend—his mother, Anna—sometimes wrote Roosevelt to commiserate over Lodge's physical ailments. In a note that Lodge had deleted from the published volume of their correspondence, Roosevelt told Lodge that his mother had confided in him about Lodge's digestive problems.[22] (In his memoir, Lodge relates, "I was taught in my youth, and very vigorously taught, that it was not good manners to discuss physical ailments in general society, and that it was the height of vulgarity to refer to money.")[23]

a matter of duty, they would have said, not self-interest — that the interest of their class, the patriarchy of the Founding Fathers, was the interest of the nation.[24]

This attitude could seem insufferably smug (then and even more so a century later), but beneath lurked more complicated forces. Roosevelt and Lodge asserted their positions with an enviable confidence and a strong sense of public service. But ease of manner, perfected over time as the Wasp ideal of "effortless grace," can be deceptive. Under the air of authority projected by both men and their kind, there lurked uneasiness, even fear. At moments the era of Wasp dominance in the last decades of the nineteenth century, as social historian Van Wyck Brooks once noted, felt a little more like Indian summer: warm, comforting, but with a slight nip in the air. The grandees of Boston's "Hub" (of the universe, as Oliver Wendell Holmes, Sr., coined the phrase) and of New York's "400" (the number who could fit in Mrs. William Backhouse Astor Jr.'s ballroom ca. 1880) seemed set in their tastes and ways — padding about on faded Turkish rugs, clipping coupons from Granny's trust fund. Yet there was a sense, even in the best households, of living on borrowed time. Some Brahmins turned inward, to their clubs and private libraries and banking houses, where No Irish Need Apply.[25] Roosevelt and Lodge believed they had a duty to face the coming storm, which is one reason why they venerated courage, why they placed such unrelenting emphasis on the duty to sally forth against danger. Life was a contest, a constant battle to be fought no matter the odds. Such was the duty seared into both men by the example of their fathers — worshipped men, seemingly so strong yet defeated by the forces of life.

Both men were refined, discerning, complex. But in their way they were bruisers. They regarded effeteness as a kind of social disease. Both men possessed, or were possessed by, a brutal streak, a bloody-mindedness, a fascination with ruthless combat. Roosevelt delighted in the rough sport of hunting, killing and gutting his prey, at times openly exulting in gore. Lodge was more reticent yet equally fascinated by raw violence. In the fall of 1895 he went to Spain with his son, Bay, where they attended a bullfight. After the first bull was killed Bay touched his father's shoulder and said, "I have had enough," and left the arena. Lodge wrote his mother that the spectacle was "brutal, savage & disgusting." But, he added, "I remained and saw three more."[26]

Reading the correspondence of Lodge and Roosevelt over a century later, it is hard not to be struck by the vehemence and almost joyous vindictiveness that Roosevelt aimed at the "goo-goos," or "mugwumps," as gentlemen reformers were also called in those days (from an Indian derivation suggesting "holier than thou"). "Oh, how I loathe the mugwumps," Roosevelt wrote Lodge in August 1887. "Those prize idiots, the Goo-Goos," he told his friend in October 1895.[27] Roosevelt especially hated E. L. Godkin, editor of the New York *Post*, who had accused him of selling out to the machine by backing Blaine in '84. Civil service reform was the great liberal cause of the day. The "educated elites"—men like Roosevelt, Lodge, and Godkin—all favored cleansing government of corruption, blaming the immigrant classes for using their newfound political power to gorge at the public trough. But Roosevelt regarded Godkin as a phony who did the bidding of aristocrats while scorning mere politicians. Noted Roosevelt in a letter to Lodge in May 1887: "The Post has devoted an editorial to me about every day; and I got in [a] neat little side hit at Godkin the other day.... How I despise the lying hypocrite!"[28] What Roosevelt hated most about the mugwumps was that they were, as he put it, "hostile to manliness." He called them "hermaphrodites"—half men, half women.[29]

Lodge would occasionally try to tone down Roosevelt's screeds, but he nursed his own grudges. He was snubbed by Moorfield Storey, Boston's leading mugwump, whenever the two men met—which was often, in insular Boston—and he was the target of a mugwump plot in June 1890 to deny him reelection to the Harvard Board of Overseers. Lodge wrote his mother that he was the victim of a "very petty political persecution" that "troubles me very little," he fibbed.[30]

Roosevelt and Lodge operated by a fairly straightforward and sensible credo: reform without power is meaningless, and power without scruple is corrupt. It is a wonder that more did not flock to their standard, but caught in the crosscurrents of class and ideology of the late nineteenth century, the two men were strangely isolated. Perhaps it was that slightly haughty air—the emanation they gave off to others (and Roosevelt fairly shouted in his private correspondence with Lodge) that they had found the one true way, and the rest be damned. Standing above the machine and the mugwumps, equally disdaining corrupt spoilsmen and effeminate dilettantes—not to mention Newport nouveaux riches and society bores, whom they also scorned—Roosevelt and Lodge formed a coalition of two. They were aware of their closed society. "What funnily varied lives we do lead, Cabot!" Roosevelt wrote Lodge: "We touch two or three little worlds, each profoundly ignorant of the others. Our literary friends have but a vague knowledge of our actual political work; and a goodly number of our sporting and social acquaintances know us only as men of good family, one of whom rides hard to hounds, while the other hunts big game in the Rockies."[31]

When not bemoaning their isolation or belittling their oppo-

TR strikes a pose. (Library of Congress)

nents, Roosevelt entertained Lodge with his tales of derring-do in the West, where he spent much of his time hunting and ranching, leaving his daughter, Alice, with his sister Bamie.[32] Writing in April 1886 on stationery embossed with the figure of a knight, he begins with a swipe at the mugwumps as "perverse lunatics,"[33] then launches into a description of how, as a deputy sheriff, he tracked down and captured some horse thieves while still finding time to read literature around the campfire ("I shall take Matthew Arnold along," he wrote Lodge before he mounted up with the posse; in his saddlebags he also carried Tolstoy's *Anna Karenina*): "I got the three horse thieves in fine style...we simply crept noiselessly up and rising when only a few yards distant covered them with the cocked rifles while I told them to throw up their hands....

"I am as brown and as tough as a hickory nut now."[34]

Lodge cautioned Roosevelt against using the pronoun "I" too often in his public writings. At the same time, he acted as Roosevelt's chief political promoter. Lodge used his influence to twice arrange jobs for Roosevelt in the public sector—as a civil service commissioner in 1889 and as a New York police commissioner in 1895. While neither position seems very prominent, Roosevelt used his social standing, his resolve, and his slashing style to become a nationally recognized figure, regarded as a comer in Republican politics and as a force of nature by the many journalists who knew him as good copy.

Lodge did not work alone. Roosevelt was a superb propagandist in his own cause and for the myth of the frontier. He often expounded on the need to rekindle the frontier spirit, once so strong, now slipping away into effeteness.[35] Encouraged by Lodge, Roosevelt in 1888 embarked on a three-volume series called *The Winning of the West*. The books (the last was published in 1896) detail the glorious march of the Anglo-Saxon "race." In the first volume, Roosevelt looks to the Teutonic invasion of ancient Rome and follows the long "blood line" to America. The Anglo-Saxons, he felt, did best when they triumphed in war—over the Irish, the French, the Spanish, the Mexicans, the Indians—and lost their vigor intermarrying with the weaker (by which he usually means Latin) races.[36] The Anglo-Saxons civilized by conquering. "The most ultimately righteous of all wars is a war with savages, though it is apt to be also the most terrible and inhuman," Roosevelt wrote. "The rude, fierce settler who drives the savage from the land lays all civilized mankind under a debt to him."[37] He brushed aside sympathy for the conquered. ("During the past century a good deal of sentimental nonsense has been talked about our taking the Indians' land," he wrote.)[38]

Roosevelt believed that regenerating this elemental spirit was a matter of life and death for modern America. He was heavily influenced by the social Darwinist theories of his professors at Harvard and Columbia Law School, which he attended for a year before going into politics. Roosevelt, to use an expression common among the social Darwinists, worried about "race suicide." The race was becoming "over-civilized"—too soft, like those mugwumps. The solution—indeed, salvation—would come from tapping into more primitive instincts, the kind brought out by sport, especially by hunting, and most of all by war. It was necessary, Roosevelt wrote, to let "the wolf rise in the heart."[39]

Roosevelt and Lodge looked to their own heredity for the conquering impulse. Roosevelt believed that Viking blood ran in his veins, that he was descended from "low Dutch sea thieves."[40] Ever prideful of his own heritage, Lodge noted that the "English Puritan was essentially a fighting man and excelled in the art of war." In his 1881 book, *A Short History of the English Colonies in America*, Lodge remarked upon the "true Puritan fashion" in which the local Indian tribes were exterminated. These Puritan fighting qualities that lived on in the Massachusetts regiments in the Civil War were now, he feared, being "refined and cultivated to nothingness."[41]

When Roosevelt was an undergraduate and Lodge a graduate student and briefly an instructor, Harvard was a hotbed of eugenics and other long-since-discredited racial theories.[42] Lodge earned his doctorate by studying histories, largely bogus, of the foundation of democracy and liberty in the dark forests of the ancient Teutonic tribes in Germany.[43] Harvard scholars were sure that Anglo-Saxons had emerged as the master race over the centuries that followed. There was, however, a problem: the "lesser" races were multiplying at a faster pace—and arriving on American shores in ever greater numbers.

Roosevelt's rallying cry to the Anglo-Saxon women of America was to get busy and have more babies. He called this competition with the immigrant classes "the warfare of the cradle."[44] Lodge's solution was to try to keep out the lesser races through tighter immigration laws. For many years Lodge sponsored legislation in Congress to exclude immigrants who could not read or write. He offered up all sorts of dubious arguments for this, including a reference to a chart of "the distribution of ability" by race in the United States, showing that, according to the *Encyclopedia of American Biography*, the "English Race" had produced more "statesmen, soldiers, and clergy" (1,542, 1,260, and 1,520, respectively) than, say, the Irish (9, 18, and 28).[45] John F. Kennedy's grandfather, John "Honey Fitz" Fitzgerald, once a congressman from Boston, liked to tell the story of being accosted by Lodge in January 1897 after the House had voted down Lodge's bill to restrict immigration. "You are an impudent young man," Lodge sneered. "Do you think the Jews or the Italians have any right in this country?" Fitzgerald responded, "As much right as your father or mine. It was only the difference of a few ships."[46]

It is startling, even shocking, to read about Lodge and Roosevelt spouting off on race and, in their approving history of ruthless forebears, appearing to endorse genocide. Each man, of course, reflected the opinions of the elites of his day, and neither was nearly as cruel nor bigoted as his pronouncements suggest. As a social Darwinist, Roosevelt was a so-called Lamarckian: he believed that racial dominance was not immutable, that over time, the lesser races could acquire the cultural traits of the superior races.[47] But more important than his faddish theorizing, he was an optimist and, at some level, tenderhearted. Latins and others might "supplant the old American stock," he wrote historian Francis Parkman in 1892. "Yet I am a firm believer that the future will somehow bring things right in the end for our land."[48] He wanted everyone to become an "American," meaning like him, but he had empathy for the poor and downtrodden. Roosevelt (much like Robert F. Kennedy many decades later) was experiential — he was ever curious, and he listened and felt as he watched the changing world around him. He was also not unsympathetic to the weak and vulnerable, having once been physically weak himself.

Roosevelt's consciousness was raised by his stint as a New York City police commissioner. Donning a cloak over his evening clothes, he would prowl the streets at night, venturing into the meanest precincts. The crusading newspaperman Jacob Riis became a close friend of Roosevelt and took him deep into the slums to see how the "other half" lived.[49] There was something in Roosevelt's character that made him wish to forgive evil, even as he morally postured. Owen Wister would hiss to his Harvard friend that "alien vermin" were overrunning the land, but Roosevelt just looked pained. Wister was reminded of a portrait by John Singer Sargent that captured Roosevelt's boyish sensitivity ("the wistfulness blurr[ing] his eyes — that misty perplexity and pain") beneath his mask of resolve.[50]

Lodge, in his Puritan rectitude, was less forgiving and his sensibility was more pessimistic, but he took on some unpopular causes. In Congress he worked hard to help the most excluded race, black Americans, who had been emancipated by Lincoln only to be shoved into peonage by Southern lawmakers as Reconstruction withered away. Though Roosevelt and Lodge regarded blacks as racially inferior, they argued that they should be treated as citizens, and in the late 1880s and early 1890s Lodge vigorously, though without success, pressed a bill to enforce voting rights in the South. He rather enjoyed becoming the lonely crusader. In January 1891 he regaled his mother with his story of facing down a "cracker" congressman, William Stone, Democrat of Missouri, slightly misquoting Hamlet: "I pry' thee, take thy hand from off my throat / For though I am not splenitive nor rash / Yet have in me something dangerous." On the floor of the House he drew applause by declaring, "I wish men to be free / As much from mobs as kings / From you as me." The "mugwump paper," the *New York Times*, highly praised him, which left him in "utter astonishment," as he told his mother.[51]

Lodge's motives may have been partly political—blacks were more likely to vote for the Republican Party of the Great Emancipator than for the Democrats. But he was nonetheless sincere in his desire to vindicate the cause of freedom for blacks for which so many brave men had died. In 1890 he wrote in the privacy of his journal: "I believe more deeply in the cause than in anything I ever thought of."[52]

Roosevelt, for all his manly bluster, needed women to care for him, to inspire him, to trim his excesses, and to pick him up when he was low. His confidante and political adviser—and surrogate mother for baby Alice after his wife's death—was Bamie. Plain, dark-skinned, suffering from a curved spine, Roosevelt's older sister was not a belle but she was smart, literate, and strong.[53] The correspondence between Lodge and Roosevelt was actually triangular: Bamie was in on all the important decisions, and when she finally married in 1895 at age forty-one, Lodge archly remarked, "Why on earth should you get married? You have Theodore and myself."[54]

Bamie and Teddy's younger sister, Corinne, were close to Edith Carow, the crying girl Roosevelt had shoved away as Lincoln's cortege passed by and the temperamental teenager

Edith Roosevelt (Library of Congress)

whom Teddy had broken with at the summer house in Oyster Bay. As a Victorian widower wishing to be "constant," Roosevelt vowed never to marry after Alice's death. But he must have feared temptation, for he asked his sisters not to invite Edith to their homes while he was visiting. One day in 1885 he ran into Edith in a hallway at Bamie's (an encounter instigated, possibly, by Bamie). Within two months they were engaged.

His wife Alice, the slender princess, had been alluring, ethereal, just beyond reach. Edith was wiser, deeper, more down-to-earth, with a reservoir of passion. She later spoke of her first intimacy with TR as her "white hour" and shocked a grand-daughter by referring to "that wonderful silky private part of a woman." Naturally a bit resentful of Alice, she also told her children that Theodore had been "bored" by his first wife.

Nannie Lodge (Courtesy of the Massachusetts Historical Society)

During their whirlwind (and secret) engagement, Edith wrote to Theodore, "I love you with all the passion of the girl who has never loved before." But thereafter, as Roosevelt biographer Kathleen Dalton observed, "their letters recorded quite a different relationship than the one T.R. had with Alice—no baby talk or childlike dependency." Edith stood up to her husband, chiding him for his bombast, nicknaming him "the Prophet Jeremiah" and managing his finances, which were a mess. (TR lost much of his fortune when his cattle ranching venture failed, and once bounced a $20,000 check to his publisher, who happened to be a brother-in-law of Josephine Shaw Lowell.) She knew her husband's vulnerabilities and hidden fears, and privately called him her "sensitive plant," after a poem by Shelley in which a plant, neglected by its gardener, becomes a "leafless wreck." And he knew her weaknesses as well—her migraine headaches, her occasional bouts of depression, her fears that he would go off and die a noble but selfish death.[55]

Cabot Lodge was perhaps even more in need of a discerning and comforting wife. Anna Cabot Mills Davis Lodge ("Nannie") was the former but not the latter. Nannie was more beautiful than Edith Carow, even more lovely than Alice Lee (to whom, inevitably in Boston, she was related; she was also distantly related to her husband, Cabot). John Singer Sargent once regretted that he had not painted Nannie, because she had the "most unforgettable...blue eyes."[56] They were a brilliant azure, like the evening sky, and not without warmth, although as time went on they could turn cold toward her husband.

Roosevelt was intrigued by Lodge's wife. Wellesley educated, Anna was able to one-up Roosevelt with her knowledge of Dickens and Shakespeare, which seemed to amuse him. She did cartwheels and ran down Cooper's Bluff at Sagamore Hill, TR's home in Oyster Bay. (A bit priggishly, Lodge struck the reference to Nannie's cartwheels from his published correspondence—he must not have wanted the reader to imagine her bloomers flashing.)[57] She was brave, too. After Nannie gave birth to their first child, Lodge wrote his mother that while she was going through a difficult labor, she said to her husband, "Don't be frightened, Cabot." Lodge added: "I am not given to tears but I assure you I can hardly think or write of this without shedding them."[58] But she could be harsh to her husband. A biographer of their grandson, the diplomat and senator Henry Cabot Lodge, writes:

She was her husband's sternest critic....He once asked her to read a speech he had prepared for a local rally. She read it and handed it back saying with charming frankness that it was very inferior stuff, would not do at all, in short was quite impossible. Lodge tossed it in the fire and wrote another. "Somewhat better," Nannie commented, "yet far from satisfactory. Really, you ought not to stand up before an audience to read that." Lodge tried a third time, and Nannie said: "Better than either of the others, though not what it ought to be. However, I suppose it is as good as you can do, my poor boy." She gave him the deflating nickname of "Pinky."[59]

Lodge's attitude toward his wife is hard to discern, though it may be revealing that he barely mentions her in his memoirs, while lavishing praise on his mother.[60] Perhaps Lodge's Hobbesian view of the world would have been softened if he had had a more forgiving and loving wife, though his Puritanism was fairly hardwired. In any case, he was not alone: he had his mother, to whom he wrote and confided at least once a week, and he had his friend Theodore.

3

Manifest Destiny

"But, of course, there won't be any war."

THE LAST DECADE of the nineteenth century was a time for flag-waving festivals, for celebrations of patriotism and country. Americans extolled, sang about, and versified national pride. The Pledge of Allegiance was written in 1892, "America the Beautiful" in 1895, and Memorial Day celebrations were becoming increasingly popular. The bitterness of the Civil War a fading memory, veterans of the blue and the gray joined in festivals of national reconciliation.[1]

The greatest of all patriotic celebrations began in the spring of 1893, in the boomtown of Chicago. There, in a grand and gleaming collection of beaux arts buildings intended to evoke Ancient Rome, the Columbian Exposition—the world's fair named in honor of Christopher Columbus—opened to the public. The so-called White City, though constructed of wood and plaster instead of marble and stone, shone at night under the glare of giant floodlamps and frequent fireworks displays. Theodore Roosevelt's wife, Edith, who visited with her husband that early summer of 1893, called the setting a "fairyland."[2]

The American attractions at the fair demonstrated the march of progress made by civilization—or, more precisely, *American*

The Chicago world's fair, 1893 (Library of Congress)

civilization—since Columbus had arrived in the New World four centuries earlier. An astonishing new invention, a giant electrical dynamo, generated power for the brilliant lights. In the vast Hall of Manufacturers and Liberal Arts, visitors marveled at such technological breakthroughs as typewriters, toilets, refrigerators, electric lamps, and artificial limbs (important in the decades after the Civil War). On display were exhibits to show how America was "civilizing" savages. In the Anthropological Building stood living proof: a full-blooded Apache related to Geronimo who had been "to Europe on a yacht" and planned to finish his education at Harvard.[3]

In a lagoon in the middle of the White City was the Wooded Island. Any of the twenty-one million visitors to the world's fair could stroll down a fragrant path of flowers and shrubs to find an authentic "Hunter's Cabin," a fitting memorial to an earlier, heartier era. Within were rifles purported to have been owned by Daniel Boone and Davy Crockett, as well as "a motley array of revolvers, knives, pipes, army blankets, playing cards, lariats, etc., scattered picturesquely through with studied negligence about the place," according to a contemporary newspaper account. A dusty prairie schooner, a covered wagon from pioneer days, stood nearby.[4]

The cabin had been built with funds raised by Theodore Roosevelt and the organization he had founded, the Boone and Crockett Club, to "promote manly sport with the rifle." Membership was limited to men "who had killed with the rifle in fair chase" some kind of "American large game."[5] The Boone and Crockett Club was a group for "men of social standing," according to the January 17, 1889, edition of *Forest and Stream* magazine.[6] Its membership, in addition to TR's friend Lodge, included historian Francis Parkman of Harvard, conservationist Gifford Pinchot, tycoons like J. P. Morgan, and future statesmen Henry L. Stimson and Elihu Root.[7]

Owen Wister was another member of the Boone and Crockett Club. Plagued by neurotic symptoms, Wister had gone west to escape his dreary bank job. He began writing stories of the cowboy life that Roosevelt loved and vigorously promoted. It was Roosevelt who introduced Wister to Frederic Remington, a former Yale football player who was becoming the great painter and sculptor of the West. Wister would later dedicate his seminal cowboy story, *The Virginian*, to Roosevelt. (Historian David McCullough has noted the irony that the myth of the West was in part the creation of three upper-class Easterners.)[8]

The Boone and Crockett bunch met most often at the University Club in Manhattan or the Metropolitan Club in Washington, D.C. In the spring of 1893, however, Roosevelt and Wister decided to hold a mini-Porcellian/Boone and Crockett reunion at the Hunter's Cabin on the Wooded Island at the world's fair. The record does not show whether the men actually slept in the cabin, in blankets on the dirt floor, but they did dine "camp fashion," as Wister put it. "Delicious fish and beefsteaks. Theodore wanted to have simpler drinks also—whiskey and beer." But Winthrop Chanler, a high-jinks-loving "Porcer" and fellow Boone and Crockett member, held out for champagne, Wister reported, "and I seconded." Champagne it was.[9] After the dinner "we went out on the lagoon in a private launch to see the fireworks illuminations," Chanler recalled. "Nothing can describe the beauty of the scene.... The water, electric-lighted white buildings.... It was simply magnificent."[10]

Champagne and a private launch to view the fireworks does not exactly seem like roughing it. But while it is easy to make fun of these gentlemen frontiersmen, their yearning for a simpler life and hardier virtues was real, their search for meaning deep and at times poignant in its urgency and occasional bewilderment. It was a strangely conflicted time, with science and reason advancing, religious superstition and myth increasingly banished to the shadows. Charles Darwin had revealed that man evolved through natural selection. Social Darwinism, the offshoot belief that the strongest races were bound to triumph over the weaker ones, was becoming an article of faith, certainly among the educated classes, who gobbled up a best-seller by John Fiske titled *Manifest Destiny*. It was, the book argued, the manifest destiny of the Anglo-Saxon race ("race" was a word used loosely in those days) to rule the world.[11]

This march of civilization was a great thing. But it came with a paradox not easily resolved. If life was about the survival of the fittest—and the fittest were surely the Americans—why did the finest, best-educated Americans so often feel weak in spirit?

Clearly, material progress did not always make for psychic well-being. In the upper reaches of Anglo-Saxon America in the last decade of the nineteenth century, there was an outbreak of nervous disorder, the "neurasthenia" that afflicted Roosevelt's mother—and Roosevelt, Lodge, Wister, and many others of their "race."*[12] Reports of impotence, homosexual acts, and a loss of virility gave rise to worries about a kind of systemic degeneracy, a weakening of the race. The anxiety of some men was exacerbated by the appearance of an assertive new breed called "the new women," who wished to smoke cigarettes and to exercise, go to college, and—perhaps most shocking of all—to vote.[14]

What was to be done to alleviate this free-floating anxiety? Get out and exercise! In the last two decades of the nineteenth century, the young men of the upper and middle classes took to sweaty gyms, lifting weights and tossing medicine balls. The country was swept by a mania for bicycling. Among those who tried to take up the two-wheeled habit was Theodore Roosevelt's wife, Edith. Her biographer, Sylvia Jukes Morris, reports that "she found the lessons difficult—'the wheel wobbles in every

---

*A rather vague malady that might be accompanied by lassitude, aches, insomnia, melancholia, and fainting spells, neurasthenia was seen as mostly a woman's disease. But in the second half of the nineteenth century many men, particularly in the leisure classes, seemed to have suffered from it as well, with symptoms that would be described today as psychosomatic. It is a curious fact, though perhaps not a coincidence, that the leading apostles of social Darwinism—the leading preachers of Anglo-Saxon superiority— were among the most neurasthenic. The philosopher Herbert Spencer, who introduced the phrase "survival of the fittest," suffered from sleeplessness and exhaustion and the belief that he was doomed to become an invalid. Darwin himself suffered from insomnia, vomiting, nausea, and eczema.[13]

direction as if it were alive'" — but pressed on with the help of an instructor holding a belt strapped to her waist.[15]

Her husband regarded sport, the more violent the better, as the next best thing to war. In 1890 Harvard had dedicated Soldiers Field (donated by Henry Lee Higginson, "Bully Higg" of the snowball fights) in memory of six Harvard heroes killed in the Civil War. Football, played with virtually no pads, was a nasty and dangerous game; the 1894 Harvard-Yale game was suspended after seven players were carried off the field, as one account put it, "in a dying condition."[16] On March 11, 1895, Roosevelt wrote Walter Camp, the great Yale football coach, to express his "disgust" with the Harvard faculty, which had voted to call for the abolition of football. Roosevelt worried that "we were tending steadily in America to produce in our leisure and sedentary classes a type of man not much above the Bengalese baboo, and from this the athletic spirit has saved us. Of all the games I like football best." Roosevelt lamented that "being nearsighted I was not able to play football in college," but noted that he had made up for this since then through other manly pursuits such as riding, cross-country, shooting, polo, "and the like." To the Yale coach, Roosevelt proudly catalogued his injuries:

I was knocked senseless at polo once, and it was a couple of hours before I came to. I broke an arm once riding to hounds and I broke my nose another time; and out on the roundup in the West I once broke a rib, and at another time the point of my shoulder. I got these injuries when I was a father of my family, and while of course they caused me more or less inconvenience, and my left arm is not as strong as it might be now, nothing would persuade me to surrender the fun and the health which I could not have had save at the risk; and it seems to me that when I can afford to run these slight risks college boys can afford to take their chances on the football field.

Roosevelt went on to recite the beneficial effects of the sporting life on college men with "sound bodies." One example was "Lodge, the senator," who with some exaggeration Roosevelt described as "a great swimmer in college, winning a championship" and more accurately as "a great horseman now."[17] Roosevelt and Lodge often rode together after the hounds near Roosevelt's house in Oyster Bay and galloped through Rock Creek Park almost every morning when they were in Washington. This was not just a matter of pleasant exercise. Lodge and Roosevelt associated horseback riding with war leaders — national saviors, the proverbial man on a white horse. As Lodge wrote, "for the development of nerve, energy and courage, so useful in all the affairs of life and so pre-eminently valuable to a people called to arms...no outdoor sport can equal riding on horseback."[18]

Whatever his claims to Walter Camp, hunting wild animals was Roosevelt's favorite sport. In his book *Hunting Trips*, he rates the challenges of hunting by degrees of peril to the hunter — from deer to panthers and grizzly bears to humans. Roosevelt had little experience as a manhunter. He had never actually killed anyone, and the opportunities for shooting bad guys or Indians in the West were fast vanishing by the 1890s.[19]

At the Chicago world's fair in 1893, one of the most popular attractions was Buffalo Bill's Wild West Show. Bill Cody had been to the East and even to the courts of Europe with his cast of plainsmen and "savages," and at the world's fair thousands of spectators ate ice cream and thrilled to his staged gunfights and roundups. The spectacle marked the somewhat tawdry end of an era. The range wars and guerrilla skirmishes between cavalrymen and Indians were over, and in Cody's extravaganza the 1890 Battle of Wounded Knee was reduced to theater, its brave veterans to bit-part actors in a carnival show.[20]

The truly enduring note at the exposition was struck by a young college professor lecturing to the American Historical Association, which held its annual meeting in the White City from July 11 to 13. In "The Frontier in American History," Frederick Jackson Turner argued that American exceptionalism was rooted in the individualism and self-reliance of the frontier settler. Jackson pointed to a little-known U.S. Census Bureau pamphlet that had declared in 1891 that the frontier was now "closed"—there was no more land to conquer and settle. What would happen to the best and most distinctive qualities of the American spirit, Turner asked, if there was nowhere left for Americans to go?

Turner's address, though factually a stretch (open space still abounded), would become during the first half of the twentieth century one of the most important and oft-quoted speeches ever made by a historian. At the time, however, it got little attention. The night of July 12 was hot; most historians tried boating or the giant Ferris wheel, or went in search of ice cream. Even Turner's parents failed to show up at his lecture.[21]

But Theodore Roosevelt was paying attention. He wrote Turner, "I have been greatly interested in your pamphlet on the Frontier....I think you have struck some first class ideas, and have put into definite shape a good deal of thought which has been floating around rather loosely."[22] Roosevelt had been thinking about American expansionism. He was writing the third volume of his treatise on the American frontier spirit, *The Winning of the West*. But he also had a more personal agenda. With conquest comes conflict, and the closing of the American frontier suggested peace upon the land. Roosevelt yearned for conflict—for the ultimate conflict of war.

But where? Mexico, perhaps? That war had already been fought once, in the war to annex Texas and California in 1846–48. In a border incident in August 1886 an American army captain was killed by some Mexican troops. Staying at his ranch at Medora, in the Dakota Territory, Roosevelt immediately wrote his friend Lodge, then a congressman: "I have written Secretary [of War William] Endicott offering to raise some companies of horse riflemen out here in the event of trouble with Mexico. Will you telegraph me at once if war becomes inevitable? . . . I think there is some good fighting stuff among these harum-scarum rough riders out here." Thus did Roosevelt first dream of the fighting unit that would make him famous, but it remained a dream: the border dispute with Mexico was soon settled.

Roosevelt continued to chafe. In his more bellicose moods it sometimes seemed that just about *any* war would do. In 1889 he wrote his British friend the diplomat (later ambassador to the United States) Cecil ("Springy") Spring Rice: "Frankly, I don't know that I should be sorry to see a bit of a spar with Germany; the burning of New York and a few other seacoast cities would be a good object lesson on the need of an adequate system of coastal defenses." Roosevelt loved hyperbole, but he was apparently serious. He wrote "Springy," "While we would have to take some awful blows at first, I think in the end we would worry the Kaiser a little."[23]

In the spring of 1895, when Roosevelt moved to New York to be a police commissioner, he seemed to have no sense of danger as he roamed crime-riddled streets in his evening clothes. With him on several of these nocturnal forays was his old family friend Robert Ferguson. Watching Roosevelt, TR's thick neck bursting from his stiff collar, his large teeth seeming to chomp his words, his muscular body in perpetual motion (Roosevelt never walked up stairs or steps; he ran), Ferguson concluded that what Roosevelt needed was "a great and glorious war" to "give effective outlet to his more natural and active inclinations."[24]

A year earlier Roosevelt had written Ferguson that he longed for "a general national buccaneering expedition to drive the Spanish out of Cuba, the English out of Canada."[25] There was no particular reason to believe the Canadians wanted the British to be driven from their shores, and in any case the Royal Navy, the most powerful in the world, would be a daunting foe to an American "buccaneering expedition." But Cuba, that was another matter.

American statesmen had been eyeing Cuba for most of the century. Stretching more than seven hundred miles from end to end, the luxuriant isle lies less than a hundred miles south of the Florida Keys—"almost in sight of our shores," wrote Secretary of State (soon to be President) John Quincy Adams in 1823, exaggerating for effect. "[Cuba's] addition to our confederacy is exactly what is wanting to round out our power as a nation to the point of its utmost interest," wrote former president Thomas Jefferson to President James Monroe in the same year. In 1848 President James Polk offered to buy Cuba from Spain for $100 million, and six years later President Franklin Pierce upped the bid to $130 million.[26] Spain indignantly refused. Cuba was its "ever faithful island," the pearl of the Antilles. For four centuries Havana had been a center of Spanish culture and wealth.

But Spain was fading. Its empire had long ago begun to rot. On Cuba there were stirrings, and on February 24, 1895, in a village at the eastern end of the island, a *grito*—a rebellious cry for liberty and independence—rang out. As historian Louis Pérez has written, "hardly anyone noticed."[27] There had been rebellions before—in 1868, 1879, 1883, 1885, 1892, and 1893. All had fizzled or been crushed, though the first one had dragged on for a decade. On February 28 brief articles appeared in American newspapers about the *grito* in Cuba, but the Spanish minister in Washington was quoted as saying, "The revolutionary movements...are wholly a matter of fiction."[28]

Teddy Roosevelt was following the developments in Cuba, and hoping. On March 19 (eight days after delineating his sporting injuries to Walter Camp), Roosevelt wrote the governor of New York and added a "P.S. private" to his letter on public school reform: "In the very improbable event of a war with Spain I am going to beg you with all my power to do me the greatest favor possible; get me a position in New York's quota of the force sent out. Remember, I make application now. I was three years captain in the 8th Regiment N.Y. State militia, and I must have a commission in the force that goes to Cuba!"

"But, of course," Roosevelt added forlornly to his postscript, "there won't be any war." Though the fighting spirit was warming in the land, the right combustibles and the right spark were still missing. The country, Roosevelt knew, wasn't quite ready for war—not yet.[29]

4

The Large Policy

"I don't care whether our sea coast cities are bombarded..."

I N THE REMEMBRANCE of war there can be a kind of forgetting. Oliver Wendell Holmes, Jr., was wounded in the bloodbath of Antietam in 1862 and feared for his sanity after the slaughter of the Wilderness campaign in 1864. Physically and emotionally exhausted, he had resigned from the army in July 1864. Later, though, he felt guilty that he had left nine months before the end of the fighting, and over time he came to idealize and romanticize the soldier's life. Even many decades later, as a U.S. Supreme Court justice, he kept his old army uniform in his closet, regularly donning it for Memorial Day celebrations and gatherings of old soldiers and the young men who worshipped them.[1]

Harvard University honored its war dead with an enormous Victorian Gothic Memorial Hall. In the lobby, plaques memorialize Harvard's fallen sons, including Robert Gould Shaw and Charles Russell Lowell. On Memorial Day, May 30, 1895, the seniors at Harvard College marched into Sanders Theater in Memorial Hall to hear Holmes, class of '61, give a speech he titled "The Soldier's Faith." Holmes evoked some of the horror of war, but more of the thrill: "If you have been on the picket line at night in a black and unknown wood, have heard the spat of the bullets upon the trees and as you moved have felt your foot slip against a dead man's body; if you have had a blind fierce gallop against the enemy, with your blood up and a pace that left no time for fear…if you have known the vicissitudes of terror and of triumph in war, you know that there is such a thing as the faith I spoke of."

He told the young men in the audience that "war, when you are at it, is horrible and dull," but he spoke of war's dreariness and waste for only a moment before returning to his theme, that the message of war is "divine." He warned against the soft life of easy prosperity and reminded the young men in the audience that they came from a great Anglo-Saxon race, imbued with a pure and noble sense of purpose, which he conjured with epic poetry:

From the beginning, to us, children of the North, life has seemed a place hung about by dark mists, out of which come the pale shine of dragon's scales, and the cry of fighting men, and the sound of swords. Beowulf, Milton, Durer, Rembrandt, Schopenhauer, Turner, Tennyson, from the first war song of our race to the stall-fed poetry of modern English drawing rooms, all have had the same vision, and all have had a glimpse of the light to be followed. "The end of worldly life awaits us all. Let him who may gain honor ere death. That is best for a warrior when he is dead." So spoke Beowulf a thousand years ago.

"Not of the sunlight,
Not of the moonlight,
Not of the starlight!

O young Mariner,
Down to the haven,
Call your companions,
Launch your vessel,
And crowd your canvas,
And, ere it vanishes,
Over the margin,
After it, follow it,
Follow the Gleam."

So sang Tennyson of the Dying Merlin.

So, too, sang Holmes to his rapt young charges.

The speech, widely reprinted, thrilled many Harvard graduates. "By Jove," wrote Roosevelt to his friend Lodge, "that speech of Holmes' was fine; I wish he could make Edward Atkinson learn it by heart and force him to repeat it forwards and backwards every time he makes a peace oration." (Atkinson was a parvenu manufacturer who had publicly argued that war was bad for business.)[2] Seven years later President Roosevelt would appoint his Porcellian clubmate Holmes to the U.S. Supreme Court at the urging of Senator Lodge.

Roosevelt and Lodge had been separated that spring of 1895 when Roosevelt moved to New York City to become police commissioner, but they reunited at every opportunity. Eleven days after he wrote Lodge to recommend Holmes's speech, Roosevelt again penned a note to Lodge, this time to say that he would soon see him back at Harvard. "At commencement, we can meet at the Porc," wrote TR.[3] (Roosevelt dearly loved the Porcellian. Some years later, when his daughter was engaged to Congressman Nicholas Longworth, then President Roosevelt bragged to

Kaiser Wilhelm II of Germany that his son-in-law-to-be was a member of "the Porc, you know.")[4]

Commencement lunch at the Porcellian in late June 1895 seems to have been a jolly affair. Holmes was there, along with Lodge, Roosevelt, and Winthrop Chanler, their friend from the Boone and Crockett Club. Champagne flowed freely.[5] That year Holmes received an honorary degree at Harvard Commencement, and Roosevelt was elected to Harvard's august Board of Overseers. Afterward Roosevelt went with Lodge to his house in Nahant, along with Chanler, a bon vivant who, according to his wife, Margaret, enjoyed crying out at parties the club's motto, *Dum Vivimus Vivamus* (While we live, let us live!).[6]

But it was not all fun and games. By autumn Roosevelt was feeling beleaguered, at once enmeshed in New York City politics as police commissioner and vilified for his "jingoism," his frequent calls for American expansionism. "Literally I am being driven to death by the work here and the responsibility," he had written Lodge on October 3. A month later he wrote, "The Boston Herald and the Evening Post have made long and vicious attacks on me for my jingo speech the other night."[7] Embarrassed by his small show of self-pity, he wrote another friend: "The strain is beginning to tell on me a little; but after all it is not enough to speak of, for I feel as strong as a bull-moose."[8] Nevertheless he continued to vent to his true friend. "I can't help writing you, for I literally have no one here to whom to unburden myself," he wrote Lodge on October 11.[9]

That year Lodge and Roosevelt had written a book together. It was called *Hero Tales*, and it was intended as moral instruction for boys. The slender volume is perhaps the clearest expression of the values the two friends, twelve-year-olds at heart, cherished—especially physical courage. There are twenty-six short biographical essays, fourteen by Roosevelt in his vivid, almost sensuous prose and a dozen by Lodge in his more didactic, imperious style. Inevitably, almost all the heroes are warriors. There is George Washington, "so exposed that bullets passed through his coat and hat"; Daniel Boone straining to "hear the approach of some crawling red foe"; Admiral Farragut shouting, "Damn the torpedoes! Go ahead; full speed!"; and a composite chapter called "The Flag Bearer" about men who would not, even at the cost of their lives, let the flag fall as they advanced against enemy fire on open ground. (This last, written by Roosevelt, is a simulacrum of the charge he would make four years later, under fire, up a far-distant hill.) The reader may find it odd that the authors included among these portraits of fire-breathing warriors a brief profile of a Harvard scholar and Boone and Crockett clubmate, Francis Parkman, whose nerves were so fragile that he could barely stand sunlight—that is, until the reader realizes that the authors identified with Parkman, the first historian to describe and extol the frontier spirit (and who, nearly blind and crippled, "triumphed over pain").[10]

The centerpiece, the most thrilling and moving portrait in the collection, is a portrait of Robert Gould Shaw. This was the hero Roosevelt first heard about from Shaw's sister, Effie Shaw Lowell, as a little boy playing at war; he was also the golden figure Lodge had watched ride off to destiny down Beacon Street. The essay is preceded by a poem in his honor written by James Russell Lowell, an editor of the *Atlantic* who had known young Shaw in the small world of Boston society:

Brave, good, and true,
I see him stand before me now,

And read again on that young brow,
Where every hope was new

"Colonel Shaw sprang to the front, and waving his sword, shouted, 'Forward Fifty-fourth!'" wrote Lodge. "With another cheer, the men rushed through the ditch, and gained a parapet on the right. Colonel Shaw was one of the first to scale the walls. As he stood erect, a noble figure, ordering his men forward and shouting to them to press on, he was shot dead and fell into the fort." The Lowell poem rang with the glory of his death:

Right in the van,
On the red rampart's slippery swell,
With heart that beat a charge, he fell,
Forward, as fits a man.

Shaw was, to Lodge, a pure specimen of everything he admired. He "had all that birth and wealth, breeding, education, and tradition could give. He offered up, in full measure, all those things that make life most worth living," wrote Lodge. "He was handsome and beloved. He had a serene and beautiful nature, and was at once brave and simple."[11]

In December 1895, just as *Hero Tales* was arriving in bookstores for Christmas, the United States threatened to go to war with Great Britain. The war scare began as a border dispute between Britain and Venezuela over some mineral-rich land in British Guyana, a place most Americans had never heard of. (American ignorance would be a near-constant in American small wars, then and later.) Invoking the Monroe Doctrine (but probably trying to divert popular attention from the aftereffects of the Panic of 1893), President Grover Cleveland sent a hot message to the British to back away from the Western Hemisphere. The British at first ignored the American leader, then haughtily rebuffed him. Cleveland, quite uncharacteristically, threatened military action. Suddenly the newspapers were full of talk of war. The *New York Times* front page for December 18, 1895, summed things up:

Preparations For War
Country Is Aroused
Want To Fight England

Army, Navy Men Profess Great Eagerness to Go to War,
Talk of Invasion of Canada

The article that ran below the headline was a good deal more sober, quoting the army bureau chief as saying that "America would make a sorry spectacle at war with England." Still, among the educated classes the fever was intense. The Union League Club of New York had 1,600 members, proclaimed one of them, and "we are 1,600 to a man behind Mr. Cleveland in this matter.... There is absolutely not one dissenting voice."[12]

In hindsight it is difficult to imagine what got into these would-be warriors. Regardless of the provocation—and the presence of some British warships off the South American coast does not seem like much of a threat to the national security—going to war with Great Britain in 1895 would have been madness. The Americans might have tried to hold Canada hostage, but they were totally outgunned at sea: Great Britain had fifty battleships, the American navy three.[13]

But a spirit of bellicosity was rising in the land. In November, before Cleveland and the British Foreign Ministry began exchanging ultimatums, when Venezuela remained only a blot on the map, Frederic Remington wrote Owen Wister, "I think I smell war in the air."[14] On December 17, Cleveland called on Congress to resist the British land grab "by every means in its power." The nation, or at least its rulers, cried hurrah. "For about a week, the country rose in a unanimous wave of presidential support," wrote historian Ivan Musicant. "Absurdist senators waved the bloody shirt. William Steward, Democrat of Nevada, asserted, 'War would be a good thing even if we get whipped, for it would rid us of English bank rule.' (America was on the international gold standard.) The *Washington Post* screamed from its editorial page, 'It is the call to arms, the jingoes were right after all.'"[15]

Roosevelt and Lodge were excited and gratified by it all. Roosevelt wrote Lodge on December 20, "I do hope there will not be any back down among our people." The military odds did not faze Roosevelt. "Let the fight come if it must; I don't care whether our sea coast cities are bombarded or not; we would take Canada."[16] He wrote his brother-in-law William Cowles: "If there is a muss I shall try to have a hand in it myself! They'll have to employ a lot of men just as green as I am even for the conquest of Canada; our regular army isn't big enough. It seems to me that if England were wise she would fight now; we couldn't get at Canada until May, and meanwhile she could play havoc with our coast cities and shipping."

Lodge was "bubbling over with delight," according to the London *Times*.[17] "I first alone in the wilderness cried out about Venezuela last June and was called a jingo for my pains," Lodge wrote his mother, who rivaled Roosevelt as his closest correspondent. "I am no longer lonely. Jingoes are plenty enough now."*[18] Lodge had written an article for the June issue of the *North American Review*, a highbrow journal of affairs, called "England, Venezuela, and the Monroe Doctrine," in which he stretched the Monroe Doctrine to declare America's "rightful supremacy in the Western Hemisphere"—a doctrine to be asserted "peaceably if we can, forcibly if we must."[20]

In Congress Lodge had been for the past nine months chief architect of something called "the Large Policy," to distinguish America's territorial ambition from that more distasteful European term, "imperialism." Lodge wanted to sprinkle the globe with American territorial possessions that would protect and open up trade. The junior senator from Massachusetts had started the course of American expansionism, as he so often did, arm in arm with Roosevelt. Back in 1890 Roosevelt had read a book called *The Influence of Sea Power on History* by Alfred Thayer Mahan. Soon he and Lodge were dissecting Mahan's theories over dinner.[21]

Captain, later Admiral, Mahan was an unlikely Poseidon. He disliked sea duty and during the Civil War his ship had showed up too late for its only battle. A tall, thin figure with an undershot chin covered up by a beard, he had a bad drinking habit (to medicate nervous headaches so severe he feared a breakdown) and a deep Christian faith. Regarded as something of a nuisance by most of his superiors, he nevertheless became the most influential naval officer in history, if ideas can be measured against exploits in battle. Drawing heavily on social Darwinist notions

---

*In a letter to his mother two months later, Lodge described the origin of the word "jingo"—from an 1870s English music-hall ballad during a war scare over Turkey: "We don't want to fight/But by jingo if we do/We've got the men/We've got the money too."[19]

of the destiny of the Anglo-Saxon race, Mahan saw sea power as the key to world dominance. Great Britain was his model and inspiration: an empire built on a great navy that protected trade across the seven seas. Mahan's ideas, coming as the European powers were carving up the "uncivilized" world and jostling against British naval supremacy, caused a global sensation. In 1894 Kaiser Wilhelm of Germany wrote a friend, "I am just now not reading but devouring Captain Mahan's book and am trying to learn it by heart." The kaiser ordered *The Influence of Sea Power on History* placed in the wardroom of every ship in Germany's High Seas Fleet. The Japanese adapted it as a text at their naval academy.[22]

Lodge would use Mahan as a preacher used the Bible. For three days in March 1895 he had held forth on the floor of the U.S. Senate to expound his Large Policy. By his desk he erected a large map upon which were placed large red Maltese crosses to signify future American possessions: Hawaii, Cuba, Puerto Rico, a canal across the Panamanian isthmus. "It is the sea power which is essential to the greatness of every splendid people," he declared.[23]

Lodge was startled, even a little overwhelmed, by the reaction in the chamber. "It was by far the most successful speech...I ever made in Congress," he wrote his mother. "I was in desperate earnest....As I spoke the Senators all came in from the cloakrooms, members of the House appeared, the messengers and doorkeepers came in. I knew I had absolute attention everywhere and I vaguely [realized] that the chamber was filled & that men were standing all around the walls....When I sat down everybody crowded around to shake my hand, something quite common in the House but which hardly ever happens in the Senate." Remembering his New England reserve but bursting with filial pride, he added, "It would be vain to say this to anyone but you, but you will be glad to hear it."[24]

The Venezuela war scare nine months later, in December, vindicated Lodge's "jingoism" in the popular press and with many of his colleagues in the Senate. On December 19, a day after the *New York Times* article, Lodge took to the floor of the Senate to argue that America could not allow Great Britain to meddle in the affairs of the Western Hemisphere by simply appropriating lands belonging to one of America's southern neighbors. His speech had caused a sensation in the press. Still, he was, as he would often seem to be, under attack from both sides: the so-called practical people, in this case the business and commercial interests, and the idealists, the loathed mugwumps, some of whom accused Lodge of playing the warmonger. On December 22 he wrote his mother on U.S. Senate letterhead, "It was painful for me to read the telegrams & letters from frightened stockbrokers & bankers sent me on Friday, asking me to eat my words and swallow my convictions."[25] On December 30 he gave a speech in the Senate intended, he wrote Anna, to "calm the people...some of whom seemed to think we had gone crazy here...& were running the country into war just for fun."[26]

Roosevelt, on the other hand, was enjoying the controversy. "Personally, I rather hope the fight will come soon," he wrote Lodge on December 27. Roosevelt was stirred up because some professors at Harvard were warning students that war with Great Britain would be a calamity. Charles Eliot Norton, professor of fine arts, denounced Cleveland's belligerent message to Great Britain as a "crime against civilization." Famously effete, Norton tried to cultivate a genteel sensibility in his students (who joked that upon arriving in Heaven, Norton would exclaim, "So overdone! So garish! So Renaissance!" and decide to spend eternity in Harvard's more tasteful Appleton Chapel).[27] Roosevelt thought that Norton embodied what he called "the Baboo kind of statesmanship"—Indian mystic, not Yankee conqueror. Wrestling with his love-hate attitude toward Harvard, Roosevelt resolved to draft a "smashing letter" to the student newspaper, the *Crimson*, attacking the "peace-at-any-price-men." But first he wrote Lodge to ask, "Do you see any harm?" Lodge evidently did not, and off the letter went, reminding Harvard men that the Monroe Doctrine had really been written by John Quincy Adams, another Harvard man. On January 19 Roosevelt wrote Lodge that he expected to be vilified by the mugwumps, but he was sorry about what he called the "cult of non-virility" creeping into the university that had produced Colonel Shaw. "I regret that some of the Harvard Professors could be led into doing what they have done. They are rapidly confirming in me the feeling that there ought to be a war."[28] At this stage of his life Roosevelt needed to divide up the world into the warriors and the weak. He could not appreciate that his old school might produce a teacher who had a more nuanced but farsighted view of humankind.

5

The Individualist

"He listened for truth from anybody."

IN CAMBRIDGE, a Harvard professor who had once taught Theodore Roosevelt worried about the growing war fever. William James was a slight figure with a full beard and a noble brow. He was a bit of a dandy, setting a style for undergraduates with his floppy ties and sporty Norfolk jackets. He sometimes hesitated when he spoke, but his words and his thoughts were alive and probing. "His eyes were said to change color with his moods," wrote historian Kim Townsend in *Manhood at Harvard*, "now tawny, now what Sarah Whitman [a flirtatious female friend] called 'irascible blue.'"[1]

James's eyes must have been flame blue on Christmas Eve 1895 as he sat writing anxious letters in his book-lined study on Irving Street, a short walk from Harvard Yard. To his friend E. L. Godkin — Roosevelt's bête noire in the mugwump press — he confessed that he hadn't "slept right for a week," ever since Cleveland's message to Congress set off the Venezuela war scare. Like Roosevelt and Lodge, he was reminded of the Civil War, but for James the echoes were not glorious but grim. "I swear it brings back the days of '61 again, when the worst enemies of our country were in our own borders."[2]

William James, self-portrait (Houghton Library, Harvard University)

William James's famous brother, the novelist Henry James, weighed in from England. An émigré living in London, Henry found most things American to be vulgar, and he rather prissily complained about "the lurid light the American newspapers seem to project...the absolute war-hunger as against this country....It stupefies me—seems to me horribly vulgar and inferior."[3] William had a sharper sense of humor than his brother, and his sensibilities were less easily offended. Still, he found the war scare horrifying.

In a letter to an English friend he tried to make a dark joke of it all, with Henry Cabot Lodge as one of the cartoon characters:

> *Well, our countries will soon be soaked in each other's blood.*
> *You will be disemboweling me, and Hodgson [an English*

statesman] cleaving Lodge's skull. It will be a war of exter-
mination when it comes, for neither side can tell when it is
beaten, and the last man will bury the penultimate one, and
then die himself. The French will then occupy England and the
Spaniards America. Both will unite against the Germans, and
no one can foretell the end—But seriously, all true patriots here
have had a hell of a time.[4]

James, such an avid student of human psychology, marveled at "how near the surface in all of us the old fighting instinct lies, and how slight an appeal will wake it up. Once really awaked, there is no retreat." James usually tried to see the positive side of things, and by the day after Christmas he had calmed down enough to write his brother that the "popular jingoism" in support of President Cleveland "has a very good side. It shows that in spite of all our party frenzy we are still a unit when it comes to a question of obedience to the executive, and that is the root of all national safety and greatness. It is true that it then presupposes that the executive should not habitually be insane!"[5]

In the January 7 edition of the student newspaper, James read with amusement mixed with alarm Theodore Roosevelt's screed decrying the "Baboo kind of statesmanship" advocated by weak-kneed professors. On January 9 James responded, trying to turn the tables on his former student. He wrote the *Crimson*: "May I express a hope that in this University, if no where else on the continent, we shall be patriotic enough *not* to remain passive... let us consult our reason as to what is best, and then exert ourselves as citizens with all our might." Rather than be passively swept up by the jingoist tide—"hypnotized by sacramental phrases" of patriotic duty—students should think for themselves and take action (by, for instance, petitioning their congressmen, as James had done, denouncing "a wanton and blustering provocation of war"). Then, in the quiet of his study, James went back to thinking and fretting. He was, he knew, trying to treat war fever with a placebo. "Reason," he once observed, "is one of the very feeblest of Nature's resources."[6]

James had taught Roosevelt comparative anatomy in the spring of 1878, during Roosevelt's sophomore year. The relationship of the two men is one of history's small what-ifs—What if Roosevelt had been a more attentive student and James a more effective teacher? What if James had become an intellectual mentor to the young Roosevelt, opening him up to a more sophisticated understanding of human nature? A budding scientist, the nineteen-year-old Roosevelt liked James's class. "Extremely interesting," he wrote Bamie in the beginning of the school year.[7] But his interest was soon to fade. Initially Roosevelt had been his usual ebullient self. (A classmate recalls Professor James "settling back in his chair, in a broad grin...and waiting for T.R. to finish.")[8] But then Roosevelt, depressed by his father's death, began to slack off, and his grade in the course dipped. James, too, was distracted. In 1878 he was shifting his academic interest from physiology to his true callings, philosophy and psychology. Just as consuming, he was in love, courting the woman who would become his wife.

Roosevelt paid closer attention to his history teacher, Norman Shaler. A proud Kentuckian, Shaler had commanded a Union regiment in the Civil War, and he was much revered by Harvard students of his time. Shaler was a disciple of Jean Lamarck, the French social Darwinist who argued that races could be improved by absorbing the culture of better races. At the same time Shaler worried that "alien races" would water down good

American stock.[9] Roosevelt received most of his intellectual grounding in racial theory from Shaler, though he appears not to have been shy about imparting a few of his own ideas. "Now look here, Roosevelt," Shaler once interrupted his young charge, "let me talk. I'm running this course."

James knew that Shaler was "a charlatan," as he put it.[10] Highly suspicious of unified, so-called scientific theories that explained all of human progress, James regarded social Darwinism as a sham. He accepted Darwin's theories of evolution, but not philosopher Herbert Spencer's attempts to torture them into a deterministic formula that conveniently rated the Anglo-Saxons as the master race. All this made James an unusual, almost lonely figure in the academic world of Harvard in the 1870s and 1880s. He was wonderfully free of cant, saved by his fresh intelligence from academic wisdom and faddishness. By instinct, he believed in the individual, not the system. He claimed to have learned a great truth from an uneducated carpenter: "There is very little difference between one man and another, but what very little there is, *is very important*." In an intolerant age, he was "the most tolerant man of our generation," Walter Lippmann later wrote. "He listened for truth from anybody."[11]

James received his "political education," he wrote, from Godkin, chief scribe of the mugwumps, who had frequently dined at the Jameses' home when William was a young man.[12] But he found Godkin too gloomy and censorious. When Godkin wanted to bash Roosevelt and Lodge for jingoism during the Venezuela war scare, James wrote, "I beseech you to be as non-expletive and patiently explanatory as you can, for thus will you be the more effective. Father, forgive them for they know not what they do!"[13]

James's biblical injunction was delivered in a self-mocking tone. He tried never to take himself too seriously, which was not easy, given the intensity of his feelings. James found his Harvard and mugwump colleagues too fussy, and he did not share their nativist fears of the alien races encroaching on Boston's shore. Indeed, from classrooms to drawing rooms he found the air too thin. In 1876, the year before Roosevelt became his student, he wrote: "Last night I went of all places in the world to Mrs. Sargent's aesthetic tea in Chestnut Street. Certain individuals read poetry, whilst others sat and longed for them to stop so that they might begin to talk. The room was full of a decidedly good-looking set of people, especially women—but New England all over! Give me a human race with some *guts* to them, no matter if they do belch at you now and then."[14]

In this active, restless spirit, James resembled Theodore Roosevelt. Like Roosevelt he had read the adventure stories of Mayne Reid, stirring tales of danger and daring like *The Boy Hunter.* He sought the strenuous life, clearing brush at his mountain retreat in New Hampshire and hiking in the Adirondacks, which provided him, one James family biographer wrote, with a "facsimile of the frontier, free of bison and hostile Indians." He had just traveled west for the first time in 1895 and had been moved by the majesty of the mountains. To his students he preached fighting the good fight—not by literal combat, but by leading an active and daring life. In an address to undergraduates that same year, on the eve of the Venezuela war scare, he quoted Shakespeare's Henry IV, shaming those who had missed war: "Hang yourself, brave Crillon! We fought at Arques, and you were not there!" He warned students against reading too much fiction, and to his eldest son, Harry, off at school, he implored, "Live energetically...live hard!" He himself was in constant motion, riding his bicycle through Harvard yard and like Roosevelt taking steps two or three at a time.[15]

But if Roosevelt was experiential, James was experimental. He believed in taking not just physical risks but mental and emotional ones. In the year ahead he would experiment with the hallucinogenic drug mescal (though he complained of a hangover and never tried it again). An insomniac, in the late 1880s he began using chloroform to put himself to sleep. Spiritualism was enjoying a revival among the elites in the late nineteenth century, and James became fascinated with psychics (however, the one he visited, a Mrs. Piper on Beacon Hill, was thoroughly respectable).[16] Prone to crushes on his female acquaintances, he impulsively kissed the Jameses' housemaid, Lizzie, in 1888 (he justified it by saying that he had never kissed anyone spontaneously, and to repress the urge seemed "churlish and inhuman"; he had no comment on Lizzie's reaction).[17] He had more serious though apparently nonphysical infatuations with some proper Boston maidens, Sarah Whitman and Rosina Emmet (the latter crush, on a woman thirty years younger, was bruising to his wife, Alice). His most significant swoon came over a young Bryn Mawr graduate he described to his wife as a "perfect little serious rosebud." James met Paulina Goldmark while hiking in the Adirondacks in September 1895, after he had returned exhilarated from his first trip to the Rocky Mountains. They met at a camp for recovering neurasthenics in upstate New York. Pauline saw herself as a "new woman" who could control her own destiny, and James marveled at how composed and unself-conscious she seemed to be—in perfect contrast to James's younger self.[18] For better and for worse, James was alive to his own feelings. A fellow philosopher recalled James's joy in those years as he ran naked under a garden hose on a hot summer's midnight.[19]

Gertrude Stein, a student at Radcliffe (the "Annex," as it was called in the 1890s), took James's seminar on psychology in 1895.

She recalled that James told her, "Never reject anything. Nothing has been proved. If you reject anything, that is the beginning of the end as an intellectual."[20]

The famous James family would later be lumped together with Brahmins like Emerson and Holmes, but they were descendants of Irish immigrants who had always felt slightly apart from the well-to-do, ingrown world of Henry Cabot Lodge—a little insecure, and the better for it. The father, Henry Senior, appears to have been a difficult man. Heir to a fortune made from construction of the Erie Canal, he dabbled in the various utopian ideas fashionable among the thinkers of Boston and Concord in the antebellum period. He finally embraced Swedenborgianism, one of the most baffling and obscure philosophies, and vaguely argued for free love. (William Dean Howells said of James's book, *Secret of Swedenborg*, "He kept it.") Henry, Senior, was said to be a great conversationalist but could be tiresome. An amateur artist, William James once illustrated the frontispiece of a philosophical tome by his father with a drawing of a man beating a dead horse.

William James lived in fourteen different houses in his first sixteen years as the family traveled, often unhappily, about New England, New York, and Europe. No matter the locale, dinnertime at the Jameses' was loud, fractious, and teasing; the neuroses of the James children were matched only by their creativity. William, it was later said, wrote philosophy as if it were fiction, while Henry wrote fiction as if it were philosophy.[21]

William was sought after by Boston hostesses, but he distrusted snobbery and intolerance. He prized Harvard's "undisciplinables"—not the smooth, slightly bored clubmen, the Porcellian swells with their Harvard "indifference," but rather the intellectuals and oddballs, "of whom I am one." He tried to be sunny, open-minded, upbeat, but as John Jay Chapman, a fellow intellectual who had broken from his own stuffy Porcellian background noted, "there was, in spite of his playfulness, a deep sadness about James."[22] He enjoyed those who lived joyously because he knew so many, even those in his own family, who lived in the dark. As much as Roosevelt and Lodge, James had been profoundly affected by the Civil War, only in a different way. William was nineteen when war broke out. According to his father, he agitated to enlist, but he didn't seem to have tried very hard. He joined a state militia for ninety days and wrapped some bandages; then he enrolled at Harvard. Henry James also stayed away from the war, entering Harvard Law School.

Their younger brothers, Wilkie and Bob, did join the Union army. Wilkie signed up with the Massachusetts Fifty-fourth as an adjutant (messenger boy) to Colonel Robert Gould Shaw. On May 28, 1863, Henry was on Beacon Hill, standing in the doorway of the home of Oliver Wendell Holmes, Sr., when the Fifty-fourth, led by Shaw, marched by on their way to death and glory.[23]

William was in the crowd, too, hearing the huzzahs, the bands playing, the soldiers singing choruses of "The Battle Hymn of the Republic." A month earlier he had visited his brother at Camp Meigs, not far from Cambridge. Charles Russell Lowell's regiment was also training there, and Colonel Shaw's nineteen-year-old sister, Effie, had come to see off her fiancé, who was moving out with his cavalry. William recalled that Effie and Charles (whom he knew from Boston society) came "whirling up on horseback," silhouetted against the setting sun. Years later, he described the scene as if it had been yesterday: "I looked back and saw their faces and figures against the evening sky, and they

Colonel Robert Gould Shaw (Boston Athenaeum)

looked so young and victorious, that I, much gnawed by questions as to my own duty of enlisting or not, shrank back—they had not seen me—from being recognized. I shall never forget the impression they made." The doomed young Lochinvar and his maiden bride-to-be "looked so much like a king and queen" that James never ventured to speak to them.[24]

Wilkie was wounded in the side and the foot in the assault on Fort Wagner. Left for dead, he was rescued by a black soldier and transported back to his parents' home, then in Newport, Rhode Island. William was at home when his brother was carried in on a warm July day, and sat by his bed for months while he cried out in his sleep for Colonel Shaw and his lost brothers-in-arms. As Wilkie fitfully dozed, William drew him

Josephine Shaw Lowell (Boston Athenaeum)

in charcoal—his brother resting facedown, mouth hanging open, vulnerable, sad. Wilkie's bravery and sacrifice made William feel "very small and shabby," he recalled.[25]

That October Emerson wrote a poem to the Massachusetts Fifty-fourth called "Voluntaries," which went in part:

So nigh is the grandeur to our dust,
So near is God to man.
When Duty whispers low, Thou must,
The youth replies, I can.

William James had replied, "I cannot." Yet the Emerson poem remained a great family favorite. No wonder James would ask his students whether they wanted to be in Crillon's place when confronted by Henry IV.[26]

All his life James would be haunted—and inspired and cautioned and instructed—by the war he missed. In a letter to his sister, Alice, in the winter of 1895, he recalled leaving his Boston club after a particularly boring and stuffy conversation. To clear his head he walked home on the cold and starry night. As he crossed the bridge to Cambridge he thought of another night many years before when, as a college student, he had left a party humming a song about the mad abolitionist John Brown ("He captured Harper's Ferry with 19 men and true / And he frightened old Virginny til she trembled through and through"). He wrote Alice, "And the contrast between the two kinds of life smote into me."[27]

James's life was a constant struggle in contrasts, between heart and head, strength and weakness, energy and lassitude. As a young man advancing up the academic ladder at Harvard, he was nearly crippled by physical ailments that were psychic in origin. He experienced periodic, sometimes constant eye strain, back pain, insomnia, and depression. His nervous system, he told his brother Henry, "is utter trash." In 1870 he suffered from a "great dorsal collapse—carrying with it a moral one." He had become, in his view, spineless. He began to contemplate suicide, or, as he put it, "the pistol, dagger, and the bowl." But he feared he lacked the courage for that, too.[28]

Actually, he had great courage, though not the sort Lodge and Roosevelt wrote about in *Hero Tales*. Over time, fitfully and with many setbacks, he willed himself to face the darkness of life, and by so doing found the light. He accomplished this through intense introspection, the willingness to experiment with his own feelings (and occasionally, selfishly, the feelings of others), and his observation of human differences. In 1890 he wrote in his pioneering magnum opus, *The Principles of Psychology*: "If the 'searching of our heart and reins' be the purpose of this human drama, then what is sought seems to be what effort we can make. He who can make none is but a shadow; he who can make much is a hero."[29]

James understood, as did the ancient Greek playwright Aeschylus, that from pain could come wisdom. He did not believe in getting on his horse and galloping away from dark care. He would become, along with Roosevelt, a great apostle of the strenuous life. He resolutely tried—quite literally, in the sense that he *resolved* to try—to look on the bright side, to find redeeming qualities. But he did not turn away from the strange and different or disturbing. Rather, he looked more closely.

In March 1865, just as the Civil War was ending, James boarded a steamer for South America. Having missed the fight, he was seeking adventure, and he found it canoeing down fetid rivers in the lush tropics, part paradise, part menacing—a world out of those Mayne Reid adventure novels he had read as a boy. He was on a scientific expedition mounted by a prominent Harvard professor and darling of the smart set on Beacon Hill, Louis Agassiz. A professor of natural history who in today's parlance would be called a creationist, Agassiz was headed to the Amazon to look for fossils that might disprove Darwin's new theories of evolution by natural selection.

The ocean voyage made James seasick most of the way down, and in Rio de Janeiro he caught a mild form of smallpox that nearly blinded him. But over the summer of 1865 he hardened his body, browned his skin, and learned to marvel at the exotica all around him. Observant and intellectually skeptical, he discovered that Agassiz, a family friend, was an old fraud who twisted evidence to prove his theories. Before long James became a Darwinian. But he had the good sense, and the rare judgment, to see through the social Darwinists as well—his fellow professors at Harvard, like Roosevelt's favorite, Norman Shaler, who were cooking up racial theories to justify their views of Anglo-Saxon superiority. James was not free of the prejudices of his age, but he was unusually—among his fellow academics, almost uniquely—open to the idea that different races had different qualities, and that one should learn from them, and not simply judge. His path began with small observations. On the beach in Brazil he noticed the "beautiful brown color" of the Indians, observing, "Their skin is dry and clean looking, and they perspire very little so on the whole I think they are better looking in that respect than other negroes or white men, who in this climate are always sweaty and greasy looking."[30] Different physiology, however, did not suggest greater or lesser character—or intelligence. That came from the individual and a thousand tiny human shadings. The white man, young James perceived, had no monopoly on truth; Brahmin gods like Agassiz could be elegant deceivers, while wisdom could come from a native shaman.

In time James evolved a whole philosophical approach to open-mindedness, to the appreciation of individual differences and a healthy disregard for neat theorizing. (It was James who gave to English-language philosophy the term "pluralism.")[31] By study and instinct, he put his principles to use. In 1888 W. E. B. DuBois entered Harvard, one of very few black students in higher education in that century. DuBois wrote that he went to college to search for the truth, and "eventually it landed me in the arms of William James of Harvard, for which God be praised.... I was repeatedly a guest in the house of William James; he was my friend and guide to clear thinking."[32]

Even as he gained intellectual confidence, James's personal life remained fraught. Returning in 1868 from a trip to Europe to shore up his shaky health, he decided to form a club—not a stuffy social club, but one for intellectuals. The model was the Saturday Club, a dining and conversation society that included such Hub luminaries as Oliver Wendell Holmes, Sr., Emerson, Longfellow, Hawthorne, and Agassiz. Known initially simply as "the Club," it met once a month, and its members included Oliver Wendell Holmes, Jr., Moorfield Storey (the future mugwump chief), Henry Lee Higginson ("Bully Higg" of the snowball fights), and John Fiske (future author of the social Darwinist manifesto *Manifest Destiny*). James had become best friends with the younger Holmes, whom he called "Wendyboy." "It used to be great fun to hear William James and Wendell Holmes…spar, or at any rate excite each other to all sorts of ideas and expressions," recalled Higginson.

The Club evolved into an even more intellectual group called the Metaphysical Club by the early 1870s. But James and Holmes grew apart. James was put off by Holmes's "cold blooded conscious egotism and conceit," he wrote his brother Henry. William memorably described Holmes as "a powerful battery, formed like a planing machine to gouge a deep self-beneficial groove through life."[33] James may have been jealous: Holmes was a thrice-wounded war veteran and already a successful lawyer, while James was still floundering about, having tried and given up medicine before turning to teaching. More significantly, perhaps, Holmes was explicitly virile and James worried that he was not.

James had not been a very suave suitor. He entertained a feeble and impossible crush on Holmes's longtime girlfriend, Fannie Dixwell. In 1876 he fell in love with Alice Gibbens but hopelessly flip-flopped about until the spring of 1878, when he finally proposed under the elms on Boston Common. The daughter of an alcoholic who killed himself, Alice was a sensitive girl. For a time during the Civil War, out of sympathy with the soldiers who slept on the ground, she had slept on the floor of her bedroom. But she was protective of William, attuned to his moods, and she suffered his enthusiasms. He called her "My Guide." In the summer of 1895, struggling with her own case of the blues, she asked her husband if he was sorry he married her. James reassured her that "that is like asking whether or not I am sorry this planet is the earth."[34]

By the fall of 1895, as he was mooning over his new friend Pauline Goldmark and the war clouds were improbably gathering over Venezuela, James had become America's preeminent philosopher. With his vivid imagination and writing style, he was fast introducing words and phrases into the cultural lexicon — "stream of consciousness," "the bitch-goddess success," "healthy-minded," "time-line," "live option," and, in the years to come, "moral equivalent of war."[35] His influence would be felt on writers as varied as Robert Frost (who came to Harvard to study under James), Robert Penn Warren, Ernest Hemingway, T. S. Eliot, and Gertrude Stein. ("The 'drama of risk,'" wrote Warren, "is at the center of the Hemingway story, as at the center of James's philosophy.")[36]

He was the era's premier student of human nature, but with self-imposed restraints. He was too focused on human consciousness — skittish about sex, he dismissed an emerging European rival, Sigmund Freud, as a "dirty fellow." He had brilliant flashes of insight but, walled off from belief in the unconscious, could not grasp some of the murkier forces of unreason. And yet by studying his own failings, by trying to come to grips with his own paralyzing fears, he saw the need for energy and action in life. "There is no more miserable being than one in whom nothing is habitual but indecision," he wrote, reflecting on his own painful experience. "There is no more contemptible type than that of the nerveless sentimentalist and dreamer, who spends his time in a weltering sea of insensibility and emotion, but who never does a manly deed."[37]

James understood and appreciated the drive to be active, heroic, even savage. But he saw the downward pull of war, and he dreaded it. As the Venezuela war scare erupted in December 1895, he worried for his country: "The good name for being a safe country that 80 years has gained us is squandered in three days and we are now as dangerous to the world as anything since Bonaparte's time." (James was apparently thinking of the War of 1812 and forgetting another foreign war, the conquest of Mexico in 1848.) On December 24 James anxiously wrote E. L. Godkin that "three days of fighting mob hysteria can at any time undo peace habits of a hundred years."[38]

The mob, James knew, was being stirred by some homegrown forces. The James brothers were leery of Harvard's veneration of war. When Harvard built the massive Memorial Hall, with its busts and plaques to Civil War heroes like Robert Gould Shaw and Charles Russell Lowell, Henry sneered that the James house on Irving Street now looked out upon a "great bristling Valhalla."[39] In a letter to Henry at the end of January, William examined the motivations of two famous sons of Harvard: "Roosevelt believes in war as an ideal function, necessary from time to time for national health. With such frank jingoes one can argue comfortably. What Lodge believes in God only knows — I fear he may *not* be temperamentally predestined to jingoism as

Valhalla: Memorial Hall at Harvard (Library of Congress)

Roosevelt is." James was made uncomfortable by that which he could not understand.

In his letter to Henry, who was living in London, he turned his attention — and his ire — to the rising jingoism of the American press, the so-called yellow press that was selling newspapers with war or the promise thereof. "The worst thing here is the insincerity, levity, and utter *irresponsibility* of the newspapers.... It makes one despair of civilization." And yet James instinctively fought against despair and tried to understand the unknowable.

6

Selling Papers

"Without a press, we shall get nowhere."

URING THE VENEZUELA CRISIS some of the most exuberantly bellicose headlines had appeared in the New York *Journal*. "Is This a Prelude to War?" the *Journal* asked on December 18, after President Cleveland's defiant message to Britain was read in Congress. The paper headlined "Wild Applause" in the Senate and reported, "The House Thundered Its Approval." Not since the Civil War had there been such excitement in the Capitol, *Journal* correspondents wrote. The veterans were dusting off their uniforms: "Grand Army Men Ready to Fight." Their womenfolk, too: "Patriotic Women Ready: The Daughters of the American Revolution Will Prove Their Devotion." The British navy was roughly twenty times the strength of America's, but the *Journal* called for a draft of the leisure classes: "Private Yachts Available for the Navy: A Splendid Fleet of Auxiliary Vessels on the Atlantic and the Pacific Coasts and the Lakes Which Patriotic Owners Could Equip for Service." There was a role for all, even if they weren't the yacht-owning type. Americans must be ever vigilant because "English Spies Have Been Here."

On December 20 the *Journal*'s front page carried a large illustration of a dapper Henry Cabot Lodge delivering what was "undoubtedly the popular speech of the day." The next day an enormous illustration showed a grinning Uncle Sam cleaning his musket after riddling a target emblazoned with England's mascot, John Bull.[1]

The New York *Journal* had, until very recently, been a small, unremarkable, unprofitable daily. In a matter of months it had been transformed into a popular, sensational—though still not profitable—daily by a tall, slightly stooped thirty-two-year-old genius named William Randolph Hearst. Hearst's father, who died in 1891, had been a rough-and-ready miner who had the good luck and savage business sense to parlay a $450 stake into a substantial interest in the Comstock silver lode and the Anaconda copper mine. George Hearst had avoided service in the Civil War and bought a seat in the U.S. Senate. His wife, Phoebe, a Missouri would-be aristocrat whose family had owned slaves, tried not to squander her husband's entire fortune bankrolling their spendthrift only son.[2] Henry Cabot Lodge wrote his mother that at a Washington dinner party he had sat beside "Mrs. Hearst—the widow of the California Senator & millionaire, a very generous & public spirited but very quiet woman with a good business head. I had some interesting talk with her on various subjects."[3] It was no mean feat to impress Lodge.

To say that little Willie Hearst was spoiled does not begin to describe the relationship between mother and son. Senator Hearst, twenty years Phoebe's senior, appears to have been more interested in his mistresses and poker. Their only son was still sleeping in his mother's bed when he was three and a half years old. Willie "can't bear for me to get out of his sight," Phoebe wrote her husband when the boy was five. In 1873, as Willie turned ten, Phoebe took her son to Europe in search of culture and consolation. Much time was spent touring castles; looking out upon Windsor Castle, the boy announced, "I would like to live there." He was not an ungenerous little prince. Phoebe informed George that after they had passed some desperate people in Ireland, Willie "wanted to give away all of his money and his clothes, too."

The senator was not so charitable when it came to his paternal obligation, and her husband's indifference gnawed at Phoebe. "We cannot help feeling great disappointment when you write so little," she told George. Willie also pined for his father, who like Theodore Roosevelt escaped family obligation to hunt in the Dakotas: "I wish I could spend a few days in the Black Hills, I would like to have a shot at some of those deer, elk, and maybe grizzly bears I heard you talk about." But the senator had no interest in his son's company.[4]

When Willie arrived at Harvard in 1882, he had blond hair parted in the middle, staring eyes, and a soprano voice. At once shy and aggressive, he tried to buy friends and later intimated that he had been elected to the Porcellian Club. He had not; the best he could do was vice-president of the Intercollegiate Base Ball Association, a position achieved after hosting a string of drinking parties in his room. "My long swiping [slang for "drinking"] has at last received its reward," he sardonically wrote his mother.[5] He kept a local waitress as a mistress and loved going to dance halls and, with his rowdy friends, throwing pies at the chorus girls. Known for staging noisy parades through Harvard Square, he was a champion prankster, at one point presenting each faculty member with a chamber pot, the professor's name inscribed in the basin. (William James received one.) Perhaps not surprisingly, the college administration tired of him. Phoebe wrote her husband during Willie's senior year,

Hearst, the Harvard dandy (right), with a friend (Bancroft Library, University of California, Berkeley)

recounting a conversation between a Harvard administrator and her son, "The Dean . . . said, 'You here again? I thought the letter I sent to S.F. [Hearst's home in San Francisco] would keep you there.'" Hearst did not graduate. She lamented her son's dissipation: "The amount he must have drank did him no good," she wrote. "Theaters, horse shows, late suppers & <u>women</u> consume two hundred dollars quickly." Hearst's capacity to spend was epic. By the time he was twenty-six he was lavishing more than $40,000 a year (about $1 million in 2010 dollars) on his personal entertainments.[6]

Yet Hearst was not without ambition. His letters to his father, mostly unanswered, were light and self-deprecating. Removed from Harvard, he tried to con his father into buying a house in Washington to launch his "brilliant entre" into politics.[7] His father didn't fall for it, but he did put his son to work on a small paper he had bought in San Francisco in 1881 to help his election bid to the Senate. The *Examiner* was a money-loser and a bore, until young Hearst arrived and found his true calling. On April 3, 1887, he gave readers a taste of what was to come when he turned over page one to a hotel fire. The headline began HUN-GRY, FRANTIC FLAMES. They Leap Madly Upon the Splendid Pleasure Palace by the Bay of Monterey, Encircling Del Monte in Their Ravenous Embrace From Pinnacle to Foundation. Leaping Higher, Higher, Higher, With Desperate Desire.[8]

Sexualized violence has long been a winning formula for mass-audience newspapers, and Hearst did not invent it (Joseph Pulitzer got there ahead of him with the New York *World*). But Hearst was especially adept at conquering that old editor's bugaboo, the slow news day. If there's no news, Hearst instructed his editors, make some (he might have said, but did not need to, even if you have to make it up). Hearst's first great "sob sister" reporter, a handsome redhead named Winifred Sweet (who went by the byline Annie Laurie), tested San Francisco's welfare net by collapsing on Market Street. As a crowd gathered, not much happened until a policeman, reeking of whiskey himself, appeared to determine whether she was drunk. She was finally taken to the hospital, where she was groped and given an unnecessary emetic. She wrote it all down in the *Examiner*, to the embarrassment of city officials. As this story suggests, Hearst's sensationalism was not without social purpose or consequence. The story caused the hospital to suspend the doctor in charge.[9]

In 1895 Hearst's mother sold the Anaconda mine for $7.5 million and gave the money to her son, who promptly used some of it to buy a newspaper in New York. The *Morning Journal* was known as the "chamber maid's delight" for its stories on society's comings and goings. Hearst accommodated the chambermaids with an enormous drawing of the wedding between the Duke of Marlborough and Consuelo Vanderbilt on page one of his first issue, November 7, 1895, but he had grander ambitions.[10] He took aim at Pulitzer, whose *World* had created a whole new era known as yellow journalism, after its yellow-tinted funny pages featuring the Yellow Kid, a street urchin who made fun of upper-class pursuits like golf or the newest luxury, the motorcar. Pulitzer's Sunday editor, Morrill Goddard, was a master at what was called "crime, underwear, and pseudo science" journalism. He would, for instance, run a feature on the anatomy of the human leg, using the garter-belted gams of chorus girls by way of illustration.

Hearst asked Goddard to meet him at the bar of the Hoffman House, a Gilded Age den of temptation where Tammany Hall did deals, businessmen conducted private assignations behind the potted palms, and a naughty portrait called *Nymphs and Satyr* beckoned from above the bar.[11] Settling into a plush red sofa, Goddard said he couldn't possibly leave the *World*. Hearst pulled out a wad of cash. Goddard protested that he couldn't come without his staff of reporters and designers. Hearst promised to hire them, too. Shortly thereafter, the entire staff of the

Sunday *World*, minus one secretary, went to the *Journal*.[12] Soon the headlines began:

He Hiccoughed For Five Days
White Woman Among Cannibals
Snakes And Their Gods
Pretty Annette's Gauzy Silk Bathingsuits
The Frightful Dreams of a Morphine Fiend

Settling into a grand suite in a building at 7 West Twenty-fifth Street, Hearst was quickly drawn to the nightlife of New York. (His mistress from Harvard, Tessie Powers, a former waitress known to Hearst's acquaintances as "the Harvard Widow" and "Dirty Drawers," was installed nearby.) He avoided the opera but faithfully attended plays and shows, especially romantic melodramas. At the same time he was a hands-on owner who relished his work. One of his editors, Willis Abbott, described his routine, later immortalized by Orson Welles in *Citizen Kane*:

> It seemed to me that his greatest joy in life was to attend the theater, follow it up with a lively supper and, at about 1:30 a.m., turn up at the office full of scintillating ideas and therewith rip my editorial page to pieces. Other pages were apt to suffer equally, and it was always an interesting spectacle to me to watch this young millionaire, usually in irreproachable evening dress, working over the forms, changing a head here, shifting the position of an article there, clamoring always for more pictures and bigger type.

The editors were frazzled by the owner's meddling, but Abbott observed that Hearst never lost his temper or even showed signs of irritation. "Hearst was to me a puzzle," he recalled. "Conducting the most brazen and blatant newspapers, he was personally shy. It was a real ordeal to introduce him to a public man, even when he himself sought the introduction, for he would invariably sit silent, with downcast eyes, leaving me to carry the conversation." He would scoff at attacks on his reputation, but his manner suggested he was not indifferent. Once, Abbott recalled, he tried to warn him against a potentially embarrassing plan of some kind. "What the devil do I care about that?" Hearst asked somewhat heatedly. "I've been in an embarrassing position ever since I came to New York, and I've thrived on it."

Indeed, he did increase the circulation of the *Journal* from 20,000 to 150,000 in less than a year. But he was still losing money after stealing away Pulitzer's staff at great cost. He tried parades and fireworks to boost circulation, but he needed something bigger, more spectacular. He needed a war.

He did not get one over Venezuela. Almost as quickly as it began, the war scare fizzled out. In early January a Royal Navy flying squadron of a dozen warships prepared to sail for the Caribbean, but before the fleet weighed anchor, great-power politics intervened. Germany threatened to go to war with Britain over a dispute in South Africa, and almost overnight Britain's strategic calculus changed. The kaiser represented a graver threat to Britain than the United States; within a week America was seen as a potential ally, a fellow English-speaking nation against German imperial ambitions. The Venezuela border dispute was shunted off for diplomatic resolution. Henry Adams, a close friend of Lodge and Roosevelt, great-grandson of John Adams, grandson of John Quincy Adams, archly observed, "The sudden appearance of Germany as the grizzly terror...effected what Adamses had tried for two hundred [years] in vain—frightened England into America's arms."[13]

Hearst was only momentarily deflated. A war against Great Britain had not been realistic; even Hearst had known that America was overmatched. In between flag-waving and bluster about Civil War veterans dusting off their uniforms, the *Journal* had warned in December that American ports were defenseless against the British navy and that the American navy was woefully underfunded and ill equipped. A *Journal* cartoonist on January 14 showed Uncle Sam floating about in a flimsy tub armed only with a flintlock pistol.[14]

Hearst could look forward to other, more manageable conflicts. As it turned out, another war was already brewing. *Journal* readers were entertained on December 8 by an article headlined "Lieutenant Churchill Describes the War." The lieutenant was Winston Churchill, and the war was the rebellion in Cuba, the conflict that had caused Theodore Roosevelt back in March to excitedly write the governor of New York, hoping for a National Guard commission in the "improbable" event that the United States should intervene. The revolution had sputtered along for nine months without much attention, save from war lovers like Hearst, Roosevelt, and Churchill.

Young Churchill was Roosevelt's spiritual brother in arms. At the outbreak of the Cuban revolution he was a twenty-one-year-old recent graduate of Sandhurst, the British military academy, and he had gone to Cuba in the autumn of 1895 as an observer with the Spanish troops because he wanted a taste of war. The *Journal* article noted that Churchill had come under fire "while bathing" in a stream—the first time he ever heard shots fired in anger. He was excited by the "wop, wop, wop" of enemy rifles but dismissive of the rebels, who showed poor marksmanship and would not stand and fight. He was more impressed with Spanish officers, who were "both brave and courteous."[15]

Churchill's Cuban adventure did not mark him deeply, other than giving him a lifelong taste for Cuban cigars. The "undisciplined rabble" that had interrupted his swim seemed to him a most unworthy foe for a properly trained imperial army.[16] But Churchill, like his Spanish hosts, underestimated the enemy. It's true that the rebels avoided toe-to-toe confrontations with regular Spanish troops. But they didn't need to stand and fight when hit and run was more effective. While Spain had put down earlier rebellions in Cuba, this one was different—better organized, more deeply rooted, more imaginatively conceived.

Its ideological leader was a slender émigré named José Martí, who would become the great martyr of the revolution and whose name still adorns revolutionary billboards in Havana over a century later. Martí's racial views were, to put it mildly, ahead of their time. In an era when scientists at Harvard were weighing skulls to determine racial superiority, Martí, white son of a Spaniard and a Cuban, believed that, as his mulatto comrade Antonio Maceo put it, there were "no whites, nor blacks, but only Cubans." With passion and eloquence, Martí envisioned a postracial society in Cuba, a color-blind *patria*. This was a deeply revolutionary concept. White landowners in Cuba had been shocked by slave rebellions in Haiti a century earlier and feared bloody uprisings by their former slave populations (slaves were not emancipated in Cuba until 1886). But as they tired of Spanish rule, some members of the Cuban elite began to accept the newly freed blacks—more than half the population of the country—as partners in revolution. Their hero, vividly described in an 1894 propaganda tract by Martí, was Salvador Cisneros Betancourt, an aristocrat who decided to bury his white daughter in the grave of a black

José Martí, the revolutionary idealist (Library of Congress)

man as an act of racial transcendence. Blacks not only flocked to the revolutionary army that sprang up in 1895, they became officers — inconceivable in a European or North American army. Their idol was Maceo, the so-called Bronze Titan, a charismatic former mule driver who rose to the rank of general.[17] Self-educated, Maceo was said to keep volumes of French literature and philosophy in his saddlebags.[18]

In his very first battle, in May 1895, José Martí rode to the head of his troops astride a white horse and was promptly shot and killed. With Martí martyred, the new rebel commander was a wily old Dominican with the grand name of Máximo Gómez. Lacking proper arms and training for his troops, Gómez did not attempt set-piece battles with the Spanish army. He fought a

General Máximo Gómez (Library of Congress)

classic guerrilla war, harassing, ambushing, sniping, and slashing and burning. His most effective tactic was to burn the farms of landowners who did not embrace the revolution. ("Blessed be the torch," Gómez decreed.) He wanted to starve the sugar industry and exhaust Spain, whose empire had long been shrinking and tottering. Spain could not keep sending soldiers forever, and Gómez was patient. His three best generals, it was said, were "June, July, and August"—the rainy season, when yellow fever killed more Spanish troops than the rebels could hope to.[19]

Gómez and the other revolutionary leaders were eager to get help. That meant awakening the sleeping giant to the north by arousing sympathy, which in turn meant stirring up America's newspapers. "Without a press, we shall get nowhere," said

Antonio Maceo, "the Bronze Titan" (Library of Congress)

Gómez.[20] In America, there was already a reasonably well-off Cuban exile community, principally cigar makers in Florida and New York. These émigrés formed a junta, a government in exile that was not recognized by the United States government but had a growing number of friends in the American press, chief among them William Randolph Hearst.

The junta—or as it was less elegantly known, the Peanut Club, after the free peanuts provided to hungry newsmen—kept a dingy walk-up office in lower Manhattan. There, reporters from the *Journal* and other New York newspapers of varying repute wandered in to be told stories of the revolution. The head of the junta, Tomás Estrada Palma—Don Tomás—told some real stretchers, and Hearst's journalists believed them, or rather published them. They made stirring, wrenching copy. (Don Tomás had the unfortunate habit of clearing his throat every time he told a lie, but no matter.)[21]

"Spaniards' Inhuman Cruelty" was the headline in the *Journal* on December 12; "Heartrending Narrative of a Butchery by Brutish Troops." The article, spun from "a letter from an eyewitness," described Spanish soldiers firing on innocent Cuban children. "Fiendish Cruelty in Cuba" blared the *Journal* four days later. And while the Cubans were usually portrayed as innocent victims, Hearst loved the exotica of the island. He was not above scaring his readers about wild Negroes on the march. "Snakes Are Their Gods," reported the *Journal* on December 29, adding "Cuban Disciples of the Devil Have Hideous Midnight Orgies."[22] Still, his sympathies clearly lay with the revolutionary army. "On to Havana!" the *Journal* editorial page cried on Christmas Day. "Cuba's Day Is Coming" was the headline a little more than a week later.[23]

Partly as a result of all this, the U.S. Congress was stirring. A wellborn young Cuban writer, Gonzalo de Quesada, was lobbying for a congressional resolution to recognize the Cuban "belligerency." This was not the same as recognizing an independent Cuban government—far from it—but as a point of international law, granting belligerency status meant regarding the Cuban revolutionaries as something more than outlaws. American arms merchants would be allowed to sell weapons and ammunition to the revolutionaries without interference by the American navy, which had been intercepting arms-laden ships sailing to Cuba for profit and adventure.[24] In January 1896, as the Venezuela war scare died down and the *Journal* went looking for new battles, Hearst naturally embraced the cause of a belligerency resolution. In mid-December, the *Journal* had already

Burning a Cuban Sugar Plantation

enthusiastically reported the junta's somewhat implausible interest in buying an American battle cruiser.[25] Now the newspaper began to press congressmen to pass a law that would make it possible for the Cubans to properly arm themselves.

The *Journal* became a handy resource for congressmen looking for evidence to support their votes. As the debate over recognizing the Cuban insurgents rattled on through the winter of 1896, the elderly and august chairman of the Senate Foreign Relations Committee, John Sherman of Ohio (brother of Civil War hero General William Tecumseh Sherman), rose on the Senate floor to quote extensively from a *Journal* report detailing the successes of the Cuban revolutionary army. The account told of Cuban cities falling before the onslaught of General Maceo, and of women soldiers—"Amazons"—who fought with machetes.[26]

These stories were wholly fictional, written by Frederick Lawrence, one of Hearst's more notorious hacks. As a reporter for the San Francisco *Examiner*, Lawrence was known for sharing the burden of covering a trial with a reporter from a competing paper. They would take turns writing the other's story, which left every other day free for recreation (which in Lawrence's case seemed to involve hanging around bars). Sent to Havana by Hearst, Lawrence seems never to have left his café table at the Hotel Inglaterra, where the foreign correspondents lazed about, swapping stories.[27]

No matter. The Senate Foreign Relations Committee reported out a resolution recognizing the Cuban insurgents as legitimate belligerents. Hearst was pleased with the response in Congress, with one important exception — the resistance of the all-powerful Speaker of the House, Thomas Brackett Reed of Maine.

7

The Czar

"A statesman is a successful politician who is dead."

A JOURNAL READER looking for Hearst's usual "crime and underwear" formula or a report on those Cuban Amazons might have been disappointed by the front page on December 2, 1895. Above the headline "The Man of the Hour in Washington," a line drawing showed some bearded or mustachioed men standing around a large, rather portly figure with smooth cheeks. "Reed, of Maine, Faces the Destiny That Is All Before Him" read the portentous caption, but Reed seemed to be facing nothing more than a gaggle of lobbyists.

The article labeled Reed, the Speaker of the House, a "political Gargantua" and "the Czar," his more common nickname on Capitol Hill. For a time, it noted, the Czar quietly ate his breakfast in the restaurant of the old Shoreham Hotel, lost in his reading and ignoring everyone around him. Finally turning to the lobbyists, he displayed "the gravity of a lion tamer." Reed stared at the men "impassively," the paper reported, his hands clasped behind his back "in a characteristic pose so well known to his admirers."[1] The image was vaguely heroic, but the tone of the article was ambivalent, as if the *Journal*'s reporter, or its publisher, was not quite sure what to make of a politician who was

Czar Reed, 1897 (Library of Congress)

seemingly so immune to popular passions or the newspaper that tried to stir them up.

Six weeks later, Reed had effectively stopped the House from voting to recognize the Cuban insurgents as belligerents, and the *Journal* was vexed. Reed, the paper observed, "holds House action in the hollow of his hand. He controls every rein of House government, and with his foot on the brake can start it, stop it, drive it when and where he will." The *Journal* correspondent reflected the impatience of his newspaper over the Speaker's intransigence, but the article also noted, with a kind of grudging admiration,

> ... that the one great force which withholds House recognition of Cuba is Mr. Reed, and yet no one need infer that

any Spanish lobby owns one hair of Mr. Reed's head. It is to the Maine man's credit, be it said, that no lobby can use him to even a slight degree. His warmest enemies never had the hardihood to even intimate as much.

For some reason, whether of the prejudice or the mind, Mr. Reed is not favorable to Cuba or America's recognition of her. He has never told why, but such is the fact.[2]

The article quoted "those who are near him" as suggesting that the Speaker "does not see why Congress should break its neck in any headlong rush to Cuba's aid.... He thinks we should save our own affairs, and deliver ourselves from peril [the effects of the Panic of 1893 were still being felt] before heading a pell-mell rescue party to tear Cuba from Spain." On January 24 and again on February 7 the *Journal* chided the Speaker for stalling, for stifling debate, and imposing a "do nothing" policy on Cuba. The *Journal* archly observed, "Mr. Reed's behavior during this session has been that of a candidate for the Presidency, and not that of Speaker."[3]

Reed was an elusive figure, not only to newspapermen but to those who worked for him. His closest aide, Asher Hinds, the parliamentary clerk to the Speaker, kept a diary. On December 14, 1895, waiting for the Speaker to begin the first session of the Fifty-fourth Congress, Hinds noted that "some of the new congressmen" were giving "furtive glances" toward the door to the Speaker's chambers. "It was easy for me to see that the Speaker was a lion with them," Hinds wrote. But the lion was human: as Reed awaited the formal summons to appear before the House, Hinds noticed that his boss was exhibiting a "feeling of nervousness." Like the *Journal* reporter, Hinds saw that Reed's "hands were clasped behind his back—a favorite attitude while speaking." It was a statesman's pose, but one that had the advantage of hiding or holding still shaking hands. As Hinds watched from his clerk's desk, Reed deflected the cloakroom chatter that he was the front-runner for the Republican presidential nomination in 1896. "Wait until you see my committees appointed," he joked to some congressmen. "A wet blanket will descend for a while."

In the Speaker's office that day there was some discussion of what to do about the Venezuela affair. Urged to take a strong position opposing President Cleveland, Reed demurred. "I am not much at the great and good man business," he said. Reed knew that the Venezuela fever would vanish when people came to their senses. Hinds recorded in his diary, "I overheard Mr. Reed say this in discussing the Venezuela affair: 'A skillful politician once said to me, It is a good rule in politics, when you don't know what to do, do nothing.'"[4] Nothing was what Reed also wished to do about Cuba, even if his closest friends in Washington—Theodore Roosevelt and Henry Cabot Lodge—had other ideas.

Thomas Brackett Reed has been largely lost to popular history, but he was physically and in every other way a giant of his day. Towering at six feet three, weighing close to three hundred pounds, he did not so much walk as roll and lurch. (A lady passerby was once heard to exclaim, "How narrow he makes the streets look!") He seemed to enjoy his singularity. In an age when most men wore beards, he was usually clean-shaven. He was unmoved by the late-nineteenth-century fad for strenuous physical exercise. Asked once to describe "the greatest problem now confronting the American people," he answered, "How to dodge a bicycle." He tried golf once or twice and lost interest.[5] While Roosevelt and Lodge were off riding to the hounds, Reed had the odd hobby of randomly riding streetcars. He would sometimes be spotted late at night on out-of-the-way streets and in far-off suburbs, always alone.[6]

Sitting in the House of Representatives, Reed could look drowsy, almost indolent, but he was far from passive. With a high-pitched, nasal New England drawl, Reed was a master of the wicked put-down. From his high chair in the House chamber, he once told Representative John Russell of Massachusetts, "Russell, you do not understand the theory of the five minute debate. The object is to convey to the House in the space of five minutes either information or misinformation. You have consumed several periods of five minutes this afternoon without doing either." With or about the pompous, he could be especially sharp-tongued. "A statesman is a successful politician who is dead," he once joked to Henry Cabot Lodge, who very much wanted to be regarded as a statesman but enjoyed the remark so much he repeated it everywhere.[7] The New York lawyer-statesman Joseph Choate once waxed eloquent after dinner: "I think I can say that I have lived a clean and decent life. I have none of the vices and a good many of the virtues, and I think I average up pretty well." There was a silence and a member of the dinner party ventured, "I wish I could say that." In his distinctive twang, Reed interjected, "Why ca-a-a-n't you? Choate did."[8]

His tongue was perhaps a little too sharp. "Reed's wit is enjoyable," noted William McKinley, congressman from Ohio and an occasional target, "especially if you do not happen to be the person at whom it is directed."[9] A writer described Reed as someone who "always preferred to make an epigram rather than to make a friend," and even a friend, Congressman Champ Clark of

Missouri, described Reed as "a self made man who worshipped his Maker."[10]

The Speaker embodied a kind of hard Yankee virtue in which pride vied mightily with humility. Born in Portland, Maine, in 1839, he was a *Mayflower* descendant but a threadbare one: his father was a Maine fisherman, and he went to Bowdoin College on a scholarship, not to become a swell with the sons of wealthy Portland shipowners, but to study Latin and Greek and Shakespeare. He disapproved of exclusive clubs and fraternities. A lonely, dreamy boy, he was like Lodge and Roosevelt a compulsive reader of history and literature. (Reed especially loved Balzac, whom he found "sad beyond tears.")[11] Unlike Lodge and Roosevelt, he was completely unromantic about the Civil War. He lost his best friend to the conflict and delayed enlisting until 1864, when he was twenty-five years old. He then joined the navy and spent a peaceful year on a gunboat, far from the action. No tales of daring and sacrifice sprang from Reed. Indeed, he seemed to delight in poking fun at his warrior years. "What a charming life that was, that dear old life in the Navy, when I kept grocery on a gunboat. I knew all the regulations and the rest of them didn't. I had my rights and most of theirs."[12]

Lodge, who served with Reed in the House for seven years, proclaimed him "easily the greatest parliamentary leader I ever saw."[13] He was a brilliant legislator. When Reed rose to speak, word would pass through the cloakrooms and corridors, and members of Congress and their aides and pages would rush to the floor and the galleries. His greatest show of force came when he ended the custom of obstructionism known as the silent filibuster. In the House, members of the minority party could stall a bill simply by refusing to acknowledge their presence in the chamber for a quorum. As the newly elected Speaker in January 1889,

Reed put an end to these shenanigans in a moment of remarkable theater. Spotting the House members who were refusing to answer the quorum call, he began directing the clerk to record their names, which he then read himself as a public proclamation of their presence. Pandemonium broke loose. Some members fled the floor or tried to hide under their desks. The House erupted into shrieks and yells as Reed forged ahead. "I deny the power of the Speaker and denounce it as revolutionary!" exclaimed a Kentucky Democrat. Congressmen began howling for recognition to speak; one of them, a former Confederate cavalry officer named "Fighting Joe" Wheeler, advanced to the front of the chamber "leaping from desk to desk as an ibex leaps from crag to crag," according to one reporter. A congressman from Texas sat down, pulled out a bowie knife, and began whetting it on his boot.

Reed stood fast, challenging any congressman who refused to be counted: "The Chair is making a statement of fact that the gentleman is present. Does he deny it?" When Representative McKinley, who relished the role of peacemaker, began to yield the floor to a Democrat wishing to protest, Reed would have none of it, and in his Yankee drawl summarized the situation as he wanted it to be: "The gentleman from Ohio declines to be interrupted." His backbone stiffened, McKinley then dutifully uttered, "I decline to be interrupted."[14] Reed prevailed; the rules were changed to end the silent filibuster, and Reed became known as Czar Reed. The *Washington Post* pronounced him the second most powerful person in the land, and talk began of him taking the next step in 1892. "They might do worse and I think they will," joked Reed. (He was right; the GOP stuck with the incumbent, Benjamin Harrison, who lost the White House to Grover Cleveland.)[15]

Reed was "ambitious as Lucifer," according to his fellow

congressman Champ Clark, but he cloaked his vanity. Even John Singer Sargent could not pierce the veil and produced a painting widely dismissed as a failure; it showed a large fat man with a vacant expression that some regarded as benign, others as sour.[16] Close observers sometimes caught a whiff of Reed's inner smoldering. A perceptive newspaper reporter observed that he "trembled in every muscle in his body" when he was gearing up for a legislative fight.[17]

Only to his diary, which he wrote in French, did Reed confess his true feelings. "Happy are those who expect nothing!" he cried in January 1889, after he won the speakership. His opponent had been McKinley, whom Reed privately disdained. "Mr. McKinley is sly, very sly," Reed wrote. "He always has his wand and his mysterious airs, which stun journalists but he is a man of little scope, believe me." In March 1895, Reed confessed to himself that the last session of Congress was "troubling, full of little things which tortured me." (The Czar had a mournful side—his only son had died as an infant—and his sadness came through in the diary.) By then he was privately planning on running for president. With his colleagues, he made light of the newspaper chatter about his possible candidacy, but in his diary he was planning to quit public life if he were not elected to the highest office. On March 30, 1895, he wrote, "I intend to go to New York if my services are not sought by an appreciative nation. There I will make some money for the little one." He had a young daughter to support, and he had a standing offer to join the Wall Street law firm of Elihu Root.[18]

Two prominent Americans were determined to make Reed president. "My whole heart is in the Reed canvass," Roosevelt wrote Lodge on December 27, 1895. Lodge virtually ran Reed's presidential campaign from his Senate seat.[19] Roosevelt and Lodge looked at Reed and saw themselves: tougher and more practical than the goo-goo reformers, yet far more virtuous and upright than the machine. Unlike the usual collection of rubes and favor seekers who populated the Capitol, Reed was the sort of fellow an educated gentleman might wish to have to dinner— highly literate, witty, a great raconteur. (Reed was, along with Roosevelt, a guest at the first dinner party Lodge gave when he moved into his new mansion on Massachusetts Avenue in 1893.)[20] Lodge and Roosevelt appreciated that while genteel, Reed was, as Lodge put it, "a good hater" who stood up to humbug and hypocrisy. To Lodge, Reed was "like Dr. Johnson," England's eighteenth-century philosophic wit: "No one was ever better to listen to, or a better listener, for his sympathies were wide, his interests unlimited, and nothing human was alien to him."[21]

Lodge had been deeply grateful for Reed's sympathy at his lowest moment, when he had been ostracized by Boston do-gooders for sticking with the GOP's corrupt presidential nominee, James G. Blaine. Feeling a touch sorry for himself as he crossed State Street one day, Lodge ran into Reed, whom he knew slightly. Reed cheered Lodge up by mocking the reformers who scorned politicians guided "only by a base desire to win."[22] The two New Englanders became close friends and would sit together in the House chamber. Describing a New Year's Eve with Reed to his mother on January 1, 1888, Lodge wrote: "He was as always most amusing & most interesting. He is a master of irony, keen, humorous, witty; full of strength & sense & when you get him alone with a literary side & a touch of sentiment that he ordinarily conceals carefully. I am about ready to say that he is the most remarkable man & the strongest & keenest mind that there is today in public life in this country."

Lodge was Reed's campaign manager when he ran for Speaker in November 1889. "I have been so absorbed in Reed's canvass that I have hardly had time to even think of anything else," he wrote his mother. Reed paid him back: "He gave me of course exactly what I asked for—a chairmanship which gives me control of our greatest measure, the election law [the so-called Force Bill, to protect Negro suffrage in the South] & the second place on naval affairs," where Lodge could agitate to build more battleships.[23]

Reed also did his best to get Roosevelt a job in the Harrison administration as assistant secretary of state. "He is a loyal friend and true as steel," Lodge wrote Roosevelt, reporting on Reed's lobbying campaign. "I am really pleased to hear about Tom Reed; I value his friendship," Roosevelt replied.[24] The secretary of state—James G. Blaine, a consolation prize—would not have the New Yorker, however, despite Roosevelt's support of his presidential candidacy in 1884. With eerie prescience given later events, Blaine worried what would happen if he went on summer vacation and left Roosevelt in charge. "I do somehow fear that my sleep at Augusta or Bar Harbor would not be quite so easy," Blaine privately wrote President Harrison. Roosevelt had to settle for chairmanship of the Civil Service Commission, a job arranged by Lodge and Reed.[25]

Roosevelt continued to cultivate Reed, even hanging his picture over the mantelpiece in his library—and then writing to tell him so.[26] "I honestly think your speeches this year have struck an even higher note than ever before," he wrote on October 14, 1894.[27] Reed was not blind to the limitations of his friends. Tiring of Roosevelt's moralizing at dinner one evening, he drawled, "Theodore, if there is one thing more than another for which I admire you, it is your original discovery of the Ten

Commandments."[28] He observed in his diary that Lodge was "sometimes a spoiled child," and, unimpressed by Lodge's ancestor worship, once uncharitably described his friend as "thin soil highly cultivated."[29]

Lodge had tried to temper Reed's sarcasm. When Reed first ran for the speakership in 1889, Lodge had visited his rooms to say, "All is going well; your election is assured but you must be careful of what you say; you must not say anything 'clever.'" Reed's eyes began to gleam. "Mayn't I say anything about Napoleon?" he impishly inquired. "No," Lodge said with a sigh. "That is just what you must not say."[30]

Lodge even attempted to gussy up Reed's plain wardrobe, persuading him to wear the cummerbund that was the style for gentlemen of the period. (Lodge preferred dark blue, Reed a less conspicuous black sash with his black suits.)[31] Both Lodge and Roosevelt undertook to introduce him to the right people, socially and politically. Lodge wrote Roosevelt in November 1894 that he had arranged "a little dinner" for Reed in New York to meet Boss Platt and Joseph Choate, the New York lawyer and diplomat whose declaration of unblemished virtue Reed had punctured.[32] With Owen Wister in tow, Lodge launched Reed into high society at a dance performance in Manhattan. "We met...about half the [F]our [H]undred, who were unintelligently interested in Reed and confusedly anxious to know *first* him, and then who he was," wrote Wister.[33]

By the late fall of 1895 Reed was off and running for the White House—but only on his own dignified terms. His chief rival for the GOP nomination was McKinley, who raised Reed's hackles with his unctuous appeals for support. "Mr. Reed rarely if ever says anything about his own aspirations for the Presidency, and then only in a joking way," noted Asher Hinds in his diary on

December 30. "But the other evening, after he had completed the making up of his committees, he talked freely for a moment about the way Mr. McKinley was promising things broadcast, in order to get support. He showed no resentment or bitterness; but his manner conveyed the idea that he thought such traffic beneath the dignity of a man seeking the Presidency."

With the speakership's immense legislative power, Reed was perfectly positioned to raise money for a presidential run. During his first session as Speaker in 1889, the term "pork" had been coined by some newspaper wags to describe congressional appropriations for projects in a member's home district.[34] Reed could have handed out pork by the ton to win friends and favors, but he refused to. Indeed, he balked at anything that smacked of buying votes. On February 2 Asher Hinds noted, "I think there are certain large political interests, especially in New York, that would like to have Mr. Reed ask help from them. But I think he is firm in his determination not to have the office unless he can get it free from such bargains as he would have to make if he consulted such interests."[35]

Roosevelt and Lodge admired Reed's integrity, even if they thought him a little too proud. They were bothered, however, by Reed's unwillingness to wave the flag over Venezuela and Cuba. At first they tried to overlook Reed's unwillingness to embrace Lodge's "Large Policy." But as Venezuela, then Cuba, thrust foreign policy to the fore in the winter of 1896, it became harder and harder for Roosevelt and Lodge to ignore a basic philosophical difference.

Reed was no jingo. America had been badly shaken by a financial panic in 1893. An economic depression had put millions out of work and exposed the sharp divide between rich and poor created by industrialization and the Gilded Age. Reed worried about social divisions that could drive the country apart, pitting rich against poor, labor against capital. In 1894 an army of the unemployed had marched on Washington, and steel and railway workers had been battling management goons and scabs in Pittsburgh and Ohio through much of the mid-decade.[36] To Lodge the unrest in the heartland was a reason to look abroad, to seek a way to release social tensions and unify the country. But Reed saw it differently. He had a keen understanding of the darker aspects of human nature; he understood and deplored war fever. He was also sensitive to human rights. Like Lodge, he wanted to protect black voting rights. Unlike Lodge, however, he did not wish to see the United States playing the role of the world's policeman, rescuing the oppressed from slavery in far-off lands, or even in ones as close at hand as Cuba. There was plenty of human suffering to attend to at home, Reed figured.

Reed had long ridiculed American adventuring. In 1891 President Harrison had threatened to send the navy to punish Chile for a minor imbroglio involving some drunken American sailors jailed after a bar fight in Valparaiso. Leaving aside the fact that America had no real navy to send, Reed mocked Harrison's sudden militarism. He acidly told a reporter, "I do not think the President ought to have written such a message to those little Chileans. They do not wish to fight us, we do not wish to fight them. What we ought to do is to charter a ship, not too large or too safe, put Harrison on board of it, and send him down to fight those Chileans. He's just about their size." (Realizing that he had crossed a line, he told the reporter, "If you publish what I have said tomorrow, I'll come to your office and kill you.")[37]

Reed's keen nose smelled hypocrisy in the growing cries of the jingoes who wanted to save Cuba from Spain. To make his point he decided to gig the southern congressmen who were getting riled up by headlines in Hearst's *Journal* and other newspapers. As it happened, a South Carolina mob had murdered a Negro postmaster. Reed saw the story and clipped it out of the paper. He then ordered a clerk to paste a headline about Cuba from elsewhere in the edition atop the South Carolina lynching story:

ANOTHER OUTRAGE IN CUBA
BODY OF A PATRIOT RIDDLED WITH BULLETS
AND THROWN THROUGH
THE BURNING RAFTERS OF HIS DWELLING

Keeping his round face completely straight, Reed handed the clipping to a South Carolina congressman who had been clamoring for intervention in Cuba. The man saw the lurid headline and began to eagerly read the story, then stopped, puzzled. "Why," he said to Reed, "this isn't Cuba." Reed turned away, but not before commenting in his Maine rasp, "No, it isn't."[38]

8

The Pleasant Gang

"Come and revolute Cuba."

O N A SUNDAY MORNING in early February 1896, Henry Cabot Lodge visited a gracious Federalist-style home on Lafayette Square, the greensward across Pennsylvania Avenue from the White House. He was there to confer with a delegation of Cubans, members of the junta, who had come to Washington to lobby for a congressional resolution recognizing the Cuban insurgents. They were meeting secretly at the home of Senator J. Donald Cameron of Pennsylvania, a member of the Foreign Relations Committee. Senator Cameron was a fool and a blowhard and an ugly drunk, but he was wealthy, and he had excellent connections to corporations that might be persuaded to support the Cuban cause. His wife, Elizabeth, was vivacious and lovely. She despised her husband, who was two decades her senior, and once told a friend that her wedding night felt like rape. A gossip columnist called the Camerons "the Beauty and the Beast."[1]

The odd little cabal at 21 Lafayette Square was joined by a man widely considered the most intellectually intimidating in Washington. Henry Adams had come to the Cameron home that day for romance. In 1896 Adams was small, bearded, and wizened, not yet sixty years old but ancient, as if burdened by the

The Adams and Hay houses (Library of Congress)

weariness of the ages, or at least the burden of legacy. In his oft-cited memoir of the Gilded Age, *The Education of Henry Adams*, the author recalls sitting in church behind his grandfather, John Quincy Adams, looking at a wall tablet dedicated to his great-grandfather, John Adams. "You'll be thinkin' you'll be president too!" his Irish gardener once called after him.[2]

Henry had spent the rest of his life trying to cast off the weight of his ancestors, while drifting ever deeper into a mystical past. Moving from Boston to Washington as a young man in the 1870s, he had observed the passing scene with a mixture of loathing and fascination, more observer than participant, at once appalled by and drawn to politics. He was a disagreeable man in many ways but clever and perceptive, and his tight little social circle was the most exclusive in Washington; among its

Henry Adams (Harvard University Archives)

core members, in addition to Mrs. Cameron, were Lodge and Roosevelt.

Adams, whose wife had committed suicide a decade earlier, was in love with Elizabeth Cameron — "Lizzie" — and once jokingly promised to have her likeness carved in the stonework above his door.[3] The affair was platonic. Aside from the age difference (Lizzie was fifteen years younger), one senses that Adams was just too tired to try for more. Writing her about Rodin's "decadent sensualities" but really about himself, Adams confessed, "I have not enough vitality left to be sensual."[4]

Adams's world-weary cynicism was profound. "Man is by nature a liar," he wrote an English friend in February 1896. "One can trust nobody and nothing." That January, he had written his

Lizzie Cameron (Library of Congress)

brother-in-law, "[John] LaFarge [the artist] is with me....He and I sit silent, opposite each other, and sigh wearily from time to time, wishing somebody would say something." And yet that same season he felt invigorated and rejuvenated by the talk of war—though not without skepticism and a self-mocking tone. He wrote the same English friend, Sir Robert Cunliffe, on February 17, "I have had real sport this winter, and feel young again. You had better sell all you have and buy with me in Cuba. I want to be a pretty Creole." He had been conspiring to support the revolution for some time. "Come and revolute Cuba," he wrote his neighbor and future statesman John Hay. "We are going to have a gay old circus."[5] In December, when the Venezuela crisis arose, he wrote an English friend, "So we are going to war! It sounds droll, to you and me. I remember how droll it seemed in '61, for my Southern friends."[6]

The tone of these letters is consistently sarcastic—and sometimes vile, even allowing for the casual anti-Semitism of his class and time. ("Bombard New York," he wrote another friend. "I know no place that would be more improved by it. The chief population is Jew, and the rest is German Jew.")[7] But Adams at his most outrageous was not without keen insight. He could feel the war fever rising, and selfishly he welcomed it as a kind of antidote to the torpor and ennui that were pressing down on him. He also sensed the inevitability of a coming clash, whatever it might be. Venezuela, he wrote in December, "was only an accident... its importance is absurdly out of proportion to the result; if it were not Venezuela now, it would be Cuba in the Spring, or Canada some other time."[8] His concern was not the where or why or how, but the when.

Adams's chief co-agitator on Cuba was Lodge. At the Camerons' on that midwinter Sunday, the two discussed ways to gin up political support for the Cubans—mostly by persuading business interests, normally averse to the disruptions of war, that there was profit to be had in a free Cuba.

Adams and Lodge were different in fundamental ways, but they were friends of long standing, products of the same fading Boston gentry. In a real sense, Adams had helped create Lodge. The younger man was a graduate student at Harvard in the early 1870s when Adams, teaching "Anglo Saxon law," took him under his counsel. Adams urged him to go into the "historico-literary" line, to become a public intellectual, and Lodge did, writing histories of his Federalist heroes George Washington and Alexander Hamilton. Adams also introduced Lodge to politics in the mid-1870s, persuading him to join a reform effort called the Party of the Centre as a check on the "Grantism" corrupting Washington. This was the core of the later mugwump movement. Politically, Adams and Lodge parted company from the goo-goos and from each other—Adams embracing a kind of medieval mysticism that grew out of his cynicism about modernity, and Lodge moving on to more practical and hardheaded politics. But the two remained close, with Adams playing the role of uncle/scold/adviser.[9]

While Adams was drawn to the romance of revolution, with its portents of doom and resurrection, Lodge was not so metaphysical. To him the unrest in Cuba was an opportunity for American expansionism, for that would establish the nation as a global power and maritime rival to Great Britain. And though the two men often talked of Cuba, they sometimes talked past each other. "Cabot is still fussing over Venezuela and England," Adams wrote his brother Brooks on January 24, 1896, as the Venezuela crisis was dying down: "I have done what I could to persuade him that he had won his stakes there, and should drop it, and go, for all he is worth, for Cuba; but Cabot is a man-child who cannot drop his toy."[10] Adams found Lodge a little pompous as well as single-minded. He once complained to a friend of being bored by Lodge's "senatorial drivel." But he regarded the junior senator from Massachusetts as an essential participant in his little salon, along with Theodore Roosevelt, who, with Edith, had been neatly folded into the Adams set when Roosevelt came to Washington as a civil service commissioner in 1889.[11]

Washington was a raw, relatively uncultivated capital city in the 1890s. L'Enfant's elegant plan still had an unfinished feel: the avenues were broad, and parks and squares dotted the city, but the effect was more patchwork than grand. Behind and alongside mansions like the one Lodge inhabited on Massachusetts Avenue were smaller and shabbier houses and even hovels "inhabited by the dregs of the negro population," wrote Margaret Chanler, wife of Lodge's and Roosevelt's fun-loving Porcellian brother Winthrop. The Roosevelts "lived in a tiny house on Jefferson Place," wrote Margaret. "[They] used to give Sunday-evening suppers where the food was of the plainest and the company the best. Theodore would keep us all spellbound with tales of his adventures in the West."[12] An invitation to the Adams household was much more prized by the socially aspiring, and rarely extended. On Lafayette Square, at the corner of Sixteenth and H Streets, Adams lived in neo-Romanesque splendor next door to his friend John Hay (their companion houses, now the site of the Hay-Adams Hotel, had been built by the eminent architect H. H. Richardson), just a short stroll from Lizzie Cameron's door. Within, sitting in a pair of low green-leather chairs before a broad window overlooking the White House, Adams and Hay (who as a young man had been Abraham Lincoln's private secretary) would oscillate between dissecting the low politics of Washington and speaking of higher things. "Presidents and cabinets wane and wax and wane again, and go, and never return; while John Hay and I sit in the window and watch. As Socrates and Pythagoras—or somebody else—used to say: one fool is much like another. So is one President," Adams wrote a friend in 1896.[13] Henry James, William's novelist brother, was a close friend of Adams and often stayed at the house on Lafayette Square on his trips back to America. In a Henry James short story, a Mr. Bonnycastle remarks to his spouse, "Hang it. Let us be vulgar and have some fun—let us invite the President!"

Adams and Hay were not as snobbish as they appeared and welcomed outsiders who could amuse. For example, Adams reported that visiting English author Rudyard Kipling "has grown rather thick with our little Washington gang," although Roosevelt found the bard of the British Empire "underbred."[14] Visitors permitted into the Hay-Adams world were highly entertained by such sights as the elderly General William Sherman (Lizzie Cameron's uncle) reenacting his March to the Sea by using his butter knife to sweep the silverware — the Rebel soldiers — from the table. Much of the teasing was good humored; Adams's circle called itself "the Pleasant Gang."[15]

The bonhomie covered over some subterfuge and sexual tension. John Hay was secretly in love with Lodge's wife, Nannie. It was not hard to understand why. Margaret Chanler described Mrs. Lodge as "the most charming woman I have ever known; an exquisite presence in this workaday world. She had unusual beauty, a pale face with regular features, and dark eyes the color of the sky when stars begin to twinkle. She had great wit; it was the only weapon she ever used in self-defense, and Cabot was a little afraid of its winged shafts."[16]

Nannie "looked as queens ought to look," said Roosevelt, "but as no queen I have ever seen does look."[17] Judging from the correspondence of Elizabeth Cameron and Henry Adams, John Hay and Nannie Lodge embarked on a decorous, discreet affair sometime in 1890, snatching moments together for "little walks," with Lizzie acting as chaperone (and alibi) and Adams enjoying the intrigue of it all. It is unclear whether Lodge — often called away or distracted by Senate business — knew or sensed he was being cuckolded. At some later point Lodge read over his diary for 1890–91 and inked out one line so forcefully that it bled onto the other side of the page.[18]

The wit and sparkle at the dinner tables of the Pleasant Gang could give way to fin de siècle gloom. In the mid-1890s the secretary of the British legation in Washington, Cecil Spring

Rice, became close to Adams, Lodge, and Roosevelt. Spring Rice enjoyed the intellectual banter, yet, he later noted, "there was something melancholy" in the talk. Some—he may have been thinking especially of Adams—spoke with a "sort of bitter despair in their minds which is hard to describe and not pleasant to listen to."

In the winter of 1896 dinner table discussion often revolved around a book written by Henry's brother, Brooks Adams, titled *The Law of Civilization and Decay*, which, as the title suggests, was very gloomy indeed. Predicting revolution and chaos, Adams lamented the weakening of the ruling class, its loss of "soldierly virtues." The tone is suggested by a letter Brooks wrote Roosevelt in February: "The whole world seems to be rotting, rotting. The one hope for us, the one chance to escape from our slavery, even for a year, is war, war which shall bring down the British Empire."[19] For his part Roosevelt found Brooks Adams a little "unhinged" and rejected his doomsday theories about the cycles of history. But he didn't disagree with Brooks's prescription of war as the cure for society's ills. On March 1 he wrote Bamie, "Have you read Brooks Adams [*sic*] 'Civilization and Decay'? It is from a false standpoint but is very strong."[20]

Cabot Lodge was close to Brooks Adams, his Porcellian clubmate. The two men had founded a dining society in Boston called the Porcupine Club, with a Latin motto that translates "The people hiss at me, but I applaud myself."[21] Lodge shrugged off his clubmate's woollier theories, but he was influenced by the notion of historic cycles of rise and decline. In the fall of 1895, on a tour of Spain, he had been stunned by the fall of a once mighty empire. "For the habitation of civilized man for 2500 years," Spain now presented "an inconceivable picture," Lodge wrote Roosevelt. "You never saw such desolate dreary plains and here and there a dying town. Even Madrid is bleak and cheerless....They are beaten, broken and out of the race and are proud and know it."[22] To Lodge and Roosevelt, Spain represented the opposite of Anglo-Saxon virtue—decadent, autocratic, spent, a cautionary tale of what could happen to a "race" that lost its martial spirit.

Lodge was ready to take Cuba off Spain's hands. He had been appointed to a special subcommittee on Cuban affairs by Lizzie's uncle, Senator John Sherman of Ohio, chairman of the Foreign Relations Committee. With Sherman's acquiescence, Lodge met secretly with the Cuban junta's delegation in Washington, who were holed up in the seedy old Ralegh Hotel and were led by the twenty-eight-year-old Cuban aristocrat-turned-revolutionary Gonzalo de Quesada. Writing his mother, Lodge described the junta as "interesting young fellows" who thanked him for his efforts "in rather pathetic fashion."[23] Adams was also in close contact with the Cubans, whom he described in his self-dramatizing way. "I am haunted by Cuban conspirators who dine with me and are pathetically patriotic and simple-hearted," he wrote a friend on February 8, 1896. The day before, he had written Brooks, "I am kept here by Cuba, which I appear to be running, for the faculty of bungling is the only faculty a legislative body possesses in foreign affairs. Of course, my share is wholly behind the scenes. Even Cabot keeps aloof from me, or I from him; for I cannot control him, and I want no ally whom I can't control."[24]

There was a certain amount of cloak and dagger involved in dealing with the Cubans. Quesada and other Cuban propagandists met once or twice with Senator Cameron or Lodge at the Cameron house on Lafayette Square, but usually addressed letters to Lizzie Cameron. She warmed to the role of secret agent, passing messages back and forth, and doing her best to keep her alcoholic husband propped up and useful to the Cuba Libre cause. She proudly reported to Adams that she had her husband, a tool of corporate interests, "worked up...to try to get some money out of the Standard Oil people in return for concessions granted [by a future Cuban republic]."[25]

Adams, whose cynicism about government was exceeded only by his cynicism about big business, was convinced that commercial interests — "the Trusts" — would wish to avoid helping Cuba because they were afraid a war would rattle the stock market.[26] Thus, the only solution was to convince the trusts that an independent Cuba would mean new markets and a new source of cheap labor. Lodge shared some of Adams's contempt for "stockjobbers" and greedy businessmen who put profit above national interest. But he was convinced, partly by Adams, partly by his own expedient political instincts, that it made sense to try to win over the business lobby to the Cuban cause.

On February 20 Lodge took the floor of the Senate to argue that "Free Cuba would mean a great market for the United States; it would mean an opportunity for American capital invited there by special exemptions; it would mean an opportunity for the development of that splendid island." Lodge also made his more familiar strategic argument for American global supremacy, noting that Cuba "lies athwart the line which leads to the [as yet unbuilt] Nicaraguan Canal," and he appealed as well to the "broad ground of common humanity."

Foreign Relations Committee Chairman Sherman was half senile and easily manipulated by the horror stories peddled by the junta to reporters hanging about the Peanut Club in New York. In the Senate he declared, "The condition of affairs in Cuba is such that the intervention of the United States must sooner or later be given to put an end to crimes that are almost beyond description." His evidence came largely from a book by a Cuban revolutionary named Enrique Donderis, who claimed that the Spaniards had executed 43,500 prisoners—a wild exaggeration. The book was a joint production of the Peanut Club propagandists and the sensationalists working for William Randolph Hearst, translated, Sherman heartily proclaimed, "by one of the great journals of the country, the New York *Journal*."[27]

On February 28 the Senate, by a vote of 64 to 6, passed a resolution recognizing the Cuban insurgents as legitimate belligerents. In April the House also went along and passed a joint resolution. Czar Reed stopped stalling because he knew he could afford to: President Cleveland, who wanted no war over Cuba, had no intention of signing it. Henry Adams was willing to take a symbolic victory, however. "Our Cuban friends are all right till autumn anyway, and we will then give them a big lift," he wrote Lizzie.[28] A presidential election was coming, along with new opportunities for Adams to conspire from his easy chair.

9

Aux Barricades!

"There will be no jingo nonsense in my administration."

THAT WINTER LODGE and Roosevelt worked hard to make sure that the new president would be Thomas Reed of Maine. In late January 1896 a worried Roosevelt wrote Lodge, "I must have a good talk with Tom Reed; if possible you must be present." A week later Roosevelt reported to Lodge, "I have seen a good deal of Reed; the weight of the struggle is very evident in his face and I can see how hard it is. The presidency is a great prize! And there is a bitter fight for it."[1]

Roosevelt's doubts surfaced slowly, reluctantly, as if he could not bear to be disillusioned by a man he regarded so highly. By late February he was beginning to wonder about Reed's zeal for that fight—any fight. On February 25 he wrote to congratulate Lodge on his floor speech pushing Cuban recognition ("one of the best things you have done") and added, "Just a line more.... What has been done in the Navy?" Roosevelt knew that Lodge was pressing for more coastal defenses and new battleships. "Surely," he wrote Lodge, "Tom Reed cannot be going to try to throw us down on a question of an addition to the naval forces and proper preparation for our coastal defense."[2]

But he was. Reed was not interested in building up a big navy, because he thought the country would be tempted to use it. Both Roosevelt and Lodge were vexed that their friend could be so timorous, not to mention ungrateful for the support he had received from the two of them. On March 9 Roosevelt wrote Bamie:

Cabot is far from pleased at the way things have gone on at Washington and, in strict confidence, he, as well as I, feel that Tom Reed has missed his opportunity this winter. He is trying to make a reputation as a conservative economist, and has merely succeeded in giving the idea that he has turned timid. He has given us no support whatever, save in the most perfunctory manner, for coast defenses and a good Navy and while I think we shall get both in the end, and that he will help us, he really has not done so with any vigor.

Roosevelt had belatedly realized that Reed would be an obstacle instead of an ally. He finished his letter to Bamie: "Tell Will [Cowles, Bamie's husband] that it is very difficult for me not to wish for a war with Spain, for such a war would result at once in us getting a proper Navy and a good system of coast defence. Your loving brother..."[3]

Four days later Roosevelt expressed his exasperation with Reed in a sharply worded letter to Lodge. Congress was balking at spending more on naval armaments, and Roosevelt was in high dudgeon, angered at the lawmakers who were not doing their all to support Lodge's Large Policy—or, in Roosevelt's favorite catchall term, "Americanism": "It is difficult for me to restrain my indignation at the cowardice of so many of the men to whom we ought to look for aid in any movement on behalf of Americanism. I must say I am getting disgusted with both Hoar and Hale [senators from Massachusetts and Maine], and I am getting pretty impatient with Reed." Roosevelt went on to whine that he had to cast his lot with the odious Boss Platt in some minor New York political squabble in order to serve Reed's presidential ambitions. Then he vented: "Upon my word I do think that Reed ought to pay some heed to the wishes of you and myself. You have been his most effective supporter; and while my support does not amount to much, it has yet been given at very serious cost to myself."[4]

In hindsight it is difficult to understand why Roosevelt and Lodge were so baffled by Reed, so slow to grasp his basic disagreement on something as fundamental as American foreign policy. It may be that Roosevelt and Lodge were so fond of Reed, so impressed by his commanding presence in the House—and by his intelligence and wit over dinner—that they chose to overlook philosophical differences for as long as possible. It is also true that Roosevelt and Lodge themselves came fairly late to a coherent foreign policy. While they shared a strong sense of manifest destiny for their "race" from at least the early 1880s, it was only during the 1890s that the two Harvard men imbibed enough of the theories of Alfred Thayer Mahan to formulate fully articulated expansionist policies. While Roosevelt had long been ready to go to war almost anywhere, his motivations were personal and atavistic, not subject to close self-examination. And while more measured and intellectual, Lodge did not give his Large Policy speech until March 1895.

In time Roosevelt and Lodge might have found a way to bridge their policy differences with Reed, though only with difficulty and with large doses of humor and goodwill. Yet there was a deeper divide between Reed and the others. Lodge and

Roosevelt were full of righteousness (and self-righteousness). Reed was proud but too acerbic and world-weary in his view of human nature to mount the secular pulpit for very long or with real conviction. And while Lodge and Roosevelt cloaked their actions in moral authority, they were willing to be expedient, to make common cause with some fairly crude characters to advance their ambitions. Reed, for all his worldliness, was not. He would not compromise his integrity to reach for higher office, no matter how much he desired it.

From his chair overlooking Lafayette Square, Henry Adams had affected a resigned amusement over the presidential contest. He called McKinley a "sad jellyfish." Reed, he regretted, was just "too clever" for the "Bankers' Party," by which he meant the Republicans.[5] Reed was indeed sometimes too clever for his own good. For a man of deep New England reserve, an emotional stoic proud of his passivity, he was remarkably undisciplined in his personal remarks. His biting comments about feckless politicians and their greedy backers came from a deep bitterness forged by a prickly sense of honor and conscience that was at war with his political ambition. Reed did wish to become president, and he not unreasonably regarded himself as the best man for the job. But the Speaker simply refused to sell favors and buy support, a scruple that did not burden his rival, William McKinley. Congressman Nelson Aldrich of Rhode Island, who later was to become a sort of high-end boodler representing the Morgan interests as Senate Finance Committee chairman (and making a vast fortune on a public salary), recalled Reed's flintiness in "the campaign of 1896."[6] With his connections to the wealthy, Aldrich received a summons to see the railroad baron Collis P. Huntington. Aldrich went to see Reed first. By all means, Reed said, go see Huntington and talk of art and music. But, Reed

William McKinley (Library of Congress)

warned, holding up his index finger, "Not one dollar from Mr. Huntington for my campaign fund!" Aldrich dutifully went and talked to Huntington, a collector of politicians as well as art. Finally Huntington cut off the high-minded conversation to express his bafflement and disgust with Reed. "Why, you can't run a campaign without money!" he exclaimed. Aldrich mournfully agreed, "I know it, but Mr. Reed will not sanction it." Huntington blurted, "Why, the others have taken it!" Aldrich realized that Huntington was covering his bets by trying to buy all the candidates, though unsurprisingly this made no difference to Reed; in fact, it may have proved a point.

Reed would not use his office to seek a higher one. ("The bill will not be allowed to come up even with that Reed button in your coat," the Speaker told a congressman seeking a favor.)[7] Without money or the willingness to obtain it, Reed's candidacy was like an army without cannon. In his diary Reed's secretary, Asher Hinds, recorded the war of attrition. "The McKinley people have raised large sums of money among manufacturers and are getting many delegates," Hinds wrote on March 8. "The presidential contest is waxing hot," he noted on March 16. "The McKinley people are making much noise and seem to be using much money."[8] Reed appeared stoical about it all. Newspaper reporters noticed that he was becoming less droll in conversation; the *Washington Post* observed that he was taking long, lonely walks down Pennsylvania Avenue "wrapped in solemn grandeur and his own greatness." Noted Hinds: "His serenity is not at all disturbed, although in the last few days I have observed perhaps a little more seriousness of demeanor." As the McKinley machine ground toward the GOP national convention in St. Louis in June, Reed began losing delegates once pledged to him from the southern states. "They were for me," Reed drawled, "until the buying started."[9]

Roosevelt and Lodge had misread Reed. Like them, he was a moralist and also a realist. But his moral outrage was aimed at political corruption, and his realism concerned human nature. He was not willing to be politically expedient to raise money for a presidential campaign, and he did not find moral purpose in pushing the nation toward war.

In politics Roosevelt and Lodge were pragmatists, not sentimentalists. Just as they had after the 1884 Republican convention, they closed ranks behind the party's choice. "I'm dreadfully sorry and sore about Reed," Roosevelt wrote Lodge after McKinley was nominated by the GOP in June. "But we must do what we can for McKinley, of course. He is an honorable man."[10]

In fact, both Lodge and Roosevelt had reservations about the GOP's candidate. In February Lodge had written Roosevelt, "It will be a great misfortune to have McKinley nominated...if I did tell you all I have learned since his campaign has progressed, you would be completely alarmed." (Later, when Lodge published his correspondence, he deleted that passage.)[11] Roosevelt was just as circumspect with Bamie shortly after McKinley was nominated in June. He called McKinley "an honorable man" but "not a strong man," and ventured, in words that would later take on greater significance, "I should feel rather uneasy about him in a serious crisis."[12]

Reed took his loss with outward equanimity. "Mr. Reed did not get the nomination for the Presidency," Hinds wrote in his diary. "If he felt disappointed he did not show it."[13] In his private communications with Roosevelt and Lodge, the Speaker displayed some bile, however. "The whole thing is a farce," he wrote Roosevelt ("dear boy").[14] Senator Redfield Proctor of Vermont had been a supposed ally who had been secretly working for McKinley. "Vermont is a nice state," Reed deadpanned to Lodge before the Bostonian headed north to campaign for McKinley. "If Proctor should die while you are there, telegraph me....Be sure, however, that he is really dead."[15]

William F. McKinley had a deceptive blandness. In a pleasing baritone he spoke in syrupy, forgettable platitudes, and he was known as a compromiser, a smoother-over, not as a take-charge leader. But he was a good vote-getter, winning the governorship of Ohio after losing out to Reed as Speaker in 1889. During the Civil War, McKinley's most notable achievement had been to drive a coffee wagon into the midst of the fighting at Antietam in order to hand out sandwiches to the combatants. He had been a brave soldier, but he had never aimed a weapon or fired a shot—and he never bragged about his experiences or even talked about the war. He had seen war at Antietam, where more soldiers died in a single morning than in any American battle before or since, and he hated it. McKinley's God was a loving one. Childless, he was devoted to his wife, Ida, a clinging semi-invalid prone to seizures. When she had an episode at the dinner table, he would gently drape a handkerchief across her face to conceal her twitching.[16]

McKinley's other partner in life was as crude and brutish as McKinley was gentle and decorous. Mark Hanna was a successful industrialist of the Gilded Age who believed that the way to get ahead was to bring together business and government, and the way to do that was to spread around cash. All questions of government in a democracy, Hanna said, were "questions of money." Hanna had plenty of money, knew how to raise more, and he used it to further the political fortunes of William McKinley. It would be misleading, however, to suggest that Hanna used McKinley as a tool of the business interests. For all his apparent spinelessness, McKinley was able to get men to do what he wanted.

In his relationship with Hanna, McKinley was undoubtedly the senior partner. And though gruff, Hanna seems to have been more affectionate than manipulative toward his friend. He appreciated McKinley's innocence, his uncontrived air of virtue notwithstanding his political flexibility. As a politician, a fellow congressman once joked, McKinley kept his ear so close to the ground that it was "full of grasshoppers." Hanna's attitude toward McKinley was "always that of a big, bashful boy toward the girl he loves," recalled Herman Kohlstaat, a newspaperman who later became a White House aide. McKinley didn't make enemies; Hanna couldn't help but make them, and he envied and admired McKinley's self-control. Together they could be an effective — sometimes darkly effective — team.[17]

Roosevelt and Lodge approached Hanna warily. "I think you ought to make every effort to see a good deal of him," Roosevelt instructed Lodge in a letter on July 30, 1896, but "he will have to be handled with some care." Roosevelt described Hanna to Lodge as "a rough man, shrewd and hard-headed" with a "resolute, imperious mind."[18] He needn't have bothered. Lodge had already encountered Hanna in a way that was too demeaning to admit even to his closest friend. According to Kohlstaat, Lodge had approached Hanna at the Republican convention in June and said, "Mr. Hanna, I insist upon a positive declaration for a gold-standard plank in the platform."

Hanna looked at the tall, thin, imperious Brahmin and said, "Who in hell are you?"

"Senator Henry Cabot Lodge of Massachusetts," came the reply, no doubt delivered haughtily.

"Well, Senator Henry Cabot Lodge of Massachusetts, you can plumb go to hell. You have nothing to say about it."[19]

Few men dared speak that way to Lodge. In his memoirs Lodge says only that Hanna "gave me no encouragement." Lodge swallowed his pride, not easy for such a proud man but a choice he had made before in the service of expediency.

In the end the GOP platform included a promise to stay on the gold standard, just as Lodge had wished. Ever pragmatic in the service of the national interest as they defined it, Lodge and Roosevelt made their peace with McKinley and his man Hanna. The latter's money-raising machine was essential to a Republican victory in the fall, and a Republican victory was essential to the preservation of the Union — or so it looked to a pair of self-appointed guardians of the state. McKinley may not have been the perfect candidate, but to say that he was better than the alternative—Democrat William Jennings Bryan—is to grossly understate the apocalyptic stakes as they were understood by Roosevelt and Lodge and most of their kind.

For Roosevelt and Lodge it was the best of times—unless it was about to become the worst. After the convention Lodge traveled straight to Cambridge, where he spoke to his class at its twenty-fifth reunion, virtually snubbing the many thin-blooded mugwumps in attendance. "This great democracy is moving onward to its great destiny," he pronounced. "Woe to the men or to the nations who try to bar its imperial march." His speech was a paean to the ideal of sports as preparation for war. "I want Harvard to play the part which belongs to her in the great drama of American life....I want her to be filled with the spirit of victory.... The time given to athletic contests and the injuries incurred on the playing field are part of the price which the English speaking race has paid for being world-conquerors."[20]

Roosevelt loved it. When Lodge came to spend the night with him in New York, he wrote Bamie that at Commencement Day, Lodge was "able to emphasize his triumph in the presence of the men who hate him most."[21]

Actually, Lodge was worn and exhausted. He may have triumphed, but at great cost. Racked by his nervous stomach, he had shed 17 pounds, a serious weight loss for a man who never weighed more than 150. He was deeply worried about William Jennings Bryan, who was leading a populist crusade, crisscrossing the country by train, seeking to save a nation, as he famously put it at the 1896 Democratic convention, from being "crucified on a cross of gold." Bryan wanted to get off the gold standard and switch to silver-backed currency, believing that this would cheapen money and thus help small farmers and the debtor class—to the horror of the bankers and industrialists who were rapidly filling Mark Hanna's coffers. Lodge was sometimes scornful of bankers and had little regard for Hanna, but he saw Bryan as a Robespierre. The Massachusetts senator had been fighting to keep undesirable immigrants out of the United States by imposing a literacy test (the measure passed Congress but was vetoed by President Cleveland). Now he worried about the enemy within, fed by an alien ideology. Lodge, who dreaded class warfare, described Bryan's call to pit mass against class "as a mean cry." "Bryanism," he exhorted in a campaign speech, was an alien menace, an evil import from the people who had cursed France with the Terror and the guillotine. Bryan's plot to appropriate wealth, he declared, had been borrowed "from across the ocean....The man who uses it is not fit to be trusted. It was the cry heard in Paris and resulted in the horrors of the Commune."[22]

Lodge was not just mouthing campaign rhetoric. He was truly worried about the fate of the Republic. One day during the campaign he visited New York to have lunch with Roosevelt and Owen Wister. The talk took a gloomy turn. How long would the American form of government endure? After a pause to consider, they agreed: about fifty years.

This may seem surprisingly pessimistic. The three men were at the pinnacle of a seemingly secure, indeed dominant social class—the "Wasp Ascendancy," as another Porcellian man, Joseph Alsop, Roosevelt's great-nephew and a leading newspaper columnist of the Cold War era, would rather longingly look back upon it almost a century later.[23] Yet the fear of Bryanism was real. Some in the upper crust made light of it: at a ball in Bar Harbor, the Maine resort of the very rich, a pageant featuring a man carrying a cross and sixteen debutantes wearing crowns of thorns was performed to mock Bryan's famous speech. But Theodore Roosevelt worried that the lower classes would soon be responding to the cry of *Aux barricades!* "What a Witches Sabbath they did hold in Chicago!" he wrote Lodge after Bryan's speech at the Democratic convention in July. A week later he wrote Bamie, "Not since the Civil War has there been a Presidential election fraught with so much consequence to the country. The silver craze surpasses belief."

Roosevelt saw the nation at the edge of a moral and social abyss. To his friend the British diplomat Cecil Spring Rice he wrote, "If Bryan wins, we have before us some years of social misery, not markedly different from that of any South American Republic." Roosevelt went on to worry that the Americans were becoming "effete" and losing their "moral spring," and—worked up enough to indulge loopy racial theories of inherited characteristics— wondering why Germans, despite their martial history, made worse New York City policemen than the Irish.[24] Writing Lodge, who was recovering from nervous and physical exhaustion on a small island near Nantucket, Roosevelt confessed that he was feeling "a little knocked up" by his work with the New York police. "Oh! How I do long for a chance to see you and to talk with you. I'd like to see a white man now and then." (Lodge struck the last sentence from the published correspondence.)[25]

The two friends reunited on the campaign trail, touring upstate New York and making a pilgrimage to Canton, Ohio, where McKinley was campaigning from his front porch (so much more dignified, they felt, than Bryan's careening about at the back of a train). Returning to Boston, Lodge went to work raising money. He particularly enjoyed shaking down "unemployed plutocrats" frightened by Bryanism. Lodge proudly proclaimed that his son-in-law, A. P. Gardner, "has wrung something like ten thousand dollars from members of the Somerset Club [Boston's most exclusive club] who never gave a dime to any public object before."[26]

Money and fear—and, Roosevelt and Lodge would insist, common sense—carried the day. "You may easily imagine our relief," Roosevelt wrote Bamie on November 8, after McKinley had solidly defeated Bryan. "It was the greatest crisis in our national fate, save only the civil war." Still, Roosevelt, lapsing into the easy bigotry of his time, wasn't entirely sure the nation was secure with the class of people who had won. "The victorious Republican leaders have taken to feasting themselves, and especially Mark Hanna, and I have been to several Capuan entertainments . . . one was a huge lunch by the Seligmans, where at least half the guests were Jew bankers; I felt as if I was personally realizing all of Brooks Adams' gloomiest anticipations of our gold-ridden, capitalist-bestridden, userer-mastered future."[27]

Roosevelt longed for national regeneration, and he yearned to play a central role in the surest means he knew of reviving the American spirit. He was feeling thwarted and frustrated as New York police commissioner, bogged down in messy city politics. He wished to return to Washington, to find a meaningful job in the new administration rebuilding the nation's sinews of war. But what job?

Lodge had been instrumental getting Roosevelt his last two government posts. Now he went to work to get him a place that suited his talents and put him in the thick of things. In the late nineteenth century, most of the federal government could fit inside the State, War, and Navy Building, a gaudy pile of Second Empire design (described by the dyspeptic Henry Adams as an "architectural infant asylum").[28] The office of the assistant secretary of the navy, a high-ceilinged suite on the second floor overlooking the White House, was perfect for a young operator like Roosevelt — a good base for shipbuilding and pot-stirring.

After the election Lodge headed out to Canton to consult with the president-elect. McKinley asked Lodge what to do about Cuba, "and we went over the whole of that very perplexing question," Lodge wrote. "It is very much on his mind and I found he had given it a great deal of thought. He very naturally does not want to be obliged to go to war as soon as he comes in." McKinley, never one to confront a problem that he could slip around, "would like the crisis to come this winter and be settled one way or the other before he takes up the reins," Lodge wrote. Lodge knew enough to realize that such an outcome was optimistic, but he reported to Roosevelt that he was "greatly pleased to see how thoroughly he appreciates the momentous character of the question."

Lodge turned the conversation to Roosevelt. McKinley was at once eager to please and cagey. He spoke highly of Roosevelt's character and service but added, rather pointedly, "I hope he had no preconceived plans which he would wish to drive through the moment he got in." Lodge could have truthfully responded, "Just a war!" but instead, he recounted to Roosevelt, "I replied that he need not give himself the slightest uneasiness on that score." Then he decorously begged the president-elect, "I have no right to ask a personal favor of you, but I do ask for Roosevelt as the personal favor." McKinley was tepidly encouraging, and Lodge was, perhaps prematurely, encouraged.

Roosevelt was overjoyed. "I need hardly say with what interest I read your letter," he responded the same day, probably the same minute he'd received word from Lodge. Roosevelt dissembled, even to his own friend (or perhaps he wrote in code his friend could understand), "Of course, I have no preconceived policy of any kind which I wish to push through, and I think he would find that I would not be in any way a marplot or agitator; but I really look upon the matter with philosophical equanimity. The main reason I would care to go to Washington is to be near you."[29]

Buoyed by McKinley, Lodge set about organizing a vast lobbying campaign for Roosevelt that marshaled prominent congressmen and political worthies, including John Hay (named ambassador to England), Czar Reed, Judge William Howard Taft, and the vice-president, Garret Hobart.[30] Reed's support in particular was essential. "It has come, I know, to the administration's ears that Mr. Reed wants him, and it is their feeling that everything must be done that Reed wants," Lodge learned from a McKinley insider.[31] Roosevelt prepared himself by inviting Captain Alfred Thayer Mahan to Sagamore Hill, his home on Long Island, to discuss maritime strategy. He also addressed the U.S. Naval Academy and updated his history of the naval war of 1812.[32] Some of this was just window dressing; most of Roosevelt's thoughts involved Cuba. "I am a quietly rampant 'Cuba Libre' man," he wrote Bamie on January 2. "I doubt whether the Cubans would do very well in the line of self-government, but anything would be better than continuance of Spanish rule." Roosevelt wanted to "send our fleet promptly to Havana."[33]

Roosevelt was incapable of doing anything quietly, and his views made their way back to McKinley. Lodge's lobbying effort stalled. One of McKinley's biggest campaign contributors, prodded by Lodge, pleaded Roosevelt's case. McKinley responded, "I want peace, and I am told that your friend Theodore—whom I know only slightly — is always getting into rows with everybody. I am afraid he is too pugnacious."[34]

A deeply frustrated Roosevelt, sick of the "ceaseless worry and interminable wrangling," began to despair of getting to the Navy Department.[35] But Lodge pressed on. He went to see John Long, the new secretary of the navy, an old friend of McKinley from Congress. Long was a sweet, charmingly self-effacing man with a musical voice and a sensitive disposition. He had declined to campaign for McKinley because he suffered from "nervous prostration," and he continued to be a hypochondriac, complaining of various ailments and wishing to spend the hot summer months on his farm on the South Shore of Massachusetts.[36] To Lodge's surprise and relief, Long said that he was all for Roosevelt. His only question was whether the job of assistant secretary was "too small for him."

Lodge informed his friend that all was not lost after all. Roosevelt felt "a little like bawling," he wrote back. "I had abandoned all idea of the Assistant Secretaryship."[37] Lodge explained that "the hitch, if there is one, is not with Long but at the White House . . . the only, absolutely the only thing, I can hear adverse is that there is a fear that you will want to fight somebody at once."[38] Roosevelt volunteered to write Long, to say that he would "work hard" and "stay at Washington, hot weather or any weather, whenever he wants me to stay there."[39]

Lodge suspected that someone was working against Roosevelt from within McKinley's circle, and he was right: Senator Thomas Platt of New York, who ran that state's Republican machine, was not so much worried that Roosevelt would get the country into war as he was that Roosevelt would interfere with his patronage at the Brooklyn Navy Yard, sometimes referred to as "Mr. Platt's Yard."[40] But Roosevelt and Lodge were nothing if not practical.

They encouraged a subtle counterargument, that the machine could remove a thorny reformer by getting Roosevelt out of New York—and they had a plum of their own to hand out. Platt had been blackballed by the Metropolitan Club in Washington, a bastion of influential men. Lodge and Roosevelt quietly arranged to have the ban removed. The club records show Senator Platt joining the club just a few weeks after Roosevelt was informed that he had been appointed assistant secretary of the navy.[41] On April 6, 1897, Roosevelt gleefully telegraphed Lodge:

SINBAD HAS EVIDENTLY LANDED THE OLD MAN OF THE SEA.[42]

With his usual weary bemusement, Henry Adams had watched Lodge and Roosevelt agitate to find purchase in the new administration. In March, when Roosevelt's boat seemed to be foundering, Adams had written a friend, "The amiable McKinley, who does not use bludgeons much, and whose ways are conciliatory and dexterous, cannot be got to appreciate Theodore's methods, in spite of all the efforts of Cabot Lodge, who is earnest to get his friends back into office."[43] For months Adams himself had been busily conspiring about Cuba, trying to arrange the "big lift" he had promised his friends in the junta back in the spring of '96. "'War in January' is the favorite nipper in the navy," Adams had jauntily written his friend Hay in late October, just before the election. In December, using Lodge's liberal interpretation of the Monroe Doctrine, Adams had secretly drafted a Senate resolution recognizing Cuban independence—a big step up from recognizing the insurgent "belligerency," and one sure to provoke a hostile response from Madrid. Adams induced Lizzie's husband to introduce the resolution in the Senate.[44] Shortly thereafter came a brief drumbeat for war stirred by a sensational report in William Randolph Hearst's New York *Journal*. "Does Our Flag Protect Women?" demanded the *Journal*'s headline on February 12. The story recounted that Cuban officials had boarded an American steamer in Havana and strip-searched a young woman alleged to be carrying dispatches from the insurgents to the junta in New York. What really caught the attention of readers was a huge drawing filling half the front page rendered by Frederic Remington (now on the Hearst payroll), showing the comely backside of a nude young woman surrounded by sinister men with mustaches. The *Journal* reported the incident, it editorialized, in hopes of stirring statesmen "from their lethargy." In response, a congressman introduced a resolution demanding that the secretary of state furnish all information relevant to "the stripping of three lady passengers on the United States mail steamer Olivette in the harbor of Habana."[45]

But in the House of Representatives, Czar Reed still held sway, and he succeeded in quieting the burst of jingoism. The Cameron resolution, passed in the Senate, quietly died in the House. Outgoing President Cleveland dreaded armed conflict with Spain. Warning McKinley, "You have a war on your hands," Cleveland went on, "If I can only go out of office...with the knowledge that I have done what lay in my power to avert this terrible calamity...I shall be the happiest man in the world."[46] McKinley was just as peace-minded, and told Cleveland so.

On March 4, 1897, a clear, windy, chilly morning in Washington, the McKinleys arose and the president-elect polished off a breakfast of porterhouse steak, broiled chicken, quail, Spanish omelet, toast, hot rolls, wheat muffins, tea and coffee. Mrs. McKinley, looking ill, tottered to her place on the reviewing stand on the East Front of the Capitol. After McKinley had

Remington's illustration for the Journal *of the Spaniards conducting a strip search (New York* Journal*)*

taken the oath of office, he delivered his inaugural address. "We want no wars of conquest," he said. "We must avoid the temptation of territorial aggression. War should never be entered upon until every agency of peace has failed; peace is preferable to war in almost every contingency." Lodge, in the audience that day, and Roosevelt, still in New York, might seize on the qualifier "almost." But speaking with Carl Schurz, a leading New York mugwump, McKinley privately insisted, "You may be sure there will be no jingo nonsense under my administration."[47] Little did he know.

10

Kinds of Courage

"You furnish the pictures, and I'll furnish the war."

WILLIAM RANDOLPH HEARST and Theodore Roosevelt had much in common. They were both Harvard men who liked fancy clothes; they were both masters of public relations; and they both desired a war for themselves and for the United States. But in spite of, or because of, these similarities, the two men disliked each other. Roosevelt tried to take no notice of Hearst, which just maddened Hearst all the more. Hearst saw himself, through his newspaper, as the champion of the little man; Roosevelt, he concluded, was too "aristocratic." Though Hearst wore splashy suits, in his newspaper he mocked Roosevelt for his showy dress—pink shirts and a black silk sash with tassles that dangled to the knees. "He has a very poor opinion of the majority," the *Journal* editorialized on January 1, 1897. "But there is one compensation: The majority has a very poor opinion of Mr. Roosevelt."

The *Journal* had sniped at Roosevelt all through his service as police commissioner. Ever the moralist, Roosevelt insisted on enforcing a law, long ignored, banning sales of alcohol on the Sabbath. (Since his brief overindulgence at the Porcellian Club, Roosevelt had been very abstemious, once more his father's son.)

Spotting a policeman taking a schooner of beer out the side door of a saloon, Roosevelt personally chased the man down (the copper had dropped the glass and run for it) and brought him up on departmental charges.[1] Roosevelt continued to close down saloons on Sunday, earning the enmity of workers, especially Irish and German immigrants, for whom Sunday was their one day to unbend. The *Journal* ran a series of articles accusing Roosevelt of using "child spies" to catch saloon owners. Roosevelt indignantly denied this even as his department announced that it would cease the practice.[2]

Roosevelt routinely accused the *Journal* of misquoting him or manufacturing his words wholesale. In late October 1896, when Roosevelt was campaigning for McKinley by attacking Bryan as a dangerous demagogue, the *Journal* reported on a conversation between Roosevelt and an unidentified stranger onboard a train to Chicago. According to the *Journal*, Roosevelt told the man he was ready, sword in hand, for the coming civil war between the protectors of property and the Bryanites: "When war does come, I shall be found at the head of my regiment." Roosevelt ventured that the coming revolt would be suppressed "as the Commune in Paris was suppressed, by taking ten or a dozen of their leaders out, standing them against a wall, and shooting them dead!" The headline over the story was: THEO. ROOSEVELT FOR HORRID WAR: He Thinks Revolution Is Being Plotted and He Wants Blood.

What had happened, Roosevelt explained in an indignant letter to Lodge, was that he had encountered an editor of the *Journal*, Willis Abbott, on the train to Chicago. Since the man was a cousin of Lyman Abbott, a highly respectable clergyman and biographer of Roosevelt's friend the Reverend Henry Ward

Beecher, Roosevelt spoke to him. "Anyone who has ever heard me speak knows that I am incapable of using such an expression as ... 'standing up the silver leaders against a wall to be shot,'" Roosevelt insisted unconvincingly to Lodge, who had heard him say more outrageous things. In a letter to the *Journal*, Roosevelt denounced the story as "a tissue of lies," but Abbott maintained that his memory of the conversation was accurately reported in the paper.[3]

Hearst proclaimed to be all for the "silver men," even though he knew that switching from the gold standard to a silver-based currency was a delusion, that "easy money" would raise prices as well as pay in a dangerously inflationary spiral. Hearst was not insincere in his pose as the workingman's friend—in some ways he anticipated Roosevelt in pushing for regulation of unfettered capitalism. But he played to working-class readers, encouraging his cartoonists to picture Hanna as a monstrous figure covered with dollar signs and McKinley as a pygmy, or alternatively as a buffoonish Napoleon asking, "Is my hat on straight?"[4]

Hearst, however, was in complete agreement with Roosevelt on one subject: that a war would be good for the country. The *Journal* dismissed McKinley's inaugural-address promise of avoiding wars of conquest as "vague and sapless."[5] If the president wouldn't start a war, Hearst concluded, he would just have to do it himself.

Hearst did not dance, ride, or drink, and at dinner parties he sat quiet and stiff, looking morose. Hostesses decided he was a bore and stopped inviting him. But he loved the bright lights. On Broadway he went to vaudeville and light theatrical romances almost every night, followed by dinner at Sherry's, a downtown

Millicent and Anita Willson with their mother (Bancroft Library, University of California, Berkeley)

celebrity oasis. Often he had on his arm not one but two show-girls, Millicent and Anita Willson, dancers in the Broadway hit *The Girl from Paris.* (Hearst had abandoned his old mistress, Tessie.) The girls lived in a boardinghouse known colloquially as a "resort"—a brothel. The truth was that he was in love with Millicent, but since she was only sixteen, her older sister served as "chaperone"—and somebody to talk with during Hearst's long silences.

Back at work, Hearst truly came alive, giddy with the thrill of a voice magnificently amplified. An editor, Harry Coleman, entered Hearst's sumptuous office (where a painting of Napoleon hung over the desk) to find him studying some page proofs for that morning's *Journal*. "Hearst suddenly spread the proofs in precise order upon the floor," Coleman wrote, "and began a sort of tap dance around and between them...with lively castanet accompaniments produced by his snapping fingers." It is a wonderful image and a revealing one. Hearst was a creative genius, a maestro, and he made an art form of popular journalism—a low art perhaps, and one not overly burdened by the truth, but one that captured the imagination of millions of readers.[6]

Hearst needed enterprising reporters, and he was willing to pay for them. He hired Mark Twain to cover the sixtieth anniversary of Queen Victoria's coronation and a boatload of writers to cover the Klondike gold rush.[7] Cuba presented a particular challenge. The Spanish authorities banned American correspondents from traveling to the front and censored their dispatches. It was illegal to mount private military expeditions to foreign countries, and such "filibusterers" were sometimes caught crossing the Florida straits and prosecuted by U.S. customs (if not sunk first by a Spanish gunboat). These impediments merely made Hearst try harder. As a publicity stunt, he was itching to send a personal emissary to the leader of the Cuban rebels. He had paid Tiffany, the Fifth Avenue jeweler, to create a gold-and-diamond-encrusted sword engraved "To Maximo Gomez, Commander-in-Chief of the Army of the Cuban Republic" on one side and "Viva Cuba Libre" on the other. The trick was to find someone, and some way, to deliver it.

In the fall of 1896 a twenty-four-year-old former Yale oarsman named Ralph Paine wandered into the *Journal* looking for adventure. Hearst opened up a long mahogany case and pulled out the sword. Paine drily told him, "I'm the damn fool you've been looking for." Paine and the sword never did make it to Cuba, however; his boat (a Florida tug captained by someone called Dynamite Johnny) was turned away from the Cuban coast after a one-shot battle with a Spanish gunboat.[8]*

Hearst had slightly better luck with the most celebrated, best-paid correspondent of the 1890s. Square-jawed and impeccably dressed, favoring Norfolk jackets, kid gloves, and a cane, Richard Harding Davis spoke in an accent that was half English, half Philadelphia Main Line. The model used by the illustrator Charles Dana Gibson as a suitable mate for the "Gibson Girl," the sweetheart of the late Gilded Age, Davis sought to embody an elegant variation of muscular Christianity, his prose full of poetic chivalry. Davis was mostly an act: born in modest circumstances, he had grown restless studying engineering at Lehigh and determined to reinvent himself. He often suffered from feelings of worthlessness and nervous symptoms, but he knew how to play the Boy Hero in an age looking for one.[9]

As soon as he took over the *Journal* in 1895, Hearst hired Davis to cover the annual Thanksgiving football game in Manhattan between Princeton and Yale for the princely sum of $500. (It was a good investment at a time when football was the rage with high society: the edition sold out.) Toward the end of 1896 Hearst hired Davis again, this time for $3,000 a month, to go to Cuba with Frederic Remington. Davis and Remington were instructed to appear late at night at the *Journal*'s offices in lower Manhattan, whence they would be secreted to the docks in a darkened, closed cab to meet their boat for the voyage to Key West. (*Journal* staffers sniggered at Hearst's propensity for such

---

*After the war was over, General Gómez was finally presented with the sword by a *Journal* reporter. He declined it, calling Hearst an "imbecile" and saying that he could have used the money the sword cost — some $2,000 — to feed, clothe, and arm his men.

unnecessary melodrama.) Davis appeared in a specially tailored tropical uniform with piping on the pant legs. Remington, who as a Yale football player had once dipped his uniform in blood from a slaughterhouse before a big game, came garbed in what he called his Duke of Marlborough outfit: a florid affair of bulging pockets, loops, and flaps that did little to hide his obesity. A racist and a bit of a boor, Remington had been hoping for a war with Spain, mostly for the excitement of it all, though he wrote his friend Owen Wister that he wasn't sure it was worth getting Americans "killed to free a lot of damn n——s who are better off under the yoke."[10]

Arriving in Key West, the two secret agents discovered that the crew of Hearst's yacht, the *Vamoose*, had gone on strike. When the captain finally hired another crew, the sleek, fast, but unstable vessel was turned back from Cuba by winter storms. So much for secrecy: Davis and Remington ended up booking passage on the *Olivette*, the mail boat to Havana, and checked into the watering hole for all visiting correspondents, the Hotel Inglaterra.

Hearst called his correspondents to Cuba "special commissioners," befitting the conviction that his newspaper was essentially a sovereign state. As envoys and not mere reporters, they were expected to travel in style. An earlier Hearst special commissioner, Murat Halstead, described his accommodations at the Inglaterra: a room with a private marble balcony and a huge four-poster bed with a headboard inlaid with mother-of-pearl. Breakfast was taken in bed on solid silver trays; the crushed ice in the bar was limitless, as was the rum.[11] It would be the same for Davis and Remington.

Until his latest pair of special commissioners arrived in Cuba, Hearst had been publishing imagined accounts of Spanish brutality to women—a Hearst favorite—and tales of the valor of the rebels, who, according to the *Journal*, bravely charged the Spanish lines shouting "*Al Machete!*"[12] In fact, aside from taking an occasional potshot, the rebels rarely attacked the Spanish troops. Disease accounted for most Spanish casualties; death from yellow fever (also called "the black vomit"), the most common of these devastating ailments, was particularly horrible. The mosquito-borne infection essentially melted soft tissues so that sufferers bled from the nose and gums, rectums and genitals, and vomited up something that looked roughly like coffee grounds but was actually stomach lining and intestine.[13] Howling and ranting as they bled from every orifice, patients had to be tied down in bed so they would not splatter the infection around the wards.

The rebel war consisted mostly of burning plantations and terrorizing anyone loyal to Spain. As in all guerrilla wars, there were atrocities. To save ammunition some Spanish prisoners were required to dig their own graves, where they were buried alive. One rebel leader delighted in using his machete to lop off the heads of "traitors."[14] The Spaniards were even more brutal. The empire had a history of bloodlust, from the Inquisition to the mass extermination of Indians in Central and South America. The word used by the Spanish general who arrived in 1896 to suppress the festering rebellion was "pacification." General Valeriano Wyler has been compared to a vicious midget; he stood four feet ten, and his eyes were sometimes described as dead. The *Journal* labeled him "Butcher Wyler" and turned up the hyperbole, even by Hearst standards: "a fiendish despot...a brute...pitiless, cold, an exterminator of men.... There is nothing to prevent his carnal, animal brain from running riot with itself in inventing tortures and infamies of bloody debauchery."[15]

At least Wyler was a soldier. While other Spanish officers lolled in Havana and insisted on imbibing chilled champagne because the Cuban water was foul, Wyler drank what his troops drank and went into the field. But he was harsh. "One does not make war with bon-bons," he said, and he determined in the most draconian fashion to starve out the rebels by depriving them of support. He ordered whole towns emptied of their citizens, "reconcentrating" them in squalid makeshift camps. The *reconcentrados* died of disease and malnourishment in droves: an estimated 170,000 people, or 10 percent of the civilian population.[16]

From the well-tended terrace of the Hotel Inglaterra it was not possible to see any of this horror, and Remington quickly grew bored. According to one of Hearst's correspondents, James Creelman, Remington sent Hearst a telegram that stated, "Everything is quiet. There is no trouble here. There will be no war. I wish to return. Remington." Hearst replied, "Please remain. You furnish the pictures, and I'll furnish the war." Years later Hearst claimed that this purported telegram was "clotted nonsense."[17] Hearst correspondents were certainly capable of exaggeration and indeed outright fiction, but the story captures the spirit of Hearst, who endlessly championed "the journalism that acts" and made no effort to disguise his desire for a war. In any case, Remington did return to New York—a relief to Davis, who was tired of the artist's need to have a cocktail before he did much of anything (not that there was much of anything to do).

In mid-January, Davis finally secured an audience with General Wyler, who did not turn out to be a butcher but rather, Davis wrote, "a dignified and impressive soldier" who received him with "courtesy and consideration." Wyler provided Davis with a private railway car for viewing the countryside as well as a valet who addressed him as "my lord." To his credit, Davis did some of the first reporting on the plight of the *reconcentrados*, but his most famous story—so famous that it would spawn countless homages and clichés—was called simply "Death of Rodriguez." In a spare but dramatic prose style that anticipated Hemingway, Davis described a young rebel proudly facing the firing squad, nonchalantly smoking a last cigarette and kissing a cross extended by a priest before the bullets flew.[18]

The *Journal* claimed that Davis had reached the rebel forces, which was not true. In a letter to his mother Davis described the trip as a "failure...I haven't heard a shot fired or seen an insurgent. I am just 'not in it' and I am torn between coming home and making your dear heart stop worrying and getting one story to justify me being here and that damn silly page of the Journal....All Hearst wants is my name." Davis sailed back in late January, filing a last dispatch—that the Spanish authorities had strip-searched a woman suspected of carrying messages to the rebel junta in New York.[19] This was the story that Remington, already back in New York, illustrated with the curvy bare bottom of a damsel surrounded by prying men, the shocking image that caused senators to shake off their "lethargy" on Capitol Hill. There was only one catch: As Hearst's competitor, Joseph Pulitzer's New York *World* gleefully reported, the woman had been searched by a matron, not men. The *World* editorialized, "Mr. Davis and Mr. Remington should be well quarantined before they are allowed to mingle with reputable newspaper men." Davis was humiliated and vowed never again to work for Hearst.[20] That was a disappointment to Hearst; he valued Davis's brand name, and while Hearst was not above making up what he could not report, he still needed reporters. He would just have to find other special commissioners—or go to Cuba himself.

*   *   *

Like Roosevelt and Lodge, William James had been thinking hard about national regeneration, about the strenuous life, and about the temptations of war. In the presidential election just past, he had worried about the "mob psychology" of the Bryanites, and he dismissed the lure of easy money as "humbug." And yet, as was characteristic, he did not resort to easy typecasting. "The Silverites are doubtless victims of a craze, but there is some good in them, and they are forcing decency upon the Republicans," he wrote his brother Henry in August 1896.[21]

That August, James had spent a week at the Chautauqua Assembly in upstate New York, the adult education-cum-family-entertainment that had become extremely popular in the late nineteenth century. He listened to the lectures on temperance and middle-class virtue, joined the wholesome sing-alongs and corny joke-telling, appreciated the good-hearted virtuousness — and felt bored and vaguely depressed by the smug conformity and mediocrity of it all. "Ten thousand people with no wilder excess to tempt them than 'ice cream soda,'" he grumbled to Henry.[22] On the train back from Buffalo he observed a man laboring on "the dizzying edge of a sky-scaling construction." The sight thrilled him. Here was the heroic worker, at the edge of his strength and endurance, *doing something brave.*[23]

James continued to search and to experiment. He gloried in a new bicycle and clambered about on mountain trails, and he had his unsatisfying encounter with hallucinogens via what he described to Henry as "a psychological Experiment with *mescal,* an intoxicant used by some of our S. Western Indians in their religious ceremonies." The drug "gives the most glorious visions of colour — every object thought of appears in a jeweled splendor unknown to the natural world" — or so James had heard tell.

His own visions were more of the floor than the heavens: "I took one bud 3 days ago, vomited and spattered for 24 hours and had no other symptom whatever.... I will take the visions on trust," he sheepishly reported to Henry.[24]

In February he wrote Henry that he had been asked to deliver an oration at the dedication of the Shaw Memorial in Boston. Henry was thrilled. It was a chance to commemorate not just Robert Shaw but their beloved brother Wilkie, who had fallen at Shaw's side and suffered terribly from his wounds. Wilkie, who had never really recovered from the war, had died young, and their brother Bob, who had also seen fighting, had become a drunk and a drifter. Both unfortunate veterans of the Civil War were much on the minds of the two older brothers who had been spared (or missed out on) the fighting. In February Henry wrote William from London: "I vibrate intensely to the 31st May. I don't know what I wouldn't give to be there. But even poor dear, dead Wilkie will be more there than I. He will be very much there, ... poor dear boy; and I can't help figuring it as a sort of a beautiful, poetic justice to him. I rejoice to know that the monument is really eminent."[25]

William, the orator-to-be, was more apprehensive. At first he half expected to deliver the usual patriotic bromides, at once soothing and uplifting. Then he thought better of it. He wanted to "break away from the vulgar claptrap of war sentimentalism," he wrote Henry. He was looking for "*Truth*," he wrote, but he was wise enough to know how elusive the truth is, especially about something so encrusted in romance as the martyrdom of Robert Gould Shaw.

On the eve of the speech he was exhausted—"fagged to death"—his voice lost to hoarseness that was no doubt psychosomatic. "At nine o'clock the night before," he recounted to

The Shaw Memorial (Library of Congress)

Henry, "I ran into a laryngologist in Boston, who sprayed and cauterized and otherwise tuned up my throat, giving me pellets to suck all morning."

Memorial Day dawned damp and misty, but thousands of flag-waving Bostonians turned out. From a battleship in the harbor a great gun boomed the signal to start the parade of veterans, soldiers and sailors. As he sat, sucking pellets, in a carriage with sculptor Augustus Saint-Gaudens ("a most charming and modest man") under the "weeping sky," James thought of Wilkie lying, wounded and wasted, under a crocheted blanket sent by a friend, Louisa May Alcott. She had sent a poem, written in her hand, "To GWJ...after being wounded at Wagner":

In the lost age of lance and shield,
Maids wrought on banner, scarf and glove
Emblems of chivalry and love
When valiant young knights took the field.[26]

Wilkie had been a sad, hurt boy, not a valiant knight. Though James had been awed by the sight of Charles Lowell and his bride, Effie Shaw Lowell, on horseback, etched against the evening sky, he knew that the celebration of war was unreal, a piece of mythology at once necessary, comforting, misleading, and possibly dangerous. Saint-Gaudens had crafted an enormous bas-relief facing the gold-domed Massachusetts State House: twenty-three black soldiers along with their young commander, riding beside his troops, an angel overhead. Shaw's death, the sculpture made clear, was not just a tragedy but a martyrdom of holy proportions.

The sentiment that Memorial Day in Boston was "pathetic," James wrote Henry—"everything softened and made poetic and unreal by distance, poor little Robert Shaw erected into a great symbol of deeper things than he ever realized himself."[27] James did not mean "pathetic" in the pejorative sense, but rather truly sad, suffused with pathos. For James the occasion was a chance to say something different—not merely to indulge sentiment and cast a warm glow over war, but to challenge his audience to think about the true nature of Robert Shaw's heroism.

When he took the stage of the Boston Music Hall shortly after noon, he felt overwhelmed. Three thousand people had jammed into the auditorium, filling the seats, the aisles, the windowsills, the outer hallway. With his voice still hoarse, James had to "shout and bellow, and you seem to yourself wholly unnatural," he wrote Henry.[28] He began by telling the familiar story of Shaw, the Fifty-fourth Massachusetts, and the attack on Fort Wagner—how the regiment fought until two-thirds of its officers and half its men had been shot or bayoneted. James's description was lyrical at moments but no different in its essential telling from all the speeches that had come before. But then his tone and his message took a new direction. "War has been much praised and celebrated among us of late as a school of manly virtue," he said, in words that could have been aimed directly at Lodge after his Harvard twenty-fifth anniversary speech of the year before, or Roosevelt at almost any time. "But it is easy to exaggerate upon this point." He explained by saying that physical courage in war, while laudable, was actually not all that exceptional. "The war tax is still the only tax that men ungrudgingly will pay," said James. "Man is once and for all a fighting animal; centuries of peaceful history could not breed the battle instinct out of us."

From James's perspective, what deserved to be praised — to be remembered for all time by orators and poets — was not Shaw's physical courage, his willingness to charge at the enemy guns. Rather, Shaw should be remembered for what James called his "lonely courage" — his willingness to leave his fancy regiment of Harvard boys, the Massachusetts Second, and take command of an untested, much doubted regiment of Negro soldiers. This did not come easily for a "blue eyed child of fortune, upon whose youth every divinity had smiled," who had "walk[ed] socially on the sunny side of life." In this "new negro soldier venture, loneliness was certain, ridicule inevitable, failure possible." Offered command of the new Negro regiment, Shaw at first had wavered, unsure what to do, James noted. But then he answered his conscience. "That lonely kind of courage (civic courage as we call it in times of peace) is the kind of valor to which the monuments of nations should most of all be reared."

James was accorded polite applause. The crowd perked up when it stood to lustily sing "The Battle Hymn of the Republic," just as the Fifty-fourth had in May of '63, marching down Beacon Street to death and glory. An old sergeant who had been shot three times but never dropped the regimental standard at Fort Wagner waved the tattered banner and the crowd exploded.

James felt deflated. "I will never accept such a job again," he wrote Henry. Of his message about civic courage he said, somewhat pitifully, "I brought in some mugwumpery at the end, but it was very difficult to manage it."[29] James may have been frustrated by trying to treat thoughtfully an occasion given over to raw emotionalism. But his speech would prove the foundation for his later work, including his formulation "the moral equivalent of war." Not always the most courageous figure himself, James understood what true courage was. His speech will resonate long after all the patriotic speeches of all the Memorial Days have been forgotten. At the time, though, it seemed a small candle flickering in the gusts of a darkening sky.

11

Romance

"All the great masterful races have been fighting races."

O N MAY 3, 1897, as William James was struggling to rede-
fine courage, Theodore Roosevelt was wiring a "personal
and private" letter to Captain Alfred Thayer Mahan.
Urgent, impatient, the new assistant secretary of the navy was
doing exactly what President McKinley feared he would do: he
was setting out his own agenda for expansion and war. "If I had
my way," he wrote Mahan, the United States would annex the
Hawaiian Islands "tomorrow." Roosevelt wanted to move quickly
on Hawaii before Japan took delivery on two new battleships
from England. We "would hoist our flag over the island, leaving
all details for after action," wrote Roosevelt, adding "I believe...
we should build a dozen new battleships." He was furious that
some lawmakers in Congress—including Thomas Reed—saw
no such need.[1] In January 1893 the islands' Queen Liliuokalani
had proclaimed "Hawaii for Hawaiians"; for her trouble she was
deposed by the American pineapple growers, aided by some U.S.
Marines, and put under house arrest in her own palace. News of
the coup dovetailed with a spurt of superficial interest on what
soon would be thought of as "the mainland." Hawaii became,
for a season, all the rage in Washington social circles. Hostesses

staged *luaus* and guests hummed a rude ditty, "Come little Liliu-o-kalani/Give Uncle Sam/Your little yellow hannie..."[2] A puppet government in Honolulu, installed by the sugar interests, was to turn the islands into an official American territory, but a treaty of annexation signed in 1897 lacked the required two-thirds vote in the Senate. Now, with Japan emerging as a Pacific naval power, Roosevelt was too impatient to wait for the politicians. He was looking for an excuse to take Hawaii.

Furiously scribbling his note to Mahan, Roosevelt turned his attention to the Caribbean, to Cuba and Puerto Rico: "Until we definitely turn Spain out of those islands (and if I had my way that would be done tomorrow) we will always be menaced by trouble there."[3] He concluded, "I need not say that this letter must be strictly private...to no one else excepting Lodge do I talk like this."

Meanwhile he was working navy back channels to be ready for the hour when war would come. Every day he took the short walk from his office in the old State, War, and Navy Building, across Pennsylvania Avenue and one block up Seventeenth Street, to the Metropolitan Club. His stride was always brisk, hastened by the prospect of vigorous debate and his lunchtime favorite, double lamb chops. The men's club, a Victorian brick structure with high-ceilinged rooms and heavy, dark paneling, served as a kind of White House mess hall before there was such a thing. Founded during the Civil War by financial men who had come from Wall Street and Philadelphia to sell war bonds and wanted a proper city club, the Metropolitan was a government unto itself. Its members included cabinet members, diplomats, and senior military officers. Roosevelt, often in the company of Lodge, dined often with Mahan, the nervous, weedy-looking, recently retired captain who was by now regarded as the most influential naval thinker in history. Roosevelt frequently helped Mahan spread his secular religion of navalism, the ideology that sea power is the key to global power. (In 1890, in a more consequential meeting than Roosevelt could possibly have realized, he had introduced Mahan to a Harvard friend, Baron Kaneko Kentaro, whose translation of Mahan's *The Influence of Sea Power on History* would directly lead to the buildup of the Japanese Imperial Navy.)[4]

Roosevelt was not planning war on the back of an envelope; he had professional help. He was in close communication with Mahan's old base of operations, the Naval War College in Newport, Rhode Island. On May 28, 1897—the day James gave his oration at the unveiling of the Shaw Memorial—Roosevelt sent this instruction to Captain Frederick Goodrich, president of the Naval War College:

> Special Confidential Problem for War College:
> Japan makes demands on Hawaiian Islands.
> This country intervenes.
> What force would be necessary to uphold the intervention, and how should it be employed?
> Keeping in mind possible complications with another Power on the Atlantic Coast (Cuba).

Less than a week later, on the morning of June 1, Roosevelt clambered aboard a fast torpedo boat, the *Cushing*, for the daylong run from Sagamore Hill to Newport. The weather was fair, the sea calm (fortunate for the assistant secretary, who was prone to mild seasickness), and the slender, wooden torpedo boat raced at more than twenty knots, spray flying, down Long Island Sound. Exhilarated, Roosevelt arrived in Newport as the sun was dipping in the west. The guns of the old battleship *Constellation* boomed a salute as the assistant secretary entered the harbor. The next day Roosevelt posed for pictures with the officers of the War College, standing on a porch that overlooks the approaches of Narragansett Bay, where John Paul Jones had set sail to fight the British in the Revolutionary War. Afterward, in a small, stuffy auditorium, Roosevelt gave his most full-throated war cry yet.

"All the great masterful races have been fighting races," he barked. "And the minute that a race loses its hard fighting virtues, then...it has lost its proud right to stand as the equal of the best." Roosevelt called for a massive, immediate buildup of the navy, quoting George Washington that "to be prepared for war is the most effectual way to promote peace." Then he continued: "No triumph of peace is quite so great as the supreme triumphs of war.... Cowardice in a race, as in an individual, is the unpardonable sin." Anticipating Winston Churchill's "blood, toil, tears, and sweat" speech at the time of the Battle of Britain by half a century, he charged his audience:

> ...there are higher things in this life than the soft and easy enjoyment of material comfort. It is through strife, or the readiness for strife, that a nation must win greatness. We ask for a great navy, partly because we feel that no national life is worth having if the nation is not willing, when the need shall arise, to stake everything on the supreme arbitrament of war, and to pour out its blood, its treasure, and its tears like water, rather than submit to the loss of honor and renown.[5]

By the time Roosevelt concluded his address, he had repeated the word "war" sixty-two times.

TR at the Naval War College (Naval Historical Center, Washington, D.C.)

Roosevelt's speech, reprinted in papers across the country, caused a sensation. President McKinley felt the breeze, though it chilled him. "I suspect Roosevelt is right," the president told a friend, "and the only difference between him and me is that mine is the greater responsibility."[6]

Right or not, Roosevelt's boss, Navy Secretary John Long, was not pleased. "He didn't like the address I made to the War College at Newport the other day," Roosevelt wrote to Captain Mahan. "I shall send it to you when I get a copy." Long was even less happy when Roosevelt essentially repeated the address to the Naval Reserve of Ohio later that summer. "The headlines and comments, for which I was in no way responsible, nearly threw the Secretary into a fit," Roosevelt wrote Lodge, "and he gave me as heavy a wigging as his invariable courtesy and kindness would permit."[7] But Long *was* kind and forgiving—"a perfect dear," Roosevelt described him to Cecil Spring Rice, and he did not want to pick too much of a fight with his eager young subordinate. Besides, Washington was getting warm, and Long wanted to go to his cooler summer home in the Massachusetts countryside. Long was certainly wary of Roosevelt's designs. "In strict confidence," Roosevelt wrote Mahan on June 9, "Secretary Long is only lukewarm about building up our Navy, at any rate as regards battleships."

But Long was not exactly an obstacle either, especially when he was out of town. With Long absent, Roosevelt got busy. On June 16 he was at the White House lobbying McKinley for a bigger navy ("Hanna backing up this like a man," Roosevelt reported to Lodge), and on July 18 he met with a group of senators and Cuban lobbyists at the Metropolitan Club to discuss Cuba Libre. He wrote Secretary Long at his farm: "There is very little for me to write you about. Everything has gone along very quietly."[8] While the assistant secretary of the navy worked up war plans and prodded congressmen reluctant to build more battleships, the secretary tended his garden in the soothing breezes of the Massachusetts South Shore.

On August 9 Roosevelt, in no rush for his boss to return, wrote Long, "You must be tired, and you ought to have an entire rest." On August 13, in a letter to Senator Cushman Davis of Minnesota, who was seeking some minor favor, Roosevelt giddily exclaimed, "At last! This time I am in sole command, and your request goes through!...Of course treat this letter as private." On August 15 he encouraged Long to extend his vacation: "I hope you are having a very pleasant time, and if things go on as they are now there isn't the slightest earthly reason for you to come back for six weeks more." Meanwhile Roosevelt busily collected and circulated the war messages of every past president (James Madison in the War of 1812, James Polk at the time of the Mexican War, Abraham Lincoln throughout the Civil War) as a way of not so subtly hinting to McKinley where his duty lay. Such heavy-handedness caused his friend Lodge to caution, "Do not on any account put them out with your name on them or as coming from you in any way, for it will look as if you were trying to force somebody's hand." That same day, August 19, Roosevelt wrote another friend, "The Secretary is away, and I am having immense fun running the Navy."[9]

His fun verged on euphoria during three days in early September. Eager to see the big guns of the modern navy in action, Roosevelt asked to go on maneuvers with the North Atlantic Fleet off the Virginia capes. Fortunately for Roosevelt's tender stomach, the ocean was glassy when the seven white ships, destroyers, cruisers, and the mighty *Iowa*, the newest battleship, staged a kind of naval quadrille for the assistant secretary: single column, double column, formation in echelon, wheeling to starboard, wheeling to port, their proud bows cleaving the long, slow swell—Roosevelt, watching from the dispatch boat *Dolphin*, was thrilled. Afterward he boarded the *Iowa* for target practice. As he stood on the bridge, bells gonged and seamen clambered to battle stations. With its eight-inch guns, the battleship shattered a wooden target floating two thousand yards away. Then, for the first time, the battleship loosed its twelve-inch guns, which were so powerful that the concussion stove in a lifeboat, shattered a couple of skylights, and knocked steel doors off their hinges. Roosevelt, wearing earplugs, was delighted. He was in his element and fascinated by the innovations, which included signaling by daylight with special Japanese-made fireworks. (Communications had not kept up with modern armament; the fleet exchanged messages with its shore base by carrier pigeon.) At night a mock battle was enacted for the assistant secretary, searchlights playing on torpedo boats as they raced in under cover of darkness. When a coxswain let go an anchor line to avoid a collision with another vessel, the assistant secretary of the navy bellowed out, "I hold you personally responsible for the loss of that anchor and chain!" (The startled sailor was later reprieved.)[10]

Roosevelt wrote Edith, who was with the children in Oyster Bay, to express his sense of awe and wonder: "I can not begin to describe the wonderful power and beauty of these giant warships, with their white hulls and towering superstructures. At night each was a blaze of light...the effect was as wildly beautiful as anything ever Turner dreamed...the immense war engines, throbbing with tremendous might...really it was almost as exciting as if we had been going into action."[11]

To Lodge, Roosevelt exulted, "I have never enjoyed three days more than my three days with the fleet, and I think I have profited from it....I was very fortunate in the weather, which was wonderfully calm. Think of it, on the Atlantic Ocean, out of sight of land, going out to dinner in evening dress without an overcoat!"[12] Roosevelt pronounced himself satisfied with the superiority of a battleship as a gun platform. Ever the public relations man, he had brought Remington with him. Just as Hearst wished to use the artist's talents to generate sympathy for Cuba Libre, Roosevelt wanted the nation's premier illustrator as a propagandist for the navy. "I can't help looking upon you as an ally from henceforth on in trying to make the American people see the beauty and the majesty of our ships, and the heroic quality which lurks somewhere in all those who man and handle them," he wrote Remington, whom he teasingly addressed as "O sea-going plainsman" (like Roosevelt, Remington was secretly uncomfortable in any craft larger than a rowboat).[13]

The man Roosevelt most wished to win over was McKinley. The president had taken up the Cuban issue, sending a diplomat to negotiate with Spain to grant autonomy to the island, but as usual McKinley's true intentions were hard to read. Roosevelt sought the chance to stiffen the presidential spine. On September 15 he wrote Secretary Long, still on his farm, to say that Washington was in the daze of "the hottest weather we have had" and mentioned that he had been to see the president. Roosevelt neglected to tell the secretary what he had discussed with McKinley during two long carriage rides and a dinner over the course of three days. He did, however, write Cabot Lodge with all the details.

McKinley had told Roosevelt that he wanted to avoid conflict with Spain and Japan, but he wasn't sure it was possible — not exactly fighting words, but Roosevelt seized on them to reassure Lodge that the president would not back off when the time came. Roosevelt declared to the president that if war came he wanted to join the fighting forces. McKinley, masking his own reaction, asked what Mrs. Roosevelt would say. Roosevelt responded that he would not consult Edith, or even his friend Henry Cabot Lodge. McKinley chuckled, but said he'd see what he could do to help if the time came. Roosevelt wasn't entirely fooled by McKinley's cheer or flattery. "Of course the President is a bit of a jollier," Roosevelt wrote Lodge, "but I think his words did represent a substratum of satisfaction."

On the second carriage ride Roosevelt pressed a piece of paper on the chief executive showing the disposition of battleships on a map, and boldly laid out a war plan to put the fleet off Cuba's coast "within 48 hours after war is declared." While the Atlantic Fleet was making short work of Spain in the Caribbean, he went on, "our Asiatic squadron should blockade, and if possible, take Manila."[14] How much of this war-gaming McKinley really absorbed is not clear. To the former Ohio congressman, the Philippines were still indistinct shapes on the far side of the globe. McKinley would later remark to a friend that he "could not have told where those darned islands were within 2,000 miles."[15]

The warm weather couldn't last forever. Before Long returned, however, Roosevelt managed to pull off one last bit of office politics—a skillful and, as it turned out, consequential maneuver to install his own man as commander of the Asiatic Fleet. The senior officer in line, Commodore John Howell, was old and fat, with the sad eyes of a spaniel. He was, Roosevelt fretted, "irresolute." Roosevelt was desperate to install his man, Commodore George Dewey, who had been a first lieutenant under David Farragut in the Civil War. A compact man with a trim white beard, Dewey was a squared-away officer with sharp creases in his trousers and a determined attitude. In the spring and summer of 1897 Dewey had lunched regularly with Roosevelt, Lodge, and Mahan at the Metropolitan Club. Unfortunately, Dewey had been recently relegated by the Navy Department to overseeing lighthouses. Roosevelt arranged a letter of support from one key senator and kept Long from seeing another in opposition, and the deed was done. The man who would become the Hero of Manila Bay was soon heading toward his destiny in the Far East.[16]

Long seems not to have suspected any chicanery. He forgave Roosevelt for a newspaper piece in the New York *Herald* that strongly suggested that the assistant had usurped the secretary's role. But if the *Herald* was an easily cleared hurdle, the same could not be said for William Randolph Hearst's newspaper. While Roosevelt was riding about in the presidential carriage, the *Journal* reported that a battleship, the *Indiana*, had suffered a cracked twelve-inch gun and a buckled hull. Roosevelt angrily denied the *Journal* reports. The steel battleship was still a relatively new creature of the sea in 1897; it was important, Roosevelt believed, that the public not have any doubts about the seaworthiness of the leviathans. Hearst, as he usually did, published Roosevelt's denial and promptly refuted it, citing a "secret" source.[17]

In August 1897, the prospects for war over Cuba seemed to be fading. Spain's conservative prime minister, determined to hang on to "the ever faithful island" at all costs, had been assassinated by an anarchist, and the new, liberal government was promising reforms to cool the rebellion in Cuba.

Hearst was frustrated and restless. James Creelman, the hard-charging newsman he had hired away from Joseph Pulitzer, recalled seeing Hearst sitting, stifled and bored, in the quiet *Journal* newsroom in early August. Most New Yorkers who could afford to had fled from the city's heat and smells to the mountains or seashore. A copyboy handed Hearst a cable from the *Journal*'s correspondent in Havana. Hearst read, languidly at first:

HAVANA.
EVANGELINA CISNEROS, PRETTY GIRL OF SEVENTEEN YEARS, RELATED TO PRESIDENT OF CUBAN REPUBLIC, IS TO BE IMPRISONED FOR TWENTY YEARS ON THE AFRICAN COAST, FOR HAVING TAKEN PART IN UPRISING OF CUBAN POLITICAL PRISONERS ON ISLE OF PINES.

Hearst put down the cable, then picked it up and read it again. He whistled softly, slapped his knee, and laughed. He called for his managing editor, Sam Chamberlain. "Sam!" he cried. "We've got Spain now!" He began issuing orders: telegraph Havana for every detail, get up a petition to the Queen Regent of Spain for the girl's release, organize all of the *Journal*'s two hundred stringers to hire carriages and begin calling on prominent women to get them to sign the petition. The girl must be saved, even if it was necessary to rescue her from prison or seize the steamer carrying her away to the African penal colony. "But that would be piracy, wouldn't it?" Hearst inquired, warming to the idea.

The *Journal* ran Evangelina's dramatic tale on August 17 and 18. A beautiful young woman from the "gentlest of families," she had come to the Isle of Pines, a small island off Cuba where Spain held political prisoners, to beg for her elderly father's release. According to the *Journal*'s lurid account, she had resisted the sexual advances of the leering prison commander and been thrown into prison herself, at a squalid Havana jail for prostitutes and madwomen. The truth, as Hearst knew, was more complicated and prosaic: she had likely been conspiring with several revolutionaries to ambush the prison commander by luring him to her rooms, and she was not languishing in a wretched prison cell. The Spanish commander in chief, General Wyler ("the Butcher" in the Hearst press), wasn't quite sure what to do with her. He considered a convent and in the end put her in relatively clean quarters on the upper story of the Havana jail, where she was decently fed and clothed.[18]

While Evangelina may not have been the "Cuban girl martyr" or the "Cuban Joan of Arc," as the *Journal* dubbed her, she was undeniably young and beautiful, and her plight, however exaggerated, resonated with a large audience. More romantic than cynic,

Hearst understood that the country was being swept by a craze for pulp romances, for tales of chivalric derring-do. The Cuban Revolution was easily rendered as metaphor, cartoons of the era showing a vulnerable young woman—Cuba—about to be ravished by a sinister, mustachioed man—Spain. Would a gallant knight—America—rush to the rescue?

On Sunday, August 22, the *Journal* banner headline read "American Women Unite to Save Miss Cisneros." Hearst had wangled sympathetic open letters to the *Journal* from Clara Barton, Mrs. Mark Hanna, Mrs. Jefferson Davis, and one from Julia Ward Howe beseeching the pope to intervene to win Evangelina's release. "The Whole Country Rising to the Rescue," the front page blared the next day. "More Than Ten Thousand Women in All Parts of the United States Sign the Petition for the Release of Miss Cisneros." (Readers were reminded "Miss Cisneros in Death's Shadow.") By the next day Hearst had even prevailed on President McKinley's aging mother to "lend her voice" to freeing the Cuban girl martyr.[19]

In the *Journal* newsroom, staffers hooted at Hearst's crusade. Characteristically, he had become a true believer in what may have begun as a stunt but quickly became an international cause celebre. Editor Willis Abbott later recorded:

I was at the office during the progress of the comedy and in daily contact with Hearst. He took the whole affair with utmost seriousness....It was the one dominating, all-compelling issue of the moment for him and he brooked no indifference on the part of his employees, most of whom in his absence cursed the whole thing for a false bit of cheap sensationalism. But Hearst felt himself to be in the role of Sir Galahad rescuing a helpless maiden.[20]

NEW YORK JOURNAL
AND ADVERTISER.

If you don't get the JOURNAL *You don't get the* NEWS.

Ent. by W. R. Hearst.—NEW YORK, TUESDAY, AUGUST 17, 1897.—14 PAGES.

PRICE ONE CENT In Greater New York; Elsewhere, and Jersey City. TWO CENTS.

MAY BAR PRINCES FROM THE CHURCH

Rumor that the Pope Will Excommunicate the Two Duellists.

CHURCH FROWNSON CODE

Fever Has Set In, and Prince Henri's Condition Is Far from Satisfactory.

HIS SURGEONS WONT TALK.

Bulletins Indicate That the Defeated Man Is by No Means Out of Danger.

ONLY CHEERS FOR TURIN

The Victor Is Warmly Received by the People of Rome, and Is Congratulated by the Italian King and Queen.

Rome, Aug. 16.—It is reported that the Pope will excommunicate Prince Henri of Orleans and the Count of Turin, as duelling is forbidden by the Roman Catholic Church.

TURIN WARMLY RECEIVED.

Rome Turns Out to Do Him Honor, and King Humbert and the Queen Congratulate Him.

(Copyright, 1897, by W. R. Hearst.)
Rome, Aug. 16.—The Count of Turin this morning received an enthusiastic welcome from the populace on his arrival.

He found anything but the following telegram from the King: "We would gladly be the first to welcome you. Congratulations on your courage and valor."

The Queen telegraphed also.

All the papers counsel the avoidance of polemics on the duel, which may provoke misunderstandings between Italy and France.

The *Journal Italia* publishes a semi-official note declaring that the Duc de Chartres has written to King Humbert, expressing his disapproval of the conduct of Prince Henri.

Alberone Withdrawn.

Paris, Aug. 16.—General Albertone, the Italian officer who had challenged Prince Henri, but who gave way to the Count of Turin, has withdrawn his challenge.

PRINCE HENRI IS WORSE.

Fever Has Set In, and the Doctor's Bulletins Are not Reassuring to the Young Man's Friends.

THE CUBAN GIRL MARTYR.

EVANGELINA BETANCOURT CISNEROS, THE GENTLE NIECE OF THE CUBAN PRESIDENT, WHOSE FATE BY SPANISH DECREE WILL BE TOO AWFUL FOR DESCRIPTION.

PITTSBURG PHIL WON A FORTUNE.

Hit the Brighton Beach Ring to the Extent of $75,000.

ALARUM HIS FIRST CHOICE

Then Backed Four Straight Winners Without Losing a Single Bet.

ECLIPSED PREVIOUS WINS.

Ed Marks Says the "Layers" Cannot Stand Such Tremendous Losses.

SMITH'S WONDERFUL CAREER.

From a Working Lad at a Small Wage He Has Become a Rich Man by Backing His Judgment on the Turf.

PITTSBURG PHIL'S WINNINGS.
Previously won this year..$300,000
Yesterday's winnings.......75,000
                           ————————
Total for 1897............$375,000

George E. Smith, alias "Pittsburg Phil," was credited up to yesterday with having won $300,000 this season from the laying fraternity. Yesterday he went down the line, at the Brighton Beach races to hunt his affections for the insider Alarum, and against him got 10 to 1, straight and 4 to 1, place. Alarum was beaten a nose to a whirlwind finish, but 4 to 1 was "juicy."

After that it was all plain sailing. The mettle plunger saw everything clear before him. Pommersmash opened at 8 to 1 and went to the post at 4 to 1. Tripping, the three-year-old Sly laid "Phil's" brother Bill Smith, trade for Mr. Jobson it opened at 4 to 1, and the lady market showed her at 5 to 1, and of this Fall took advantage. Then came the fast Sly Baby flinge, and against him in the Sea Gift Handicap the price was shorter, 5 to 1 man, who cut out four of his money the opening price, or even 4 to 3, at which figure winny stars closed, to a good price.

The last of the valley of good things with which the chap was measured was John's leaky is generated suit, two years old, by Archipelago at the Highlands, which was purchased not long ago by J. W. Silverton, the man who got hold of the "Kandy-race" incline, because he is said to take his income out of these stable, with them all night. If buyley had been in the race of John Dryden or J. W. Impera not only pure colored bird but he would have been a 2 to 1 shot, for Metical III, who was made favorite, was attempting to give him nine pounds.

A Remarkable Day.
As Stanton owns and trains him leaky...

NEW YORK JOURNAL
AND ADVERTISER.

While Others TALK. The Journal ACTS.

While Others TALK. The Journal ACTS.

NO. 5,446. • Copyright, 1897, by W. R. Hearst.—NEW YORK, THURSDAY, OCTOBER 14, 1897.—16 PAGES.

PRICE ONE CENT In Greater New York; Elsewhere, Jersey City. Two cents.

EVANGELINA CISNEROS REACHES THE LAND OF LIBERTY.

The Beautiful Young Cuban Girl, Rescued by the Journal from Hideous Recojidas, Arrives in New York on the Seneca.

She Slipped Aboard the Vessel Disguised as a Boy and Hid in a Closed Berth Until Far Out at Sea.

Left the Seneca at Quarantine on a Journal Boat and Is Now at the Waldorf Forgetting the Squalor of Her Havana Prison.

EVANGELINA CISNEROS, once well nigh a prisoner among the meanest wretches in the hideous Havana prison, is a guest at the Waldorf Hotel. Surrounded by all the luxury and elegance that fortune can furnish, she is alternately laughing and crying over the events of the past week.

She went, less than a week, ago but the Journal correspondent broke the bars of her cell and led her to liberty over the flat roofs of the Cuban capital. It is the memory of those thrilling few minutes that meant for her a lifetime of captivity or a future of peace and liberty that most often recurs to her now. She arrived yesterday on the Ward line Seneca, and was taken from the steamer by a Journal boat at Quarantine, thanks to the courtesy of the Government and the Quarantine authorities.

When the Seneca sailed from Havana there figured on the passenger list one, Juan Sola. A girl who signed the name Juana Sola to the declaration created by the Customs House people was the nearest passenger to making good the lost one. Her declaration was that she brought along durable things into the country. If ever that declaration was truthfully made, it was made in the case of this brown-eyed, chestnut-haired girl who put so anxious to please the man who made her sign.

The little girl Juana who was the simple red gown she had upon sketches up so simple out of clothes such as a plasterer's those were the clothes that Juan Sola wore. When he was slipping back to Havana with a big hat slouched over the chestnut hair that even danger of discovery could not tempt her sign to conceal it lay tighter between a roll, laughing pair of lips that...clenishly, maybe, blew a cloud of smoke into the face of the Chief of

Police, who was watching this plank, and made the fixtures of the young man very indistinct indeed.

There was no reason the Chief of Police should scan the closely the young man with the big cigar. Juan Sola's passport had been duly issued by the Spanish Government, and, as far as the papers showed, there was no reason to suspect him. Of course, Juan Sola was the girl the Journal correspondent had rescued from Recojidas, and the bone of a whose escape was on every tongue in Havana—the girl for whose capture the police had for three days been breaking into houses and guarding the roads, and yet she passed under their noses, with no disguise but a boy's suit of clothes and a big cigar.

"Ay madre," gasped Evangelina Cisneros yesterday, rolling her big brown eyes, "but that cigar was almost as bad as the prison. They did not come nearer killing me in Recojidas than that cigar did on the steamer. The whole world swam around me. The boat seemed to the toward me. The water was yellow and the sky was black! Ay de mi, how can men smoke them?"

Nothing could be seen of the beautiful little Cuban girl as the Seneca steamed opposite Quarantine to permit the boarding of the Health Officer. The other passengers, after the fashion of ocean travelers, grouped amidships to scan the vessel of the tyrant who had left him this power to lock them all up in Quarantine, and who looked as if he would enjoy doing it. The girl was hidden away in her own stateroom, wondering what manner of reception awaited her in the big city whose sky line broke the horizon ahead. She was entirely alone—Juana Sola in very truth. The people on board were kind to her from the moment she revealed her identity, but at this moment, when she realized that she had reached the haven of refuge, to gain which she and her gallant rescuers had risked death itself, she fled from the new-found friends and would not even look out the door of her stateroom.

The Journal boat accompanied the Health Officer's cutter to the side of the Havana steamer. On board it were a number of the girl's friends, including Mrs. J. Ellen Foster, of the National Relief Association, the dear Journal man, Karl Decker, Mrs. Senator Quaid, Rev. Samuel Silva, Mrs. John M. Thornton, Mrs. J. C. Burrows, and other ladies equally prominent, who all had offered to chaperon the little exile, and who in now her companion at the Waldorf. One cell blind was aboard the Journal

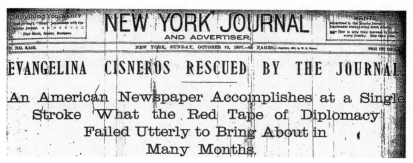

(*New York* Journal)

Just as he had tried to deliver his Tiffany sword, Hearst sought back-channel assistance. Karl Decker was a blond, handsome, six-foot Virginian, the son of a Confederate cavalry colonel and the sort of adventure-seeking young gentleman who seemed to be attracted to Hearst's "journalism that acts." In late September Hearst sent Decker on an improbable mission to rescue Evangelina from her prison cell in Havana. Incredibly, he succeeded. The *Journal* devoted thousands of words to the dashing deed: how Decker and Evangelina slipped messages to each other (the signal to go ahead was for her to wave a white handkerchief; to caution her, he would light a cigar); how Decker rented a room directly across from her cell window; how she drugged her cellmates with opiates in their coffee; how Decker slid a twelve-foot ladder across to her cell and cut the bars with a hacksaw, bending them with brute strength; how the pair escaped into the night.[21]

The story was even true, or mostly true; Decker neglected to inform readers that he had bribed the guards, who arranged the theater of the escape as a way to save face. (According to Abbott, Decker spent years fruitlessly trying to get Hearst to reimburse him for the bribes; possibly Hearst didn't want to know about them.)[22] Two days after her escape, dressed in boy's clothing, chomping on an unlit cigar and with her hair pulled up under a hat, Evangelina boarded the steamer for Key West.

The *Journal* celebrated her arrival in New York on October 13 with a great wallow of self-congratulation. "Evangelina Cisneros Reaches the Land of Liberty!" cried the banner headline. "The Journal's Motto: While Others Talk, the Journal Acts," Hearst inscribed on the editorial page, which bore his name in large letters. The lead editorial asked: "We have freed one Cuban girl— when shall we free Cuba?"[23]

With his love of spectacle, Hearst presented Evangelina — the promised dark-haired Saint Joan — to a wildly cheering throng at a mass open-air rally in Madison Square. The *Journal* ecstatically described the scene:

> Evangelina Cisneros and Karl Decker are standing hand in hand. He is pressing her forward, in silent deprecation of his own claim to that uproarious greeting. The people are crying as if mad. The search light lights up both figures vividly, and the face of each is deathly white.... Fireworks are bursting and hissing in the air, the band is playing the Cuban anthem, every man on the stand has doffed his hat, and the shouting of the crowd continues. The girl stands like a beautifully chiseled statue, motionless, awed. She is a mere child, and her mind cannot grasp all this.[24]

At dinner at Delmonico's, society matrons lined up to meet or at least look at Miss Cisneros, who was wearing a white couturier gown courtesy of W. R. Hearst. The grand impresario barely showed up, however. According to one magazine account, "the man who footed the bills came into the room where [Miss Cisneros] stood among the palms, shyly shook hands with the heroine whom his wonder machine had created, and then excused himself and hastened away in his automobile."[25] Evangelina proceeded to Washington, D.C., where she shook the hand of President McKinley, and then faded into obscurity, marrying a dentist. Done with her, Hearst quickly moved on, searching for new romantic heroes.

Henry Cabot Lodge was every bit as romantic as Hearst, though he hid his sensitivity from all but a few close friends behind a dour and disapproving manner. Lodge disdained the yellow press in general and Hearst in particular, though they were working toward the same expansionist ends. Lodge's dreaminess showed in more subtle ways, in his love of romantic poetry and art, and in his well-concealed desire to cast off the mantle of duty, if only for a time. In Washington, while he ground away in the Senate, he allowed himself to dream of summers on Tuckernuck Island, a shingle of sand south of Cape Cod where he retreated for as long as possible in July and August. Excusing himself from a brief visit with his mother in early August 1892, he explained his flight to Tuckernuck: "I needed the rest badly & here I get constant outdoor air & exercise in & out & on the water—nothing to do & idle books to read."[26]

Lodge observed Episcopal ritual, but he showed little religious faith. Rather, he found spiritualism in nature, in the beauty of the changing seasons that he observed on his long rides with Roosevelt, and especially in the brilliant sea light of his summers off the Massachusetts coast. Such appreciation was echoed in Lodge's son, named George after Lodge's father but known as Bay, who once wrote a poem about Tuckernuck:

... on the naked heap of shining sand
Th'eternity of blue sea pales to spray:

The holy voices of the sea and air
Are sacramental, like a peaceful prayer... [27]

Bay was a charming, sensitive boy who rejected his father's sense of puritan duty and the burden of his name by becoming a poet. (A Harvard professor, giving Bay a D grade, commented, "Mr. Lodge, *you* ought to do better than that.") Lodge had worried about his son. "He...seems to have no interests or ambitions & to love mere stupid idling beyond anything," he wrote Henry Adams in 1893, when Bay was still at Harvard. But he indulged Bay as a kind of alter ego, a benign doppelganger allowed to express the sentimentalism and sense of wonder that Lodge himself held in check. Some thought that Lodge actually indulged his son too much. Edith Wharton, who became a friend of Bay, observed that young Lodge was kept "in a state of brilliant immaturity." [28]

Tuckernuck seems to have been a kind of spiritual retreat for father and son. (Nannie stayed mostly in their summer house on Nahant.) The island was owned by an eccentric friend of Lodge, Sturgis Bigelow, who was a Buddhist and had considered becoming a Shingon priest in Japan. On sunlit Tuckernuck, warmed by the Gulf Stream that meanders off the New England coast, buttoned-up Brahmins could unbutton—literally casting off their inhibitions and their clothes. "Surf, Sir! and sun Sir! and nakedness!" Bay wrote Bigelow before heading for the island one summer. "Oh, Lord! How I want to get my clothes off—alone in natural solitudes!" [29]

Bay's father desperately needed some natural solitude in the summer of 1897. Under the pressure of work, his digestive system had failed again. "I am very tired & need rest," he admitted to his mother in June. [30] Roosevelt worried to a mutual friend that he was "really alarmed" by Lodge's nervous exhaustion.[31] In August, showing unusual sensitivity, he wrote Lodge: "I am very much pleased that you are loafing, and I am sure that you will very soon be yourself again. Any man who throws himself with such intense energy into his work as you do, and who therefore accomplishes so much, must pay the penalty in one way or another, especially if he not only *does* things, but *feels* them."[32]

Lodge was feeling pressure from all sides. He has been portrayed by revisionist historians as a tool of the nascent military-industrial complex, but in fact his correspondence shows that he was constantly fencing with the moneyed interests, many of whom were his social peers and did not hesitate to chide him.[33] Lodge did argue that trade follows the flag, but he scorned businessmen who put profits before the national interest. And they, in turn, attacked him, especially when he sounded too much like his friend Roosevelt, praising war as a cure for national malaise. "I regard war not as a sort of foot-ball, but as a serious thing," Charles Francis Adams (brother of Henry and former president of the Union Pacific Railroad) wrote Lodge, in a typical letter from a businessman during the brief war scare of December 1896. "The only remedy I see for the exciting state of affairs," Adams continued, "is a return of business prosperity; for I have always noticed that when people are employed and prosperous they cease to be Jingoes."[34]

Lodge's most painful exchanges came not with his old Harvard friends or State Street bankers but with Thomas Reed. In late August, as Roosevelt was playing the role of hot-weather navy secretary and Hearst was plotting to save Miss Cisneros, Lodge gently prodded Reed to back more congressional funding for the navy and coastal fortifications. Lodge took the position that a stronger defense was an insurance policy against war.

Reed responded with a clever and telling counterargument. "Over insurance," Reed wrote Lodge, "creates what the insurance men call Moral Hazard"—an invitation to the overinsured man to become reckless because he is certain of a bailout. Reed argued that heavy defense spending invited conflict, since leaders would either become complacent in the arrogance generated by seemingly overwhelming force or reckless in the cocky belief that no opponent could possibly triumph. Either way, devoting such substantial resources to this cause would create a perilous situation. Lodge shot back that Reed was indulging in "casuistry," using logic to defend a false premise. "We are not overinsured," Lodge insisted. "We practically have no insurance at all, or at best very little, and our risks are enormous. I am very sorry that your extreme pro-Spanish prejudices should warp your otherwise just mind."

Did Lodge really think Reed was guilty of "extreme pro-Spanish prejudices"? Perhaps Lodge was teasing—he also jibed at Reed for misspelling "cynical" (Reed had it "cynicle"). But Reed's tone in response was not light, for he understood the high stakes involved. Reed wrote back, apologetic about being "too brash in my way" but warning that an accident could lead to war if tensions rose between Spain and America over Cuba.[35]

Reed, too, had witnessed America's growing naval power, but he regarded great fleets differently from Roosevelt or Lodge. In August he had been in his Portland, Maine, hometown when the Atlantic Fleet "steamed out of Casco Bay and anchored in stately procession." It was "a spectacle, not only of beauty, but of power," wrote Reed. Ever the student of history, however, he also noted that these vessels would before long become obsolete, which would require a new round of costly shipbuilding. "With the increasing wealth and knowledge of mankind will come greater storehouses of power and monsters more death-dealing in capacity, and those will continue to come until war shall be no more." A utopian day when men lay down their arms, Reed knew from his own deep and dark knowledge of human nature, would never come. Though he was not religious, he was gloomy enough to envision a more apocalyptic ending.[36] In the shorter term, his political instincts told him, the war spirit was rising.

12

The Stolen Letter

"I am not at all easy about Edith."

YEARS LATER, after his friend had died, Lodge would regret-fully write in his journal that Reed had "set himself against the evolution of the country & the forces of the time."[1] Lodge was right: the Speaker had been out of step with the nation he wished to lead. Americans, Reed had felt, needed to attend to their affairs at home—an economic boom and bust, a growing gap between rich and poor, human rights violations measured by scores of lynchings—before they sought new worlds to conquer or downtrodden peoples to save and civilize. But though Reed's thinking was rational and logical, it missed the mood of his countrymen. In part because Americans were fearful of enemies within, they went looking for enemies abroad. War and conquest have served to distract nations from their internal contradictions and conflict for as long as nations have existed. American excep-tionalism did not exempt the nation from the laws of human nature. The historian Richard Hofstadter has written of "the psychic crisis of the 1890s." As William James put it more sim-ply in a letter to a friend, "War must come."[2]

Roosevelt, Lodge, and Hearst did not by themselves cause that war, but this was not for lack of trying.

*   *   *

The last months of 1897 brought a lull in the Cuban crisis. After the assassination of Spanish hard-liner Antonio Cánovas del Castillo in August, the new liberal government had wanted to make peace with the rebels in Cuba and to avoid a confrontation with the United States. Wyler was relieved of his Cuban command in October and recalled to Spain, and the Spanish government, under diplomatic pressure from the McKinley administration, began talking about freeing the *reconcentrados* and offering some form of autonomy to the "ever faithful island." In a message to Congress, McKinley called on Americans to give the Spanish reforms a chance to succeed. Hearst's *Journal* predictably scorned the president's statement as "lacking in virility, worse than mild...timid...cringing."[3]

Roosevelt, however, was grudgingly admiring of McKinley. "I am forced to admit that the President has handled this Spanish question so as to avoid the necessity of war and yet to uphold the honor of the country," he wrote a New York lawyer in mid-November. Yet his need for war—some war, maybe any war—remained, so he continued to prod Secretary Long. "The Secretary has been a dear, as he always is; I only wish I could poison his mind to make him a shade more truculent in international matters," Roosevelt wrote Bamie. (Privately, Long was unimpressed by Roosevelt's hard sell. "He bores me with plans of naval and military movement, and the necessity of having some scheme of attack arranged for instant execution in case of an emergency," the secretary confided to his diary.)[4]

Roosevelt was not oblivious to the impression he often made. He knew he could come across as a bully and a blowhard, and it bothered him to be thought of as more talk than action. He wrote John Hay, who was now ambassador to England, "I have a horror of bluster which does not result in a fight; it is both weak and undignified."[5] His solution, predictably, was not to bluster less frequently but rather to seek a real fight, one that he could join, preferably on horseback and leading the charge. His determination was single-minded to the point of obsession. He did not appear crazed or even neurotic; he was, as ever, ebullient and in control of his impulses — but those impulses were very strong. He would raise his sails and tack with the gale.

Tender and sentimental, Roosevelt was a good family man. Still, his obligations to his family and his almost primal need to prove himself in war were bound to clash eventually. An autodidact, he could do several things at once: run the navy; write books (at the time, a volume on American ideals); read books (an average of one a day); exercise maniacally; roughhouse with his children; and be a decent and faithful husband. Edith was sometimes worn out by her Theodore, but she gave him great latitude. Having waited to marry him while his affections strayed elsewhere, she knew how to be patient. In 1894 Roosevelt had wanted to run for mayor of New York, but Edith dissuaded him, partly for financial reasons. Seeing his resulting depression, she had vowed never again to thwart his ambition. She felt "terribly," she had written TR's sister Bamie at the time. "This is a lesson that will last my life."[6]

The Roosevelts were not rich, at least by Gilded Age standards, a sizeable portion of Roosevelt's inheritance having vanished with losses sustained by his cattle ranch in the Dakotas. A worrier about the family finances, Edith—pregnant with her fifth child in the autumn of 1897—did her best to make do. She doled out an allowance to her husband, which he spent without noticing. She even furnished their rented house at 1810 N Street with hand-me-down pieces of "Mesozoic or horsehair furniture," as she put it.[7]

Roosevelt and children at play at Sagamore Hill (Theodore Roosevelt Collection, Houghton Library, Harvard University)

The Roosevelts had just settled into the house when Edith went into premature labor. "Very unexpectedly, Quentin Roosevelt appeared just two hours ago," Roosevelt wrote Bamie that morning of November 19. "Edith is doing well. By the aid of my bicycle I just got to the Doctor & Nurse in time!" But he did not stay for long. After seeing his tiny new infant, he rode his bike back to the office and resumed his correspondence about the coming war. He indulged his fatherly pride and attended to dynastic obligations for just a moment: "I have a new small boy just two hours old, whom I have entered for Groton," he wrote Captain Frederick Goodrich. Then it was back to business: a confidential letter to William Kimball, a retired captain and former head of the Naval War College, written with what he described as "a frankness which our timid friends would call brutal." The reason for going to war with Spain was not just humanitarian or in the "self-interest" of the United States, Roosevelt wrote, but rather for "the benefit done our military forces by trying both the Navy and Army in actual practice"—like a war game or peacetime maneuvers, only conducted with live ammunition under conditions so real that sailors and soldiers would die, though presumably in low numbers. "It would be a great lesson, and we would profit much by it," he wrote, revealing a realpolitik few government officials would commit to paper, then or now. He went on: "I believe that war will have to, or at least ought to, come sooner or later; and I think we should prepare for it well in advance. I should have the Asiatic squadron in shape to move on Manila at once."[8]

Having done his part to replenish the Anglo-Saxon race and prepare for battle, Roosevelt cheerfully joined his family to celebrate Thanksgiving with the Lodges. "Mrs. Theodore is remarkably well & the baby strong & thriving," Lodge wrote his mother on November 28. "Theodore has been in every day & dined with us on Thanksgiving. He is in high spirits & full of energy & enthusiasm, as reviving & sweeping as a breeze from the hills & as affectionate as ever."

Righteous in so many things (though, in the manner of ancient prophets, more than a little cold-blooded), Roosevelt continued his moralizing. He ordered the Brooklyn Navy Yard to substitute cocoa for beer in the canteen, and he gently chastised the Harvard football captain for inspiring his team to remove the *H* from their sweaters after losing to Yale. It was a "hysterical" reaction, Roosevelt wrote a friend, a bit of melodrama smacking of primitive cultures whose dishonored warriors sacrificed themselves after defeat on the battlefield.[9] Such finger-wagging could have made Roosevelt insufferable, but he was such a boyish enthusiast that his earnestness and bombast were bearable, and sometimes unintentionally entertaining.

Among the highlights of the season was Roosevelt's discovery of a "new playmate," as he exulted to Lodge, a Harvard-trained surgeon and former army Apache fighter named Leonard Wood. Tall, muscled, pigeon-toed, yet with the gait of an athlete, Wood "combined, in a very high degree, the qualities of entire manliness with entire uprightness and cleanliness of character," Roosevelt later wrote.[10] Most impressive, Captain Wood had won the Medal of Honor, the award for gallantry that Roosevelt thirsted for the way a camel does water. Wood, who was serving in the White House as McKinley's personal surgeon, "walked me off my legs" on a scramble through nearby Rock Creek Park, Roosevelt approvingly reported to Lodge.[11] In the chill of late autumn the three men got together to form a slightly ridiculous tableau: the assistant secretary of the navy, the junior senator from Massachusetts, and the White House surgeon, kicking a football around an empty lot. "I wish you could see the Senator punting," Roosevelt wrote Lodge's son-in-law Augustus Gardner on December 1.[12]

Roosevelt longed for a greater game. On Christmas Eve, while his family gathered around him, Roosevelt wrote General C. Whitney Tillinghast, commander of the New York National Guard:

> *This is just to wish you a merry Christmas and to tell you that I shall not forget to warn you if I think there is any danger of trouble. As I said before, if there is trouble I shall go down in the New York contingent, whether it is to Cuba, or Canada, or Haiti, or Hawaii; and I shall ask you and every other friend I*

*have to help me arrange matters so that I can go — although I
don't believe there will be any difficulty on that score.*[13]

In early January, Edith became very ill with what her doctors
called some sort of grippe. Roosevelt was supposed to go to New
York, but he canceled his plans in order to stay with his ailing
wife. He was "exceedingly put out," he wrote a friend. "It is the
first time I have ever missed a Boone and Crockett dinner."[14]
This was a rare selfish display of petulance. Roosevelt could
be very attentive to his family. "Big Bear" to his "bunnies," he
loved telling his children ghost stories and engaging in pillow
fights. ("You must always remember," Cecil Spring Rice would
famously say about TR in the White House, "that the President
is about six.")[15] On January 12 the assistant secretary wrote
Captain Goodrich asking him to reschedule an appointment
because "Saturday afternoon and Sunday are the two days that I
devote mainly to the children, and it would break their hearts if
I mix it up with something else."[16] Even so, Edith recalled that
her husband always seemed to be gone when she was pregnant,
and she was usually depressed during her confinement. Her own
father, an alcoholic, had often been absent. Edith wore a cloak
of detachment, but she keenly felt Theodore's frequent absences.
And, of course, war trumped all.[17]

Edith remained bedridden, and her illness worsened. The tim-
ing could not have been more unfavorable. Events were quicken-
ing, and her husband's crowded hour was fast approaching.

In Havana on January 12, rioting broke out. Pro-Spanish loyalists smashed the printing presses in the offices of newspapers
that were backing autonomy from Spain. Spain's offer had not
brought peace to the troubled island. Lines were hardening: the

rebels were emboldened, believing that Spain was on the verge of defeat, while the loyalists bitterly opposed the idea of an autonomous colonial government. The war had more or less ground to a halt; both sides were exhausted. There was a coffin shortage. Máximo Gómez, the rebel commander, proclaimed a "dead war" and predicted that the Spanish forces would soon give up. Although some Spanish commanders showed little fight and retreated to the cities, the rebels lacked the men or arms for a last frontal attack on Spanish strongholds.[18]

The New York *Journal* excitedly—and falsely—reported that mobs were attacking American citizens in Havana. NEXT TO WAR WITH SPAIN, blared Hearst's front page, wildly predicting U.S. armed intervention within forty-eight hours.[19] Only Roosevelt was ready for that. But as a precaution, the U.S. envoy in Havana, Ambassador Fitzhugh Lee (Robert E. Lee's nephew) sent a prearranged signal, "Two dollars," requesting that the American warship USS *Maine* coal up and prepare to sail from Key West to Havana harbor.

On the morning of January 13 Roosevelt walked into the office of Secretary Long and shut the door. That night Long wrote in his diary, "he told me that, in case of war with Spain, he intends to abandon everything and go to the front." In words later excised from his published journal, Long wrote:

The impetuosity and fierceness with which [Roosevelt] insists upon this are rather amusing. He has gone so far daft in the matter that he evidently regards it as a sacred duty which he owes to his own character, to improve every opportunity of dying with malaria, or being played out with a hospital fever in this bushwhacking fight in Cuba. I tried to persuade him that if it was his country which was at stake, or his home should be defended, such a course would be worthwhile. I called him a crank, and ridiculed him to the best of my ability, but all in vain. The funny part of it is, that he actually takes the thing seriously.[20]

Just as Roosevelt seemed about halfway to Cuba, Edith's illness pulled him back. "I am not at all easy about Edith," Roosevelt wrote Bamie on January 17. His wife, he reported, "does not seem to get much better; she has very bad neuralgic pains, and is weak." He uneasily described her as "an invalid"—the word often used to describe his fragile mother, Mittie.[21]

Edith was not the only family member showing signs of infirmity. On January 13 Roosevelt had written a friend with some disappointment that little Teddy, age ten, was probably not up to that Sunday's family scramble through Rock Creek Park. "Ted has dreadful headaches each day," he wrote Bamie on January 17.[22] The blinding headaches worried Roosevelt greatly—he feared his son was showing the same early symptoms displayed by his younger brother Elliott, a broken wastrel and alcoholic who had died at the age of thirty-four.[23]

Roosevelt's little boy was not the only one who struggled to keep up in the rough-and-tumble scrambles in Rock Creek that turned competitive when Captain Wood showed up to test the Roosevelts with his Indian tracker's stamina. Alice, TR's child by his first wife, remembers the hikes and other family outings as a little too rugged. "Oh, those perfectly awful endurance tests masquerading as games!" she recalled.[24]

Roosevelt was very affectionate with his oldest son but determined to make him into a little soldier. He described him as "manly" when he was a toddler and delighted that he carried a tin sword everywhere.[25] He read him the *Nibelungenlied* to awaken his Norse spirit and gave him his first real gun at age nine and a pony named General Grant.[26] (Father and son could not wait until daylight to try out the new rifle. Adjuring little Theodore not to tell his mother, big Theodore fired the gun into the ceiling of his bathroom.) Teddy would recall that as they walked in the streets of Washington, his father would stop to diagram famous battles in the dust.[27] The lessons took. "I'll be a soldier!" the nine-year-old exclaimed to his father the day Roosevelt finished writing *Hero Tales*. Like his father, little Teddy was raised to be a Christian soldier. "Can God fight?" he asked him when he was five years old.[28] Roosevelt *père* had no doubt concerning the answer.

Ted was determined to live up to his father, an impossible task. Looking into the mirror, TR bemusedly recalled, little Teddy would howl, "Ted got no mufstache, Ted got nothin' but a mouf." Then he would put on his father's big shoes and clump around the house.[29] A game little boy, he wore thick glasses and was "clumsy," according to Roosevelt. He followed his father like a little pet and napped on the hide of a grizzly Teddy Senior had shot.[30]

Roosevelt's letters in late January alternate between agitating for war and fretting over his family's health. On January 20 Edith seemed better, but "the wretched Ted continues just the same." On January 25: "Edith is a *little* better; Ted no better." January 31: "Edith had a relapse while I was gone.... Ted is a little worse, and I am going to have a consultation about him." Roosevelt began dreaming once more of riding away on that swift horse that leaves grief behind. "I long at times for the great rolling prairies of sun-dried yellow grass," he wistfully wrote a hunting friend in mid-February.[31] Little Teddy must have sensed, as children do, that his father wished to be off again, away from the sickroom.

If he had stopped to reflect, Roosevelt might have perceived the real reason for his little boy's psychosomatic headaches. In the way that family cycles repeat themselves, the son's suffering was heir to the father's. Roosevelt's own asthma attacks had begun when *his* father was long absent, working off his guilt over buying a substitute to fight in the Civil War. But in the winter of 1898 Roosevelt's heart and mind lay elsewhere, and his family knew it. As Edith continued to complain of acute neuralgia—nervous pain—and Teddy of crushing headaches, Roosevelt wrote Hermann Speck von Sternberg, the German military attaché in Washington: "Between ourselves I have been hoping and working ardently to bring about our interference in Cuba," he confided. "If we could get the seven Spanish ironclads together against our seven seagoing ironclads on this coast we would have a very pretty fight; and I think more could be learned from it.... I am glad Mahan is having such influence with your people, but I wish he had more influence with his own. It is very difficult to make this nation wake up."[32]

But the nation, including President McKinley, was beginning to stir. The president's interest was pricked by rumors that Spain might make a secret deal with Germany, which was bristling with imperialist ambition. America's ambassador to Haiti reported that four German warships had entered the Caribbean. Was the kaiser maneuvering to snatch Cuba like a piece of falling fruit? On January 24 the president—with one eye on the German naval presence—finally gave the order to dispatch the *Maine*, the armored cruiser that was standing by in Key West, to Havana: just a friendly visit, Spain was assured.[33] At the same time, Protestant preachers full of civilizing moral uplift for heathens and Catholics flooded the White House with letters urging McKinley to rescue Cuba. "You have no idea," McKinley's brother Abner wrote a friend on January 25, "of the pressure on William from religious groups." In San Francisco, Mark Hanna was denounced by a Baptist church for holding back the president.[34] On Capitol Hill, congressmen were speechifying again about intervention to help the Cuban rebels. On January 31, Henry Cabot Lodge wrote a friend, with more prescience than he could have possibly realized, "There may be an explosion any day in Cuba which would settle a great many things."[35]

At the Spanish embassy in Washington, the ambassador could also sniff something burning. He cabled Madrid: "The change in sentiment has been so abrupt, and our enemies, influenced by it, so numerous, that any sensational occurrence might produce a change and disturb the situation." The ambassador— Dom Enrique Dupuy de Lôme, minister plenipotentiary and envoy extraordinaire of His Catholic Majesty—was a reactionary. He disliked the liberal government's softening on Cuba. On January 26, the day after the *Maine* moored in Havana harbor, Dupuy de Lôme, glittering in his gold braid and finery, attended a diplomatic reception at the White House. The Executive Mansion was dowdy and rundown, the carpets worn threadbare by the crowds allowed to wander through every day before 2:00 p.m., and the floor beams shook (army engineers worried about a cave-in).[36] The air was redolent with the flowers supplied by a massive greenhouse where today the West Wing stands. After dinner McKinley paid special attention to Spain's rather haughty envoy, inviting him to sit at his table for brandy and cigars. "I see that we have only good news," said McKinley, ever the jollier. (The rioting had at last quieted in Havana.) Dupuy de Lôme's answer is unrecorded, but if he smiled, his expression was insincere. He felt contempt for the American president. In December he had written a friend, the editor of a Madrid newspaper who was visiting Havana, remarking that McKinley was "weak and catering to the rabble, and, besides, a low politician." The president, he wrote, was trying to have it both ways, seeking to appease the peace faction while posturing for the jingoes. The letter suggested that Spain's own step toward conciliation over Cuba was cynical, a sham. Certainly Dupuy de Lôme did not believe that Cuba should be granted independence.[37]

In Havana, a secret agent of the revolutionary junta sneaked into the editor's hotel room and stole Dupuy de Lôme's letter. The purloined document, with its official crest and flowing handwriting, was smuggled north to the Peanut Club in lower Manhattan, where Horatio Rubens, the junta's lawyer, recognized its propaganda value and leaked it to the group's closest friend in the American press, William Randolph Hearst.[38]

Hearst was thrilled. He was not simply interested in selling newspapers; by now he was personally caught up in a rescue fantasy that would deliver Cuba from the cruel embrace of decadent Spain. Like Roosevelt, he feared that protracted negotiations and half measures would preempt a quick, decisive war. He had been fretting over the concessions by the liberal government in Spain, worried that compromise would avert the final confrontation. Cuba, he believed, was starving while the politicians fiddled. "Cuba Turned into a Great Charnel House...No Food in Sight...Women and Children the Principal Victims...Horrors of Camps...Everyone is a Beggar" headlined one eyewitness account in the January 12 *Journal*. It was a vivid tale, and it was true. Hearst also correctly read the public mood. On January 19 he reported that the House of Representatives — the "People's House" — was chafing against the Speaker's control. "Free Cuba Shakes Sway of Reed; House in Uproar Against the Czar" blared the *Journal*. These headlines were true, too. A cartoonist showed

Reed mocked by the Journal *(New York* Journal*)*

an obese Reed sitting on a large, smoldering box labeled "The House," above the words "Things Are Getting Hot for Speaker Reed."[39] The Spanish press did not help Reed's cause when it praised him as Spain's friend. "He is a Yankee," the *Heraldo* of Madrid editorialized, "who deserves not to be one."[40]

In pursuit of headlines and heroics, Hearst was spending a fortune. The *Journal*'s proprietor kept seven full-time correspondents in Havana, plus a small fleet of boats carrying messages and contraband back and forth. His crusade had become international news, especially since the Evangelina Cisneros rescue. In early February British newspapers reported that Karl Decker, Evangelina's deliverer, was headed back to Cuba aboard the newest Hearst yacht, the *Buccaneer*. When Spanish authorities boarded the vessel in Havana, they found not Decker but another correspondent, Julian Hawthorne, son of Nathaniel and author of best-selling romances—the chivalric tales Hearst loved and used as templates for his journalism. The Spanish police also discovered seven small artillery pieces Hearst was trying to smuggle into Cuba. Professing to be outraged by the Spanish seizure, Hearst declared it "the Spanish-*Journal* War," but he was no doubt secretly delighted.

Hearst greeted the arrival of the *Maine* on January 25 with the headline "Our Flag at Havana at Last" and an editorial urging that all Cuban ports be immediately occupied by the U.S. Navy. The scoop of the stolen Dupuy de Lôme letter was cause for still greater exultation. "Worst Insult to the United States in its History" was the banner headline in the February 9 *Journal*, which splashed a facsimile of the letter, with the ambassador's distinctive handwriting, over its entire front page. The *Journal* immediately launched a "Go Home de Lome" campaign. Other newspapers picked up the cry, emphasizing that the ambassador had challenged McKinley's manhood, a fighting insult in an age so sensitive to masculinity.[41] Realizing that he had outlived his usefulness, Dupuy de Lôme cabled his resignation to Madrid.[42]

Roosevelt disdained Hearst, but he was heartened by the leaked letter. On the night of February 9, as Washington was buzzing over the *Journal*'s scoop, a Frenchwoman named Henriette Adler was the inadvertent victim of Roosevelt's passion on the subject. At a diplomatic reception at the White House, she recalled, she was listening with some amusement to newly minted jingoes mispronouncing the words "Cuba Libre." Suddenly she was backed into the wall by a "burly gentleman" engaged in animated conversation with another gentleman. Theodore Roosevelt was hotly arguing with Mark Hanna, McKinley's adviser and financier, now a senator from Ohio. Roosevelt was getting worked up about McKinley's tentativeness over Cuba when his flailing elbow caught a rose sewn on the shoulder of Miss Adler's dress, ripping the decoration off. *"Mon dieu!"* exclaimed Miss Adler. Speaking rapid French, Roosevelt profusely apologized. Notwithstanding her shock, Miss Adler was charmed by this man with "flashing teeth and sparkling eye glasses," she recalled. Fortunately, Nannie Lodge was standing nearby. Mrs. Lodge provided a pin, and a pair of senators, backs turned, formed a screen while the two ladies repaired the garment. The conversation then resumed, hot as ever. "I hope to see the Spanish flag and the English flag gone from the map of North America before I'm sixty!" insisted Roosevelt. Hanna, his chin sunk in his white tie, stared back. "You're crazy, Roosevelt," he said.

Later that evening Hanna accompanied Miss Adler to supper. He was still stewing over Roosevelt. Puffing on his cigar, he grunted that, thank God, they hadn't put Roosevelt in the State Department. "We'd be fighting half the world," he said, brooding over his champagne. He wasn't happy about sending the *Maine* to Havana, either. It was, he said, "waving a match in an oil well for fun."[43]

In Havana harbor on the night of February 15, 1898, the USS *Maine* swung at her mooring in the flood tide. She was a "second class battleship": an armored cruiser originally designed for sail but now steam powered for Captain Mahan's new age of steel fleets clashing at sea. All was *tranquilo* in the harbor, where commercial steamers and a couple of warships rode side by side in the still, fetid water off the Old City. Finishing a letter to his wife, the *Maine's* commander, Captain Charles Sigsbee, paused to listen to the lilting sound of taps trumpeted by a bugler who, Sigsbee thought, had added a few flourishes to his nightly rendition. Returning to business, he picked up his pen to write a letter to Assistant Secretary of the Navy Roosevelt, recommending against equipping battleships with torpedoes. (Roosevelt, he knew, welcomed the torpedo as a lethal new weapon.) The night was unusually hot for February; heavy clouds hung in the black sky. Sigsbee had changed his dress blue wool jacket for a lighter garment, and he was trying to unwind from his day—a trip to a bullfight, lunch for Clara Barton of the Red Cross in his wardroom, a cursory inspection of a nearby Spanish warship (he had noticed her brightly varnished, highly flammable woodwork; it would be aflame, he thought, in the first ten minutes of a close action). Onshore a few hundred yards away were the distant sounds of revelry. Although it was Carnival, the men of the *Maine* had been denied shore leave and were cooped up in their stifling quarters below, save for a few officers smoking cigars on deck.

Sigsbee heard a sound "like a rifle shot." Then came, he later recalled, a "bursting, rending and crashing roar." His cabin was plunged into darkness. Stumbling onto the poop deck, he collided with a breathless marine who dutifully reported what was obvious: there had been an explosion and the ship was sinking. The marine private, observing military etiquette as the deck canted beneath them, gave the time—9:40 p.m. They could hear a strange whistling moan—the sound of air escaping from compartments belowdecks, where hundreds of men remained trapped as the water rose.

Sigsbee leaned out over the rail, straining to see while his eyes acclimated to the dark. Eventually he could make out white

The USS Maine *blows up.*

objects bobbing in the water: the bodies of a few dead or wounded American sailors thrown from the ship in the blast or flushed out where the hull had cracked open. Sailors from the nearby *Alfonso XII,* the Spanish warship Sigsbee had earlier observed, rowed alongside, risking their lives to pick up survivors as ammunition cooked off all along the sloping deck and twisted superstructure of the shattered *Maine.* "Captain, we had better leave her," urged an officer, who was preparing to abandon ship. Sigsbee stepped into a small boat and looked back, only half comprehending, at the sinking tomb that held the bodies of more than 250 of the *Maine*'s 355 sailors and officers.[44]

Sigsbee was taken to a nearby steamer, the *City of Washington.* In the captain's stateroom he wrote out a message to be wired to Washington:

MAINE BLOWN UP IN HAVANA HARBOR AT NINE FORTY
TO-NIGHT AND DESTROYED. MANY WOUNDED AND

DOUBTLESS MORE KILLED OR DROWNED. . . . PUBLIC
OPINION SHOULD BE SUSPENDED UNTIL FURTHER
REPORT.

For once Hearst had not gone to his office after the theater.
He arrived at his apartment in the early-morning hours of February 16—"quite late," he recalled—to find his butler waiting with the message that his office had called. As Hearst later told the story, he called in and learned that the *Maine* had been blown up in Havana harbor. "Good heavens!" Hearst exclaimed. "What have you done with the story?" An editor replied that the story had gone onto page one. Hearst asked, "Have you put anything else on the front page?" "Only the other big news," was the reply. "There is not any other big news," Hearst afterward claimed he shot back. "Please spread the story all over the page. This means war."[45]

13

Remember the *Maine*

"He has gone at things like a bull in a china shop."

OR ONCE HEARST had been scooped on Cuba. He wasn't alone: only one paper—Joseph Pulitzer's New York *World*—had run an eyewitness account of the sinking of the *Maine* in its paper on the morning of February 16. Nearly as frustrating, Hearst's wee-hour instruction to blow out page one and print nothing but the *Maine* story had come too late to catch that morning's edition of the *Journal*.

Hearst was galled to be beaten by his archrival, but the next morning more than made up for his laggardly start. "Destruction of the Warship Maine Was the Work of an Enemy," ran the top headline stripped across page one. Beneath was a drawing, wholly imagined, of the *Maine* anchored over a sinister oblong—a giant "submarine mine, or fixed torpedo"—wired to a Spanish fortress onshore. A later edition screamed "The Warship Maine Was Split in Two by an Enemy's Secret Infernal Machine." The next seven pages of the newspaper, an agglomeration of rumor and wild prediction, dealt entirely with the wreck of the warship and the inevitable consequence, as Hearst saw it. The next day "The Whole Country Thrills with War Fever" claimed the *Journal*'s banner.[1]

(New York Journal)

This, too, was an exaggeration. Some papers vied with Hearst to bang the drums, but others denounced press sensationalism. Religious groups toned down their earlier cries for intervention and sided with businessmen calling for a wait-and-see approach.[2] Some argued logically that it made no sense for Spain to destroy an American warship; such a provocation would be madness for a country that had nothing to gain from American intervention. Whether some renegades or rebel provocateurs managed to plant a mine beneath the ship was another question, but the most knowledgeable experts were doubtful. The day after the *Maine* blew up, the navy's leading authority on explosive ordnance, Philip Alger, a professor at the U.S. Naval Academy, told the Washington *Star*, "No torpedo such as is known in modern warfare can of itself cause an explosion as powerful as that which destroyed the *Maine*. We know of no instances where the explosion of a torpedo or mine under a ship's bottom has exploded the magazine within."

A far more likely cause, Alger pointed out, was an accident. There had been a dozen reports of spontaneous coal fires in the bunkers of warships. The coal bunker on the *Maine* was right next to the gunpowder magazine (intentionally placed there, on the theory that the coal-filled bunker would provide another layer of protection from an incoming projectile). The bituminous coal used by the *Maine* was known to be particularly combustible. It was entirely possible, Alger suggested, that a coal fire had started up and burned hot enough to detonate the magazine:

Magazine explosions...produce effects exactly similar to those effects of the explosion on board the *Maine*. When it comes to seeking the cause of the explosion of the *Maine*'s magazine, we should naturally look not for the improbable or unusual causes, but those against which we have had to guard in the past. The most common of these is through fires in the bunkers. Many of the ships have been in danger various times from this cause and not long ago a fire in the *Cincinnati*'s bunkers actually set fire to fittings, wooden boxes, etc., within the magazine and had it not been discovered at the time it was, it would doubtless have resulted in a catastrophe on board that ship similar to the one on the *Maine*.[3]

Hearst ignored such cautions. MAINE IS A GREAT THING. AROUSE EVERYBODY. STIR UP MADRID, he wired his correspondent in London, James Creelman.[4] Despite the *World*'s scoop, the *Journal*'s circulation passed the one million mark on the day after the *Maine* went down in Havana. Here was a chance to drive it higher still. Although the *Maine*'s victims (those whose bodies could be recovered) were solemnly and respectfully buried in Havana, the *Journal* headlined on February 21, "Havana Populace Insults the Memory of the Maine Victims," and repeated on February 23, "The Maine Was Destroyed by Treachery."[5] Promoting "the journalism that acts," Hearst offered a $50,000 reward "for the detection of the perpetrator of the Maine outrage" and found three senators and two congressmen willing to go to Havana as "*Journal* commissioners" aboard a Hearst yacht, the *Anita*.[6] Hearst tried to hire some divers to inspect the wreck of the *Maine*, but they were turned away by Spanish authorities. The *Journal* instead printed a rumor: "War! Sure! Maine Destroyed by Spanish...This Proved Absolutely by Discovery of the Torpedo Hole!"[7]

In Washington an uneasy quiet prevailed. Silent crowds stood outside the White House and gathered in the lobby of the secretary of the navy's office, where a scale model of the *Maine* was displayed, the tiny naval ensign on the fantail lowered to half mast. President McKinley told Senator Charles Fairbanks of Indiana, "I don't propose to be swept off my feet by the catastrophe."[8] Secretary Long, who had been awakened at 1:00 a.m. on the morning of February 16 by a messenger bearing news of the *Maine*, complained in his journal of losing a night's sleep, tentatively concluding: "My own judgment is, so far any information has been received, that it was the result of an accident."[9]

Roosevelt took the contrary view. "Assistant Secretary Roosevelt Convinced the Explosion of the Warship Maine Was Not an Accident" read the headline just below the banner in the February 17 *Journal*. There was no elaboration in the article, and

Roosevelt, who almost automatically disavowed any statement attributed to him by a Hearst publication, disavowed this one, too.[10] But Roosevelt was not shy about his opinion with naval officials that day, and they may have leaked his views to reporters hanging about the Navy Department. In his private correspondence he was no less certain than Hearst. On February 16 he wrote Benjamin Harrison Diblee, a Porcellian brother:

> *Being a Jingo, as I am writing confidentially from one Porc man to another, I will say, to relieve my feelings, that I would give anything if President McKinley would order the fleet to Havana tomorrow. This Cuban business ought to stop. The* Maine *was sunk by an act of dirty treachery on the part of the Spaniards* I *believe; though we shall never find out definitely, and officially it will go down as an accident.*[11]

Roosevelt was very anxious that the sinking of the American warship *not* go down as an accident. He had good reason to believe that in fact the *Maine* had been destroyed because of a design flaw—and a powerful motive to cover up any such finding, not just because he wanted war with Spain, but because he feared a backlash against the navy's backbone, the modern battleship.

By interesting coincidence, he had before him on his desk that morning a letter from Lieutenant Commander Richard Wainright, executive officer aboard the *Maine*. The letter suggested that the secretary of the navy appoint a board of officers to look at the precautionary measures taken by the navies of other nations—England, France, Germany, and Italy—to insulate their powder magazines from incendiary heat, including the heat produced by a fire in a coal bunker. Roosevelt was well aware of the pattern of coal fires in other warships and was familiar with the design of the *Maine*, in which the bunkers were separated from the magazine by nothing more than a steel bulkhead that would grow white-hot when heated by a coal fire.[12]

Roosevelt had been forewarned. Some senators were fretting that the modern battleship, full of machines and high explosives, was inherently vulnerable to disaster—a floating "volcano," according to Senator Eugene Hale, chairman of the Naval Affairs Committee. Secretary Long had picked up on these apprehensions, and he fretted about the volatility of battleships in his private diary ("our great battleships are experiments which have never yet been tried") and in conversation with Roosevelt.[13] At the time, Roosevelt handwrote Long a gentle response suggesting that some accidents were inevitable in modern ships but no reason to stop building them. He also shrugged off the misgivings of several congressional lawmakers, including his old friend Tom Reed. "I was informed that both Speaker Reed and Senator Hale had stated that we must cease building any more battleships, in view of the disaster to the *Maine*," Roosevelt wrote Long on February 19. "I cannot believe that the statement is true, for of course such an attitude, if supported by the people, would mean that we have reached the last pitch of national cowardice and baseness."[14]

Spain had proposed a joint investigation of the sinking, but Roosevelt successfully urged Long to rebuff the proposal. Instead the navy appointed its own board of three officers to formally investigate the explosion. In the Senate there was some debate over calling for a congressional investigation. When William Mason of Illinois suggested that the navy—and Theodore Roosevelt in particular—could not be trusted to seek the whole truth, a thin, dapper figure quickly arose from his desk on the

Senate floor to defend the integrity of the assistant secretary: "I think those who know Theodore Roosevelt would be slow to believe he would seek to conceal the truth in regard to this disaster," declared Senator Lodge.[15]

No evidence has ever emerged that Roosevelt improperly tried to influence the formal naval inquiry into the sinking of the *Maine*. But he did seek to silence Professor Alger, who had laid out the case for a coal-bunker fire in the Washington *Star* the day after the explosion. Roosevelt wrote Captain Charles O'Neil, chief of the Bureau of Ordnance, asking, "Don't you think it inadvisable for Prof. Alger to express opinions in this way?" He added, a bit disingenuously, "The fact that Mr. Alger happens to take the Spanish side, and to imply that the explosion was probably due to some fault of the Navy...has, of course, nothing to do with the matter."[16] It is significant that when the court of inquiry met in closed session during the last week of February and the first two weeks of March, the judges never called on Professor Alger—or, for that matter, any other outside technical expert on ordnance or explosives.[17]

At the house on N Street in the chill of late February, the doctors came and went. They passed an anxious Roosevelt, spinning between marital obligation and martial ambition. Cabot Lodge worried about his friend and offered to take in two of his healthier younger children, Ethel and Archie, to ease the burden on Edith. Roosevelt's eldest child, Alice—feeling neglected and protesting that she did not love her stepmother—was sent to her Aunt Bamie's in New York.[18]

Medicine was still quite primitive in the 1890s, and psychological understanding even more so. Edith reported to her sister Emily that three different doctors put little Ted through "every test" but "they cannot seem to put a name to his trouble."[19] Lodge noted the anxiety in the Roosevelt household and on February 6 remarked to his mother that "the protracted worry is beginning to tell on Theodore."[20] On February 12 Lodge wrote her again, in some perplexity:

> *The doctors say there is no internal trouble with Edith which was feared & yet she does not seem to mend or only slightly. Then poor little Ted seems to have broken down nervously, suffers from continual pain in the head & is a source of great anxiety. We have succeeded in getting the two younger children over here at last & that is a great gain & quiets the house for the invalids, but I confess I should like to see signs of more definite improvement in both cases.*[21]

In the days after the sinking of the *Maine,* Edith took a serious turn for the worse. "Edith had more fever yesterday, and though she went down again last night she seems so weak that I have concluded to get Dr. Osler, the great Baltimore expert, in for a consultation," Roosevelt wrote Bamie on February 25. "I have not felt the loss of the Maine nearly as much as I would if I had not had so much to worry over in my own home."[22] But the consultation of Sir William Osler, a Canadian physician then based at Johns Hopkins, was "anything but reassuring," Lodge reported to his mother the next day. "They fear trouble arising from the confinement which may necessitate an operation. Poor Theodore is in great distress of mind & we are all very anxious & depressed as you may suppose."[23]

The anxiety in the Roosevelt house was matched, if not exceeded, in the homes of other important men around the city as the government was forced to face the prospect of war with

Spain. "My sleep utterly broken and much nervous trouble," Secretary Long recorded in his diary on February 21. He believed that President McKinley was no better off, writing, "Am sorry to find him more oppressed and care-worn than at any time I have been in the Cabinet. Am afraid he is in danger of over-doing."

In an age of experimentation and medical quackery, Long stumbled on a new-technology solution for his aches and pains: an electric massage machine that jiggled the patient's stomach and legs.[24] While Long was jiggling, Roosevelt used the secretary's absence to move the United States Navy to a war footing.

Far from distracting Roosevelt from his naval duties, the family crisis seems to have energized him, just as Long's absence liberated him. Writing and signing documents and telegrams, he spent the twenty-fifth of February moving ammunition to ships, authorizing the unlimited enlistment of seamen, and ordering guns from the Navy Yard to be shipped out for sea action. He wrote yet one more letter to General Tillinghast of the New York National Guard to say that if war came, "pray remember, that in some shape I want to go." Then he telegraphed halfway around the world a message that represented America's first real step toward war:

DEWEY, HONG KONG:
ORDER THE SQUADRON, EXCEPT THE MONOCRACY [an ancient paddle-wheel steamer], TO HONG KONG. KEEP FULL OF COAL. IN THE EVENT OF A DECLARATION OF WAR WITH SPAIN, YOUR DUTY WILL BE TO SEE THAT THE SPANISH SQUADRON DOES NOT LEAVE THE ASIATIC COAST, AND THEN OFFENSIVE OPERATIONS IN THE PHILIPPINE ISLANDS. KEEP *OLYMPIA*

[a cruiser and Dewey's flagship, due for overhaul]
UNTIL FURTHER ORDERS.

ROOSEVELT

Long's mechanical massage and leisurely afternoon off seem to have been a tonic. "I had a splendid night last night," he wrote in his diary on Saturday, February 26. But his mood soured when he reached his office that morning to discover the paper trail left by Roosevelt. "He has gone at things like a bull in a china shop," Long peevishly recorded in his diary. "[T]he very devil seemed to possess him yesterday afternoon." Then, in words he later excised from the published version of his journal, he wrote: "His wife is very ill, his little boy is just recovering from a long and dangerous illness, so that his natural nervousness is so much accentuated that I really think he is hardly fit to be entrusted with the responsibility of the department at this critical time."[25]

In truth, Long overreacted to Roosevelt's order to Dewey. The assistant secretary had not been behaving like a bull in a china shop, but rather putting into effect war plans long conceived and agreed to, at least in principle, by Long himself—that if war with Spain seemed imminent, the Pacific squadron would prepare to seek out and destroy the Spanish fleet at Manila. It is significant that Long did not reverse Roosevelt's action. Nonetheless Long, a sensitive and decent man, correctly surmised that Roosevelt was showing nervous strain from his family crisis. Edith's temperature had not dropped below 101 degrees for a month. It was a "plain case of exhaustion," guessed Henry Adams's friend Lizzie Cameron, but in fact the situation was more serious.[26] Edith's pelvis was swelling. Dr. Osler, an expert in abdominal surgery, thought she was suffering from an abscess and told Roosevelt that his wife was "critically ill" and needed an operation right away. But Roosevelt held off. He wrote Bamie that two other doctors, a family doctor named Magruder and Roosevelt's friend and "playmate" Leonard Wood, "very wisely, are going to see whether an operation can not be avoided." Roosevelt warned Bamie, "Don't in any letter speak of the possible 'operation'; I don't think it will be necessary to have one, and to talk of it would merely make Edith nervous."[27] The nervous one was Roosevelt: the odors of the sickroom held a particular repulsion for him; they summoned memories of the loss of his first wife and mother in one wrenching night and day.

Edith's condition continued to worsen, until she was too weak even to listen to Roosevelt read to her. Now truly alarmed, he summoned a gynecologist, who "demanded immediate action." As the surgeon was summoned, Roosevelt recounted to Bamie, "I held her hand until the ghastly preparations were made."

The operation was a success. "She behaved heroically; quiet, even laughing," Roosevelt wrote Bamie.[28] Roosevelt's friends were later critical of him for initially choosing the advice of Wood and Magruder over the world-famous Osler. "Such cattle for doctors I have never known," Lizzie Cameron wrote Adams. "Theodore surrounded her with a lot of perfectly incompetent doctors, taxidermists and veterinarians, good sportsmen and excellent athletes, but medically null," wrote Winty Chanler to his wife, Margaret. Still, Edith was "now out of the woods and mending rapidly."[29]

Edith's operation occurred on the night of March 7. By March 9 Roosevelt was beseeching General Tillinghast again, "in a great quandary," because he was afraid that if he went into the service he'd end up "guarding a fort and no enemy within a thousand miles of it." Perhaps he could raise his own regiment: "I have a man who rendered most gallant service with the regular Army against the Apaches" — Wood — "whom I would very much like to bring in with me." Roosevelt was worried that Spain would dispatch a fleet of torpedo boats to attack the navy. "We should fight this minute in my opinion, before the torpedo boats get over here," he wrote Mahan on March 14. "But we won't . . . very possibly we won't fight until the beginning of the rainy season [June], when to send an expeditionary force to Cuba means to see the men die like sheep [from disease]." To William Astor Chanler (Winty's brother), Roosevelt despaired on March 15, "I shall chafe my heart out if I am kept here instead of being in the front, and I don't know how to get to the front."[30] He wailed to Bamie on March 16: "McKinley is bent on peace, I fear."

Roosevelt's screeds did not make him welcome at the White House; he lamented that he had become persona non grata, which only added to his stress. "I hope never to see another such winter," he wrote Brooks Adams. "We have had to send all the children away from the house." Edith, he reported, was "crawling back to life," but slowly.[31] Five different doctors were unable to find anything physically wrong with little Teddy, so it was decided to send him to New York, to stay with Bamie and be treated by Dr. Alexander Lambert, a "neuro. specialist," Edith reported to her sister Emily. Edith appears to have had an inkling of what was troubling Teddy — "nervous prostration" — but his father, while tender with the boy, was oblivious to his own role in causing little Ted's psychological disturbance: the whipsawing from paternal absence to intense paternal pressure, relentlessly masculine, just like his own father. There was no obvious solution. Edith could see that the man of the house really wanted to be off proving his manhood on a distant shore. She confided to Emily, "We have all been on such a strain since the 'Maine' disaster. It has told on Theodore's health and he has

The Court of Inquiry (Library of Congress)

been troubled with insomnia."[32] This was a home, it seemed, where a (literally) healthy balance was impossible.

Roosevelt clung to his faith that the board investigating the sinking of the *Maine* would find that the cause was "outside work," not an accident. A subconscious slip in a letter on March 6 to his brother-in-law Doug Robinson suggests he suspected the real cause. Thinking perhaps of those coal bunkers side by side with the *Maine*'s powder magazine, he concluded that "with so much loose powder round, a coal may hop into it at any moment."[33] Still, Roosevelt was not overly alarmed, having receiving confidential reports that the court of inquiry was headed for a more agreeable conclusion. Seizing on a shred of evidence—that the keel had bent upward in an inverted V— the board concluded that the explosion had been initially caused by an underwater mine. (More than seventy-five years later, a formal U.S. Navy investigation under Admiral Hyman Rickover determined that the far more likely cause was a coal fire followed by an internal explosion—exactly the assessment of Professor Alger, suppressed by Roosevelt, and the finding of a separate inquiry conducted by the Spanish at the time, in March 1898.)[34] Captain Sigsbee was exonerated. (The navy's true judgment may be detected in his next assignment, the command of an old converted freighter.) Meanwhile, one member of the court, Captain F. E. Chadwick, quietly made sure to insert extra steel bulkheads between the coal bunkers and the powder magazine aboard his own battleship, the *New York*.[35]

McKinley wanted to hold back the report, even though it merely exonerated the navy without assigning the responsibility to Spain or anyone else. He sensed that the tiniest of sparks could set off a terrible blaze. "We are not prepared for war," he cautioned his advisers.[36] But inevitably the report leaked to the press. Hearst's *Journal* was dissatisfied with its indefinite conclusion on the question of culpability. "The suppressed testimony shows Spain is guilty of blowing up the *Maine*," huffed an editorial.[37]

Roosevelt said as much to any reporter within range. Ordering the navy's peacetime white ships to be painted battle gray on March 24—the very day the report was delivered to the president—Roosevelt was already in full war mode. His machinations were aided by new technology: a long-distance telephone was installed in his office, and the instrument, reported the *New York Times*, was "in almost constant use."[38] On Saturday night, March 26, Roosevelt hobnobbed with reporters at the Gridiron Dinner, an occasion for skits, songs, and general hilarity between Washington correspondents and the politicians they covered. At the club's sixteen-course midwinter banquet, reporters had staged a fake boxing match between Senator Lodge and an opponent of civil service reform. The theme for this night's bash was war. The menu showed a warship flying the Gridiron flag heading for "To-Morrow Castle." (Havana harbor is protected by Morro Castle.) The evening's special guest, Roosevelt was jokingly promoted to Vice-Admiral of the Gridiron Navy. But he was not in a kidding mood. Teeth showing, but not in a smile, he turned to President McKinley's closest ally and backer, Mark Hanna, who was also seated at the head table. "We will have this war for the freedom of Cuba, Senator Hanna, in spite of the timidity of the commercial interests," Roosevelt growled. "It was a very dramatic moment," reported the Gridiron Club history, "and there was no one present at the dinner who did not thoroughly understand that war was inevitable."[39]

If only Roosevelt could make it come sooner! "I'd give all I'm worth to be just two days in supreme command. I'd be perfectly willing then to resign, for I'd have things going so that nobody could stop them," he wrote Bamie on April 1.[40] Roosevelt was helped by Hearst's *Journal* ratcheting up the pressure on Hanna, whom the paper referred to as "President Hanna" to suggest his power over McKinley. Hearst dusted off cartoon images from the 1896 campaign to charge that McKinley was the pathetic tool of the craven commercial interests — represented by Hanna, who was depicted covered by dollar signs. In three-inch type a front-page headline read HANNA VS. HONOR. The paper had the audacity to quote Roosevelt praising the *Journal* as a "great influence" on the country. Roosevelt denied the quote, as he routinely did whenever the *Journal* printed one of his indiscretions. Nonetheless, he and Hearst were writing on the same page.[41]

With his love of stunts, Hearst proposed recruiting a regiment of giant athletes — heavyweight boxers, football players, and baseball sluggers — to overawe the pitiful Spaniards. Frank James, brother of the bandit Jesse, offered to lead a company of cowboys, while "Buffalo Bill" Cody declared that with thirty thousand Indian braves he could rid Cuba of Spaniards in sixty days.[42]

Suppression of the truth, the outmaneuvering of the president by war-hungry subordinates, and the incessant publicity over the *Maine* were having an effect. A great welling-up of patriotism, mixed with a desire for revenge, spread from coast to coast. "Remember the *Maine!*" was heard on street corners and from church pulpits, in town halls and on college campuses, sometimes followed by "To Hell with Spain!" — a war cry first printed in the *Journal* that began appearing on buttons and matchbooks, throat lozenges and penny candy. College students at Lehigh began holding impromptu drills. Mass meetings in Buffalo called for a declaration of war. The *Nevada Appeal* of Carson City accurately reported, "Many people are for war on general principles, without a well-defined idea of why or wherefore."[43] In Kansas, reported the young editor of the *Emporia Gazette*, American flags were "fluttering everywhere."[44]

No clear or immediate answer was forthcoming from the president. McKinley was working on a message to Congress laying out a course of action before the legislators could seize the initiative and declare war on Spain. "He is in a very trying situation," Long jotted in his diary on April 4. "He has been robbed of sleep, overworked, and I fancy that I can see that his mind does not work as clearly and directly and as self-reliantly as it otherwise would."[45]

It was about this time that Roosevelt began joking, with a vehemence that no doubt got back to the president, that McKinley "has no more backbone than a chocolate éclair." With some, including friendly newspaper reporters, Roosevelt used Henry Adams's description of McKinley: "a jellyfish."[46] McKinley was not nearly as weak and hapless as he was portrayed by Roosevelt—or by the biting cartoons of Hearst's *Journal*, or by his critics at the time, or by skeptical historians in later years.[47] Since taking office a year earlier the president had shown both firmness and finesse in pressing Spain to make concessions on Cuba, an effort that led to Spain's declaration of partial autonomy at the end of 1897. He continued to negotiate with Spain even as the war cries echoed from Capitol Hill. But he was caught in an impossible bind between Spain, which would not let go, and the Cuban rebels, who would not give up their demands for complete independence.

McKinley never quite grasped that Cuba was, for most Spaniards, a sacred object. In Spain's popular mythology the "emerald island" was a gift from God to Spain for the *reconquista* that drove Islam from Europe in the fifteenth century. As the Spanish empire crumbled over time, memories of the *siglo d'oro*, the golden century, only grew stronger. The Spanish people knew that they would be outmanned and outgunned in any war with the Americans, but they entertained a foolish faith in the Spanish *guerrillerismo*, the indomitable spirit shown by guerrilla bands against the Napoleonic invasion of Iberia in the early nineteenth century. They were animated as well by a fierce sense of *punctilio*: better to be defeated than to be seen backing down. Perhaps a little more realistic, in their negotiations Spain's diplomats stalled and played for time, hoping, wishing that some European monarch might come to their rescue. McKinley's minister to Madrid, Stewart Woodward, constantly complained of *mañanaism*, the Spanish unwillingness to act before they absolutely had to.[48] The attitude of the Spanish public, and the absurdity of their situation, was shown by a bullfight staged in Madrid shortly after the sinking of the *Maine*. Into the ring were sent a bull, representing Spain, and an elephant, representing the United States. The bull didn't do much but snort, and the elephant just stood there impassively. Nothing happened, and the deflated crowd filed out.[49]

For their part, the Cuban rebels were stubbornly defiant. They did not want to settle for half measures, for autonomy or an armistice. They wanted freedom now—complete independence from Spain—and, for that matter, independence from the United States. The revolutionary army that had been put on its back by General Wyler's draconian "reconcentration" policy had regained strength after his departure in the fall of 1897. Spanish troops were retreating to garrisons in the cities, leaving the rebels free to roam the countryside.

Hoping to persuade the rebels to enter into a cease-fire with Spain, McKinley had summoned Horatio Rubens, the New York lawyer for the junta, to the White House shortly after the sinking of the *Maine*. In his private office on the second floor, McKinley walked restlessly about, the tails of his frock coat swinging, his eyes black with determination, according to Rubens's recollection. "You must accept an immediate armistice with Spain," the president demanded. "To what end, Mr. President?" Rubens asked. "To settle the strife in Cuba!" McKinley cried. "But is Spain ready to grant Cuba independence?" the junta's lawyer asked. "That isn't the question now," the president insisted, his voice rising. "We may discuss that later. The thing for the moment is an armistice." Rubens declined. "Absolute independence from Spain," he insisted. He compared Cuba's situation to America's versus Great Britain in 1776 and 1812.

McKinley stared at Rubens and turned to look out the window at the Potomac, glistening to the south beyond the trees.

"Isn't this a beautiful view of the river?" he asked. "Beautiful," agreed Rubens. Then, hoping to move the president, Rubens laid out some enlarged photographs of emaciated and diseased Cubans held in Spain's *reconcentrado* camps. According to Rubens, McKinley looked "gingerly" at the photos at first, then more closely. "Finally," Rubens wrote, "I noticed tears began to course down his face. When he could trust his voice, he said, 'I hope you will say nothing of the effect of this sight on me.'"[50]

McKinley was wrought up by more than the pictures of suffering women and children. Feeling misunderstood and put upon, he feared that the public had developed amnesia during the generation that had passed since the Civil War. And he believed that Cuba was unready for independence. It was all very well for the mob and their elected representatives to clamor for Cuba Libre, McKinley believed; but it was his responsibility as president to look beyond the war cries and calls for revenge and ask just what would Cuba, free of Spanish domination, look like? Were the Cubans, about half of whom were recently freed slaves, capable of self-governance? McKinley had little desire to make the island an American colony, but he feared that Cuba could become another Haiti, which had descended into chaos after slave revolts in the late eighteenth century.

Secretary Long, who shared the president's views, laid out the argument against Cuban independence in a "personal and confidential" letter to a friendly newspaper correspondent on April 15. "We can't recognize independence on the part of a people who have no government; no capitol; no civil organization; no place to which a representative of a foreign government could be sent," Long explained.[51]

In an era when the educated classes were obsessively worried about their virility or lack thereof, it must have been painful for

McKinley to listen to the jeers. Wrote a versifier named Frank A. Putnam:

> *A mighty people proud and free, await their captain's battle call;*
> *Their captain bends on coward's knee; his nerveless hand the*
>   *sword lets fall.*
> *The heroic deeds that reft our chains arouse in him no answering*
>   *fire;*
> *Trembling, he schemes for sordid gains and sees a race in rags*
>   *expire.*[52]

There were uglier expressions of the public mood. McKinley and Hanna were burned in effigy by mobs in Virginia. Theater audiences in New York hissed at the mention of the president's name and tore his picture from the walls while singing "The Star-Spangled Banner" after every performance.[53] The *Journal* pictured the president in a bonnet and apron.

McKinley was described by intimates as haggard, his eyes bearing the dark circles of insomnia. There were suspicions that he was dipping into the patent narcotics used to treat his epileptic wife. Attending a musicale at the White House one night, Herman Kohlstaat, the newspaperman friendly with McKinley, was summoned to meet privately with him in the Red Room. Sitting on a large crimson-brocade lounge, McKinley rested his head on his hands, elbows on knees. He complained of not sleeping, and vowed that Congress was trying to drive him into a war with Spain. "He broke down and cried like a boy of thirteen," Kohlstaat wrote in a memoir. According to the newspaperman, he put his hand on the president's shoulder and tried to reassure him that the country would back whatever course he took. After a while McKinley asked Kohlstaat, "Do my eyes look very red?

Do they look like I've been crying?" Kohlstaat advised the president to blow his nose "long and hard" as he reentered the room to make his guests think he merely had a cold.[54]

Leonard Wood had told McKinley that he wished to serve his country not as a surgeon to the president but once more as a soldier in the field. McKinley knew that Wood and Roosevelt had become close friends and, no doubt, coconspirators in the cause of war. One morning when Wood dropped in to see the president, McKinley, trying to make light of the situation, asked, "Well, have you and Theodore declared war yet?"

Wood answered, "No, Mr. President, we have not, but we think you will, sir."

Recalling the carnage he had witnessed at Antietam many years before, McKinley turned serious. "I shall never get into a war," he said, "until I am sure that God and man approve. I have been through one war; I have seen the dead piled up; and I do not want to see another."[55]

14

The Trophies of Miltiades

"Is he quite mad?"

ONE VOICE WAS oddly missing from the public clamor over Cuba in the late winter and early spring of 1898. While Theodore Roosevelt badgered the president to wage war and made no effort to be discreet about it, his friend Cabot Lodge gave no interviews and delivered no speeches. The two men were "in the closest touch throughout this period," as Roosevelt put it in his memoirs. But Roosevelt was fundamentally an optimist, open to the world for all to see, while Lodge was a pessimist and deeply private for such a public man. In December Roosevelt had joked to a friend that Cabot would come to the christening of his baby boy Quentin "with gloomy reluctance, as it is against his principles to sanction anything so anti-malthusian as a sixth child."[1] The distinctly different characters of the two men showed through on the eve of war, even as they remained friends and allies.*

---

*Senator Lodge was in the office of the assistant secretary of the navy on Saturday, February 25, on the day Roosevelt ordered Dewey to prepare to sail to Manila to hunt the Spanish fleet. The two were not conspiring together to start a war, as it was sometimes later alleged; Lodge had just wandered in to say hello and found Roosevelt furiously signing orders.[2]

The senator from Massachusetts was playing an inside game. Ever the loyal party man and mindful of his own political survival, he feared the Republicans would break apart over Cuba. "With the [party] split in two, we shall be defeated at the polls, and your humble servant among others will go down in the wreck," he confided to Sturgis Bigelow, his landlord on Tuckernuck Island. The Republicans were dependent on backing from big business, and most wealthy merchants and investors were reflexively antiwar. Lodge was always getting fretful letters from the moneyed interests ("I have not met a man...in the aristocratic upper crust in which you & I are imbedded, who considers that we have any justifiable cause for war. Below that crust...the wish for war is *almost* universal," moaned one fellow Brahmin). Lodge patiently debated old friends like Henry Lee Higginson, warning him that failing to intervene in Cuba would give the Democrats an opening in the next election. "The course which you are advising leads straight to free silver and Bryanism," he warned Higginson, evoking the horrors narrowly averted in 1896. Lodge was exasperated by his banker friend. "How much he has changed since the days when he was a free-soiler and fought for the Union. Age and wealth are great sedatives to prevent action," Lodge despaired to a friend.[3]

At the same time, Lodge gently nudged McKinley toward intervention in Cuba. The senator, who was constantly making the two-mile carriage ride between Capitol Hill and the White House, worried that McKinley would lose control of Congress, which he feared would stampede to war before the administration could come up with a plan for armed intervention. Lodge held a higher opinion of McKinley than did his friend Roosevelt; he was more sensitive to the political pressures and far less prone to cork off with his own views. But the constant need to dance attendance on the president took its toll. On April 3 he wrote his mother:

> *This has been a week of intense strain & suspense, both very hard to bear & very wearing on the nerves. I have been with the President almost every day & have done all in my small way that I could to help him keep Congress from breaking away & acting without him. It has not been easy work & the pleasure has not been enhanced by frantic telegrams from frightened brokers & bankers calling upon me to stand by the President as if I was fighting him.*[4]

Lodge's uncharacteristically poor grammar ("as if I was") suggests the agitation he felt, even as he dashed off his weekly epistle to his mother. Adding to his burdens was the worry always felt by parents of young men on the eve of war. His precious boy Bay, the cultivated young poet, was twenty-four years old and determined to fight if war came. "The agony of mind to his mother & myself you can guess," Lodge wrote his mother. "I will not dwell upon it. But he comes of fighting stock. It must be I suppose & we bow our heads. This never leaves my thoughts & yet the work of every day must go on."[5]

In the House of Representatives, Thomas Reed was also feeling under the gun, though he tried not to show it. The press had been sniping at him for months — and not just the yellow press. Respectable papers lashed Reed for refusing to spend more to build up the navy. The New York *Herald* ran a large cartoon of the grave ghost of General George Washington tapping a fat, slightly addled-looking Speaker Reed on the shoulder. Reed is clutching a gavel stenciled "Anti-National Defense." Washington is holding a copy of his Farewell Address, in which the founder cautioned that spending money on national defense could avert the far higher cost of war. The caption under the Speaker's image read "Our Great Objector."[6]

Asher Hinds recorded his boss's efforts to brush off the press. "The Speaker does not want war and does not believe there will be war, although the sensational journals are doing their best to bring it about," Hinds wrote in his diary on February 28, two weeks after the *Maine* went down. He went on to quote his boss: "'How we are infested with rats and mice,' said he [Reed] the other day, speaking of one of the sensation writers. 'But it is so in the ways of all the world. You no sooner build a fine house than the rats and mice get into it.'"[7]

In early March, Reed could not stop Congress from shouting through $50 million for national defense. In the House, the legislation was introduced with a rebel yell by Congressman "Fighting Joe" Wheeler of Alabama, the former Confederate cavalryman who had jumped from desk to desk in an attempt to get to Reed when the Speaker had upset the quorum rules.[8] "It seemed as though a hundred Fourth of Julys had been let loose in the House," noted Hinds in his diary. The next day Hinds glimpsed a quietly bitter little scene. The Senate passed the $50 million defense appropriation "without debate," wrote Hinds. "Senator Henry Cabot Lodge came over and told the Speaker with an air of glee, I thought," wrote Hinds. "The Speaker responded something about the trophies of Miltiades which I did not catch." Hinds may have missed the remark but Lodge, a student of the classics, surely did not. Miltiades was a Greek general who, flush with victory against the Persians at Marathon in 490 BC, led a punitive mission against an ally of Persia, a small island nation that was supposed to be a pushover. The mission was a fiasco and Miltiades was defeated and disgraced; he died of his wounds in prison.[9]

Like a hero in another Greek tragedy, Reed could see his own powers diminishing but seemed helpless against the fates. In January the New York *Journal* had written almost gloatingly about Reed's own party stirring against him over Cuba.[10] Hearst's paper, as it occasionally did, had the facts right: Reed was losing his ability to dominate the House, to keep the jingoes at bay through procedural maneuvering and sheer force of personality. Joe Cannon, chairman of the House Appropriations Committee and a potential Reed rival, did not even consult with the Speaker before sending the $50 million defense bill to the House floor. As he boarded the streetcar that evening to head back down Pennsylvania Avenue from Capitol Hill, Cannon was accosted by the lumbering Reed. "Joe, why did you do it?" asked Reed (meaning not only why did he introduce such a massive spending bill, but why did he end-run the Speaker). Cannon offered some excuses, and Reed listened. "Perhaps you are right, perhaps you are right," said Reed, shaking his head, and the two men never discussed the matter again.[11]

As the war tide gathered force, Reed was reduced to sarcasm. In mid-March Senator Redfield Proctor, who had visited Cuba, gave a careful description of the misery and suffering caused by Spain's reconcentration policy. Delivered in a flat voice, without apparent emotion, Proctor's speech was devastatingly effective. The descriptions of starvation, disease, cruelty, and hopelessness silenced the Senate chamber. Reported by the newspapers, the speech changed minds of voters still unsure about intervening in Cuba. Proctor was a self-made millionaire with standing in the business community. The antiwar sentiment on Wall Street ebbed; businessmen began to accept the inevitability and even the virtue of war with Spain. Reed, whose skin was much thinner than he liked to admit, had not forgotten how Proctor had betrayed him by switching his support to McKinley in the 1896 presidential campaign. His remark, when he heard of Proctor's speech, was particularly sour. Proctor had made his fortune in the Vermont marble business. "Proctor's position might have been expected," Reed drawled. "A war will make a large market for gravestones."[12]

By the end of March, Reed was cornered, forced to use obscure legislative precedents to keep the House from debating a declaration of war. Some fifty members of his own party, dubbing themselves the Reconcentrados, began to meet secretly to discuss how to break the Czar's hold. In the House, "peace" became an epithet; Reed had to gavel for silence when the now jam-packed galleries hissed at the word.[13] On April 6 reporters gathering around Reed's breakfast table at the Shoreham Hotel chatted with the Speaker about a letter from a former governor of New York who was asking Reed why he couldn't do more to dissuade members of the House from calling for intervention and war. "Dissuade them!" said Reed with a cold smile. "Dissuade them! The Governor is too good. He might as well ask me to stand out in the middle of a Kansas waste and dissuade a cyclone. It can't be done with success."[14] Reed was beaten and he knew it.

By Monday, April 11, huge crowds overwhelmed the Capitol building. Dressed in their Easter finery, they awaited the formal delivery of the president's message to Congress on the Cuban situation.[15] "Summer has come with a burst & the city is beginning to wear its spring look," Lodge wrote his mother. The cherry blossoms had fallen, and tulips and magnolias were in full bloom. "But," Lodge wrote, "there is no thought to anything but the Spanish question & the coming war."[16] McKinley's message was full of high-flown language ("in the name of humanity, and in the name of civilization") but it was ambiguous, maddeningly so to warhawks. The president called for Congress to authorize armed intervention, but he did not ask for a declaration of war against Spain, and he seemed to leave the door open for further negotiations. To the frustration of the Cuba Libre lobby and their many friends, he did not call for the independence of Cuba or the recognition of the rebel government. (Practically speaking, there was no rebel government to recognize, as the rebels' commanding general, Máximo Gómez, privately admitted; the country was racked by looting and the sacking of towns by starving rebel soldiers.)[17]

Read by relays of droning clerks, McKinley's seven-thousand-word message was greeted by only polite applause in the House. Among the unimpressed was the owner of the New York *Journal*. McKinley's speech, editorialized Hearst's sheet, "profoundly disappointed the American people; instead of a call to arms" the president had "sounded a summons to retreat."[18]

Capitol Hill seethed for a day. Then, on April 13, an open revolt broke out against Reed's rule. House Democrats, eager to get a jump on the Republicans by calling for a measure to recognize Cuban independence, began standing and yelling to be heard by the Speaker, who calmly sat in his chair on an elevated platform. As the members grew increasingly restive, a Republican congressman from Pennsylvania called a Democrat from Georgia a liar. The Democrat heaved a large bound volume of the *Congressional Record* at the Republican, and suddenly the aisles filled with lawmakers shouting, tugging and pulling, then swinging wildly. A congressional page was knocked out by a blow to the jaw. In the galleries women screamed. From his chair Reed pounded his gavel. ("Like the Olympian Jove on a cloud, sat a big, pallid man, with an egg-like head, wielding an ivory gavel as a blacksmith wields a hammer," recounted the reliably florid *Journal*.) No one paid any attention. Finally Reed ordered the sergeant-at-arms to intervene. Grabbing a large pole topped by a solid-silver American eagle, the retired army colonel waded into the mob. Some members just laughed at this show of authority and went on wrestling. The eagle was knocked askew. Only when they were worn out did the congressmen stop fighting. The scene was an embarrassment to Congress and to Reed. The next day the *Times* of London reported:

> Men fought; "Liar," "Scoundrel," and other epithets were bandied to and fro; there were a half dozen personal collisions; books were thrown; members rushed up and down the aisles like madmen, exchanging hot words, with clenched fists and set teeth; excitement was at fever heat. Not for years has such a scene occurred. The Speaker, after vainly striving to restore order, directed the Sergeant-at-Arms to use the silver mace, the emblem of authority of the House.... Mr. Henderson, of Iowa, Republican, a war veteran, from the midst of the fighting, surging crowd appealed to members to observe order and not disgrace the American Congress. They hissed him. Finally some semblance of order was restored.
>
> Such is the body in whose favour the President on Monday abdicated his rightful authority and to whom he entrusted the fortunes of his and their country.[19]

Ever supportive of his boss, Asher Hinds gave a more benign account in his diary:

> We had in the House today while the proceedings were going on a very lively row, which took all the Speaker's

coolness and mastery to quell.... The affair occurred on my side of the Speaker's chair, and within a few steps of where I sit. I transmitted the order to Sgt. at Arms Russell to take the mace (members call it the "goose"—it is surmounted by a silver eagle) and go and stop them. He was considerably tossed about for a time. Young Halstead, chief page on our side, tried to separate the combatants and got hit on the jaw. This is the only casualty.[20]

Hearst's *Journal* blamed Reed for "imparting his gag tactics into a great historic occasion" and accused him of reducing the House to an imitation of "the French Chamber of Deputies." But enough of politics and politicians, the *Journal* implored—"the time has come for the soldiers and sailors to do the talking."

Theodore Roosevelt shared Hearst's impatience. In a new pocket diary he had purchased to record the history he could see in the making, Roosevelt wrote of his estranged friend, "Reed is malignantly bent on preventing all preparation for war."[21] On the morning of April 14 he sent Lodge a note imploring him to push for Congress to recognize Cuban independence. "Otherwise we shall have more delay and more shilly-shallying." On the other side of the Capitol, the House had passed a resolution essentially backing the administration, authorizing armed intervention but saying nothing about a declaration of war or independence for Cuba. "You must have no part in it," he instructed, in words that were sterner than he normally used in his private correspondence with Lodge.[22]

Roosevelt was perhaps sensing that the senator from Massachusetts was a little too loyal to McKinley. The day before, Lodge had broken his long silence on Cuba to back McKinley with a speech on the Senate floor. Before the packed and hushed

FOR FREE CUBA.

Eloquent Plea in Senate by Henry Cabot Lodge.

Declares We Must Have Reparation for the Maine.

He Arraigns Spain for Her Course in Cuba, for Duplicity in Her Dealings With the United States, and Puts the Responsibility for War, if War It Is to Be, Upon Her — In the Face of a Great Crisis He Urges Unanimity of Action and Loyal Support of the President.

(New York Journal*)*

galleries Lodge stood trim and erect in his tailored charcoal suit and high white collar. He took the role of statesman, calling on the Senate and the nation to support the president. His tone was more sorrowful than angry; he suggested that if Congress had only paid for more battleships (as he had long urged), Spain might now be backing down. Notwithstanding McKinley's forlorn wish to keep diplomacy alive, he warned against further negotiations with Spain. "We have been wandering too long as a country amid the delusions and snares of diplomacy. Let us now come out into the clear light of day and look the facts squarely in the face," he proclaimed, his grating voice suffused with the moral certainty of his Puritan ancestors.[23]

Lodge (New York Journal*)*

All that week, as the dogwoods budded and the excited crowds swirled about Capitol Hill, the House and Senate hotly debated, stopping only for impromptu choruses of "The Battle Hymn of the Republic." They were ready to fight Spain. But what to do with Cuba once the fighting was over? Many were wary of recognizing an independent Cuban government. On the other hand, only a few lawmakers (and not even Lodge, the great expansionist) wished to annex Cuba as a colony or territory. Some of this reluctance was principled: the Cubans had fought their revolution and should be free. Some hesitation was rooted in nativist fear: most Americans did not want to absorb a Catholic, half black population.[24] After some muddled debate, Congress passed the Teller Amendment, which renounced any intention of annexing Cuba. The measure was offered by Senator Henry Teller of Colorado, who had reportedly received a $2 million bribe from the junta—the rebel government-in-exile was determined to keep Cuba from becoming an American colony. (Teller had another motive for keeping Cuba outside the borders of the United States: the profits of Colorado's sugar-beet farmers would be threatened if Cuban sugar did not face a tariff on foreign imports.) Finally, eight anxious days after McKinley delivered his message to Congress, the House and Senate, with a chorus of whoops and hollers, passed a joint resolution calling for Cuban independence. President McKinley, his cheek to the gale, signed it.

The outcome was a policy mishmash and a prescription for trouble. The American people wanted war—but their government was divided and unsure about its ultimate strategic aims. Congress had voted for Cuban independence, but the president (and, for that matter, many congressmen) were doubtful that Cuba could govern itself. More than a century later, diplomat and historian Warren Zimmerman would write in his account of the period, *First Great Triumph*, "That fatal ambiguity has scarred American relations with Cuba ever since."[25]

At 7:30 a.m. on April 21, America's ambassador in Madrid, Stewart Woodward, was notified that Spain had broken diplomatic relations with the United States. Woodward hastily burned or collected his papers and, carrying a six-shooter in his hand, caught the 4:00 p.m. express train to Paris. Angry Spanish mobs stoned the train. Across the ocean at dawn that morning, inside the Virginia Capes, the North Atlantic Squadron slipped its moorings and the battleships and cruisers, destroyers and torpedo boats, sailed out to sea and swung south toward the Caribbean.[26]

"We are in it for all we are worth," Cabot Lodge wrote his friend John Hay, who as ambassador to London had been lining up the support of Great Britain. "But it is a terrible business.... Bay will go — there is no stopping him. I hope to get him a place in the navy, but, alas, you can imagine how our hearts are low & how hard it has been not to cry out for peace at any price & to live up to one's deep convictions of public duty.... My son in law [Augustus Peabody Gardner, husband of Lodge's daughter Constance] means to go — alas again — and then I have been assailed as a 'jingo'!"[27] To his mother he wrote, "It is hard but we must face it as bravely as we can."[28] Mixed in with Lodge's genuine anxiety was a certain amount of moral posturing. One senses that he was proud, and perhaps a little thrilled, that his son ("he comes from fighting stock") felt the call of duty. As a senator he had been positioned to keep his son out of the trenches: he now arranged, through Secretary Long, to get Bay commissioned as a cadet aboard a warship, the *Dixie*, commanded by Nannie Lodge's brother, Charles Davis.[29] Lodge also gave his family house on the shore at Nahant over to the army, "free gratis for nothing," for use as a signal station.[30]

Lodge's donation was politically astute, if somewhat ludicrous from a military standpoint. There were wild fears of the Spanish navy appearing off the East Coast, bombarding American cities. In his diary Secretary Long grumbled about the irony of "Senator [William] Frye, who has been a blazing jingo, shouting for war" asking for a warship to protect the Maine coast "which he represents."[31] Others made light of such fears. Winthrop Chanler, Roosevelt's and Lodge's Porcellian friend, drily joked that, should the Spanish army invade New York City, "they would all be absorbed in the population... and engaged in selling oranges before they got as far as 14th Street." But Chanler, too, was swept along in the hysteria. "War-War-War-Extras are being shouted under the Club windows," Chanler wrote his wife from the Knickerbocker Club in Manhattan. "I was surprised to find so many men who say they can't sleep at night for thinking, thinking, thinking."[32]

On Saturday, April 23, President McKinley called for 125,000 volunteers to swell the 28,000-man regular army. A million volunteers answered the call. One was Roosevelt. On the rainy morning of Monday, April 25, he walked into Secretary Long's office and formally announced his intention to resign as assistant secretary of the navy in order to join the army as a colonel in a volunteer regiment. Long, who had known this decision was coming for some time, penned a few kind words about Roosevelt in his diary, then cut loose with perplexity and frustration over his departing deputy:

He has lost his head to this unutterable folly of deserting his post where he is of most service and running off to ride a horse and, probably, brush mosquitoes from his neck on the Florida sands. His heart is right, and he means well, but it is one of these cases of aberration — desertion — vainglory; of which he is utterly unaware. He thinks he is following his highest ideal, whereas, in fact, as without exception everyone of his friends advises him, he is acting like a fool. And, yet, how absurd all this will sound, if, by some turn of fortune, he should accomplish some great thing and strike a very high mark.*[33]

---

*Long added to his diary at the end of this page, before it was published: "Later, P.S. Roosevelt was right and we, his friends, were all wrong. His going into the Army led straight to the Presidency."[34]

Long was right about the universal disapproval of Roosevelt's friends. "Is his wife dead? Has he quarreled with everybody? Is he quite mad?" Henry Adams wrote Elizabeth Cameron.[35] "I really think he is going mad," Winthrop Chanler wrote his wife. "The President has asked him twice as a personal favor to stay in the Navy Dept., but Theodore is wild to fight and hack and hew. It is really sad. Of course, this ends his political career for good. Even Cabot says this." (Chanler apparently felt his own Anglo-Saxon blood rising, for he promptly followed Roosevelt, joining up — improbably, given his complete lack of military experience — as an adviser to the Cuban army: "Cabot has got me passes which practically put the army and navy of the U.S. at my disposal, so that I can leave when I get tired of it or sick or anything," he explained to his wife.)[36]

Another member of the Henry Adams circle, the artist John La Farge, told a family member that Roosevelt was "behaving very badly in leaving his family for a junket like this; he is going *because he wants to*; that's what is so deplorable in a husband and father."[37]

Roosevelt's motivations for leaving his post and his family to go off on a quixotic adventure — he was far more likely to be bitten by a disease-bearing insect than to be shot at by Spanish bullets — indeed come off as selfish, if not daft. But Roosevelt did not act heedlessly or impulsively. He crafted a series of sober, carefully considered letters to his friends, often employing the same language, to explain himself. He wrote one:

I can assure you that I am quite disinterested in this. I am not acting in a spirit of recklessness or levity, or purely for my own selfish enjoyment. I don't want to be shot at any more than anyone else does; still less to die of yellow fever. I am altogether

*too fond of my wife and children, and enjoy the good things
of this life too much to wish lightly to hazard their loss, or to
go away from my family; but the above is my duty as I see it.
It is very hard to have to act against the wishes and strongly
expressed advice of all of my best friends — you, Lodge, Sturgis
Bigelow and the rest.*[38]

In such correspondence Roosevelt's usual bombast was gone.
He even made an attempt at self-awareness, or at least was honest enough to know he could not truly plumb the depths of his own psyche. "I don't want you to think that I am talking like a prig, for I know perfectly well that one never is able to analyze with entire accuracy all of one's motives. But I am entirely certain that I don't expect any military glory out of this Cuban war, more than what is implied in the honorable performance of duty," he wrote Paul Dana of the New York *Sun*, one of several newspapermen Roosevelt regarded as intimates. Roosevelt's fear of being seen as a tin soldier emerges again and again in these letters. "One of the commonest taunts directed at men like myself is that we are armchair and parlor jingoes who wish to see others do what we only advocate doing," he wrote Sturgis Bigelow.[39] For two years, he explained to Dana, he had been trying to get the United States into a war ("to accept the arbitrament of the sword, if necessary"). Now that the war had arrived, he felt honor bound to practice what he preached.[40]

That need for honor was likely deeper than his letter to Dana acknowledged. Consciously or not, Roosevelt may have been seeing his father's ghost. In later years his daughter by his first wife, Alice Roosevelt Longworth, who possessed a sarcastic blade worthy of Tom Reed, could get a rise out of her father merely by taunting him about his own father's failure to fight in the Civil

War.[41] Roosevelt was determined to redeem the family name. But he still had to think hard about what to do and to measure the consequences for his family as well as himself.

As it happened, the relation of father and son — his relationship with his *own* son — was much on Roosevelt's mind as he pondered his course in the early spring of 1898. Dr. Alexander Lambert, a Cornell public health doctor and friend of Bamie's (and an unusually skilled physician for his time) had undertaken the care of little Ted, who was still racked with nervous headaches as he lived in seclusion with Bamie at her Madison Avenue apartment. Roosevelt's correspondence with Lambert during this period is revealing. Showing psychological insight more normally associated with a later generation of doctors, Lambert wrote Roosevelt that the father was at least partly responsible for his son's nervous disorder; the boy had been unsettled by too much pressure to become a manly little warrior. Judging from Roosevelt's response to the doctor, Edith had been arguing much the same to her husband: that he needed to ease up on the little boy. Roosevelt had resisted his wife's judgment and implicit criticism, until Lambert weighed in with his letter of advice to Roosevelt. On March 29 Roosevelt replied, "Dear Alec, I shall give plain proof of great weakness of character by reading your letter to Mrs. Roosevelt, who is now well enough to feel the emotions of triumph." Roosevelt raised the white flag and pledged to Lambert: "Hereafter I shall never press Ted either in body or in mind. The fact is that the little fellow, who is peculiarly dear to me, has bidden fair to be all the things I would like to have been and wasn't, and it has been a great temptation to push him." It's far from obvious that Ted Jr. felt driven to surpass his father — more likely, Roosevelt was thinking about (or in modern psychiatric parlance, transferring) his own duty to outdo his father as a man.[42]

Ted Jr.'s first buck (Theodore Roosevelt Collection, Houghton Library, Harvard University)

One of Roosevelt's shrewder biographers, Kathleen Dalton, suggests that Roosevelt was promising anything to get out of the house and go to war.[43] But he may have also wished to save Ted from the curse of growing up believing that his father wanted to fight and ought to have, but did not out of a softhearted but misguided solicitude for his family. In this sense he would be relieving his son of certain oppressive burdens.

The Roosevelt household was slowly recovering as both springtime and wartime arrived in Washington that April. All the children came back from Aunt Bamie's or the Lodges', and Edith was able to rise from her sickbed. On impulse one warm day early that month, Edith took a carriage to surprise her husband at the

Metropolitan Club, where she knew she would find him eating lunch. Spotting Leonard Wood coming out of the club, she sent him back in to fetch her husband. "I wish," Edith told Ted Jr., "you could have seen his face of surprise and delight."[44]

Edith supported her husband's decision to go to war; the whole family did. "I can never say what a help and comfort Edith has been to me," Roosevelt wrote his sister Corinne on May 5, as he was preparing to ship out.[45] In true Roosevelt fashion, little Kermit, age nine, knocked down and bloodied a schoolmate who suggested that his father might not come back alive.[46] But ultimately, whether his family was supportive — or needed him at home — was irrelevant. He was going. Many years later, as president, he admitted as much in a letter to another friend, his military attaché Archie Butts:

> *When the chance came for me to go to Cuba with the Rough Riders, Mrs. Roosevelt was very ill and so was Teddy. It was a question if either would ultimately get well. You know what my wife and children mean to me; and yet I made up my mind that I would not allow even a death to stand in my way; that it was my one chance to do something for my country and for my family and my one chance to cut my little notch on the stick that stands as a measuring rod in every family. [Here he was unquestionably thinking of his father.] I know now that I would have turned from my wife's deathbed to have answered that call.*[47]

15

Hot Time

"You must capture vessels or destroy. Use utmost endeavor."

I F THEODORE ROOSEVELT's modus operandi was to deny or
brush past inner turmoil, William James's instinct was to stop
and examine himself and the contradictions within. The great
turn-of-the-century philosopher and psychologist was his own
laboratory subject. He knew what fools heroes could be. And yet
he idolized the instinctive, plunge-ahead action hero. "We draw
new life from the heroic example," he wrote in his masterwork
The Principles of Psychology. James worshipped what Emerson
called "the lords of life"—the men who face down danger and
embrace challenge—and he pitied or simply scorned the pro-
crastinator and equivocator. James's introspection drew not a
little on his bouts of self-loathing. As literary historian R. W. B.
Lewis has observed, James was conscious of an "inward hollow-
ness," the sadness of a man caught between thought and action.
T. S. Eliot, borrowing from Brutus's soliloquy in *Julius Caesar,*
would later capture James's dilemma in his 1927 poem "The
Hollow Men":

Between the idea
And the reality

Between the motion
And the act
Falls the Shadow[1]

James was not ambivalent about democracy. Unlike most of his fellow mugwumps, he had not viewed William Jennings Bryan as some kind of Robespierre. While he found the populists crude, he understood that they reflected the real concerns of Americans who had been left behind in the Gilded Age. Nor was he upset by labor unrest or the waves of immigration—all natural stages, he believed, in the progression of a people's republic. James was not a prig; he was open to the raw, sometimes uncouth spirit of democracy. And he was a true patriot, if benignly paternalistic at times.[2]

That spring of 1898, it took James some time and anxious thought to work out his feelings about the war. On April 8, with the country on the verge, he defended his Harvard colleague Charles Eliot Norton, who was being vilified in the press for counseling students not to enlist in the military, and if necessary to buy draft substitutes, as their upper-class fathers had done in the Civil War.[3] "Pray don't get your facts from the papers," James cautioned a friend who wrote to complain indignantly about Harvard's notoriously overcivilized professor of art history. James believed that Professor Norton, who was receiving anonymous death threats accusing him of aiding the enemy, was actually showing a kind of bravery in his outspoken pacifism.

For his part, James was a little surprised to find himself *welcoming* the war—indeed, he impetuously exclaimed to a friend, "the war is undoubtedly the very best thing that could have befallen us." He thought war might serve as a positive catalyst, that its exigencies would reawaken a reformist spirit in the land

and, he wrote his brother-in-law and fellow intellectual William "Mack" Salter, "make America put our very best qualities foremost. We mugwumps will have a magnificent chance, on the new basis, in making all the virtues of the country *line up* in meeting the emergencies that are sure to arise." James wanted to believe the rhetoric flowing from Capitol Hill, that America had no interest in conquest or in exploitation. He was savvy enough to know that high-minded words have a way of masking baser motives. Still, the mere act of believing could make heroes out of men. "*The things* a man or nation *fights for*, or thinks he fights for, or pretends he fights for, are, after all, the measure of his place on the scale," he concluded.[4] He was gratified that the war was being waged for the sake of "humanity."

James was an optimist as well as a patriot. Wars were terrible and tragic, but the two closest to James's experience—the conflicts that shaped his sense of national identity, the American Revolution and the Civil War—had stimulated great progress. Men had fought not just for the sake of bloodlust but for the freedom of man—only white men in the first case, to be sure, but all humanity in the second. Armed conflicts to make men free were more noble than base, James believed.

And yet James, too, knew well the personal cost of war, etched in the suffering face of his wounded brother Wilkie. He knew that in the cause of glory men could behave shamefully. Nothing excited man's inner passions more than rushing forth, sword in hand, to avenge a wrong and free the innocent. James revered (and envied) the man on horseback—the Shaws and Lowells he had watched ride off to war. But he also knew what horror could flow from charging blindly into the guns.

Ultimately, James's true gifts lay not in reasoned analysis but in his intuition and impulse, his ability to cut through received cant to sense the deeper forces lurking. At the same time he was a late-Victorian gentleman who lived a safe and orderly, indeed cosseted, life. The outbreak of the war against Spain aroused in him contradictory and incomplete thoughts. He was flailing a bit—his friend and fellow Harvard philosopher George Santayana compared him to an "impetuous bird...flying aloft, but always stopped in mid-air, pulled back with a jerk by an invisible wire tethering him to a peg in the ground."[5] Such strands wove a thicket of complications. James was a believer in what he called "the old *Vox Populi*," but he feared the public was being manipulated by the "howling" press, particularly the yellow press. "The abominations of the press have literally surpassed all belief, and the word WAR in enormous capitals repeated for two months past on every front page of the 'great dailies' has at last to produce its suggestive effect," he wrote his brother Henry. War "must come, to relieve the tension," he explained. "The 'people' are really crazy for it, now, for its own sake." He singled out as "*absolutely insincere* villains" certain editors—"those of the New York *Journal* (a Harvard graduate millionaire named Hearst) and *World* ought to be hung higher than any criminals." (James may have recalled that he was one of the professors upon whom the undergraduate Hearst bestowed a chamber pot, its bowl decorated by the professor's photograph.) He was smart enough to spot another pitfall in the rush to fight Spain. "If war comes, what we *shall* do with Cuba, no one knows," he wrote Henry.[6]

James watched the war clouds gather from the boardwalk of Atlantic City, then a newly popular vacation spot where he had gone to earn a lecture fee. He found the "enormous flimsy cardboard town" to be a hollow place, though the sea air was "first rate" and the "surf strong today," he wrote his wife, Alice, on April 19. In his hotel room he munched on a fresh russet apple brought from home, and it reminded him of "the moral flavor of life." Feeling a pang of homesickness, he vowed to travel no more for paid lectures, and told Alice that he wished that he did not have to go on that weekend to speak at Bryn Mawr College outside Philadelphia. He may have been guilty of protesting too much to his faithful Alice. On that same day he wrote Susan Goldmark, one of the vivacious Goldmark sisters, to say that he held hope of seeing "the fair Pauline," the youthful object of his middle-aged crush, on his visit to Bryn Mawr.[7]

Buffeted by contradictory emotions—his mixed feelings about war, his inconstant feelings toward his wife—in his correspondence James displayed a jumble of common sense and wishful naivete. Writing from London, where the headlines also blazed, brother Henry expressed his "horror" that Spain might "bombard" Boston, but William calmly reassured him that such an attack was highly unlikely.[8] With Alice, he stuck to his theme that war would at least force America out of its "isolation" and possibly prove "educative." He was being too hopeful, and he probably knew it; one senses that he was playing the reassuring father figure with his brother and spouse. At the same time, in a letter to Mack Salter he was shrewd enough to "suspect" that only the "slimmest" evidence linked Spain to the sinking of the *Maine* and wise enough to again lament "the odd thing" that America was going to war without a plan for Cuba after Spain was driven from the island. How to reconcile such contradictory feelings? He tried to be optimistically, if wryly, philosophical: "Still, this blindness and instinctiveness is, I suppose, a measure of the greatness of our destiny!"[9]

Halfway around the world, American sailors were applying the final coat of dull gray paint to the last ship of the U.S. Navy's

Asiatic Squadron, anchored in a small bay on the Chinese coast.[10] Thanks to Assistant Secretary Roosevelt's warning cable of February 25, the seven warships were all fully provisioned and coaled. At about 7:00 p.m. on April 25, Commodore Dewey received a telegram from Secretary Long:

WAR HAS COMMENCED BETWEEN THE UNITED STATES AND SPAIN. PROCEED AT ONCE TO THE PHILIPPINE ISLANDS. COMMENCE OPERATIONS PARTICULARLY AGAINST THE SPANISH FLEET. YOU MUST CAPTURE VESSELS OR DESTROY. USE UTMOST ENDEAVOR.

In his autobiography Dewey would later write: "In the Hong Kong Club it was not possible to get bets, even at heavy odds, that our expedition would be a success. . . . I was told, after our officers had been entertained at dinner by a British regiment, that the universal remark among our hosts was to the effect: 'A fine set of fellows, but unhappily we shall never see them again.'"[11]

At the time, Dewey was privately much more sanguine about the coming battle. "I think it will be short work for us," he wrote his son in March. As Dewey's biographer Ronald Spector noted, the commodore's "judgment may have been influenced somewhat by Farragut's 'damn the torpedoes' attitude," but he also knew from experience that the underwater mines guarding the passages to Manila were probably decayed by the tropical seas and in any case useless in deep, fast-flowing water. Not unreasonably, he regarded the Spaniards as hapless.[12]

As the marine band aboard the flagship *Olympia* played "El Capitan," Dewey set course for Manila. While the little fleet steamed across the calm South China Sea, the bandsmen in their starched white uniforms worked through their repertoire:

Admiral Dewey (Library of Congress)

"Yankee Doodle Dandy," "Marching Through Georgia," and a new standard that would become a kind of theme song for the soldiers and sailors of the Spanish-American War, "There'll Be a Hot Time in the Old Town Tonight."[13] Eager for combat, crews began stripping wood that might catch fire and throwing it over the side. (The mess boys on one ship became a little carried away and threw most of the dining tables overboard, forcing the men to eat off the deck.) Dewey, one of the few officers who had actually seen battle (during the Civil War), took a calmer view and simply covered most of the *Olympia*'s woodwork with canvas and splinter nets. But he was no less determined to lead the way. When one of his officers (as it happened, his nephew Lieutenant William Windner) suggested that a supply ship enter the channel to Manila Bay first in order to set off any mines, Dewey declared, "Billy, I have waited sixty years for this opportunity. Mines or no mines, I am leading the squadron in myself."[14]

Flashes of heat lightning illuminated the heavy clouds over Manila Bay in the predawn hours of May 1. Otherwise, all was dark. The ships of the American fleet steamed past the island of Corregidor at the mouth of the bay, while the men lay tensely by their battle stations. Following centuries-old custom, decks were sprinkled with sand so sailors would not slip in their own blood. (The men complained that the sand got in their mouths and eyes.) A light shone in the distance...a few shots flashed from a nearby battery. Misses. An American ship returned fire. Silence.

Dressed in a tweed golfing cap, Dewey paced the bridge of the *Olympia*. He had thrown up his breakfast. In the gray light of dawn he could see the enemy fleet. With Spanish pride they were flying the empire's massive gold-and-red battle flags; with Spanish defeatism they had anchored close to shore so they would sink in shallow water. Shells sailed overhead while the Americans closed to 5,500 yards, and Dewey coolly gave the order to the *Olympia*'s captain that would make him famous: "You may fire when ready, Gridley." The scene that followed seemed more in keeping with opening day at a ballpark than with modern warfare. Flags broke out along the yardarms of the American ships, and bands aboard the *Olympia* and *Baltimore* struck up "The Star-Spangled Banner" while officers and sailors stood at attention. A great cheer went up, followed by the roar of cannon.

The carnage on the Spanish ships was terrible. Aboard the flagship, the *Reina Christina*, a shell landed on the officers' dining table that doubled as a surgery, slaughtering the wounded where they lay. Shrapnel whizzed through the rigging of the American ships as they paraded back and forth pouring shells into the Spanish fleet, but casualties were light—six wounded, none dead. At one point Captain Gridley informed Dewey that

The Battle of Manila Bay

ammunition was running out, and Dewey ordered the fleet to withdraw for breakfast. "For God's sake, don't let us stop now. To hell with breakfast," cried out a crewman. Gridley had been misinformed; the *Olympia* had plenty of ammo, and, breakfast over, returned to wrecking the Spanish fleet. The sailors were giddy with battlelust. An officer found the men in one powder magazine dressed in gunny sacks for skirts, doing the hula while they sang "There'll Be a Hot Time..."

The one-sided battle was over in time for lunch. All seven Spanish ships were burning or sunk, with over four hundred dead. In a final gloat, the marine band aboard the *Olympia* played Spanish songs, including the popular "La Paloma." Hearing the mocking tune across the water, the Spanish colonel in charge of a shore battery shot himself.[15]

"VICTORY!! Complete! Glorious!" cried the New York *Journal* on the morning of May 2 in the largest typeface available.[16] But

257

Hearst, not for the first time, was getting a little ahead of the facts. To prevent a call for Spanish reinforcements, Dewey had had the undersea telegraph cable between Manila and Hong Kong cut, and it took a week for a full account of the battle to reach Washington. Public suspense was immense; reports had filtered out through Madrid of a Spanish defeat, but at considerable cost to the American fleet. "Great nervousness is felt in Washington because nothing is heard from Dewey," the *Journal* reported on May 7.

That rainy morning in Washington a messenger awakened Secretary Long with news of a secret cable. The message was titled "McCulloch" — the name of Dewey's dispatch boat, which had finally made its way to Hong Kong. Long rushed into his office to read the ciphered message, patiently waited while the censors deleted sensitive details, and called a press conference. He emerged into his reception room to find a tumult of reporters. In his pleasant singsong voice, Long read the censored version, apparently without noticing that the reporters weren't paying full attention. In fact, they had already been handed an uncensored version by a visitor to the office that day — Lieutenant Colonel Theodore Roosevelt of the First U.S. Volunteer Cavalry, who had stopped by his old haunt at the Navy Department to wind up a few affairs. Peering over the shoulders of the cryptographers as they worked, Roosevelt had made some notes and passed them out to reporters, a final act of insubordination toward Long, who with his characteristic gentle good humor did not seem to mind.[17]

America went mad for Dewey and victory over Spain. A play titled *The Bride Elect* was playing at the Knickerbocker Theater on Broadway, and the show included the chorus "Unchain the Dogs of War!" Every night the audience stood to roar out the words with the cast. Demand for American flags exceeded supply; mills could not make them fast enough. The Stars and Stripes were everywhere, even on the cover of the sedate *Atlantic Monthly*, the favorite magazine of Boston mugwumps.[18] In Madison Square, Hearst threw a party in honor of Dewey that was attended by 100,000 people; they ate ice cream formed in the shape of battleships. Dewey's name was everywhere—in songs and poems, on chewing gum and cigarettes, even on the birth certificates of newborn boys. A laxative advertised with the commodore's portrait bore the legend "The 'Salt' of Salts." At the Metropolitan Club in Washington, a new item appeared on the menu: *Poulet Sauté à la Dewey*.[19]

Dewey was seen as the embodiment of "Anglo-Saxon valor," living proof that the "race" had not gone soft. The commodore (soon to be admiral) fostered the myth with newspapermen of the diffident hero so cool and superior that he could order his men to pause for breakfast in the heat of battle.[20] Privately, Dewey was not modest at all. His victory at Manila Bay, he wrote his son, "is one of the most remarkable naval battles of the ages" (an outrageous boast given the mismatch of the two fleets). Friends sought so many gold buttons from his uniform as keepsakes (or relics) that his white jacket was stripped bare, and he had to borrow buttons from other officers. In the Senate, Henry Cabot Lodge led the vote to bestow a bronze medal on every sailor in the Asiatic Squadron and to present Dewey with a diamond-encrusted, gold-hilted sword from Tiffany, much as Hearst had wanted to do for Máximo Gómez. Dewey, who happily accepted the offer, found the sword too heavy to wear except at White House receptions.[21] Even Henry Adams awakened from his nap. "As for war, it is a God-send to all the young men of America," he wrote Lizzie Cameron from Vienna, where he was touring. "Dewey's shooting has startled even Austria. We are already an Asian power!"[22]

Adams's drollery aside, Europe was taking notice. Great Britain, which less than three years earlier had been toying with war against the United States over Venezuela, buzzed with pro-American spirit. At the queen's birthday on May 24, a British regiment toasted both the Union Jack and the Stars and Stripes with the boast "Their colors never run."[23] Mr. Dooley, the fictional Irish barkeep of political satirist Finley Peter Dunne, tried to prick the balloon by wondering whether the Philippines were islands or canned goods. Still, American expansionism, once the province of Senator Lodge and a few of his closest friends, became the talk of the nation.[24]

Roosevelt wanted a little credit, too:

> *Washington, May 2, 1898*
>
> *My dear Commodore Dewey:*
>
> *Let me congratulate you with all my heart upon your magnificent work. You have made a name for the nation, and for the Navy, and yourself; and I can't say how pleased I am to think that I had any share in getting you the opportunity which you have used so well.*
>
> *Faithfully yours,*
> *ROOSEVELT*

"Didn't Admiral Dewey do wonderfully well?" Roosevelt wrote his old ranch manager, William Sewall. "I got him the position out there in Asia last year, and I had to beg hard to do it; and the reason I gave was that we might have to send him to Manila. And we sent him—and he went!"

On the same day he cabled his congratulations to Dewey, Roosevelt sent a telegram to Brooks Brothers, the gentleman's clothier in New York:

ORDINARY CAVALRY LIEUTENANT COLONEL'S UNIFORM IN BLUE CRAVENETTE.[25]

Congress had voted to raise three voluntary cavalry regiments "from among the wild riders and riflemen of the Rockies and the Great Plains," as Roosevelt would colorfully describe them in a later memoir.[26] In his newly purchased pocket "war diary," Roosevelt wrote on May 6: "Commissioned as Lt. Col. 1st U.S. Volunteer Cavalry. Wood as col., by my choice. The colonelcy was offered to me."[27]

It was indicative of Roosevelt's lingering insecurity that he felt a need to announce that the higher rank had been offered to him first. His decision was a wise one, though. Wood was Roosevelt's friend, family doctor, and playmate; hero of the Apache Wars; and a soldier's soldier, and Roosevelt was prudent to put himself under the command of someone who knew how to organize as well as fight, particularly since the army was nowhere near ready. During the several weeks between resigning as assistant secretary of the navy and joining his regiment, Roosevelt had set about learning the plans of the War Department. The task was "simple," Roosevelt drily, if hyperbolically, recorded in *An Autobiography*. "They had no plans."[28] Roosevelt's chief emotion during this period of waiting (and fretting and fidgeting) seems to have been indignation. His first entry in his war diary, for April 16, reads in part: "I have the navy in good shape. But the army is awful. The War Dept. is in utter confusion. Alger has no force whatever, & no knowledge of his department."[29]

A panic over the whereabouts of the Spanish fleet that had quickly followed the public's giddiness over declaring war had not made the military's job any easier. Roosevelt fumed over congressmen demanding navy ships to protect their cities along the coast and scoffed at wealthy people who wanted them anchored off their summer homes. He noted scornfully that Proper Bostonians were transferring their wealth to safe-deposit boxes in Worcester, well inland.[30]

Roosevelt was not venting only in his private musings. In his diary entry for May 5, Secretary Long described a visit from his former deputy: "He shouts at the top of his voice and wanders all over creation."[31] Roosevelt could barely contain himself when he called on a senior army general and found the man not slaving at his desk, but posing in a new uniform. The officer asked Roosevelt's opinion on the position of the pockets—were they attractive?—and told him he must procure some black boots for standing on hotel piazzas. Roosevelt gruffly replied that he had no intention of standing around in hotels, and in his memoir pointedly noted that he had never bought a dress uniform, "nothing but my service uniform."[32]

For his part, Secretary of War Alger seemed to sit in his office all day greeting old friends and visitors. Colonel Wood, by contrast, was a dynamo of organization and a wizard at outfoxing the bureaucracy. He went to the chief of ordnance to make sure his regiment would be armed with Krag-Jorgensen rifles, which burned smokeless powder. (Lacking enough modern rifles, the army was planning to outfit regular troops with "Krags" but volunteer troops with pre–Civil War era rifles that belched smoke. Wood understood that an outfit equipped with such relics would in all probability see little action, so he insisted on more modern weapons for his men; fortunately, the chief of ordnance was an old friend.) There were not enough sabers to go around, so Wood ordered machetes, more useful for cutting away Cuban jungle. With its genius for planning, the army was preparing to send men to the tropics in blue wool, but Wood ordered "stable uniforms," brown canvas fatigues for the undignified work of cleaning out stables, but of lighter weight and cooler than the heavy blues.[33]

There was no shortage of volunteers for the expeditionary force against Cuba. Indeed, the army was overwhelmed by offers of help. Among those turned away: "Buffalo Bill" Cody, notwithstanding his offer to raise an army of thirty thousand Indian braves, and a Colorado matron named Martha Shute, who proposed raising a cavalry regiment made up solely of women.[34]

Roosevelt had been thinking about raising a band of "harum scarum rough riders" since a border incident with Mexico in 1886. According to Roosevelt the idea of organizing a cowboy regiment had originated, a bit incongruously, with his German friend, later ambassador to the United States, Baron Hermann Speck von Sternberg. The former Prussian army officer made the suggestion one day while the two men were talking about the Wild West and amusing themselves target shooting at Roosevelt's estate in Oyster Bay.[35] Pony Express riders were first called "rough riders," and the term had later been employed by Buffalo Bill's Wild West Circus. Roosevelt later protested that the name Rough Riders was a press creation, and he sniffed that the label had been cheapened by the "hippodrome," but at the time he didn't protest very much.[36]

The First Volunteer Cavalry numbered over a thousand men. About fifty of them were well-to-do easterners (and three were New York City policemen).[37] It became a source of enormous and everlasting satisfaction for Roosevelt that he was able to recruit not only cowhands and ranchers but gentlemen sportsmen. Newspaper reporters gleefully saw the potential for good copy in his regiment of cowboys and "swells." Lincoln Steffens, one of the new breed of investigative journalists for whom President Roosevelt would later coin the term "muckraker," beseeched Roosevelt to list for publication some of the "swellest" names in his troop. A bit haughtily, but unable to suppress his pride and desire for publicity, Roosevelt telegraphed back on May 4:

HARDLY KNOW WHAT YOU WOULD CALL THE SWELLEST NAMES. THINK IT WOULD BE A LITTLE BIT BAD FOR THE MEN TO SAY WHICH THEY WERE, BUT THERE ARE A NUMBER OF KNICKERBOCKER AND SOMERSET CLUB, AS WELL AS HARVARD AND YALE MEN GOING AS TROOPERS, TO BE EXACTLY ON A LEVEL WITH THE COWBOYS.[38]

In his memoir *The Rough Riders*, he rattled them off like Emerson's young Lords of Life: Woodbury Kane, Harvard footballer, polo player, America's Cup yachtsman; Dudley Dean, "perhaps the best quarterback who ever played on the Harvard eleven"; "Yale men like Waller the high jumper, and Garrison and Girard; and with Princeton men like Devereux and Channing, the football players; with Larned, the tennis player; with Craig Wadsworth, the steeple-chase rider; with Joe Stevens, the crack polo player; with Hamilton Fish, the ex-captain of the Columbia crew..."[39] To sister Corinne he wrote, "I have about 25 'gentlemen rankers' going with me—five from the Knickerbocker Club, and a dozen clean-cut, stalwart young fellows from Harvard, such fine boys."[40]

Wood had gone ahead to San Antonio to establish a training

camp for the regiment. Anxious that his young Lancelots might not submit graciously to the discipline of KP and cleaning latrines, Roosevelt gathered most of the easterners at an army depot in Washington before they shipped out and lectured them sternly: They must not shirk the lowliest duty, and they must not complain, ever. If they could not accept these terms, they should step aside now. "Not a man of them backed out," Roosevelt later wrote. "Not one of them failed to do his whole duty."[41]

Roosevelt had just time to take some last rides through the blooming countryside with Edith, whose health had continued to improve; to play with his "cunning" children; to buy extra life insurance; and to commune with the Lodges. "The Lodges are much broken, especially Nannie, as Bay went to his ship today," Roosevelt wrote Bamie on May 8. "But really we're all fake heroes; we sha'n't see any fighting to speak of." His pessimism about this sprang from worries about whether the fighting might last long enough. Again and again in his last letters before departing Washington, including one to President McKinley, he returned to his fear that he would not see action before the war ended. He was secretly relieved when the Spanish Atlantic fleet, rumored to be at large, was reported back in Cádiz. That meant no decisive naval battle could prematurely end the war—before Roosevelt could get there.[42]

Roosevelt arrived in San Antonio at 7:30 a.m. on May 15, having closely studied a slim book called *Drill Regulations for Cavalry, United States Army, 1896* on the train ride from Washington.[43] He was dressed in a fawn-colored uniform with canary yellow facings and accompanied by his "man," a black servant named Marshall.[44] He had not even had time for a brief pilgrimage to the nearby Alamo, where his hero Davy Crockett had died in combat over a half century earlier.

A few Rough Riders were gathered at the station, warily eyeing their new lieutenant colonel. One Oklahoma trooper recalled that the men were suspicious: Roosevelt was said to be a rich cop from New York—not a promising résumé to hardscrabble westerners who sometimes lived outside the law. Worse, he wore glasses; he looked more like a "dude" than a soldier. But Roosevelt had heard it all before. In the Dakota Territory he had been mocked as "Four Eyes" and for shouting "Come hither!" to ranch hands.[45] It had not stopped him then, and he was determined not to let it stop him now.

Roosevelt fell in love with his regiment, or the idea of his regiment, almost overnight. By May 19 he was writing Lodge, "You would be amused to see three Knickerbocker club men cooking and washing dishes for one of the New Mexico companies.... The dust, heat and mosquitoes prevent existence being at all sybaritic. I am heartily enjoying it nevertheless."[46] So, apparently, were most of the East Coast men, some of whom reportedly had brought walking sticks, golf clubs, evening clothes, and, in at least the case of one greenhorn private from Fifth Avenue, his valet. All luxuries were discarded or sent home while the men drilled under the hot Texas sky. There were a few mishaps. A try at a cavalry charge led by Roosevelt turned into a stampede. Several riders were thrown as their horses collided and bucked and reared.[47]

By and large Wood let Roosevelt train the men.[48] Known as "Old Poker Face" for his low-key sternness, Wood was a seasoned commander, an old hand at garrison life who understood that good sanitation counted for more than fancy horsemanship. He seemed unbothered by the cult of Roosevelt fostered by the press. He had arrived in San Antonio a fortnight before

Roosevelt to be greeted by a big sign that read "This way to Camp of Roosevelt's Rough Riders." He said not a word.[49]

Returning to camp from town one day, Wood encountered Roosevelt in a buoyant mood, saying that the day's drill had gone so well he had bought his boys some beer. Again, Wood said nothing, but that night at the officers' mess the colonel described what could happen when officers began drinking with their men, and suggested that no officer who did so was worthy of his commission. Silence fell over the table. That night Roosevelt went to Wood's tent and apologized profusely.[50]

On Sunday, May 22, the Rough Riders mounted up at the local state fairground for a reading of the Articles of War. A photograph of the occasion shows Roosevelt on his horse in the first rank of officers, his mount lined up slightly ahead of Wood's, as if he couldn't wait to lead the charge. It was the sort of mild effrontery Wood wisely tolerated. He could see that the men were warming to the boundless energy and bursting democratic spirit that the lieutenant colonel's upper-class manners could not disguise. Under fluffy white clouds that Sunday morning, the men sang "Onward, Christian Soldiers" and "A Mighty Fortress Is Our God." Town girls lined up to kiss them. Some of the men had names like "Rattlesnake Pete," and a few arrived with notched pistols. The more unruly were starting to slip out at night to get drunk; Sergeant Hamilton Fish, the former Columbia crew captain, reportedly had to hold off an assault on the beer stand at the fairgrounds. Wood appreciated that he needed to get his men to the fight or else, as he put it, they would start to fight each other.[51]

"Wood is the ideal man for Colonel," Roosevelt wrote Lodge on May 25. Some of the other officers "are very poor." Roosevelt added, "I wonder how Bay is enjoying himself? I do not suppose either he or I will see much fighting." But he swept away incipient self-pity with purpose. He was determined to use his connections to make sure he would not be left out. "If they begin to send troops to Cuba, I shall wire you to see that we go. We are all ready now to move, and will render a good account of ourselves. I earnestly hope that no truce will be granted."[52]

That same day deliverance came. A telegram arrived from the War Department inquiring when the First Volunteer Cavalry would be ready to leave. Wood telegraphed back AT ONCE. The sound of shouting brought troopers running out of their tents to see Wood and Roosevelt "embracing like schoolboys," as one account put it. Roosevelt broke into a little jig, dancing in front of his colonel with his hat in his hand and his hand on his hip. The men took up their cry:

Rough, tough, we're the stuff,
We want to fight and we can't get enough!
Whoopee![53]

16

The Rocking-Chair Period

"I want to go, but I should be a fool."

H OW DO YOU LIKE the *Journal's* War?" Hearst asked his readers on May 8, the day his newspaper published the official dispatches of Dewey's great victory in Manila. He printed the rhetorical question twice, as the "ears" on either side of the newspaper's logo, just beneath his latest, war-swollen circulation claim: 1,468,759 more readers than any other paper in the country.[1]

With his staff, too, Hearst spoke of "our war."[2] He was not just showing off. From the *Journal* building Hearst loved to stage fireworks displays and paid for bands to lead patriotic marches at lunchtime—that is, until the crowds broke into off-color beer songs, and free concerts had to be canceled. But Hearst also had grander designs. In a memoir, his fast-talking European correspondent James Creelman reprinted a copy of a signed letter he had received from his boss that suggests the scale of Hearst's hubris, as well as his willingness to spend freely to flout international law. Spanish admiral Manuel Camara had entered the Mediterranean in late May with a large fleet bound for Suez and ultimately to attack Dewey's small squadron at Manila. At his office in London the *Journal's* man received the following missive:

New York Journal
W. R. Hearst

May 28, 1898

Dear Mr. Creelman,

*I wish you would at once make preparations, so that in case
the Spanish fleet actually starts for Manila we will be prepared
to buy or charter some English tramp steamer on the Eastern
end of the Mediterranean and take her to some narrow and
inaccessible portion of the Suez Canal and sink her where she
will obstruct the passage of the Spanish fleet.*[3]

Creelman never did have to arrange this outrageous demonstration of "the journalism that acts." The fleet turned around and steamed back to Cádiz to protect the Spanish coastline from American attack. But there can be no doubt that Hearst would have willingly written the check and risked the international uproar. In addition to demonstrating Hearst's patriotism, the ensuing flap would likely have sold even more papers than the rescue of Evangelina Cisneros.

Revisionist historians have gone to some pains to disprove the notion of "Hearst's War." The war fever that consumed the country in the spring of 1898 had many causes, to be sure, of which the yellow press was only one. It may be that McKinley did not even read "the yellows," as one historian has pointed out. But it is also true that he read six or seven daily newspapers heavily influenced by Hearst's publication — not just the polemical headlines but the reporting turned up by Hearst's correspondents. A good deal of that reporting was factually unreliable or sensationalized, but it was not wrong about the suffering of the Cuban people. Congress derived most of its knowledge from newspapers, the only real information source of that time;

meanwhile, the Spanish saw the American press, particularly the *Journal*, as sorcery. Prime Minister Antonia Cánovas del Castillo told Creelman, "The newspapers in your country seem to be more powerful than the government."[4]

Hearst was willing to reach deep into his mother's pockets to finance the *Journal*'s coverage. In February he began flaunting his "war fleet"—the yachts *Anita* and *Buccaneer*, and the tug *Echo*. The flotilla grew to include about a dozen dispatch boats and steamers owned or chartered by Hearst plying the Caribbean as the invasion of Cuba neared.[5] According to Hearst editor Willis Abbott, the newsroom virtually emptied as men were sent to cover the war; by the end the *Journal* had dispatched forty reporters, editors, and photographers to Cuba. The expense far exceeded the revenue from circulation gains. It was a good thing the war did not go on for two years, wrote Arthur Brisbane, editor of Hearst's evening paper, because the *Journal*—along with its competitors—would have been bankrupted.[6]

The war inflamed the already fierce rivalry between Hearst's *Journal* and Joseph Pulitzer's *World*. Pulitzer canceled his annual summer vacation in Bar Harbor and spent heavily to catch Hearst, as the two papers soared over the million mark in daily circulation. But the crafty Brisbane, a brilliant newspaperman whose salary was dependent entirely on circulation, outfoxed Pulitzer. Newspapers of that era routinely lifted stories from one another. When Brisbane took over Hearst's *Evening Journal*, the editor joked that he had only two correspondents, and one of them was paid to stand outside the *World* to snatch up a copy of every edition so the *Journal* could lift its contents (without, of course, ever crediting the other paper). As Hearst began spending with abandon, the roles reversed. Unable to keep up with Hearst's war machine, Pulitzer's paper began filching more and more news content from its rival. So Brisbane decided to play a little trick. He solemnly printed a report that an Austrian artilleryman, Colonel Reflip W. Thenuz, had been killed in the Spanish trenches. The *World* promptly published this information as if it were its own reporting, and Brisbane snapped the trap. Reflip W. Thenuz, Brisbane informed the public, was an anagram for "We pilfer the news." The *Journal* cheekily began soliciting design proposals for a "Thenuz Memorial."[7]

Readers laughed, none with more glee than Hearst. This was exactly the sort of prank he had loved since his days on the Harvard *Lampoon*. But he was far more than a practical joker. His critics saw in him a pathological wantonness and compared him to a wicked child who sets his family's house ablaze because he wants to see the fire engines arrive. E. L. Godkin accused Hearst of the basest cynicism, of exploiting suffering on a grotesque scale. The mugwump editor was especially put off when the wife of a senator junketing to Cuba as a *Journal* "commissioner" died of a heart attack and Hearst had the gall to say she had died of a broken heart from seeing so many suffering children. Such critical clucking made no real impression on Hearst, who saw himself as a romantic hero, not an exploiter. Yet occasional sniggers likely had more impact. Taunting a man as a girl or as a mere boy was a vicious put-down in an age that prized manliness defined by strength and gallantry—as Hearst knew from the japes of his own cartoonists mocking McKinley in a bonnet. A local gossip sheet, the *Town Topics*, took to calling Hearst "Willy Boy," a figure in short pants playing at war while real men fought.[8]

More galling to Hearst was Theodore Roosevelt's sudden fame as a Rough Rider. Hearst's newspaper had been wallowing in the spectacle of clubmen and cowboys training together for war ("Another Millionaire Joins Teddy Roosevelt's Terrors," the *Journal* headlined on May 10, over a picture of Joseph Stevens, son of a French duchess, on his polo pony).[9] But Roosevelt, always maddeningly a step ahead of Hearst, had gotten a jump on getting to the looming fight, and Hearst needed to catch up.[10]

In late May the *Journal*'s proprietor wrote McKinley offering to create and equip, at his own expense, a cavalry regiment—and to enlist himself as a private. Seeing more risk than reward in encouraging Hearst, the president declined. Hearst next turned to the navy, offering his 130-foot yacht, *Buccaneer*, as a fully armed gunboat, with Hearst in command. The navy gladly took the yacht, guns and all, but told Hearst he would have to apply for a commission.[11] Dutifully journeying to Washington, Hearst was kept waiting outside the office of Secretary of War Alger and finally told his application would be taken up in due course by a review board. Hearst was embarrassed and vexed: waiting on a bench in a public reception room was painful for such a shy man. Hearst could not understand why his fellow plutocrat John Jacob Astor, Jr., who had given the navy a yacht and the army an artillery battery, had been rewarded with a commission as a lieutenant colonel while Hearst hadn't even been made an ensign. (His navy commission finally came through after the war was over.) In all likelihood Hearst was being punished by the administration for all those mocking cartoons of McKinley and Hanna during the 1896 campaign.[12]

As usual, Hearst took matters into his own hands and turned to Creelman, who had recently returned from London in order to join the Hearst forces advancing on Cuba. Creelman's orders were to charter a steamer and outfit her as a flagship worthy of the commander in chief. Hearst's men loaded enough food and supplies aboard the *Sylvia* for an invasion, along with medicine chests (acetate of lead for mosquito bites, petroleum jelly for sunburn, and rhubarb pills for indigestion) and chemicals for a darkroom. The two Willson sisters, Hearst's inamorata Millicent and her older sister Anita, came along, dressed in sailor suits. Also onboard were two motion picture cameramen. With his genius for moving the masses, Hearst had seen the potential of Thomas Alva Edison's kinescope, a kind of magic-lantern precursor to the movie camera. As a regular in burlesque houses, Hearst had recently witnessed the sensation caused by a crude movie of two battleships doing nothing more than steaming along in grainy black and white. Audiences had gone wild over this, and over a fuzzy three-minute film of the funeral procession for the dead sailors of the *Maine*.[13]

If Hearst wrote his mother to say good-bye, there is no record of it. What we do have is correspondence between Phoebe Hearst and her treasurer, Edward Clark, in which Mrs. Hearst expresses her displeasure that Willie is spending $5,000 to $10,000 to arm a yacht for the navy—money he does not have, she protests. Her son had already lost roughly $8 million in the three years he'd owned the *Journal*. She also worried that her son would get himself killed sailing to Cuba. She should have "no anxiety as to his safety," the treasurer tried to reassure her. The military would not let him get close enough to the fighting. Not for the first time, the moneyman underestimated the ambition of Mrs. Hearst's boy.[14]

Even Henry Cabot Lodge, well into middle age at forty-eight, felt the pull. He and his Brahmin contemporaries were hearing an old drumbeat. The martial spirit was rekindling in Henry L. Higginson, the businessman who until recently had opposed intervention in Cuba largely for commercial reasons. "God!" he exclaimed, in a babbling stream of consciousness. "I believe the whole country would enlist if need be. Where I sit in the [Knickerbocker] club—sports—loafers—athletes—dandies—raised in cotton wool—a rose garden—scoffers—what you please—a little club—& 40 men have already gone, 11% of the club, which has many old men.... Of course, I feel like an old fool, feel so & long to go into the service." Lodge replied only slightly more soberly, "It is splendid and most uplifting the way our boys are going in everywhere. I want to go, but I should be a fool, I suppose, and only fill a place some younger man could fill better, while here I can be of some use."

That he could be of use was of no doubt. Lodge was overjoyed that his Large Policy was becoming American policy, embraced by the White House and Congress alike "at last," as he gloated to Roosevelt on May 24. Lodge wanted to "sweep" up Cuba, Puerto Rico, the Philippines, and Hawaii, annex them all.[15] "The people do not want to give up anything," he wrote one friend. "The American flag is up and it must stay," he wrote another.[16] Lodge was amused to learn that the commercial interests, especially the big mill owners, were coming around. "[They] see a pecuniary advantage to themselves in empire. That settles the question," wrote Lodge's Boston friend and frequent correspondent George Lyman.

There was but one holdout. "The opposition now comes exclusively from Reed, who is straining every nerve" to thwart expansionism, Lodge wrote Roosevelt.[17] Prodded by the pineapple growers, Congress was about to turn Hawaii into a U.S. territory. Lyman wrote Lodge that Speaker Reed's opposition "has been a matter of extreme regret and annoyance to all his friends. I can't understand it."[18] He also teased Lodge about the consequences of mixing empire with democracy. "By the way," he deadpanned, "when we get the Philippines, I suppose you will have seated on one side of you a little black pigmy from the hills of those islands, and on the other side, a cultivated negro from Hawaii."[19]

Lodge saw in the war against Spain another advantage: the chance to finally heal the wounds between North and South by uniting the country in common cause. To that end he persuaded Secretary of War Alger to allow the men of the Massachusetts Sixth Infantry, on their way from Boston to Washington, to disembark from the train and march through the city of Baltimore. In the spring of 1861 in slave-owning Baltimore, some of the first blood of the Civil War was spilled by angry mobs attacking the same regiment as it passed through the city on the way to defend the nation's capital. This time around the regimental band played "Dixie" and the crowds cheered wildly. A floral tribute was presented with the inscription "Maryland and Massachusetts: Flowers Not Bullets."[20] Lodge wrote his mother that day, May 22, that he had slipped away from his duties in Washington to witness the spectacle. "It was 'roses, roses all the way'—flags, cheers, excited crowds," Lodge reported. "Tears were in my eyes. I never felt so moved in my life. The war of 1861 was over at last."[21]

On Sunday, May 29, the First U.S. Volunteer Cavalry boarded trains for the long trip from San Antonio, Texas, to Tampa, Florida. From there they would embark for Cuba. For four hot, dusty days, through "interminable delays," Roosevelt recorded in his diary, the trains creaked through the southeastern United States. And yet the procession felt like a victory march. Huge crowds lined the tracks. "They brought us flowers; they brought us watermelons and other fruits, and sometimes jugs and pails of milk," Roosevelt recalled in his memoir. "Everywhere we saw the Stars and Stripes, and everywhere we were told, half-laughing, by grizzled ex-Confederates that they had never dreamed in the bygone days of bitterness to greet the old flag as they now were greeting it, and to send their sons, as now they were sending them, to fight and die under it."[22]

Roosevelt occupied his "few spare moments" reading a book called *Superiorité des Anglo-Saxons* by a French military expert, Edmund Demolin, who extolled the American spirit of individual initiative while lamenting the deadening "militarism" of the Europeans.[23] Roosevelt needed little encouragement in this department; he was well practiced at clashing with (and working around) military bureaucracy. Still, he was bracing himself. He understood that America's sleepy little army of Indian trackers was readying, none too efficiently or expertly, for one of history's most challenging military exercises, the amphibious invasion of a hostile foreign shore.

The Rough Riders arrived in Tampa on June 5 to find an army undisciplined and unready. "No words can paint the confusion," Roosevelt jotted in his diary.[24] A single train track was backed up for miles outside the sandy Florida resort town and its port. No one was there to greet the Rough Riders or to tell them where to camp. For twenty-four hours no food was forthcoming; officers had to provision their men out of their own pockets.[25] Earlier arrivals had set up sloppy, filthy camps; another volunteer regiment had made the tenderfoot's mistake of digging latrines just to windward of the tents. Wood, by contrast, was a model of order and discipline. He quickly set up ranks of tents, along with kitchens and "sinks" that were "as neat as a surgeon's tray," according to Richard Harding Davis, the dapper correspondent who, along with the rest of the press corps, quickly descended on the Rough Riders' camp to see how the cowpokes and "gentlemen dudes" were getting along.[26]

Embarking for Cuba at Port Tampa (Theodore Roosevelt Collection, Houghton Library, Harvard University)

The temperature was in the nineties, but a low haze occluded the sun, and mercifully few mosquitoes were carried in on the sea breeze.[27] A mile away, like a palace rising from the desert, stood an enormous structure topped with silver minarets. The Tampa Bay Hotel was a Moorish monstrosity known as "Plant's Folly," named after railroad tycoon Henry Plant, who wanted to entice the wealthy to travel by rail to the sandy, piney Gulf Shore. As peacocks strutted in the exotic gardens, the piazzas, normally empty in summer, filled with officers and foreign military attachés in colorful uniforms and pith helmets, gossiping and scanning the bulletin board for messages, waiting for something to happen. This was "the rocking chair period of the war," wrote correspondent Davis.[28]

Davis, who was on assignment for the New York *Herald,*

introduced the British military attaché, Captain Arthur Lee, to Roosevelt. ("Good heavens, don't you know Theodore Roosevelt? You must meet him this very minute," Davis told Lee. "He is the biggest thing here and the most typical American living.")[29] Roosevelt, who privately scorned Davis as a poseur and "a cad," was more like the reporter than he cared to admit. Both were dandies and expert self-promoters, and in any case the two men were useful to each other. Roosevelt made sure the correspondent was always nearby; he hoped that Davis would make him a legend. Familiar with the society swells among the Rough Riders, Davis was helpful in another way: the men of Troop K—the eastern dudes—used his room at the hotel to bathe.[30]

Not a professional soldier, Roosevelt was used to distinguishing between gentlemen and nongentlemen, not officers and men. He promptly offended regular army officers by inviting two enlisted men to his dinner table (both were New York clubmen; one was his family friend Bob Ferguson). But his most frequent and welcome companion was Edith, recently arrived by train from New York.

For several weeks Edith had been stoically playing the role of warrior's wife. "I do not want you to miss me or think of me for it is all in a day's work and we have had more happiness in eleven years than most people have had in a lifetime," she wrote her husband on May 23. She was relieved to report that little Ted was better, though clingy, and that she would soon move him from his quarters with a nurse to a bed in his father's dressing room. "The children vary their prayers for you tonight," she told him. "Kermit petitioned that the war should not last, as it was an expense to the country. Ted scornfully commented, 'costs so many brave men you should say.'"[31]

Edith arrived in Tampa on June 2, eager for some fleeting time with her husband before he embarked for Cuba. The next morning she wrote her sister, "I am writing in my thinnest nightgown in a comfortable room with a bath room adjoining." Roosevelt, who had not slept much for four days, had been awaiting her under the hotel rotunda. "He has grown thin but looks very well and rugged," wrote Edith. She fed him, bathed him, and took him to bed. Colonel Wood had made a dispensation for Roosevelt to spend the night with his wife. Edith's doctor as well as Roosevelt's commander, he knew that Edith had been unable to enjoy the marital bed during her long confinement recovering from childbirth and infection. Nevertheless, at 4:00 a.m. Roosevelt crept out in time to join his troops for reveille.[32]

On June 6 Edith and all the diplomats and foreign attachés who had made their way to Tampa were invited to watch cavalry troops staging a charge across the flat sands. The Rough Riders galloped past waving machetes instead of sabers. Richard Davis was moved by the sight of two thousand men on horseback moving in orderly ranks; he knew he was witnessing something that could not last, a vestige of a vanishing age of warfare.[33]

That morning Roosevelt learned that the Rough Riders would not be riding in Cuba after all—there was room only for their officers' horses on the transports. Far worse, Roosevelt believed for an hour or two that he would be stranded in Tampa—a "bitter" moment, he recalled. But then came new orders. He was relieved to report to Lodge that he would be among the six hundred or so Rough Riders embarking. He was philosophical about his men losing their mounts. "We should be glad to go on all fours rather than to not go at all," he wrote Lodge.[34] Four Rough Rider troops (about three hundred men) were left behind. Roosevelt saw some of the abandoned men weeping.[35]

The Fifth Army Expeditionary Force was commanded by

an old Indian hunter, Brigadier General William Shafter. The obese, gouty Shafter, whose fighting days were long behind him, was bewildered by changing messages from Washington. "When will you leave? Answer at once!" demanded headquarters in late May.[36] But "hurry up" was quickly followed by "not so fast." Shafter, it seemed, was caught in the crossfire between impatient politicians who wanted war — and right away — versus overcautious military men complaining that the army was short of ammunition and transport. Though the top brass could not say so very loudly, they also dreaded arriving on a tropical island just as the fever season was beginning.

The wild card was the Spanish fleet, which for a time disappeared from view somewhere in the Caribbean. The American navy had engaged in some desultory shelling of Cuban forts (in one case while the ship's band on deck played a German operetta), but the real prize — the fleet of Admiral Pascual Cervera y Topete — had escaped them. Cervera knew his once powerful, now decrepit flotilla was doomed and that his mission was quixotic, driven more by pride than realistic hope. But he kept the Americans guessing until, at the end of May, his ships were sighted slipping into the well-protected harbor at Santiago de Cuba, Cuba's second city, located at the southeastern end of the island. A sudden flurry of orders and counterorders emanated from Washington, adding to the already considerable confusion in Tampa.[37]

General Shafter was sipping coffee after dinner at the Tampa Bay Hotel on the evening of June 7 when he was summoned to the telegraph office. "You will sail immediately..." the White House commanded.[38] At the Rough Rider camp the men raced to fold their tents and gather their belongings. By midnight they were assembled at the rail line, waiting for their assigned train to the port of Tampa, eight miles to the south.

No train came. At 3:00 a.m. the men were ordered to move to a different position. Still no train. At dawn Roosevelt and Wood halted a coal train headed north and commandeered it. After some strenuous negotiations with the engineer, the six hundred men and officers clambered aboard, hauling their officers' horses up the gangway, and chugged south. Hearing the hallooing and yelling of the Rough Riders (now caked in coal dust), a soldier in a volunteer regiment spotted Roosevelt, grinning broadly as he stood in the open door of a freight car, his blue bandana flapping in the breeze.[39]

Chaos greeted them at the end of the line. The track spur extended onto a mile-long harbor quay, with ships docked and moored all around. The heavy-laden freight cars were somehow missing the bills of lading listing their contents. Some ten thousand soldiers jostled about, separated from their equipment and supplies with no way to find them.

Wood and Roosevelt had been told if they did not secure a ship, they risked being left behind. Searching anxiously through the milling crowd, by accident the Rough Rider commanders found the harbormaster, and the overwhelmed official blithely told them to take the steamer *Yucatan*, moored out in the harbor. Somehow Wood found a small launch and headed out to the ship while Roosevelt marched the men toward the gangway. Informed that the *Yucatan* had already been assigned to two other regiments—the Army's Second regulars and the New York Seventy-first volunteers—Roosevelt looked around and quickly realized there would not be room enough on the old tramp steamer for all three regiments, or even half that many men.

Never one to walk when he could run, Roosevelt promptly double-timed his troops around the volunteer regiment. He ordered a detachment of Rough Riders to surround the gangplank in order to keep the Army regulars away. It was a sticky moment: Roosevelt was outranked by the commander of the regulars. Spotting Wood slowly pulling toward the berth aboard the *Yucatan*, Roosevelt "played for time," as he later recalled. He engaged in a shouted dialogue with his commander (actually Roosevelt couldn't hear Wood, who was too far away), and bluffed that Wood—who outranked the regular army man—had ordered him to hold the gangway. (It was all "rather lawless," Roosevelt later admitted, or perhaps boasted, to Lodge.)[40]

The Rough Riders climbed aboard the *Yucatan* along with a few companies of regulars. As the New York volunteers disconsolately marched away from the overcrowded pier, Roosevelt saw two young men standing on the boardwalk holding a large, unwieldy camera. Roosevelt asked who they were. They were the Vitagraph Company, wishing to go to Cuba to take moving pictures of the war. At moments like this Roosevelt's mind worked exactly like William Randolph Hearst's. "I can't take care of a regiment," he said. "But I might be able to handle two more."[41]

His six hundred men were aboard, but there they sat, day after sweltering day, under the semitropical sun. A false sighting of the Spanish fleet by an edgy navy lookout had left the deeply unhygienic vessels and their human cargoes festering at anchor in Tampa Bay. Roosevelt and the other officers lived in relative comfort in a cabin on deck, where they were served fresh meat and vegetables. (Roosevelt had his manservant, Marshall, onboard.) But Roosevelt noted to Lodge that he had to step over soldiers lying on deck, while down in the lower hold the scene was "unpleasantly suggestive of the Black Hole of Calcutta." The water around the ship was a "sewer." The men were issued "horrible stuff" called "canned fresh beef" that was "nauseating" and inedible, even to the half-starved.[42]

Roosevelt wrote Bamie that he feared an outbreak of disease, and he beseeched Lodge (as he routinely did in his private correspondence) to use his influence with the White House: "Do, old man, try to see that the expedition is no longer deferred."[43] On the fifth day Roosevelt's friend Winthrop Chanler found him sitting at a table in a little hotel on the pier, where Roosevelt had gone in search of news. Wearing the uniform of a colonel in the Cuban army, Chanler was in Tampa looking for his own passage to the island. The two club brothers commiserated. Roosevelt was "dirty and hungry," Chanler reported to their mutual chum Lodge, "unable to get anything he wanted....He gnashed his teeth at the whole disgraceful performance of embarkation." And yet, Chanler wrote, "I cannot but feel that his political future has been benefited rather than hurt by his sacrifice."

On the sixth day, June 13, word came: the coast was clear, the Spanish threat judged a false alarm. With men cheering and shouting on deck and in the rigging, the thirty-two transports carrying the Fifth Army weighed anchor and set off. The *Yucatan* nearly collided with another transport but slipped safely down the channel. Correspondent Davis noted that the public had given up on a grand farewell. "Only three colored women and a pathetic group of perspiring stevedores and three soldiers" waved good-bye.[44]

The mighty armada made it all the way to the foot of the bay, where it anchored for the night. Finally, on June 14, as Roosevelt recalled, "We were all again under way, and in the afternoon the great fleet steamed southeast until Tampa Light sank in the distance."[45]

For a week the ships heaved and rolled south and east, the black-hulled merchant vessels lumbering along in three columns, protected by a dozen warships clad in their dull gray paint. At night the brilliantly lit convoy would have made perfect targets for Spanish torpedo boats, had there been any.

"Today we are steaming southward through a sapphire sea, wind-rippled, under an almost cloudless sky," Roosevelt wrote his sister Corinne on the second day out. On deck the Second Regiment's band played the ubiquitous "There'll Be a Hot Time"—"where you knowed ev'rybody and dey all knowed you, / and you've got a rabbit's foot to keep away de hoodoo," sang the troopers, mimicking minstrel singers. As the band swung into "The Star-Spangled Banner" the men stood and somberly took off their felt campaign hats.

Roosevelt's mood was ecstatic, almost messianic. "It is a great historical expedition, and I thrill to feel that I am part of it," he wrote Corinne. "If we fail, of course we share the fate of all who fail, but if we are allowed to succeed (for we certainly shall succeed, if allowed) we have scored the first great triumph in what will be a world movement."[46] After sunset Roosevelt stood at the rail with Captain William "Bucky" O'Neill of Arizona, a former sheriff who had become a friend. It pleased Roosevelt that O'Neill had not only faced down desperados but had also read deeply in the classics and could discuss "the mysteries which lie behind courage." (Roosevelt had spotted O'Neill as a soul mate when he overheard the sheriff discussing Aryan word roots and Balzac with the Rough Riders' surgeon, Dr. Robert Church, a former Princeton football player.) O'Neill, who had taken many risks in life, told Roosevelt that he felt the odds were now against him. But as he looked out at the Southern Cross in the black night sky, he mused, "Who would not risk his life for a star?"[47]

On the morning of June 20 the men saw the blue-green mountains of Cuba rising from the sea and stood transfixed by the land they had been sent to liberate. The rainy season was coming, and the perfect weather turned gray; low clouds and squalls swept in. A small boat came alongside bearing a navy ensign with a message for the ship's master. The men watched, smiling, as Roosevelt broke into one of his jubilant heel-toe dances. "We land tomorrow!" he cried. "Whoopee!" In the officers' mess that night a toast was drunk: "To the officers — may they get killed, wounded, or promoted." At 3:30 a.m., before the first light of dawn, the bugles sounded.[48]

17

Hurrying to Empire

"Here were champagne and lively companionship."

W HILE ROOSEVELT WAS steaming across the Caribbean dreaming of the "first great triumph" of a "world movement," Reed was losing his struggle to hold off a new era of American expansionism—or as he called it, imperialism. Reed used the loaded word to evoke the "land hunger" of the European powers vying to carve up the nonwhite world. He tried to point out the irony of a nation created in the name of freedom seizing colonies of its own. Reed was hardly alone in seeing the hypocrisy—in Boston an "Anti-Imperialist League" was forming—but the Speaker was increasingly isolated in official Washington. In May, while congressmen wildly celebrated Dewey's victory at Manila Bay, Reed had been somber. "This is a serious matter," he said to a newspaperman. "Dewey ought to sail right away from that place. It'll make us trouble for all time to come if he does not."[1]

McKinley, while naturally cautious, had his finger in the political wind. The president covetously eyed Hawaii. "We need Hawaii just as much and a good deal more than we did California," he told his aide George Cortelyou on May 4.[2] The obstacle was Reed. From his chair, the Speaker refused to call on anyone offering the

Hawaii annexation resolution. A few lawmakers still feared the Czar. (The most strident Senate proponent of expansionism in the name of Anglo-Saxon supremacy, Albert Beveridge of Indiana, shied away from trying to change the "Gibraltar-like mind and will of the Speaker.")[3] But the newspapers—the respectable press as well as the yellow journals—were in full cry against Reed's dictatorial domination of the People's Chamber.[4]

Reed knew that his intransigence was untenable. A decade earlier he had built his name and his power by arguing the unfairness of the minority thwarting the majority to smash the old silent filibuster. Now he looked like a single man defying the will of the many. In June he dropped his resistance to the annexation of Hawaii, and on June 15 the bill passed the House by a vote of 209 to 91.[5]

Reed was not present in the House that day, indisposed with some unnamed illness. By custom the Speaker did not cast a vote on legislation before the House. In April, when the House had overwhelmingly passed the joint resolution authorizing armed intervention in Cuba, Reed had privately lamented to one of the six congressmen who voted no that he envied "the luxury of your vote." But on the occasion of the Hawaii vote, Reed resorted to an extraordinary gesture. He instructed another congressman, John Dalzell of Pennsylvania, to announce to the chamber that if the Speaker had been able to be present, he would have voted no. The *Nation*, which in the past had criticized him as a despot, was moved to applaud Reed's integrity: "Courage to oppose a popular mania, above all to go against party, is not so common a political virtue that we can afford not to pay our tribute to the man who exhibits it." Reed pretended to be nonchalant about his crushing defeat. In early July reporters who sought him out at his rustic cabin on the Maine seashore learned that he had abandoned the bicycle for walking. He was said to be "without a care in the world." The Buddha wished to be Zen-like, but he was actually depressed. He was pondering his retirement from public life.[6]

William James wished, as always, to believe the best about his country. "The European nations of the Continent cannot believe that our pretence of humanity, and our disclaiming of all ideas of conquest is sincere," he wrote a friend on June 15, the day the Hawaii annexation bill passed the House. "It has been *absolutely* sincere." But James worried about what he called "the psychologic factor." Once "the excitement of action is set loose...the old human instincts will get into play with their old strength, and the ambition and sense of mastery which our Nation has will set up new demands." For a mere professor of philosophy and psychology far from the corridors of power, James could be uncannily prescient about the geopolitical future. In his letter to his French friend François Pillon, he peered ahead:

> *We shall never take Cuba; I imagine that to be very certain — unless indeed after years of unsuccessful police duty there, for that is what we have made ourselves responsible for. But Porto Rico, and even the Philippines — are not so sure. We had supposed ourselves (with all our crudity and barbarity in certain ways) a better nation morally than the rest, safe at home, and without the old savage ambitions, destined to exert great international influence by throwing our "moral weight" etc. Dreams! Human nature is everywhere the same; and at the least temptation all the old military passions arise and sweep everything before them.[7]*

Writing from his cool study in Cambridge on that warm June morning, James added, "I am going to a great popular meeting in Boston to-day where a lot of my friends are to protest against the new 'Imperialism.'" At three o'clock that afternoon, James was one of several hundred proper Bostonians who squeezed into the city's historic meeting place, Faneuil Hall, for the first session of the Anti-Imperialist League. The newspapers the next day reported a great deal of speechifying by mugwump worthies, led by Moorfield Storey, Lodge's old foe. There were many virtuous declarations, such as, "Resolved: That our first duty is to cure the evils of our own country," as the room grew as stuffy as the Brahmins speaking there.[8] James was unmoved and a little put off. Though he counted himself a mugwump, he bridled when snobbery undermined idealism. He enjoyed needling his expatriate brother Henry and scolds like E. L. Godkin when they condescended to the cruder passions of the unwashed masses. Yes, foreign conquest was a betrayal of the principles of 1776, James heartily agreed. But so was aristocratic prejudice against the "alien, inferior, and mongrel races." James the pluralist disdained the sneers of his fellow mugwumps, especially Godkin, who described the Cuban rebels as a "motley" crowd no more capable of understanding "our religion, manners, political traditions and habits, and modes of thought" than "the King of Dahomey."[9]

Hearst got to Cuba first, arriving off the coast on June 18, before Roosevelt and the convoy bearing the Fifth Army. The steamship *Sylvia*, chartered from the Baltimore Fruit Company by the enterprising Creelman for his boss, had been made over into a suitable flagship for the press wars. Down below in the darkroom was enough equipment to start a "photograph supply shop," according to J. C. Hemment, a photographer hired by Hearst. Also onboard, reported Hemment, was "a printing machine and the material necessary to print the first paper in Cuba after it came into the possession of the United States." On the way to Cuba the *Sylvia* had stopped in Jamaica, where Hearst and his entourage went to the local racetrack and bought polo ponies to serve as mounts in the campaign ahead. After a rough crossing, the *Sylvia* encountered the American navy blockading Santiago. Clambering up a sea ladder aboard the flagship *New York*, Hearst demanded to see the commander, Admiral William Sampson — one baron to another. Sampson did not quite see the parity but allowed a brief audience. He was "stiff" and "severe," Hearst later reported. The admiral apparently had not admired the *Journal*'s coverage of the *Maine* affair. The *Journal* later described him as "a rear admiral, always in the rear."[10]

What Hearst really needed were passes and permissions for his correspondents to move freely with the American army. When the invasion armada finally arrived off Santiago on June 22, Hearst, attired in navy blue blazer and yachting cap, set out in search of the *Seguranca,* the steamer being used as General Shafter's headquarters. After his small steam launch had blundered about in the night, caught in the beams of searchlights and repeatedly challenged by anxious lookouts, Hearst finally located the *Seguranca* and General Shafter. The commander in chief was wearing only pants and a light blue shirt, his three-hundred-pound body sweating profusely in the tropical heat. Shafter looked decidedly worried about the prospect of putting seventeen thousand men ashore and keeping them safe from yellow fever long enough to drive out the Spaniards. It seems the McKinley administration had decided to cooperate with Hearst. "The thing to do with a dirty sheet was to wash it," Secretary of War Alger had counseled

McKinley.[11] Shafter was courteous to Hearst and gave him the necessary permissions.

Waiting for war may have been hell for the soldiers packed aboard their ships, but on the *Sylvia* the party was just getting started. Billy Blitzer, a pioneering motion-picture cameraman who would later work with D. W. Griffith, came aboard Hearst's flagship from another of his yachts, the *Anita*. "Here were champagne and lively companionship," Blitzer recalled. "The *Sylvia* had just arrived that morning and they were all anxious to go sightseeing." He was delighted to see the Willson twins onboard, still dressed in their sailor suits (according to Blitzer the "male attire" was a disguise so navy personnel would not notice the two chorus girls in the nearby press boat). He was also delighted to be part of this scene. "We were in a delirious state of being under fire in war time," he wrote with mild exaggeration (the navy was firing on the coast, but nobody was firing back), "and we got more friendly than we would have at home; the crew mixed with the guests and vice-versa."

The invasion of Cuba was lent an air of gaiety by the constant playing of military bands.* Shortly before 9:30 on the morning of June 22, men of the Fifth Army were singing along with the regimental bands' umpteenth rendition of "There'll Be a Hot Time in the Old Town Tonight" when the warships opened up with a twenty-minute salvo on the landing zone. Unbeknown to the Americans, the Spanish had already fled: the navy was

---

*On their return home many of the bandsmen landing in New Orleans hocked their instruments to buy liquor and other entertainments. One of the locals who purchased an unclaimed trumpet at a pawnshop was Louis Armstrong.

Roosevelt and Richard Harding Davis (Theodore Roosevelt Collection, Houghton Library, Harvard University)

firing on Cuban rebel troops in a harbinger of things to come. Fortunately, the rebels did not sustain many casualties because the firing was not all that accurate.[12]

As usual, no one was in charge. A score of steamers milled about miles offshore, discharging troops into over a hundred small boats. The scene reminded Richard Harding Davis of a regatta, with the racing shells waiting for the starting command.[13] There was no order or plan to the landing. "We disembarked higgledy-piggledy, just as we had embarked," recalled Roosevelt. "Soldiers went here, provisions there; and who got ashore first largely depended on individual activity."

Confusion and hesitation on the part of others always seemed to favor Roosevelt. By happy coincidence his former naval aide, a Lieutenant Commander Sharp, was spotted alongside, aboard the navy's converted yacht the *Vixen*. As assistant secretary of the navy, Roosevelt had arranged for Sharp to have command of the vessel, and the young officer ("a first class fellow") was eager to repay the favor. He sent over a "black pilot," recalled Roosevelt, who guided the *Yucatan* to within a few hundred yards of the shore. Other ships and boats followed, Roosevelt recalled, "like a flock of sheep."[14]

The American army was landing at Daiquiri, the site of a defunct ironworks and "a squalid little town" of rusty corrugated shacks, noted Roosevelt. There was no harbor to speak of, just an indentation in the coast, and the docking facilities were at best precarious. The iron pier was too high for the small boats, and a smaller, slimy wooden-plank dock—splintering, rotting, and half dismantled by the departing Spanish—tested the agility of soldiers weighted down by bedrolls and weapons. A boat capsized and two soldiers drowned, despite the heroic efforts of Captain "Bucky" O'Neill, who dove in fully clothed in an attempt to save them. The first casualties of the war, the victims were "buffalo soldiers," African Americans who wanted to stay in the army after the Civil War and were often posted to remote Indian territory far from white communities. (Black soldiers were included in the invasion force in significant numbers on the mistaken theory that their tropical bloodlines would make them immune to yellow fever.)[15]

Once on the beach, Roosevelt snorted with indignation. The navy's method of disembarking the officers' mounts was to drive them plunging into the sea, to swim for shore. Some frightened horses headed in the wrong direction, until an astute bugler trumpeted the cavalry charge, whereupon they staged an about-face. Many animals drowned, including Roosevelt's own Rain-in-the-Face, crushed by a heavy wave in the surf.[16]

Landing at Daiquiri

Atop a green and rocky hill overlooking Daiquiri stood a Spanish blockhouse. In the early afternoon an American flag suddenly fluttered from a small flagpole at its peak. From the freighters arrayed on the shining sea below, steam whistles shrieked and hooted; in the boats and on the beach, men shouted themselves hoarse. Bands aboard ships began to play "The Star-Spangled Banner."[17] The flag had been the inspiration of Edward Marshall, one of the *Journal*'s correspondents, and a small band of Rough Riders. Marshall had actually arrived before the invasion, aboard a tug from Hearst's private flotilla, and he was eager to plant an American flag on behalf of his paper. At the summit of the craggy hill at Daiquiri, he encountered a few Rough Riders with the same idea and a grander flag—a silk Old Glory hand-sewn by patriotic womenfolk in Arizona.

Descending from the peak onto the beach, Marshall encountered Roosevelt. He was "boiling" with anger, Marshall recalled. The captain of the *Yucatan* had sailed off without unloading the

Rough Riders' supplies. Roosevelt had nothing but a light mackintosh and his toothbrush. Fortunately, "Old Four Eyes" had sewed several extra pairs of eyeglasses into his hatband, but he was missing a saddle for Texas, his surviving horse. Always eager to extend a favor from the Empire of Hearst, Marshall gave him a saddle; the Hearst team had a surplus. "In Colonel Roosevelt's distress I came to his rescue," he recalled. "He rode it into battle the next day and into oblivion, for it has never been heard of since."[18]

Santiago de Cuba, an ancient city of thirty thousand people, was about twenty miles away. The Fifth Army's plan, such as it was, was to march down the *camino real*, the royal road (actually a muddy rut), and take Santiago from the east. The commander of the cavalry was General Joseph "Fighting Joe" Wheeler, the same gnomish ex-Confederate cavalryman who, as an Alabama congressman, had tested the patience of Speaker Reed. "A regular gamecock," was Roosevelt's description. Wheeler's orders were to follow behind General H. W. Lawton, commander of the Second Infantry. Damned if he was going to follow an infantryman, and a Yankee, into battle, Wheeler was determined to outflank his own infantry.

At 3:00 p.m. on June 23, the Rough Riders began the march to Siboney, a squalid town on the coast seven miles away. Most had not slept well, thanks to mosquitoes, red ants, and giant orchid-colored land crabs that were not dangerous but hideous and decidedly creepy to anxious men spending their first night in the tropics. The march was brutal. The horseless Rough Riders had jokingly renamed themselves "Wood's Weary Walkers" in honor of their commander. Bowlegged cowboys fell by the wayside under the scorching sun. But Wood pressed them on— and about a mile from Siboney, the Rough Riders walked past the infantry, who were dropping from the heat in even greater numbers. Wood wanted the honor of hitting the enemy first.[19]

In Siboney that night, Davis, who had attached himself to the best story—Theodore Roosevelt—painted a surreal scene. Under the moonlight, naked men laughed and shouted as they splashed in the waves. The sounds reminded Davis of the amusement park at Coney Island.[20] Some of the men had carelessly dropped their blanket rolls on the long, hot march. Now they found these bedrolls draped over the shoulders of the Cuban *insurrectos*, the rebel force that had come to greet their liberators. The Cubans were already eagerly scavenging (and sometimes stealing) the supplies of the far better equipped *norteamericanos*.

The American troops were shocked by their new allies. The rebels were ragged and emaciated, and, more off-putting, roughly half of them were black. Even more disturbing, some of the black rebels were *officers*. For an American soldier in the late 1890s, especially those from the South in the new era of Jim Crow laws, the idea of putting black men in charge of white men was extremely hard to accept or even fathom. The black units in the American army, including those in Cuba, were entirely commanded by white officers. The Cuban revolution's attempt to create a postracial society ("No blacks or whites, but only Cubans") was at least a half century ahead of the consciousness of the average American soldier.[21]

Some of the North Americans saw the Cubans as exotic. In the lower ranks, soldiers got busy concocting lurid rumors—the Cuban soldiers traded bullets for prostitutes and played soccer with the skulls of dead Spaniards.[22] American higher-ups quickly scorned the Cubans as venal or useless. "They are the most worthless...lot of bushwackers extant," Captain Frank McCoy wrote his parents. "What they want is to see us do the work and them reap the fruit," wrote Major James Bell.[23] Roosevelt was just as dismissive in his memoirs: he described the Cubans as "a crew of as utter tatterdemalions as human eyes ever looked on.... It was evident, at a glance, that they would be no use in serious fighting." Second Lieutenant John H. Parker, in command of the Gatling gun detachment, was particularly vivid: "[The Cuban] is a treacherous, lying, cowardly, thieving, worthless, half-breed mongrel; born of a mongrel spawn of Europe, crossed upon the fetiches of darkest Africa and aboriginal America. He is no more capable of self-government than the Hottentots that roam the wilds of Africa or the Bushmen of Australia. He can not be trusted like the Indian, will not work like a negro, and will not fight like a Spaniard."[24]

Misunderstanding and cultural differences immediately soured relations between the Cuban rebels and the Americans. The Cubans were insulted when Americans tried to use them as manual laborers. More important, they could not understand why the Americans were so determined to make frontal assaults on enemy positions. For decades the Cubans had fought an on-and-off guerrilla war in which direct contact with the better-armed enemy was deemed suicidal. The rebels believed in hit-and-run ambush. Far from being useless, their guerrilla tactics were essential in keeping Spanish forces pinned down or diverted as the Americans plowed toward Santiago.[25]

The Americans were in a hurry. General Shafter had been reading his history, and he knew the story of Lord Vernon's expedition against Santiago in 1741. Landing at Guantánamo, about forty miles from Santiago, the British encountered little Spanish opposition—but tropical diseases killed over two thousand troops. Sixteen miles short of Santiago, Lord Vernon was forced to withdraw. Shafter believed the Americans must take

Santiago quickly, before the rainy season bestowed its curse of yellow fever.[26] Roosevelt, too, was worried about disease — not so much for others, but that it might fell him before he had a chance to face enemy fire.

The rainy season brought torrential late-day downpours. At nightfall at the Rough Rider encampment outside Siboney, Roosevelt dried himself by a fire with some officers and enlisted men, among them Captain Allyn Capron and Sergeant Hamilton Fish, one of the "gentleman rankers." In his memoir of the Rough Riders, Roosevelt recalled, "I caught myself admiring the splendid bodily vigor of Capron and Fish.... Their frames seemed of steel, to withstand all fatigue; they were flushed with health; in their eyes shone high resolve and fiery desire."[27] Wood approached Capron with welcome news: in the morning the captain and his company, L Troop, would have the lead as the Rough Riders moved against the Spanish. With perhaps a premonition, Capron responded, "Well, tomorrow at this time the long sleep will be on many of us."[28]

Toward midnight, Wood outlined the plan of battle to Roosevelt. Their commander, General S. B. M. Young (fortuitously, a fellow Boone and Crockett Club man who had promised to get Roosevelt and Wood to the fight) would take a column of regulars, dismounted cavalrymen, along the main road. With Capron's L Troop walking point, Wood would lead the Rough Riders on a jungle path along a ridgeline that roughly paralleled the thoroughfare. The two forces would meet up at the first line of enemy defenses, about four miles from the coast, where the road crests as it cuts through the hills. The pass was known as Las Guasimas, after a clump of nut trees that grew there.[29]

Roosevelt lay down to sleep, or tried to. Two years earlier he had written a friend confessing that he "betrayed altogether too much nervousness" before facing a fight. His wife had spoken to him about his anxious expression, and so had more virile types. After he shot a grizzly bear out west, a fellow hunter told him "he would have believed, if the bear had happened to get away, that I had been afraid of it." Once, before riding to the hounds at Meadowbrook, a fellow sportsman had "chafed" him about his apparent uneasiness. But Roosevelt knew that when it came "down to actual fighting... then I should be perfectly cool and collected." He had no need for dreams, for such fantasia and reality would meet in the morning, when, at long last, he set off to hunt "the most dangerous game" — man.[30]

18

Ambush

"We've got the damn Yankees on the run!"

Siboney, Cuba, June 24, 1898

THE TROPICAL DAWN broke like "an egg," recalled Edward Marshall, the New York *Journal* correspondent assigned to follow the Rough Riders. One minute it was dark; the next, light. Marshall doubted that either Wood or Roosevelt had slept. At 6:00 a.m. both officers were still wearing their long yellow slickers from the night before. Wood "looked worn and haggard, and his voice was cracked and hoarse. Roosevelt was as lively as a chipmunk, and seemed to be in a half dozen places at once." Wood was impatient to get going—he did not want the other column of troops under General Young to reach the enemy first.[1]

The men had to climb about five hundred feet to the path along the ridgeline leading in from the sea. Footsore and exhausted, some just lay down with their packs, unable to go forward. Even Roosevelt grumbled to himself that Wood was setting a fast pace. But Roosevelt the nature lover perked up when the troops began marching single file along the bridle path leading to Las Guasimas. "The tropical forest was very beautiful, and it was a delight to see the strange trees, the splendid royal palms and a tree which looked like a flat-topped acacia, and which was covered by a mass of brilliant scarlet flowers," he later wrote of his march into battle.[2] Marshall recalled "the oppressiveness of the heat, which made us gasp and sweat," and found something eerie about the surroundings. This had once been cultivated farmland, until the revolution swept by, burning and looting. Through the dense and tangled foliage they could glimpse a mansion house, abandoned and overgrown.

Amid the chatter of birds they heard the plaintive call of the cuckoo. Marshall froze; the sound of the cuckoo had been used as a signal by Spanish sharpshooters during a brief engagement with a detachment of U.S. Marines who had landed at Guantánamo a few days earlier. However, no one else seemed worried. The men down the line were gabbling about how they'd like a cold beer. Wood ordered, "Silence in the ranks!" but the chattering resumed. Roosevelt wandered over and began chatting with Marshall about a lunch they had shared with his boss, Hearst, at the Astor House in New York. Suddenly Roosevelt was distracted when he noticed a strand of barbed wire in the fence hemming the bridle path. "My God!" Roosevelt exclaimed. "This wire has been cut today!" Marshall asked what made him think so. "The end is bright," he said, "and there has been enough dew, even since sunrise, to put a light rust on it, had it not been lately cut."

Just as he spoke, one of the regiment's doctors came blundering along on a mule, making a racket. Roosevelt, jumping up to quiet him, "made more noise than he did," Marshall recalled. "Then came the first shot."[3]

They had marched into an ambush. In the advance guard, Sergeant Fish and Captain Capron—whose "splendid bodily vigor" Roosevelt had admired just the night before—were cut down. The Rough Riders could not see who was shooting at them, but they could hear the sound of Mauser bullets cutting through the air, a sound like z-z-z-z-z-eu and then chug when the bullet struck flesh. Men were spinning around and falling, their canteens and gear clinking and clanking as they went down in a heap. Wood—"Old Icebox"—seemed completely cool. (Actually, he was perfectly aware of the danger and regretting that he had not taken out a $100,000 life insurance policy for his family.)[4] Wood calmly gave orders, including one telling the men to stop swearing and start shooting.[5] "Colonel Roosevelt, on the contrary, jumped up and down, literally, I mean with emotions evidently divided between joy and a tendency to run," Marshall recalled, but Wood steadied his overexcited deputy and ordered him to take a squad into the bush on the right flank. Roosevelt collected himself; his initial panic fled and he became the brave, steady soldier under fire he hoped he would be. (He had but one slight and comical misstep: his sword got caught between his legs, making him stagger as he tried to run into the jungle.)[6]

Roosevelt and his troopers were trapped by dense growth as the Mauser bullets zipped through the leaves. They could not see the enemy. Were they being fired on by their own troops? Roosevelt was peering around a palm tree when a bullet thudded into the trunk, sending a cloud of dust and splinters into his ear and eye. In the span of three minutes nine of his men were hit. Roosevelt began to think of an old fox hunting song:

Here's to every friend who struggled to the end . . .[7]

He was rescued, improbably, by a reporter—Davis, who, with his eye on the big story, had come limping along beside

The Fight at Las Guasimas

Roosevelt. Davis was suffering from painful sciatica and could barely walk, but he was dressed for battle in a custom-designed blue coat and puttees, with binoculars hanging around his neck. It was Davis "who gave us our first opportunity to shoot back with effect," Roosevelt recalled. He had directed "some volley firing at points where I rather doubtfully believed the Spaniards to be, but had stopped firing and was myself studying the jungle-covered mountain ahead with my glasses, when Davis suddenly said, 'There they are, Colonel, look over there; I can see their hats near that glade.'" Davis pointed down into a valley to their right. Quickly, Roosevelt ordered his men to pepper the valley with shots, and "suddenly" the Spaniards sprang from their cover and ran, disappearing over the far hill.[8]

Roosevelt headed back to the trail. Pushing forward, he encountered the body of young Fish, eyes glazed. There was no time to stop for the dead and wounded, though he worried what the vultures and land crabs might do with them. He soon found Wood, who ordered him to lead his troops into the high grass and "rather open forest" on the left. "A perfect hail of bullets was sweeping over us as we advanced," Roosevelt recorded. Still unsure where the enemy lay, he took a carbine from a wounded man "and began to try shots with it myself," though he had no clear target.[9]

To the right Roosevelt could hear cheering. The Rough Riders had bumped into the advance guard of General Lawton's troops moving up the *camino*. Now the Spaniards were breaking ranks and fleeing. General Joe Wheeler forgot which war he was fighting and yelled, "We've got the damn Yankees on the run!"[10] Colonel Wood, showing again why Roosevelt cherished him as the embodiment of nineteenth-century manly virtue, cried out, "Don't shoot at retreating men!"[11]

And then it was over. Roosevelt picked up some shiny Mauser cartridges as keepsakes for his children.[12] He was briefly jolted when a trooper told him that Wood was dead, but he found his commander standing in a clearing with Generals Wheeler and Young. When the brass congratulated their volunteer colonel on a job well done, Roosevelt felt a rush of relief, though he tried to look composed. He had not really been sure what he was doing through most of the battle, but he had modeled his posture on that of Wood—never be seen in a prone position. His men had seen him erect, never flinching.[13]

The battle had lasted ninety minutes. The Rough Riders lost eight dead and had thirty-four wounded, a casualty rate (measured as killed plus wounded) roughly twice that of the rest of the regiment, or so Roosevelt was proud to boast. About a thousand American troops had driven fifteen hundred Spanish soldiers from the ridgeline, though historians have concluded that the Spaniards had never intended to stand and fight, but rather planned to withdraw. Overall, sixteen Americans died and fifty-two were wounded, versus ten Spanish killed and twenty-five wounded.[14] Roosevelt was revolted when he found that vultures had already torn the eyes from some of the Spanish dead. "Bucky" O'Neill, the literate Arizona sheriff who had joined Roosevelt in starlit philosophizing aboard the *Yucatan*, "turned to me and asked, 'Colonel, isn't it Whitman who says of vultures that "they pluck the eyes of princes and tear the flesh of kings"?' I answered that I could not place the quotation," Roosevelt recalled.[15] Cuban rebel soldiers who had not been in evidence during the battle materialized to scavenge bedrolls again, this time those discarded by the Rough Riders as they went into combat.[16]

"Every man behaved well; there was no flinching," Roosevelt wrote Corinne that night. "The fire was very hot at one or two points where the men around me went down like ninepins." Usually bluff and cheerful, he liked to be direct about gruesome sights in nature, to a degree that approached the macabre. To Corinne: "The woods are full of land crabs, some of which are almost as big as rabbits; when things grew quiet they slowly gathered in gruesome rings around the fallen....The vultures were wheeling overhead by the hundreds."[17]

Early news accounts described the battle as a bloody ambush, a "gallant blunder."[18] Roosevelt, with his eye on posterity, soon set about correcting this version of events. He appears to have deftly used correspondent Davis, just as Davis had used him. In a private letter to his family written at the time, Davis related, "We were caught in a clear case of ambush."[19] His early articles in the New York *Herald* conveyed a sense of giddy troops suddenly surprised.[20] But by the time he was writing his widely read account for *Scribner's Magazine*, Davis had put a finer gloss on the battle, emphasizing the "vast difference between blundering into an ambuscade and setting out with a full knowledge that you will find the enemy in ambush, and finding him, there and then driving him out of his ambush and before you for a mile and a half into full retreat."[21] Roosevelt may have conferred with Davis on presenting the battle in a more favorable light than was cast by his early dispatches. The record hints at inducements: Roosevelt took the unusual step of mentioning Davis — a reporter, not a soldier — in official dispatches and offered Davis, a man he had privately described as a "cad," a captaincy in his regiment anytime he wanted it.[22] In a private letter to McKinley and in his later memoirs, Roosevelt went to great lengths to argue that the Rough Riders had not been caught by surprise. He claimed that they were deploying flankers *before* the shooting started, which suggests readiness for the fight, but eyewitness accounts do not back him up, and Roosevelt's pleadings have an air of protesting too much. Like a lawyer arguing "in the alternative," he also blamed the Cuban scouts for disappearing and giving no warning.[23] Davis later wrote a fawning letter to Roosevelt disputing the ambush theory, forgetting, perhaps, that he had been one of the first to advance it. The satirist Peter Finley Dunne's Mr. Dooley had some fun mimicking Roosevelt's account of his arrival in Cuba: "We had no sooner landed in Cubia than it became nicessry f'r me to take command iv th' ar-rmy which I did at wanst. A number of days was spint be me reconnoitring, attended on'y be me brave an' fluent body guard, Richard Harding Davis."[24]

Davis later played the battle as the vindication of the swells.

Noting that the clubmen among the Rough Riders had been mocked in the popular press for their "imaginary valets and golf clubs," Davis described them charging the Spanish the way Princeton rushed Yale down a chalk-lined gridiron—"through the high hot grass at Guasimas, not shouting, as their friends the cowboys did, but each with his mouth tightly shut, with his eyes on the ball, and moving in obedience to the captain's signals." He made a particular hero of the Rough Riders' surgeon, Robert Church, the former Princeton football star who, soaked with blood, had carried four men off the battlefield under "unceasing fire." (Church was decorated with the Congressional Medal of Honor.)[25]

Colonel Wood made the prudent decision not to formally punish the one officer who ran away—Adjutant Tom Hall, a West Point grad who was detested by the men as a fussy martinet. Wood explained to one of his captains that if "we bring that man to a court martial, the bravery of the five hundred will be forgotten and the cowardice of one alone will be remembered." Wood reminded the complaining captain that Frederick the Great ran away in his first fight. "Quite true, sir," protested the captain, "but this son of a bitch will run away in every fight." In the first flurry of shots, Hall had seen a man go down and mistakenly believed the victim was Wood. Instead of staying with his men, the staff officer had jumped on a horse and dashed all the way back to Siboney, crying that the commander had been mortally wounded in a terrible ambush.

The man Hall had seen go down was actually Edward Marshall, the *Journal* correspondent.[26] Placed under a tree, Marshall was lying on a stretcher with a bullet lodged near his spine. His wounds were serious, though not fatal. He was surrounded by wounded men moaning in pain when he heard someone begin to sing:

My country, 'tis of thee,
Sweet land of liberty,
Of thee we sing.

Marshall and the others joined in:

Land where our fathers died,
Land of the pilgrims' pride…

In the morning the Rough Riders buried their comrades in a common grave. Roosevelt was profoundly moved by the death of young Fish, later saying that he reminded him of Robert Gould Shaw, the martyred Civil War hero of his boyhood.[27] That night he wrote a condolence letter to Fish's family, who were fellow Knickerbockers, and sent them the young man's watch, a family heirloom engraved "God Gives." At the grave, a quartet sang "Nearer, My God, to Thee," and all the regiment joined in singing "Rock of Ages."[28]

As Roosevelt was singing hymns to the dead, Hearst was landing at Siboney, four miles away. J. C. Hemment, his photographer, recorded the strange, "picturesque" scene that greeted them on the beach. Stripped naked, the "colored regulars," the black buffalo soldiers of the Tenth and Eleventh Cavalry, were gamboling in the surf, playing "all kinds of pranks and tricks." Standing nearby, watching in "amazement," were the Cuban rebels, "wretched and emaciated." Hearst and his entourage proceeded to the newly established headquarters of the *Journal*: a "cozy little Cuban dwelling" next door to the home of the American Red Cross, where Clara Barton, the already iconic nurse, had set up shop. Always prepared—and better prepared than the army—Hearst was able to provide the Red Cross with a large cargo of ice.

In his role as press sovereign, Hearst had come ashore to pay an official visit to General Calixto García, commander of the Cuban rebels. Dressed in a white-duck suit and a wide-brimmed Panama hat, the general was holding forth on the veranda of "an odd little Cuban shanty painted blue and white, with red tiles on the roof and tropical plants growing up the sides," Hemment recorded. James Creelman, the veteran correspondent who had interviewed both the pope and Sitting Bull, did most of the talking. Hearst was, as usual, shy and mostly silent. García, a sweating old man, took off his hat to reveal an angry scar on his forehead. On the verge of capture during an earlier revolution, García had shot himself in a failed attempt at suicide.

Famous for his temper—an aide was instructed to murmur an Ave Maria whenever he appeared on the verge of eruption—García was gentle and solemn with the *Journal* delegation. He presented Hearst with a Cuban flag riddled with Mauser bullet holes as a token of thanks for all the American publisher had done for the cause. Then he shouted the battle oath of his forces, *"Cuba Libre!"* and even the tongue-tied Hearst took up the cry.[29]

Climbing to the top of the hill overlooking the American fleet, spread in a semicircle just offshore, Hearst took pencil to paper and filed a dispatch. "It is satisfactory to be an American and to be here on the soil of Cuba, at the very threshold of what may be the decisive battle of the war," he wrote. His three-thousand-word piece was a bit purplish in places ("smells of stagnant and fermented vegetation ground under the feet of a thousand fighting men rise in the swooning hot mists through which vultures that have already fed on corpses of slain Spaniards wheel lazily about the thorny, poisonous jungle"), but on the whole the reporting is straightforward, mostly an account of his interviews with Admiral Sampson, General Shafter, and General García.[30] To his mother that same day he wrote, "I am at the front and absolutely safe, so don't worry." He proudly quoted General García as saying that "the *Journal* had been the most potent influence in bringing the United States to the help of Cuba and that they would always remember the *Journal* as a friend when friends had been very few." Hearst couldn't resist pointing out that "other proprietors are safely at home." He hastily added, "and I will be soon." But first he had to see a battle.

Roosevelt and his men camped in a marshy open spot by a clear stream five miles from Santiago. He wrote Corinne that he was "in excellent health, in spite of having been obliged for the week since I landed, to violate all the rules for health." He was sleeping in clothes drenched with sweat and rain, drinking unboiled water, and subsisting on "hard tack"—hard biscuit—bacon, and coffee without sugar. His servant Marshall, an old buffalo soldier, had vanished before the fighting but now turned up "too sick to be any use to me."[31] Soaked by daily downpours, his men had no dry clothes and, worse, no tobacco; some were smoking dried grass roots and manure.[32] Frustrated with the army's incompetence, Roosevelt organized an expedition to Siboney to buy for his men beans and canned tomatoes, which he paid for out of his own pocket, ignoring the regulation that canned vegetables were for officers only.[33]

His first letter to Lodge began as a model of manly modesty and self-justification:

Camp 5 miles from Santiago, June 27, 1898
Dear Cabot,
    Well, whatever comes I shall feel contented with having
left the Navy Department to go into the army for the
war; for our regiment has been in the first fight on land,
and has done well.....

He reported that "our regiment furnished over half the men and half the loss." The Spaniards "shot well," but "our Cuban scouts and guides ran like sheep at the first fire. The smokeless powder made it very hard to place the men who were shooting at us; and our men at times dropped thickly when we could not tell where to fire back." Roosevelt ended with a jab at General Shafter, his commander in chief. "Shafter was not even ashore! The mismanagement has been maddening. We have had very little to eat. But we care nothing for that, as long as we got into the fight. Yours ever, Theodore."

On that same day, June 27, Shafter finally hove into view, carried in a groaning buckboard.[34] The heat was hard on his obese body; he felt dizzy and nauseated. Straining men hoisted the general aboard a mule that looked smaller than he did, and the animal heaved and staggered up a conical-shaped hill called El Pozo, from whose summit the American commander could survey the next battlefield.

Ahead was a lush green valley. Through it the *camino* snaked along for about two miles to a high ridge: the San Juan Heights. With binoculars Shafter could clearly see a long, yellowish trench of freshly dug earth along the ridgeline, topped by a Spanish blockhouse that looked oddly like a Chinese pagoda. Peering through the glasses, Shafter could make out the sombreros of Spanish soldiers and the blue coats of their officers. Just beyond,

visible at night by its lights, was the city of Santiago. Below San Juan Hill was a grassy clearing—a murderous field of fire for the defenders on the heights.

Mindful of Lord Vernon's lost struggle against yellow fever a century and a half earlier, Shafter wanted to get on with the assault on the city and its ten thousand troops. He was worried about more than disease. Cuban scouts reported that a Spanish relief column—some eight thousand men—was marching for Santiago (the actual number was less than half that). Unless the *insurrectos* could waylay them, the reinforcements were expected to arrive by July 2 or 3, and Shafter had little faith in his Cuban allies.

Nevertheless he made no attempt at a fine-tuned strategy. Shafter planned to send a division led by General Lawton north to capture the town of El Caney, cutting off a small but well-defended Spanish garrison along with Santiago's water supply from the mountains. The rest of his force of roughly fifteen thousand would march up the *camino* and launch a frontal assault on the San Juan Heights. When two top commanders became ill with tropical fever, Wood was promoted, which meant Roosevelt—to his "intense delight"—would inherit command of the Rough Riders.[35]

Roosevelt was happy with Shafter's straight-ahead tactics. As a reader of Mahan, he was familiar with Admiral Nelson's dictum: that in a sea battle a commander can do no wrong maneuvering his ship alongside the enemy.

At three in the afternoon of June 30, Shafter gave the order to move out. The traffic on the rain-choked *camino* was chaotic, and the Rough Riders did not reach the jumping-off point until well after dark. The jungle was thick on each side, and the men moved slowly, cursing the heat and the confusion. Bandsmen threw aside their brass instruments as deadweight.[36] At 9 p.m., Roosevelt recorded in his diary, the Rough Riders pitched camp. After setting his pickets, he curled up on his saddle blanket under a raincoat. He later claimed to have slept, but probably not soundly: in his memoir of the time he wrote, "except among hardened veterans, there is always a certain feeling of uneasy excitement the night before a battle."[37]

In any case, he was up well before dawn on July 1, 1898— "the great day of my life," as he would call it for years to come.[38] His later description of the setting was characteristically theatrical though not exaggerated, and no doubt captured his sense of exaltation: "It was a very lovely morning, the sky of cloudless blue, while the level, shimmering rays from the just broken sun brought into fine relief the splendid palms which here and there towered above the lower growth. The lofty and beautiful mountains hemmed in the Santiago plain, making it an amphitheater for the battle."

The hard battle was supposed to come against the garrison at El Caney to the north, where the infantry was already advancing; indeed, Roosevelt could hear guns in the distance. The artillery pieces he could see being wheeled to the top of El Pozo, just ahead, were supposed to make a diversion. After El Caney fell all the troops would advance on the San Juan Heights, but the Rough Riders were to be held in reserve, behind the regular cavalry. Roosevelt worried he might not get into the fight. Despite his deep knowledge of history he forgot, for the moment, an old rule of war, that the best military plans rarely survive contact with the enemy.[39]

19

The Crowded Hour

"Holy Godfrey, what fun!"

MOST OF THE wartime letters between Roosevelt and his wife were destroyed. But snatches survive, and one passage, which an archivist was able to decipher though it had been blacked out with ink, suggests the tenderness between them. After Edith received her first batch of correspondence from her husband in Cuba, she wrote him back, "Last night, I slept better because I held your dear letters to my heart instead of just having them under my pillow. I felt I was touching you when I pressed against me what your hand had touched."[1] Edith still felt weakened from her illness of the past winter and feared that she had no recuperative power, but she was stoical. While apart her husband, too, tried not to think of how he missed his family, for fear it would "unman" him.[2] But the stiff upper lip cost Edith. Her heart beat so hard that she suffered from a "heart enlargement" that put her to bed and improved only when her husband came home. She fought back tears and "helplessness," and wrote her sister, "I think of the women in the Civil War who lived through four years of this."[3] To her husband she confessed, "Always I have a longing and missing in my heart but I shall not write about it, for it makes me cry."[4]

Her children were a comfort. On the morning of July 1, as Roosevelt prepared to go into battle, Edith lay on a chaise lounge on the piazza at Sagamore Hill, "Kermit cuddled beside me and Archie sitting on my legs," she wrote her husband. "We are all beginning to long for a letter. All the children say at intervals, 'Oh, when shall we hear from father?'"[5] To her sister Emily, she wrote, "I find it absolutely essential for me not to break down for the sake of the children."[6]

Little Ted remained a worry. He had been proud that his father was going into battle and longed to be his "batman," his servant, and to clean his guns, but in late June he suffered a relapse of his neurasthenic headaches. Ted had been sleeping in the same bed as his mother—rather "restless[ly]" she reported to her sister.[7] Roosevelt instructed Edith that if he did not return home alive, she should give his sword and revolver to Ted and Kermit, the eldest boys. When Edith read them the letter, she related to her husband, "They both put their heads in my lap and sobbed bitterly."[8]

The scene on the top of El Pozo on July 1 was a conclave of professional and amateur war lovers. Frederic Remington was there, making sketches of the four artillery pieces. One of the teamsters hauling the guns was Tom Mix, who would become Hollywood's first cowboy star of the silent screen. Colonel John Jacob Astor, rumored to be worth some $100 million, owed his presence to the purchase of a commission as an artillery officer (he bought the artillery as well). Lieutenant John Pershing of the Ninth Cavalry, known as "Black Jack" because he commanded a company of black soldiers, was standing nearby; he would go on to command the American Expeditionary Force to France in the First World War. Missing was the commander of *this* expeditionary force. General Shafter had awakened unable to arise.

He blamed the heat and his gout, and was forced to rely on messengers reporting to his cot.[9]

At about 6:30 a.m. the American guns opened up, spouting a great cloud of white smoke over El Pozo. The newly promoted General Wood, standing with Roosevelt, remarked on the foolhardiness of stationing a large force of men directly behind the artillery—that is, in the line of fire if the Spanish shot back. "Hardly had he spoken," Roosevelt recalled, "when there was a peculiar whistling, singing sound in the air." With a boom a shell exploded, spraying shrapnel everywhere. Wood and Roosevelt leaped on their horses and began shouting at their men to disperse. A second shot burst overhead, then a third. Roosevelt felt a twinge of pain and looked down to see a bump "about as big as a hickory nut" rising from his wrist. A man nearby lost his leg, and Wood's horse was pierced through the lungs. A shell landed on a farmhouse, and "the Cubans scattered like guinea hens," Roosevelt noted. One of the many newspaper reporters who had been loitering about grabbed Richard Harding Davis by the arm and exclaimed, "Isn't this awful?" Davis nodded. "Very disturbing, very disturbing," he replied.[10]

Taking a cue from the Cubans, Roosevelt's men scattered into the underbrush. When the bombardment ceased after about twenty minutes, Roosevelt experienced "no little trouble" rounding them up and forming a column. He arranged them in rows of four and marched them, or tried to, toward the battlefield. It was slow going. The men passed groups of infantry halted by the side of the road, and were themselves halted several times. There seemed to be no order or plan. "Our orders had been of the vaguest kind, being simply to march to the right and connect with Lawton [the infantry commander besieging El Caney]—with whom, of course, there was no chance of connecting," Roosevelt recalled. Lawton's men were at that moment pinned down by unexpectedly stiff resistance several miles away: "No reconnaissance had been made, and the exact position and strength of the Spanish was not known." Arrayed along the San Juan Heights, the Spanish soldiers were firing down on the Americans "in desultory fashion," Roosevelt wrote in his memoir of the Rough Riders.[11]

Shafter's one misbegotten stab at gathering intelligence was to float a hot-air balloon above the advancing force. Lookouts were to spot the Spanish gunners and shout down coordinates from the balloon. But the balloon served as a target for the enemy. As his men reached the ford at the San Juan River, Roosevelt was horrified to see the balloon bearing down on their position, attracting a hail of fire. He hustled the Rough Riders across the river and moved them down the firing line to the right. Other troops were not so lucky; the junction of the *camino* and the river became known as Bloody Ford.[12] Davis, who was there, described men "gasp[ing] on their backs, like fishes in the bottom of a boat."[13] Caught and increasingly desperate, they could not move forward into the exposed grass at the base of San Juan Hill, and they could not move back into the flood of troops still pouring down the narrow road. Men, most of whom were raw recruits just a month or two from civilian life, were falling everywhere. Spanish sharpshooters in the trees zeroed in on a temporary medical station, shooting the wounded where they lay.[14] A private in a national guard regiment, Charles Post, felt his feet slipping in the mud on the road and realized to his horror that there had been no rain that morning — the moisture was blood.[15]

Roosevelt managed to get his men to a sunken lane where they could crouch down out of the worst of it. But the firing was intensifying. The Mauser bullets drove "in sheets" through the trees and high grass as the Spanish fired volleys, Roosevelt said. One of his troopers, a Harvard-trained lawyer named Arthur Cosby, recalled that the shooting started slowly, "like the first drops of a rainstorm," but then swelled into a "steady deathly static." When the balloon was finally punctured and collapsed, a bitterly sardonic cheer went up.[16]

Now, at long last, Roosevelt was surrounded by noble death. He was resting on a riverbank, talking to a young West Pointer named Ernest Haskell about cavalry tactics, when the lieutenant failed to answer his question; he had been shot in the stomach and was soon dead. The colonel's first orderly, "a brave young Harvard boy, Sanders," dropped from the heat (and later died of fever). Roosevelt summoned another trooper to act as orderly and instructed him to return to El Pozo to get orders for an advance. The young man stood, saluted, and pitched forward, shot dead through the neck. Down the firing line "Bucky" O'Neill was practicing the noble if quaint rule that officers should always be seen standing under fire. He was walking up and down, smoking a cigarette. One of his sergeants implored him to lie down: "Captain, a bullet is sure to hit you." O'Neill took the cigarette out of his mouth, blew some smoke, and replied, "Sergeant, the Spanish bullet isn't made that will kill me." As he turned back around, a Spanish bullet entered his mouth and tore through the back of his head.

The minutes ticked by; the sun grew hotter; the bullets continued to rain down. Never a patient man, Roosevelt was trying to remain calm, or at least project calmness. He still had no orders. He was about to indulge a Nelsonian disregard for military discipline and "march towards the guns" when at last a lieutenant colonel arrived to give him the command "to move forward and support the regulars in the assault on the hills in the front."[17]

As a boy Roosevelt, like his friend Cabot Lodge, had read Sir Walter Scott's Ivanhoe novels. He remembered Scott's famous saying: "One crowded hour of glorious life is worth an age without a name."[18] Writing to Lodge a few days later, he recounted, "Then came the order to advance, and with it my 'crowded hour!'" His memoir would echo this: "The instant I received the order I sprang to my horse and then my 'crowded hour' began."[19]

Roosevelt had intended to walk into battle with his dismounted soldiers, but he quickly rationalized that in the terrible heat he would need his strength, and on horseback he could be more easily seen by his men. Of course he would also present a bigger target for Spanish snipers, who were trained to aim for officers, but at this moment Roosevelt was blind to risk. Indeed, he consciously made himself gaudier. He was dressed in his usual uniform of khaki trousers and blue flannel shirt with yellow suspenders and brown felt hat. He tied his blue-and-white-checkered bandana around his hat so it would float behind as he rode, a warrior's headdress — and a bull's-eye.

"I started in the rear of the regiment, the position in which the colonel should theoretically stay," Roosevelt recalled. Military doctrine also dictated that infantry should not make frontal assaults over open ground on defended fixed positions. But Roosevelt was thinking about Ivanhoe, not about those books on military drill and tactics he had dutifully crammed on the train to El Paso. He rode up and down the line, cajoling his troops to rise and shaming stragglers into action. Finding a man cowering behind a bush, he ordered him to stand. The man seemed to hesitate. "Are you afraid to stand up when I am on horseback?" Roosevelt jeered. The man stood and immediately fell, shot with a bullet Roosevelt believed, naturally, to have been aimed at him.[20]

The Rough Riders, five hundred strong, moved into the tall grass at the foot of a hill about the height of a ten-story building. At the top they could see a farmhouse and a huge iron kettle (for boiling sugarcane), and men in trenches shooting down at them. The Rough Riders were supposed to be supporting the regulars, but they—buffalo soldiers of the Ninth Cavalry— were lying prone in the grass. They had no orders to advance. Roosevelt sought out their captain and told him he thought the hill could not be taken by firing on it, and that only a rush would succeed. The captain replied that he could not attack without orders. When asked where his colonel was, the captain did not know. "Then I am the ranking officer here, and I give the order to charge," Roosevelt blustered. The officer looked unsure how to proceed. "Then let my men through, sir," said Roosevelt.*

Waving his hat, swearing and joking, Roosevelt rode back and forth rallying his men. Two "coloured soldiers" from the Ninth regulars "threw down" a fence, and Roosevelt trotted back into the lane, splashed through a stream, and when he was abreast of some ranch buildings at the top of the hill, he turned his steed and began to bound up the slope, which inclined gradually at first, then more sharply, at roughly a forty-five-degree angle. All around him men were yelling. A Pawnee named William J. Pollock let loose a war whoop that the men long remembered.[22] Unevenly, tentatively at first, the line surged forward—not just the Rough Riders, but infantry and dismounted cavalry all along

---

*The captain, Henry Anson Barber of Cambridge, Missouri, confirmed the essentials of Roosevelt's account in a letter mailed to his wife at the time.[21]

Remington's painting of the charge up Kettle Hill (Courtesy of the Frederic Remington Museum)

the base of the San Juan Heights, volunteers as well as regulars. Roosevelt was not the only commander to spur his men forward: the rush, along a ragged line stretching more than half a mile, seems to have been a case of spontaneous combustion, as if the men had been pent up too long—though Roosevelt would later get most of the glory.[23]

The press corps was watching from El Pozo. "By God, there go our boys up the hill!" someone cried out. Stephen Crane, author of *The Red Badge of Courage* and now a correspondent determined to prove his bravery, was listening to the foreign military attachés talk. "It is very gallant, but very foolish," one said. "They can't take it, you know," said another. "Never in the world. It is slaughter, absolute slaughter." The Japanese military representative just shrugged his shoulders and said nothing.[24]

Richard Harding Davis found himself stifling the instinct to call to them to come back. There were no flashing bayonets, no massed fighting men, just soldiers in muddy brown or blue, in groups of two or three, running, stumbling, sometimes creeping up a hill. The men seemed to have difficulty moving, as if they were wading waist-high in water. He described Roosevelt's "blue polka-dot handkerchief" floating out straight behind his head "like a guidon"—the regimental colors carried into battle.[25] Davis would later write, "No one who saw Roosevelt take that ride expected him to finish it alive." He was the only man on a horse, a huge target well ahead of his troops. (Rough Riders would reminisce, "At San Juan, he didn't say, 'Go on'; he said, 'Come on!'") In the hot grass, under a brilliant noonday sun, in a shower of fire, he galloped ahead. A bullet scraped his elbow, another knicked his horse. Somehow his glasses were knocked off, and he had to fumble in his pocket for an extra pair.* But he knew exactly where he was going and what he was doing; he was in a state of vertiginous euphoria. "I had not enjoyed the Guasimas fight at all, because I was uncertain as to what I ought to do. But the San Juan fight was entirely different," he later wrote in *An Autobiography*.[27]

Reaching a wire fence forty yards from the top, he jumped off his horse and turned it loose. A huge Arizona miner named Henry Bradshar, who had attached himself to Roosevelt after the first two orderlies fell away, ran up and shot two Spaniards as they were emerging from their trench. The enemy, perhaps a hundred soldiers, was in full flight.

At the top of what became known as Kettle Hill, Roosevelt

---

*Roosevelt omitted from his memoirs any mention of his glasses getting knocked off. One version suggests his wire-rims were shot off by a bullet from behind fired by one of his own men, or that he had momentarily turned away from the enemy, facts that would be inconvenient or awkward to explain.[26]

was quickly joined by a melee of men from different regiments who planted their yellow silk guidons (and later argued about who got there first). Across a shallow valley to the west Spanish troops in firing pits along the ridge of the San Juan Heights, about a third of a mile away, were still shooting at them. Roosevelt and his men took cover behind the giant iron kettle and watched the drama playing out on a larger hill to the left. Led by the white-haired General Hamilton Hawkins, the infantry was advancing up the steep incline under heavy fire. Suddenly the men could hear a drumming sound over the rattle of carbines. It was the *bap-bap-bap* of the Americans' Gatling guns, primitive machine guns, pouring bullets on the Spanish redoubt. That seemed to turn the tide: Spanish soldiers in their pinstriped white-and-pale-blue uniforms began jumping from the trenches and running out of the pagoda-shaped blockhouse at the top of the highest hill.

Roosevelt wanted to be in on the kill. Shouting to his men to follow, he vaulted over a low wire fence and began to run down the far side of the hill, into the valley that separated Kettle Hill from the San Juan Heights. Five men followed; two were quickly hit. After about a hundred yards Roosevelt realized that almost no one was following. Angry, thwarted, he returned to the top of the hill and began "bitterly" taunting his men as "cowards." They rather sheepishly, and unconvincingly, claimed not to have heard his command to charge. For once Roosevelt sought permission from higher authority in the person of General Samuel Sumner, who had arrived on the scene, for an order to advance. Getting it, he rallied his men. This time — grinning, Roosevelt later claimed — they followed.[28] Down into the valley they ran, now a mass of soldiers from several regiments, and up the San Juan

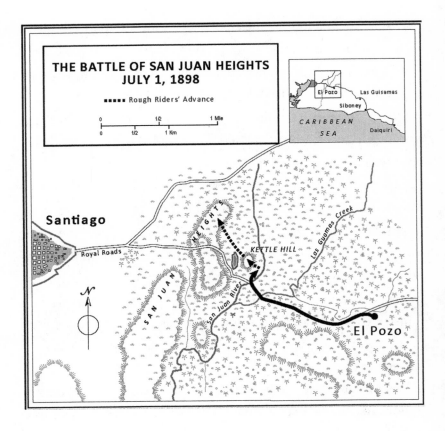

THE BATTLE OF SAN JUAN HEIGHTS
JULY 1, 1898

■■■■■ Rough Riders' Advance

0   1/2   1 Mle
0   1/2   1 Km

El Pozo   Las Guisamas
Siboney
CARIBBEAN
SEA   Daiquiri

Santiago

Royal Roads

HEIGHT

KETTLE HILL

Los Guamas Creek

SAN JUAN

San Juan River

N

El Pozo

Heights. Roosevelt was in ecstasy. "Holy Godfrey, what fun!" he shouted to Bradshar, who faithfully trotted along beside him.

Spotty fire met them. As Roosevelt, huffing in the heat, trotted past a small pond in the valley, a spent bullet struck his left hand. His elbow was still bleeding from the bullet that had grazed him on the charge up Kettle Hill. Delighted to be wounded again, however lightly, Roosevelt raised his bleeding hand and cried, "I've got it again boys, I've got it again!" Then he turned to a more seriously wounded trooper who was staggering along behind him and said giddily, "You needn't be so damn proud!"[29]

They reached the Heights in time to see the last Spanish soldiers fleeing. As he and Bradshar were running up "at the double,"

Roosevelt and his men on top (Library of Congress)

two Spaniards "not ten yards away" leaped out of the trenches and wildly fired their Mausers at them. Roosevelt reached into his holster and drew his pistol—a Colt .45 service revolver, salvaged from the USS *Maine* and given to him by a brother-in-law, navy captain W. S. Cowles. As the two assailants "turned to run, I closed in and fired twice, missing the first and killing the second," Roosevelt wrote.

Roosevelt did not shoot the soldier in the back. He later said he "shot the man in the left breast as he turned."[30] Shooting a fleeing man may not have been exactly the heroic moment Roosevelt had yearned for, but he had at last stalked and killed that "most dangerous game." He had proved his physical courage beyond all doubt. In the Darwinian terms he liked to employ, he had shaken off the torpor of overcivilization and tapped his innate savagery. "All men who feel any power of joy in battle,"

The Rough Riders in the Spanish trenches on San Juan Heights, looking back at Kettle Hill (Theodore Roosevelt Collection, Houghton Library, Harvard University)

Roosevelt would later write, "know what it is like when the wolf rises in the heart."[31] He had effaced any stain left on the family escutcheon by his beloved but draft-dodging father.

Roosevelt's bloodlust did not subside right away. He encountered an old family friend, Rough Rider Bob Ferguson, and announced that he had just "doubled up a Spanish officer like a jackrabbit." The two men walked along the line of trenches peering down at the crumpled bodies in their light-blue pinstriped uniforms (which looked "like pajamas," according to Private Post of the New York Seventy-first, the national guardsmen arriving just after their ordeal at Bloody Ford). "Look at these damn Spanish dead!" Roosevelt exclaimed to Ferguson. In his memoirs he observed, clinically but a bit ghoulishly, "Most of the fallen had little holes in their heads from which their brains were oozing."[32]

Four days later Ferguson described the scene in a letter to Edith, or as he addressed her, "Dear Mrs. Theodore." An old hunting buddy, Ferguson had seen his friend exult in the chase, but on San Juan Hill, Roosevelt seemed to have departed the mortal sphere in his glory over the "power of joy in battle." Ferguson wrote Edith: "No hunting trip so far has ever equaled it in Theodore's eyes.... I really believe firmly now they can't kill him."[33]

Six hours earlier, as they rested beside the road awaiting orders to begin the assault on San Juan Hill, Private Post and his fellow national guardsmen had seen a man dressed in civilian clothes ride by on a horse. The man was slightly too large for his mount; Private Post had noticed that his legs dangled well below the horse's belly and that the man was wearing white socks that were curiously out of kilter with his otherwise natty ensemble—jaunty flat-brimmed straw hat with a scarlet hatband that matched the fellow's necktie.

The mismatched dandy was William Randolph Hearst. Young Post recognized the *Journal*'s proprietor because before enlisting in the national guard, he had been an illustrator for the *Journal*. "Hey, Willie!" Post cried out, and the other men took up the greeting, for Hearst was a well-known figure to New Yorkers. "Hey, Willie!"

Hearst "never moved a muscle," Post recalled. "He never cracked a smile." The artist-turned-national-guardsman thought perhaps Hearst was maintaining a "poker face," though it's more likely that the *Journal*'s owner was just shy and possibly nervous on the day of battle. When Hearst's star correspondent James Creelman rode up, some men, recognizing him—for Creelman was also a celebrity—cried out, "Hey, Jimmy!" Not at all bashful, Creelman flashed a toothy white smile beneath his black beard. He waved just as a trumpeting of bugles signaled the order to move out.

"Boys, you're going into battle. Good luck!" exclaimed Creelman. Ever his boss's keeper, he turned to Hearst and whispered something. As Post later recounted, Hearst "almost smiled," and awkwardly waved his scarlet-banded hat. "Good luck," he said mildly, in his high, thin voice. "Boys, good luck be with you." Then, wrote Post, "he stiffened again."[34]

Hearst's day had begun well before dawn. A servant from the *Sylvia* had packed a picnic hamper with silver, china, and chicken sandwiches. Hearst put on his hat and necktie and stuck a pistol in his belt. Climbing onto his too-small mount, he joined the flow of soldiers toward the battlefield. Accompanying him with Creelman was photographer J. C. Hemment; an old Harvard friend, Jack Follansbee; Colonel Honoré Laine of the Cuban Army, whom Hearst had drafted as a guide; and a servant. (When another photographer found Hemment eating his lunch along the trail, the servant was holding an umbrella to shield him from the sun.)[35]

At El Pozo around 6:30 a.m., the *Journal* delegation rode past the Rough Rider regiment. "As we passed by them, we recognized many a well-known face," recalled Hemment, who remembered the Fifth Avenue swells from his work as a society photographer. "Several of them saluted us as we went along towards this battery on the hill." The journalists were navigating the unfriendly trail—Creelman recalled the smell of jungle rot and the revolting land crabs, Hemment the "Spanish swords," long-leaf cactus that sliced trousers—when they heard the American battery opening up atop El Pozo.

A few minutes later, as shells from the return fire of the Spanish guns began to explode in the air around them, a Rough Rider officer cried out, "What in the hell are you fellows doing? Don't you see that you're drawing fire from those batteries? For God's sake men, get off your horses!"

As Hemment recalled, Hearst turned his horse to face Hemment's own and offered a shy smile. "Well," he said, "I guess possibly we are drawing the fire, but we are not the only ones around here." Hearst and the others quietly dismounted. The question "Let us go back?" hung in the air unasked, Hemment later wrote. None of the Hearst men wanted to look like a coward.[36] "Shrapnel shells were bursting over us in large numbers; men were being struck down besides our very selves," recalled Hemment. The photographer noted that the men did not go down theatrically—there was "no Rialto business. A man was hit, and he simply sagged down in a heap, sinking into the low bushes without a murmur, without a word."

Hearst and his party pushed on—but not toward San Juan. The night before, a general had whispered to Creelman that the big fight would be at El Caney, the village two miles north that was protected by a stone fort called El Viso. General Lawton had marched on El Caney with 5,400 men, and the Hearst entourage hastened along after them.[37] The siege was supposed to be a quick one. Lawton's orders were to take El Caney and march his men down to join the assault on the San Juan Heights. But the five hundred or so Spanish regulars at El Viso were well dug in on a conical hill topped by the fort. The battle, which was supposed to be over by 10:00 a.m., was still raging at noon, and the Americans were suffering heavy casualties. An infantry captain came upon the scene of about a hundred men lying in a sunken road behind the firing line. He asked another officer if they were the infantry reserve taking cover. "No, sir," came the reply, "by God, they are casualties." The captain gingerly stepped over the wounded men, appalled by their suffering in the noontime sun. Many simply bled to death.

At about 1:00 p.m., from his cot General Shafter gave the order to disengage. Lawton ignored it. His small battery of four artillery pieces had finally zeroed in on the fort. The guns shot away the flagstaff at El Viso, to cheers from the beleaguered Americans, and began knocking holes in the fort. As the firing from the fort slackened, the Americans crept closer.

Incredibly, the man who led the final charge was a reporter from the *Journal*. As Hearst watched from Lawton's artillery battery, Creelman had ventured to the front lines. Perched high on a hillside, Creelman noticed a "wrinkle," as he called it, in the topography that would allow the Americans to move closer to the fort undetected. "This was hardly the business of a correspondent," he later acknowledged, but he mentioned his observation to a commander, General A. R. Chaffee. Creelman soon found himself in the novel role of pathfinder, showing the soldiers where to snip barbed wire so they could slip into an enemy trench full of dead or dying Spaniards. Puzzled by the silence after so much firing, Creelman ventured into the fort itself. He entered a charnel house. "The dead and the wounded lay inside in every conceivable attitude," he wrote. Some were crying in pain. A soldier held a ramrod affixed with a white handkerchief. Speaking French to Creelman, a grimacing, white-faced officer surrendered his troops, those who were still alive.

Creelman wanted more. He had seen the Spanish red-and-gold flag flying over El Viso, and he coveted it as a trophy of war for his newspaper. He stepped outside the fort to find the flag lying in the dust. Picking it up, he defiantly, giddily, waved the banner toward the village below, where Spanish troops still hid in the houses and huts. As he returned with his prize, shots rang out. Creelman felt a blow, as if he had been struck by a fist, and spun around. A bullet had torn through his upper arm and entered his back.

Draped with the Spanish flag he had so foolishly sought, Creelman was carried down the hill and left to lie in the sun. His vision swam, and he noticed a strange yellow glare. He drifted off. Someone knelt beside him and placed a hand on his feverish brow. "Opening my eyes, I saw Mr. Hearst, the proprietor of the New York *Journal*, a straw hat with a bright red ribbon on his head, a revolver at his belt, and a pencil and notebook in his hand," Creelman wrote in a memoir. "The man who had provoked the war had come to see the result with his own eyes and, finding one of his correspondents prostrate, was doing the work himself."

Creelman could still hear the "tinging of Mauser bullets" not far off, but Hearst patiently interviewed his wounded man, taking down the details on his notepad. For a moment Hearst acknowledged Creelman's obvious pain. "I'm sorry you're hurt," he said. Creelman recalled that his boss's face was radiant with enthusiasm. "But wasn't it a splendid fight?" exclaimed Hearst. "We must beat every paper in the world."[38]

With that, Hearst mounted a fast horse and raced to the coast. At Siboney he wrote out a story that was taken aboard the *Sylvia* and thence to Jamaica, where it was wired to New York to appear in the *Journal* on July 4—the first eyewitness account of the assault on El Caney. "The Battle of Caney—by W. R. Hearst" read the large page-one headline. Hearst described his own movements, noting telling little details like the piece of shrapnel that pierced the canned beef he had intended to eat for lunch. "The Editor of the Journal Describes the Great Struggle as He Saw It on the Battlefield," proclaimed the subhead. An illustration showed Hearst taking dictation from the bandaged Creelman.[39] Hearst not only took the byline but seems to have forgotten all about his wounded ace correspondent. On July 5, Creelman wrote this rather pathetic letter to his boss:

Dear Mr. Hearst:

After being abandoned without shelter or medicine and practically without food for nearly two days — most of the time under constant fire — you can judge my condition. My shoulder was as you know. That I am here and alive is due simply to my own efforts. I had to rise from my litter and stagger seven miles through the hills and mud without an attendant.... Mr. [Jack] Follinsbee [sic] stayed one night with me and got a fever. We are both here without cloths [sic]. I must get to the United States in order to get well. I expect no gratitude but I do expect a chance for my life.

Faithfully yours,
James Creelman[40]

Hearst would not see Creelman's letter for several weeks. While Creelman was staggering through the mud, Hearst was aboard the *Sylvia*, shadowing the American fleet and waiting for the Spanish to sally forth.

20

Matters of Honor

"Did I tell you that I killed a Spaniard with my own hand...?"

B Y MIDAFTERNOON ON JULY 1, Roosevelt was the ranking officer of a mélange of about four hundred men from different troops—regular and volunteer, infantry and cavalry, white and black—hunkered down on the ridgeline known as the San Juan Heights. They could see in the near distance, less than two miles away, whitewashed buildings of the city of Santiago. The Spaniards had regrouped and were still shooting from a tree line a few hundred yards down the slope. Occasionally a man would be hit and sometimes killed.

"None of the white regulars or Rough Riders showed the slightest sign of weakening; but under the strain the colored infantrymen (who had none of their officers) began to get a little uneasy and drift to the rear, either helping wounded men or saying that they wished to find their own regiments," Roosevelt recalled. He jumped up, pulled out his service revolver, and called on them to halt. In a scene that was widely witnessed, he complimented the soldiers as brave men but threatened to shoot them if they did not return to the line. "This was the end of the trouble, for the 'smoked Yankees'—as the Spaniards called the colored soldiers—flashed their white teeth at one another, as they broke into broad grins, and I had no more trouble with them, they seemed to accept me as one of their own officers," Roosevelt wrote.[1]

When that account appeared a year later in a story Roosevelt wrote about the Rough Riders for *Scribner's,* there was a bitter reaction in the small but influential African American newspapers printed in the United States. As Jim Crow legally relegated black people to inferior status in the South, blacks could hardly be blamed for ambivalent feelings about the war against Spain. Whites from North to South saw the war as a way to reunite the blue and the gray, to patch over the wounds of the Civil War. Naturally, it seemed to blacks that this war was an excuse to forget why the war to free the slaves had been fought in the first place. Knowing that the officer corps would be kept lily-white, some blacks resisted recruitment, saying, "No officers, no soldiers." But others wished to show that they were citizens, too, and men—even in the cause of carrying what Rudyard Kipling would memorably versify as the White Man's Burden.[2]

Though nearly a quarter of the expeditionary force was black (those "immunes" sent to Cuba on the wrongheaded assumption that they would not succumb to tropical disease), the black soldiers were treated shabbily. In Florida they were kept out of bars and hotels; in one grotesque incident, drunken soldiers from Ohio snatched a black two-year-old from his mother and used him as target practice, to see how close they could shoot without killing the infant. The shaken child and hysterical mother survived, but black soldiers, outraged and humiliated, went on a rampage in the city of Tampa on June 6, setting off an ugly race riot that was kept out of the newspapers. On the voyage to Cuba the black regiments—veteran buffalo soldiers in the

Ninth and Tenth Cavalry, raw recruits in the Twenty-fourth and Twenty-fifth Infantry—were kept belowdecks in the most squalid conditions.

Nonetheless the black soldiers fought bravely and well at Las Guasimas and at San Juan. Roosevelt seems to have recognized this, for he wrote that even his southwestern troopers regarded the "smoked Yankees" as comrades and were willing to "drink out of the same canteen."[3] So it is curious that in his published recollections he condescended to the black soldiers, describing them as utterly dependent on their white officers. The confrontation at the top of San Juan Ridge seems to have stemmed from a misunderstanding—the black soldiers (not "infantrymen" but troopers from the Tenth Cavalry) were not shirking. Rather, they had been sent to the rear to get rations and entrenching tools.[4] Roosevelt's racial attitudes were moderate, but only relatively speaking. The spirit of the age was captured by a British military attaché who, upon reaching the top of Kettle Hill, exclaimed to Roosevelt, "It's a great day for us Anglo-Saxons!"[5]

Lacking the proper tools, Roosevelt's troopers began digging trenches into the ridgeline with bayonets and empty meat cans. One of the Rough Riders found some shovels in the Spanish officers' quarters, as well as a pot of boiling stew, which Roosevelt shared with his ravenous men in tiny, evenly divided portions. By midnight the trench digging was done, and the Rough Riders dropped off to sleep, shivering in their sweat-soaked shirts. They had long since shed their bedrolls. A Spanish blanket was found for Roosevelt, and he shared it with his orderly Bradshar and Lieutenant David Goodrich, scion of the rubber company and former captain of the Harvard crew. Before he lay down to sleep, Roosevelt pulled out his little leather pocket diary and wrote with a pencil:

Rose at four.
Big Battle.
Commanded regiment.
Held extreme front of firing line.[6]

At dawn a shell burst overhead, showering the men with shrapnel and killing or wounding five of them. In his memoirs Roosevelt would later lament the death of Stanley Hollister, a Harvard track star, and Theodore Miller, a Yale man and the son of the founder of the Chautauqua camp meetings that William James had found so antiseptic and dull. At the time, however, he showed no emotion.[7] Roosevelt would later proudly if not quite accurately claim that the Rough Riders suffered proportionately the worst losses of any of the thirty-four regular and volunteer regiments—89 of 490 men killed or wounded—and that the loss rate among officers participating in the attack was especially high (about one in four), which was "as it should be." This was inaccurate: the Rough Riders' casualty rate for July 1 was later put at 15 percent, behind the black Tenth Cavalry—17 percent—and two infantry regiments that lost more than a fifth of their men assaulting San Juan Hill.[8] But whatever the count, Roosevelt was thrilled by the sacrifice of his alma mater and the implicit rebuff to Harvard's mugwump faculty and administrators. From his tent a month later he would write Harvard's president Charles Eliot, "I cannot say how proud I am of the Harvard men who are with me."[9]

Atop the San Juan Heights the Americans huddled in trenches, moving about on their knees to avoid the occasional potshot. Torrential downpours kept them soaked. There was not enough food, and their commanders safely back at headquarters at El Pozo seemed paralyzed, unsure whether to advance or retreat.

Racked by fever and doubt, General Shafter was stretched out on a door in his tent, far from the front lines. He telegraphed Washington to say that he was considering withdrawing the troops to a safer position. He was appalled by the losses so far, which he estimated at about four hundred killed or wounded (the true number was even higher, nearly fifteen hundred casualties, or 10 percent of his total forces). And he was haunted by hobgoblins of Spanish reinforcements racing to the rescue from nearby garrisons. In Washington, President McKinley wanted his generals to press on, but the army and navy engaged in a standoff: the army wanted the navy to attack the Spanish forts at the head of Santiago harbor, and the navy wanted the army to do it. Taking the ancient stone forts would invite heavy casualties. Neither service wanted to take the chance.[10]

Roosevelt heard the talk of retreat and would have none of it. He told his commander General Wheeler, "Well, General, I really don't know whether we would obey an order to fall back."[11] Fighting Joe "expressed his hearty agreement" and vowed to resist such an order, Roosevelt recalled. But the fight had gone out of other officers, and morale was slipping among the troops. By the morning of July 3, "one smelt disaster in the air," Davis wrote. "The alarmists were out in strong force and were in the majority." No one had slept much for three days, tobacco had run out, and the men were filthy, weak, cramped, suffering from sunstroke, and wondering whether every headache was the onset of malaria or, worse, yellow fever. "My clothes smell so that I can't use them as a pillow," Davis wrote his mother.[12]

Roosevelt tried to buck up his men with his bluff good cheer, but a letter he wrote Henry Cabot Lodge that day betrays his anxiety and uncharacteristic despair:

Outside Santiago, July 3, 1898

Dear Cabot:

Tell the President for Heaven's sake to send us every regiment and above all every battery possible. We have won so far at a heavy cost, but the Spaniards fight very hard and charging these intrenchments against modern rifles is terrible. We are within measurable distance of a terrible military disaster; we must *have help.... Our General is poor; he is too unwieldy to get to the front. I commanded my regiment, I think I may say, with honor. We lost a quarter of our men. For three days I have been at the extreme front of the firing line; how I have escaped I know not; I have not blanket or coat; I have not taken my shoes off even; I sleep in the drenching rain; and drink putrid water. Best love to Nannie.*

Yours ever,

Theodore

As Roosevelt wrote those words, deliverance was already on the way—not from McKinley or the hopelessly snarled military bureaucracy in Washington, but from the solons of the dying Spanish Empire.

The potshots Spanish troops were directing at the Americans were faint spasms from a mortally wounded beast. Spain had lost the war, and the Spaniards knew it. With Santiago's water supply cut off when El Caney fell, its people, already famished and diseased, were also drinking putrid water doled out of rapidly emptying cisterns. Yet simple surrender was out of the question. At the end of their four-hundred-year-long colonial reign, the Spaniards were preoccupied with honor. They had to put up a fight, no matter how futile.

In Santiago's splendid sheltered harbor, the Spanish battle

squadron rode at anchor, well protected by the guns of Morro Castle at its narrow mouth. Outside the harbor, a far superior fleet of American warships waited in blockade. In Havana the royal governor, Captain General Ramón Blanco y Arenas, worried about his reputation back home. "If we should lose the squadron without fighting," he told his commander in Santiago, General Arsenio Linares y Pombo, "the moral effect would be terrible, in Spain and abroad." By telegraph Blanco ordered the navy to weigh anchor and engage the Americans in a final sea battle.[13] The commander of the fleet, Vice Admiral Pascual Cervera y Topete, thought the order was "madness" and suicidal, yet he obeyed.

Sunday, July 3, dawned foggy, but the sun quickly burned through and turned the Caribbean an iridescent blue. The winds were light; not far offshore the American ships could be seen rolling in the slow southern swell. Admiral Cervera ordered the signal "*Viva Espana*" hoisted from his flagship, the *Infanta María Teresa*. As the battleship steamed out of the harbor, Captain Victor Concas y Palau, Cervera's chief of staff, refused to step inside the ship's armored conning tower, "in order, if I should fall, to set an example to my defenseless crew," he recalled, capturing perfectly the peculiar mix of Spanish pride and defeatism. Standing on the bridge in his dress uniform, Concas requested permission from Cervera to open fire on the American ships that were already closing in. Cervera nodded. As the buglers called men to action, Concas was overwhelmed with emotion. The trumpeting, he later recalled, was "the last echo" of the bugles "sounded at the capture of Granada [the *reconquista* of Spain from Islam]. It was the signal that the history of four centuries of grandeur was at an end and that Spain was becoming a nation of the fourth class." At the time Concas turned to Cervera and said, "Poor Spain!" The admiral just looked pained, and shrugged.

Aboard the blockading American battleships—the *Texas, Brooklyn, New York, Oregon, Iowa,* and *Indiana*—the officers and sailors, in dress whites, were observing the Sunday morning ritual, the reading of the Articles of War, followed by prayers and a hymn. With a cry from the lookouts, signal flags began fluttering from mastheads—Signal 250, "Enemy Ships Escaping." A great cheer went up from men bored by thirty-four unbroken days of blockade duty. A mad scramble ensued, officers buckling on their swords and gunners stripping to the waist, just as man-of-war men had readied themselves in centuries past.

Aboard the *Brooklyn,* Associated Press correspondent George Graham watched with appalled awe as the Spanish fleet—the flagship *Infanta María Teresa,* followed by the battleships *Vizcaya, Cristóbal Colón,* and *Almirante Oquendo* and the destroyers *Plutón* and *Furor*—emerged from the harbor channel by Morro Castle at roughly ten-minute intervals. The parade was at once solemn and gaudy. While the American warships had been daubed in dull gray, the hulls of the Spanish warships were painted glossy black, the superstructures buff white. The brightwork was varnished and painted, and gold figureheads were freshly gilded. Enormous silk battle flags streamed boldly. Brightly colored awnings shaded the decks as if for a garden party, and the men stood at attention on the yardarms.[14] Aboard the USS *Texas,* Captain Jack Philip marveled at the ships sailing out to their doom "as gaily as brides to the altar." Then he gave the order to open fire.

The heavily varnished paneling in Admiral Cervera's stateroom quickly ignited when the American salvos began crashing in. On the bridge the stoical Captain Concas recalled "shells were bursting all around us." He fell, badly wounded, along with two aides—the only men still alive outside the armored conning tower. The *María Teresa* began to belch black smoke. Slowly the burning vessel turned toward shore and made for a small cove, where she beached before she could sink. Rocked by explosions, the *Vizcaya* also ground onto a sandbar. The men on the *Texas* began cheering, but Philip called out, "Don't cheer, boys, the poor devils are dying."

One by one the ships of His Imperial Majesty were burned, sunk, grounded, scuttled. There were odd touches of gallantry. To give some drowning Spaniards a float, a crewman on the *New York* threw overboard the chaplain's wooden pulpit, wrenched from the deck where an hour or so earlier the crew had assembled to worship. Over on the *Iowa* the crew carried the badly wounded commander of the *Vizcaya*, Captain Antonio Eulate, aboard. The marine guard presented arms; Eulate struggled to straighten up and unbuckle his sword. He kissed the hilt and presented the ceremonial blade to Captain Robley Evans, who, in the tradition of victorious captains honoring the courage of the vanquished, graciously declined.

The endgame was ragged. The *Colón*, the last ship to be hunted down, slowly lost speed. The engine-room crew, drunk on brandy, had mutinied. When the ship surrendered, American sailors found the stokers' bodies in the boiler room; they had been shot by their officers for shirking.

The battle was over by 1:00 p.m. Only one American sailor died, his head blown off by a Spanish shell, his remains splattered on the American Flying Squadron commander, Commodore Winfield Scott Schley. The Spaniards lost 323 killed and 151 severely wounded, about a fifth of the ships' men and officers. Admiral William Sampson, the overall fleet commander, who had missed the battle because he was ashore bickering with General Shafter, nonetheless claimed the glory. He wired

A Spanish warship burns off Santiago.

Washington: "The fleet under my command offers the nation as a Fourth of July present the whole of Cervera's fleet."[15]

Aboard the *Sylvia*, William Randolph Hearst watched the sea battle from a safe distance of three or four miles. He had been a little too eager several days earlier, when the American fleet had bombarded Morro Castle. With Hemment on the bow with his camera, Hearst had ordered *Sylvia* close to shore, hoping to get a good shot of American shells striking the ancient citadel. Several of the missiles landed uncomfortably close, and then one — a twelve-incher — actually skipped over the *Sylvia*. Hearst wisely retreated.

He could not resist inspecting the still smoldering wrecks of the Spanish fleet on the Fourth of July. At 5:00 a.m. the *Sylvia* drew alongside the *Vizcaya* so that Hearst and his entourage could see up close the twisted metal and gaping shell holes. They recoiled at the grotesquely misshapen charred bodies. Hearst boarded the Spanish battleship and as a trophy of war took a lump of molten metal (later kept on his desk as a paperweight).

A detachment of marines from the *Texas* came by to shoo Hearst away from the battle zone. "What were you doing on the ship?" the officer in charge demanded. "Just looking about, sir, at the results of the battle," Hearst answered ("meekly," he later self-deprecated). "Can't you mind your own business?" said the officer. Hearst found his confidence. "Not very well, sir, and be a good newspaperman!" he shot back.

Indeed he could not stay away. Using high-powered binoculars purchased in New York, he spied a motley group of men on the beach. Dressed for the occasion in blue flannel blazer and yachting cap, he leaped into action, ordering the *Sylvia's* launch swung out and steering for shore. Armed with a pistol, he outraced a boatload of marines from the *Texas*. The men on the beach were Spanish sailors, survivors of several vessels including the flagship *María Teresa*. Hungry and half naked, they were only too glad to be captured.

Hearst assembled his prize — twenty-nine prisoners of war — on the deck of the *Sylvia*. As his yacht steamed past the *Texas* (and some fuming marines), Hearst assumed his favorite role, impresario of the unexpected. In honor of Independence Day, he led the Spanish prisoners in three cheers for "George Washington and Old Glory." Then he tried to find a naval officer who would take the Spaniards off his hands. The captain of the *Oregon* declined. "Keep 'em," he said, obviously displeased by Hearst's grandstanding. "You took 'em. You can take care of 'em." Eventually discharging his catch to the captain of the *Harvard*, a converted cruiser, Hearst demanded a receipt, which he later hung on his office wall.[16]

In an editorial on July 6 entitled "American Manhood Tested

Spanish sailors captured by Hearst, and his receipt (New York Journal*)*

by War," the *Journal* ventured to answer the question that had so troubled the social Darwinists who predominated in America's intellectual class—the readers of Roosevelt's *Winning of the West*, who fretted about overcivilization and the corrupting effect of the "lesser races":

> This year's Fourth of July found the American Republic bigger and richer than ever before. But what about its quality? Is this the American stock, with its new mixture of the blood of all the races of Europe, as good as it was through the Dark and Bloody Ground of Kentucky, or when Jackson was laying low the veterans of Wellington at New Orleans? Let Manila and Santiago answer. As far as the fighting quality goes, the experience of this war proves that instead of deteriorating the American race is steadily improving.

Hearst was a jingoist and prone to pseudoscientific theorizing. But as the publisher of a mass-circulation newspaper, many
of whose readers were recent immigrants, he could be a crudely
unifying force.

The suicide of the Spanish fleet at last made surrender unavoidable, but there was still time for haggling. The too-proud Spanish and the uncertain Shafter engaged in a desultory negotiation
that stretched on for a week, then two weeks. In Washington,
President McKinley decided that he wished to be a true war
president and demanded unconditional surrender. The Spanish insisted they be allowed to keep their arms, and as always
played for time. A wretched procession of starving civilians was
permitted to leave the besieged city. Roosevelt forbade his men
to share their feeble rations, but prostitutes traded their favors
for hardtack from the American soldiers. The men on the front
lines tried to amuse themselves in more wholesome ways as well.
On July 4 the military bands swung into stirring tunes (the
Rough Rider band played "Fair Harvard"), and when an enormous thunderstorm burst in late afternoon, the men stripped
and played leapfrog in the rain.[17]

But disease was coming. The first cases of yellow fever—the
dreaded black vomit—appeared on July 6; within a week 150
cases had been detected. Clara Barton arrived and, trying not
to embarrass the naked men lying in the wards, pulled down
her hat and averted her eyes as she walked by. She did the best
she could with insufficient medicines, but illness would claim far
more American lives (771) than would Spanish bullets (243).[18]

Roosevelt was beside himself with rage at his dithering commander. "Not since the campaign of Crassus against the Par-
thians has there been so criminally incompetent a General as

Shafter," he steamed in a letter to Lodge on July 5. Then he summoned his deep and sustaining resources of self-regard. "I don't know whether the people at home know how well this regiment did," he went on. "I am as proud of it as I can be; and these men would follow me anywhere now."

He need not have worried about how he was regarded back home. He had taken care on that score by cultivating Richard Harding Davis, whose dispatches made Roosevelt seem like the hero of the entire battle. Ever alert to Roosevelt's public image, Lodge had been clipping newspaper stories, and in a letter he enclosed a sampling, along with his joyous congratulations. "You again brilliantly distinguished yourself at San Juan on Friday," Lodge wrote on July 4. "You are one of the most popular persons in the war and deserve to be. Pray God you come out all right. We have been living with our hearts in our mouths."

Lodge had been following the war as closely as possible in the telegraph age. He had been anxiously waiting at the War Department on Saturday, July 2, when Shafter had sent his "disheartening dispatch," as Lodge described it to Roosevelt, recommending that the hard-won ground of his troops be abandoned so they could withdraw to a safer position. "I was perfectly appalled by the utter lack of efficiency, organization or plan there displayed by the head of the Department [Secretary Alger]. I was a rank outsider and have no military education or experience, but I could have taken those questions up which they were muddling over and settled them in an hour," Lodge wrote his friend on the front line.

Lodge had also been hovering about the White House, plumping to make Roosevelt a general—McKinley, ever the pleaser, said he would see to it—and bracing the president against softening on expansionism. In his frequent letters through the month of July (delivered to Roosevelt a week later), Lodge privately expressed his fear that McKinley might be "timid" about annexing the Philippines. He boasted that his son Bay had been commended for handling his guns well on his warship in a naval bombardment of a Spanish fort. One of many in Roosevelt's circle who had questioned the judgment of a thirty-nine-year-old signing on for combat duty, Lodge admitted that he had been "all wrong about your going into war." But he advised his friend to "look after" his regiment "and not run ahead of it in every charge that is made."[19]

Lodge's pride in his protégé was tinged with political opportunism. "I hear talk all the time about your being run for Governor and Congressman, and at this moment you could have pretty much anything you wanted," he wrote. It was the second time he had raised the possibility of political reward to Roosevelt. "The newspapers are nominating you for Governor of New York," Lodge had written on June 29—even before Richard Harding Davis described Roosevelt charging up San Juan Hill.[20]

Davis, whose dispatches were widely picked up or copied by other newspapers, loosely conflated Roosevelt's assault on Kettle Hill with the attack on the higher, better-defended San Juan Hill captured by General Hawkins and his infantry. Davis's carelessness—and Roosevelt's persistent failure to correct it—would provoke years of squabbling and jealousy. Understandably peeved at Roosevelt's penchant for headlines, the regular army in its official reports diminished his role in the battle.[21]

This was a problem for Roosevelt, because the prize he eyed was not immediately the governorship of New York, but rather the Medal of Honor. On July 7 he wrote Lodge that "General

Wheeler says he intends to recommend me for the medal of honor; naturally, I should like to have it." He never got it in his lifetime. Despite an ardent campaign bordering on the embarrassing (in his 1913 *Autobiography* he was still publishing testimonials), Roosevelt failed to persuade the top brass that his actions on July 1, 1898, were not just gallant but exceptionally gallant, as the medal requires. The army dismissed him as brash and impertinent, a glory hound, while Secretary Alger regarded him as a relentless self-promoter.*[22]

While Roosevelt agitated for his honor, the Spaniards play-acted for theirs. The Spanish commander arranged for a token bombardment of Santiago so he could report back to Madrid that his troops laid down their arms only under fire. Finally, on July 17, the Spanish surrendered, or rather capitulated, as the official documents put it. The word for surrender—*rendición*—was not used in deference to Spanish insistence on the less pejorative *capitulación*.[23]

The surrender ceremony in the central square of Santiago was more sorry than grand. Shafter did not dismount from his horse because he was afraid he would be unable to get back on. Trumpets sounded, and there was a good deal of saluting and handshaking between American and Spanish officers. The Rough Riders gave Roosevelt three cheers. But it was impossible to ignore the stench of dead horses and the vultures circling over the desperate city.[24]

Excluded from the surrender ceremony were the Cubans, the people for whom the war had been fought. Shafter did not trust the *insurrectos* to behave. Learning that his forces would be

---

*President Bill Clinton finally awarded Roosevelt the Medal of Honor posthumously, in 2001.

barred from entering the city of Santiago, Cuban general Calixto García sent this message, touching in its wounded pride
and appeal to American history, to the American general:

> *A rumor, too absurd to be believed, ascribes the reason for*
> *your measure and of the orders forbidding my army to enter*
> *Santiago, to fear of massacres and revenge against the*
> *Spaniards. Allow me, sir, to protest against even the shadow*
> *of such an idea. We are not savages ignoring the rules of*
> *civilized warfare. We are a poor, ragged Army, as ragged and*
> *poor as the Army of your forefathers in their noble war for the*
> *Independence, but as the heroes of Saratoga and Yorktown, we*
> *respect too deeply our cause to disgrace it with barbarism and*
> *cowardice.*[25]

Shafter may have felt a pang of guilt, for he agreed to permit
García, though not his troops, to attend the surrender ceremony.
But through the usual failures of communication, García was
turned away at the outskirts of Santiago at gunpoint by a soldier whose orders were to block any Cubans from entering the
city. The guard was a Rough Rider, a family friend of Roosevelt
named Edward Emerson, who later wrote that he did not recognize the general.[26]

Heartbroken, García resigned. He had long feared that all
those American shouts of *"Cuba Libre!"* would not lead to a
Cuban government and that the Americans would take charge
of the island, at least for a long while. It had been the old general
who had welcomed Hearst to his headquarters on the beach in
Siboney and given him a bullet-holed Cuban flag in the hope
that the *Journal* would pressure Washington to let the Cubans
rule themselves.[27] But his hope was forlorn; Hearst did not

believe the Cubans were ready for self-government, though he was not quite as adamant as Shafter, who exclaimed, "Self government! Why these people are no more fit for self-government than gunpowder is for hell."[28]

Shafter thought the Cubans were inept allies, and was furious that they had not prevented a relief column of several thousand Spanish soldiers from reaching Santiago in early July. His contempt was unjustified. Using their usual hit-and-run tactics, the Cuban guerrillas had slowed and harassed the advancing column, killing twenty and wounding seventy Spanish soldiers. The Americans needed the Cubans as scouts and skirmishers. The Cubans needed the Americans to destroy Spanish naval forces and strongholds. Contrary to the claim of some historians, the revolutionaries were not on the verge of victory when the Americans barged in. "Only the Americans could have destroyed the Spanish army at Santiago, and to claim otherwise is delusional," writes historian John Tone, author of the most balanced scholarship on the Cuban military.[29] But hardening racial attitudes made it difficult for the Americans to believe that the Cubans were capable of self-defense or self-governance. Roosevelt's and Lodge's old clubmate Winthrop Chanler was explicit in his prejudice. Ever the adventurer, Chanler had joined up with the Cuban army with the rank of colonel and had been wounded while landing there. He wrote Lodge that the Cuban army in the west of the island was better than the forces in the east (around Santiago) because "in the East the black element predominates....The men Theodore saw run like sheep are the same men who robbed our soldiers."[30]

For his part Roosevelt regarded the Cuban insurgents as worthless. He passed along his doubts about the Cubans to

Lodge, who in turn spoke to McKinley. As Lodge informed a friend, Henry White,

Theodore writes from Santiago that the Cubans behaved badly, fought badly. There are accounts which are more favorable, but this is the general drift of our information. The country is I think satisfied that the Insurgents have not got a government and cannot make one. The President I think feels very strongly about Cuba. . . . He means to take firm military possession and not withdraw the troops until the island is in perfect order and a stable government established.[31]

With the surrender of the Spanish army, the Rough Riders were moved to a camp in the foothills, supposedly a healthier spot, though "fever is making perfect ravages among us," Roosevelt wrote Lodge. "I now have left less than half of the six hundred men with whom I landed." Pooling his personal funds with money from other Fifth Avenue swells, he was able to buy his starving men some beans and cans of tomatoes. "Their clothes are in tatters," Roosevelt reported. "They have not changed their underclothes since they landed a month ago."

Roosevelt announced that he himself felt "as strong as a bull moose," and that he was not afraid of the "Yellow Jack." "I don't think I should die if I caught it, and in the next place should the worse come to the worst, I am quite content to go now and to leave my children at least an honorable name (and, old man, if I do go, I do wish that you would get that medal of honor for me anyhow, as I should awfully like the children to have it and I think I earned it)." Roosevelt told Lodge he was "just wild to see you and spend an evening telling you various things" for "this has been, aside from Edith, *the* time of my life; but there have been many grim features to it, and you're the only man to whom I can write of them."

And write he did, pouring out over many pages his complaints about the incompetence of the top brass and the squalor of camp life. "However, enough of grumbling," he paused in one letter. "Did I tell you that I killed a Spaniard with my own hand...?"[32]

21

Spoils of War

"We're a gr-reat people.... An' the best iv it is, we know we ar-re."

A S YELLOW FEVER spread among his troops, Roosevelt, still feeling healthy, found ways to divert himself. The American ambassador to Cuba, General Fitzhugh Lee, invited him to tour Morro Castle at the head of Santiago harbor. Growing bored, Roosevelt eyed a wreck a few hundred yards out in the channel and suggested to his subordinate, Jack Greenway, a former Yale athlete, that they swim out and take a look. The two men disrobed and dove in, and as Greenway later told the story, they were splashing along when they heard General Lee begin to yell from shore. Roosevelt asked if Greenway could make out what the ambassador was shouting. "Sharks," replied Greenway, wishing he were back onshore.

"Sharks," replied Roosevelt, blowing out a mouthful of water. He continued to swim toward the wreck, spurting out words between breaths: "They" stroke "won't" stroke "bite." Stroke. "I've been" stroke "studying them" stroke "all my life" stroke "and I never" stroke "heard of one" stroke "bothering a swimmer." Stroke. "It's all" stroke "poppycock." Escorted by a phalanx of sharks (at least, in Greenway's telling), the two reached the wreck. "I felt better," Greenway recalled, until he remembered they had to swim back.[1]

Roosevelt's fellow officers were stewing about how to get off the pestilential island. Nobody wanted to be the one to suggest a flight to safety—they were all regular army officers with careers to consider. Roosevelt, on the other hand, was a volunteer. He was also the one with good press contacts. Somewhat recklessly, Roosevelt agreed to act as messenger.

One day in early August the newspaper correspondents were sitting around the old Anglo-American Club in Santiago, where the sugar traders had sipped rum in more peaceful times, when Roosevelt blew in. He was wearing a pair of jodhpurs and exuding high spirits. By now newsmen were accustomed to his cheerful bragging about his regiment; he spoke the way a father talks when his "boy has scored the winning touchdown in a big football game," recalled the *Journal*'s Ralph Paine (the former Yale oarsman recruited by Hearst to present a sword to General Gómez).[2]

From his pocket Roosevelt pulled a draft of a "round robin" letter he was preparing to be signed by all the top commanders, beseeching General Shafter to get the army out of Cuba before the force was obliterated by fever. "What do you boys think of it?" Roosevelt asked.

The letter appeared in several American newspapers a few days later. Roosevelt strongly suggested in his *Autobiography* that it was leaked with Shafter's connivance, which may have been true. But leaking the letter was a very risky and impertinent step, embarrassing to the top brass in Washington. An even more pointed personal letter to Shafter, signed by Roosevelt and also leaked, essentially accused the War Department of letting the army die "like rotten sheep" while Washington dithered.

Secretary of War Alger was indignant when the story broke.[3] "It looks as if Roosevelt, in his impetuosity, has raised the devil by getting together a town meeting of officers in Santiago and preparing the most doleful account of soldiers there," Navy Secretary John Long complained to his wife, Agnes. The letter created a "panic" not just in Washington but across the country, Long wrote.[4] Roosevelt's "impetuosity" could not have helped his chances to win the Medal of Honor. The irony is that Alger had already instructed the army to draw up orders withdrawing the troops to the United States. Roosevelt's poke had been unnecessary.[5]

On August 7 the Rough Rider band played "The Star-Spangled Banner" as the steamer *Miami* slid past Morro Castle into the blue Caribbean and swung east, then north toward home. Roosevelt's quarters resembled a "chicken coop," he recalled, and the food and water were bad, but the sea was calm and the officers sat around telling stories. The Civil War tales spun by General Wheeler reminded them that, relatively speaking, their war had been but a skirmish. The Rough Riders, who had burned their stinking, germy uniforms, celebrated their exodus by gambling away their paychecks and selling whiskey to the stokers in the boiler room. On learning of this recklessness, Roosevelt Solomonically banned the whiskey selling but not the gambling.

At Montauk Point on Long Island on Monday, August 15, as the *Miami* was warped in by tugs, a large crowd pressed along the wharf looking for a bronze-faced man in khaki. They yelled when they saw him: "Hurrah for Roosevelt! Hurrah for Teddy and the Rough Riders!" Someone shouted up from the pier, "How are you, Colonel Roosevelt?" Roosevelt bellowed back, "I am feeling disgracefully well!" Then, surrounded by gaunt and careworn men, he checked himself. "I feel positively ashamed of my appearance, when I see how badly off some of my brave fellows are." Still, he could not resist: "Oh, but we have had a bully fight!" Disembarking, he was surrounded by reporters. He showed them the pistol he had used to kill the Spaniard.[6]

Roosevelt announced that he was ready to go back to Cuba and take Havana, but he was too late: Spain had reached a formal peace treaty with the United States three days earlier. Now eager to return home and see his family, he was thwarted by a five-day quarantine for yellow fever.

So Edith came to him. Jacob Riis recalled seeing a hooded and cloaked Mrs. Roosevelt, rattling along on a buckboard through the Montauk hills while thunderheads blackened the afternoon sky, on her way to meet her "husband-lover."[7] A young officer smuggled Roosevelt out of the camp that night. The rendezvous was brief, and Edith, ever discreet, allowed only in her private correspondence that her husband looked well "but very thin" (he had lost about twenty pounds).[8]

Roosevelt reached home on August 20 at eight in the evening. The normally sleepy Long Island town of Oyster Bay gave him a riotous welcome with fireworks and bands and a large crowd waving welcome-home banners and pushing to get a look at "Our Teddy." Edith, who disdained the nickname, was the stoic once more. She found her house overrun with reporters and camera "fiends." "It is something horrid," she wrote Emily, "but it will not last long."[9] She was being optimistic. The cult of Roosevelt had begun.

Crowds followed him down the street when he went to New York City. The mail poured in, one letter addressed only with a drawing of a Rough Rider wearing glasses. In his correspondence to Lodge from Cuba, Roosevelt had expressed reticence about running for governor, but he began maneuvering almost as soon as he stepped off the boat. On August 17, less than forty-eight hours after his arrival, while he was still in quarantine, he telegraphed Lemuel Quigg, head of the Republican Party in New York:

CAN YOU GET HERE TOMORROW OR FRIDAY. CAN PUT YOU UP FOR THE NIGHT. WOULD PARTICULARLY LIKE TO TALK OVER MATTERS WITH YOU.[10]

The day after Roosevelt had arrived in Oyster Bay, he left Sagamore Hill to meet with Senator Thomas Platt, his old political nemesis, at the Fifth Avenue Hotel in Manhattan. The two foes danced around each other. Platt had his doubts about Roosevelt, whom he could not control, but Quigg had persuaded the bosses that Roosevelt's celebrity was a juggernaut. Roosevelt flirted with running as an independent just to keep Platt uncertain, then accepted the machine's support.[11]

When Lodge came to visit, Roosevelt's affection overflowed. "I don't believe you realize old man, what a keen, keen pleasure it was to see you at Sagamore. Next to Edith and the children there is no one whom I so desired to see (and never is anyone)."[12] Lodge teased Roosevelt ("I don't know how Dewey took Manila without you") and confidently predicted to their friend Winthrop Chanler that Roosevelt would be elected governor.[13] To make some much-needed money and burnish the legend, Roosevelt was already at work on a six-part series on his triumphs for *Scribner's*. Finley Peter Dunne's Mr. Dooley joked in his usual argot that it should be called "Alone in Cubia."[14]

But while Roosevelt could not resist the temptation of self-glorifying publicity, his affection for his men was real, as was theirs for him. At the end of August he returned to Montauk to disband his unit and muster them out. In the slanting light of late summer, he swam in the still-warm surf and joined his cowboys in their stamping Indian dances around the campfire. Twice he delivered farewell addresses. He began the second, "Officers and men, I really do not know what to say" and then rambled on, pouring out his love and brio, praising his men, cowboys and socialites alike, as true Americans, bidding them to continue in the world's fight. The men gave him a beautiful small statue, Remington's *Bronco Buster,* and many wept openly. Finally, in mid-September, the Rough Riders were dispersed. "So all things pass away," Roosevelt told Jacob Riis as they lay on the grass by his tent under a starry sky, watching a meteor streak past. "But they were beautiful days."[15]

The political life to which he returned was sordid. Roosevelt dodged between the machine and the mugwumps, between the regular Republicans and the reform Independents, disliking both. His political foes leaked the charge that he was not a legal resident of New York because he had not paid taxes there, and he had to hire the famous Elihu Root—the same lawyer who made Thomas Reed a standing offer to join his firm—to ensure his eligibility for office with some clever argle-bargle. By September 26 he was writing Lodge, "I have, literally, hardly been able to eat or sleep during the last week, because of the pressure upon me."[16] Roosevelt appears to have experienced some kind of postwar depression, but he soon shook it off. Nevertheless he informed Senator Platt that he would not run for governor after all. "Is the hero of San Juan Hill a coward?" sneered the senator. That did it. "By Gad!" Roosevelt shot back, "I'll run."[17]

On August 20 Hearst welcomed Admiral Sampson's victorious fleet to New York. "Welcome to the Sea Kings!" trumpeted the

Roosevelt bids farewell to the Rough Riders (Theodore Roosevelt Collection, Houghton Library, Harvard University)

Journal. ("The Heroes Have Come Home," ran the subhead, "But The Ships Have Their War Paint on Yet. Europe, Please Take Notice.") Hearst took credit for persuading local businessmen and politicians to declare a holiday, and thousands of New Yorkers lined the west shore of Manhattan to see the mighty warships parade up the Hudson. Hearst arranged for the massive fireworks he loved and floated the *Journal*'s "war balloon" above Grant's Tomb, with observers aboard to signal the progress of the fleet north from Staten Island with periodic bursts of confetti. (The same balloon had floated above the *Sylvia* to allow Hearst's reporters to watch the naval battle off Santiago.)[18]

Though he loved such spectaculars, Hearst stayed in the shadows. He was down, overcome with his own postbellum *tristesse*. The navy had finally awarded him his commission—as an ensign—in August, after the war was over.[19] He rightly sensed that he was being toyed with. If only he had found his way into uniform! He was also feeling guilty about abandoning poor Creelman at El Caney. Arriving back in New York in late July, he sulked. All day long he sat in his hot suite in the Waldorf, consumed by regret. He wrote a doleful letter to Creelman at his family home in Ohio, where his star correspondent was recovering from his wounds. "I feel like hell myself," confessed Hearst, half sardonic, half downcast. "I sit all day in one place in a half trance and stare at a spot. I'm afraid my mighty intellect is giving way. Anybody can have Cuba that wants it." He was bitterly jealous of Roosevelt. Although Hearst rarely opened up to anyone, he poured out his angst in a letter to his mother:

> *I guess I'm a failure. I made the mistake of my life in not raising a cowboy regiment I had in mind before Roosevelt raised his. I really believe I brought on the war but I failed to score in the war. I had my chance and failed to grab it, and I suppose I must sit on the fence now and watch the procession go by. It's my own fault. I was thirty-five years of age and of sound mind — comparatively — and could do as I liked. I failed and I'm a failure and I deserve to be for being as slow and stupid as I was. Outside of the grief it would give you I had better be in a Santiago trench than where I am. . . . Goodnight, Mama dear. Take care of yourself. Don't let me lose you. I wish you were here tonight. I feel about eight years old — and very blue.*

Self-pity does not get much more abject than that. Hearst may have been as blue, as desperate for his mother's comfort, as the letter suggests. Possibly he was bracing her for the bill that was coming due. Hearst's fleet, his army of correspondents, his constant extras, balloons, fireworks displays, and all the rest were taxing his mother's resources, notwithstanding her still-profitable silver mines. Painfully, Hearst cut back, laying off staff under orders from his mother's accountant.

He needed a new cause, a new way of capturing the public mood and retaining (or even boosting) circulation now that the war was over. Yes, the war had been short and glorious, and empire beckoned. But there was a bit of a sour taste to the celebration. Deflated himself, Hearst picked up on the disgruntlement. The *Journal* campaigned against the squalor in the army camps, the shoddy uniforms and sickening food, especially so-called embalmed beef, canned beef preserved with odious chemicals. As it became clear that many more American soldiers had been killed by sickness than by enemy bullets, Hearst got so wound up that by the end of August he was denouncing Secretary of War Alger as a "murderer."[20]

The *Journal* had lionized Roosevelt in war, but once he decided to run for governor, Hearst's jealousy seeped into his newspaper. Though he had journeyed to the battlefield in Cuba, Hearst had felt like a bystander, a mere spectator in his yachting clothes. He wanted like Roosevelt to be in the arena. In September Hearst wrote his mother asking for her financial support if he ran for governor. But no one asked him to run. In relatively short order Hearst would become a self-made politician, but he could not transform himself overnight. Not surprisingly, in the meantime he turned on Roosevelt, lampooning the Republican candidate for governor as a bucktoothed cowboy pretender, as an overgrown child, as a tool of the machine. Infuriatingly, Roosevelt ignored him—and was able to do so with impunity.[21]

"What a wonderful war it has been," Lodge wrote John Hay, the man who (possibly unbeknown to Lodge) had cuckolded him a few years earlier. "What a navy we have & what good fighters our soldiers are. Nothing but victory & at such small cost." Lodge mildly joked about Roosevelt's boasting but added that "he has a right to shout as much as he likes."[22]

Hay, who was in London as America's ambassador to Great Britain, agreed on all counts. He had written Roosevelt to congratulate him on his "crowded hour" (they all seemed to be quoting Sir Walter Scott, author of their youth); to acknowledge that he had deplored Roosevelt's decision to go to war; and to admit that he had been wrong. "You obeyed your own demon, and I imagine we older fellows will all have to confess that you were right." Hay went on to use a phrase that would be long remembered: "It has been a splendid little war," he wrote.[23] Less commonly quoted are the words that followed: "...begun with the highest motives, carried on with magnificent intelligence and spirit, favored by that Fortune which loves the brave. It is now to be concluded, I hope, with that fine good nature, which is, after all, the distinguishing trait of the American character."

There is a wonderfully smug assumption in those words, a foundation stone of American exceptionalism: that the essential American character is better—somehow more decent—than that of other nations. America had by and large been content to be better than other nations and *apart* from them—separated by vast oceans from their scheming and greed, their power-mad intrigues born of ancient dynastic rivalries and national hatreds. America was purer: refugees from the fallen Old World sought redemption in the New. But now, partly by the accident of war fever, partly by the larger designs of Lodge's Large Policy,

America was joining in the scramble for imperial dominion. Men like John Hay entered this contest with the bland assumption that America would be different, more moral, less likely to be seduced by the temptations of conquest and booty—that it would uplift rather than beat down. These were not completely naive assumptions. America was a beacon of hope: not in absolute terms, but certainly relative to other nations it was the land of the free. John Hay was hardly a dreamy idealist. Secretary to Abraham Lincoln during the Civil War, he was experienced as a diplomat, as a newspaper publisher, and as an author of popular novels. He was a worldly, sophisticated, and wise man. But he was a bit of a dilettante and no strategist; he found Lodge and Mahan somewhat ponderous. He had not thought a great deal about the consequences of America as a world power, in part because it was such a new idea. Like McKinley, Hay barely knew how to find the Philippines on a map. At ease hobnobbing with British royals and debating trade or war with peers of the realm, he knew next to nothing about what would eventually be called the "developing" or "third world." Such regions were merely foreign and exotic countries, shapes on a map populated by inferior creatures and awash in uncommon tongues. It is obvious from the correspondence of Hay and his friend Adams, and their correspondence with Lodge and Roosevelt, that even these men of the world were making up their ideas about what to do with America's newfound power as they went along.

Adams had been among those who'd conspired to bring about a war to liberate Cuba. But he viewed the actual conflict from a great distance and with his customary jaundiced weariness, part affected, part real. Back in February he had been touring Egypt, musing upon the decline of empires as he watched a jackal sniff about the tomb of a pharaoh, when he first heard of the sinking of the *Maine*.[24] In May, as the war was breaking out, he wrote Hay from a hotel in Belgrade, "Naturally, I have stayed here in order to escape the bother of noise and idiocy that always begins a war." To his unrequited love Lizzie Cameron, he archly observed, "As for the war, it is a God-send to all the young men in America. Even the Bostonians have at last a chance to show that they have emotions."[25]

Hay was just as droll with Adams but much more engaged in the world, at least via a European conduit. Hay was present at the creation of what became known as the Special Relationship between the United States and Great Britain. "For the first time in my life I find the 'drawing room' sentiment altogether with us," a somewhat astonished Hay had written Lodge from London in early April, on the eve of war. "If we wanted it—which of course we do not—we could have the practical assistance of the British navy."[26] Soon after their huff over Venezuela in December 1895, Great Britain and her former colony began to see a common interest, the alliance of what Cabot Lodge, in his frequent correspondence with Hay, called "the English Speaking People" (an expression that would gain greater currency from the pen of Winston Churchill). At first the Anglo-American alliance seemed narrowly aimed at countering the growing robustness of German naval power. In the next century, as championed by Churchill and his partner, Theodore Roosevelt's younger cousin Franklin, the bond of the English Speaking Peoples would be endowed with grandeur, some arrogance, and much goodness, too, as it fostered the global spread of individual freedom and the rule of law. But all this lay in the future. As ambassador to the Court of St. James's (the formal appellation of the U.S. ambassador to Great Britain),

Hay was startled to see how warmly he was received by America's former masters across the sea. "This is in strict confidence—at the last levee, all the royalties stopped me, shook hands and made some civil remark," he wrote Lodge. "The Spanish ambassador coming next to me was received merely with a bow."

Wanting to be near his friend Hay, and perhaps to draw a little closer to the new epicenter of world power, Henry Adams leased an enormous Elizabethan mansion in the English countryside in the summer of 1898. It was "the size of Versailles," Adams deadpanned, and could sleep forty people. Adams lived there like a pasha, entertaining visiting statesmen and turning his villa into "a sort of country house to the [American] Embassy." Lizzie Cameron appeared at Adams's rented manse to re-create her salon on Lafayette Square. His neighbor in the English countryside was none other than Henry James. William's keen-eyed novelist brother would come over to take tea and to observe the asexual affair between Adams and Mrs. Cameron. "Women have been hanged for less—and men have been too, I judge, rewarded with more," he quipped.[27]

On August 14, two days after the peace accord between Spain and the United States had been signed, a White House telegram arrived at the London embassy. The message informed Hay that he had been appointed secretary of state by President McKinley. As much a complainer and neurasthenic as his friend Adams, Hay was plunged into depression by the momentous telegram. He moaned that the responsibility would kill him within six months. Adams retorted that he had no choice—having taken a favor from the president (assignment to the London embassy), he was compelled to accept a call to duty.[28]

After steamrolling the opposition to his Large Policy in

Washington, Lodge treated himself to a few days on Tuckernuck island and then repaired to the house in Nahant he had loaned to the Signal Corps for the duration of the war. The house was intact but its once-lovely green lawn had been torn up by over-zealous cadets.[29]

War had caused Lodge to gloat but also to worry. He had feared for friends and family at the front. The anxiety had been "almost unbearable," he had written his mother.[30] He had also confided to Josephine Shaw Lowell his angst over his friend Theodore; his son Bay (on a warship that was supposed to sail to Spain for a final naval battle); his brother-in-law, who was also Bay's captain; and his son-in-law, who was with the army headed for Puerto Rico (Spain's last significant possession in the Carib-bean). Effie Lowell, sister and bride of Harvard's martyred Civil War heroes, could sympathize, Lodge felt. "I know that you can appreciate the days of anxiety through which Mrs. Lodge and myself are passing," he wrote. Always, memories of a Civil War boyhood loomed large.[31]

After Santiago, the Spanish navy, or what was left of it, hid in Spanish ports while Puerto Rico fell to the Americans after mere skirmishing and with almost no casualties. Bay, though a lowly naval cadet, was permitted the honor of hoisting the American flag at the Spanish surrender in Ponce. With the safe return of all his loved ones in August, Lodge was able to relax and crow some more. He quickly turned his Nahant house into a trophy gallery decorated with a Spanish saber, a Puerto Rican machete, the porthole of a Spanish ship, and a giant Spanish flag—all "judiciously looted," as Lodge put it, by Bay. Lodge boasted to his friend Sturgis Bigelow that he was going to make every Spaniard in Washington march beneath the Spanish royal ensign, which he had draped over a hallway.[32]

"We have risen to be one of the world's great powers," Lodge proclaimed. Now came the hard question of what to do about it. At moments America's rush to relieve Spain of her empire had seemed almost like opéra bouffe. In July an American warship, the *Charleston*, stopped in Guam, a small Spanish possession in the western Pacific, and began shelling the Spanish fort. "Whereupon, the Spanish governor in full uniform came off [approached the warship in a small boat] and said that he regretted that he had no powder with which to return the salute," Lodge wrote Roosevelt, hoping to share a good laugh over bumbling Spaniards and the follies of war.[33] But both men knew that empire was no laughing matter, and in the giddy aftermath of victory over Spain, difficult decisions loomed. America was on the verge of acquiring millions of dependents with darker skins and different cultures, many of them at odds with each other, and of acquiring the territory of imperial rivals who were not only intent on carving up the world, but quite probably each other.[34]

Having bungled relations with the indigenous rebel force in Cuba, the United States proceeded to do the same in the Philippines. Faced with widespread insurrection long before Admiral Dewey arrived with his fleet, the Spaniards had been as cruel and as clumsy as they had been in Cuba. Repression was medieval: the Spanish authorities strangled rebels with a device called a garrote, twisted slowly with a large iron screw. Emilio Aguinaldo, the Filipino rebel leader, was a charismatic young man (not yet thirty) with a babyish, pockmarked face and a strong sense of his destiny. He called himself the "generalissimo."[35] At first Dewey treated Aguinaldo respectfully, as an ally against Spain. The "generalissimo" was encouraged by American diplomats to believe that the United States was on his side. Rebel soldiers, alongside a smaller American contingent, enveloped

Aguinaldo

Spanish-controlled Manila. But then, just as in Cuba, the rebels were cut out. Seeking to accommodate the overweening pride of the Spanish, the Americans looked for ways to allow the enemy to lay down arms while saving face. In August a mock battle was conducted (with a little too much eagerness; America lost more men than in the real naval battle of Manila Bay). As had been planned, Spain then surrendered to the United States—but not to Aguinaldo. As the Spanish governor explained, he preferred to surrender to white men than to "niggers." (American soldiers as well as their commanders also commonly called Filipinos this.) Aguinaldo and his rebel commanders were excluded from the negotiations and the surrender ceremony.[36]

Acquiring the Philippines was an afterthought. The idea did not seem to have occurred to Lodge, chief apostle of expansionism, until after Dewey's victory at Manila Bay, and Adams and Hay were also not quite sure what to do with the islands. "You have a new game to play," Adams wrote Hay, "[and I] don't quite feel as though I know the value of the cards or of the players."

Adams's own proposal was modest: acquire a coaling station in the islands, nothing more.[37] More dramatically, Lodge considered giving half of the islands to Great Britain. Although his personal tastes had always been Anglophile, his politics had been consistently Anglophobe; he and Roosevelt had long enjoyed bashing the British and dreaming, somewhat preposterously, of an invasion of Canada. But now Lodge imagined a great Anglo-Saxon hegemony that far transcended the original war aim of Cuba Libre: "Race, blood, language, identity of beliefs & aspirations all assert themselves.... To the drawing together of the English Speaking People all over the world & of the two great nations seems far more momentous, more fraught with meaning to the future of mankind than the freeing of Cuba or the expulsion of Spain from this hemisphere," he wrote John Hay.[38]

Lodge was always careful, however, not to use the word "imperialism," and he genuinely wanted America to take a higher road than had the European powers, including Great Britain. He wanted the United States to train native peoples "in the principles of freedom" and to learn self-government. He hoped that America would stand above "corruption" and "jobbery"—that it would raise up, rather than exploit, the islands. He made economic arguments for annexing the Philippines, but mostly for political reasons: to persuade the commercial interests, dominant in the Republican Party, to come aboard.[39]

Lodge intensely lobbied President McKinley, who listened, cautiously at first. Ever keen to the political breezes, McKinley decided to tour the country to test public opinion. McKinley was canny—he could see economic opportunity in expansionism as the great powers set to carving up China. The Philippines would be a key staging area, and if America did not seize the islands, Germany or Japan would. But McKinley wanted to make sure the people were behind him.

In October he toured six midwestern states in ten days. He cast America's duty in moral terms, the opportunity as providential. In Omaha he asked, "Shall we deny ourselves what the rest of the world so freely and so justly accords to us?" The audience roared "No!" In Iowa he declared, "Territory sometimes comes to us when we go to war in a holy cause, and whenever it does the banner of liberty will float over it and bring, I trust, blessings and benefits for all the people." McKinley prayed over the question of acquiring the Philippines. He later described the process to a group of Methodist clergymen: "I walked the floor of the White House night after night until midnight; and I am not ashamed to tell you, gentlemen, that I went right down on my knees and prayed Almighty God for light and guidance more than one night."

Late one night, he told the preachers, he had had an epiphany ("I don't know how it was, but it came"). Giving back the islands to Spain would be "cowardly and dishonorable." Giving them to France or Germany would be "bad business." The islands could not be left alone—they were "unfit for self-government." So there was nothing left to do but "to take them all, and to educate the Filipinos, and uplift and Christianize them." McKinley did not acknowledge, or perhaps did not know, that most Filipinos had long since been converted to Catholicism.

McKinley's self-righteous sermonizing was more fodder for Mr.

Dooley, Finley Peter Dunne's fictional Chicago bartender: "We're a gr-reat people.... We ar-re that. An' the best iv it is, we know we ar-re."[40] On October 26, Secretary of State Hay sent a cable to American negotiators in Paris: they were to demand that Spain turn over the entire Philippine archipelago to the United States.[41]

22

A Certain Blindness

"Are we to have a Mongolian state in this Union?"

O N A BRIGHT afternoon in the fall of 1898 three philoso-
phers stood in the airy library of a house on Quincy Street,
at the edge of Harvard Yard. As the yellow leaves drifted
down outside and autumn light streamed into the large, book-
lined room, the owner of the house, Professor George Herbert
Palmer, stood with his back to the window, "evidently enjoying
the pleasant rays of the setting sun," recalled his Harvard colleague George Santayana. But the third philosopher, William
James, was plunged into darkness. He was "terribly distressed,"
recalled Santayana. "James said he had lost his country."

James told the others that he could understand the U.S. intervention in Cuba; the island had suffered from the oppression of
the Spaniards. But the annexation of the Philippines — what could
excuse that? To James, McKinley's decision to demand owner-
ship of the distant archipelago was somehow un-American.
James had long sustained a faith in American exceptionalism. He
believed, or wished to believe, that Americans were less prone to
the corruption and greed of their European forebears. He could
not excuse the president's imperialistic grab for territory in the
name of freedom and Christian morality.

Palmer did not wish to have his pleasant afternoon spoiled, so he smiled and murmured academic banalities—yes, he saw James's point, but every thesis had its antithesis, and the synthesis would ultimately be for the public good. Santayana, fatalist from the Old World, mourned for his quixotic Spain but regarded James as an innocent. In his memoir Santayana wrote that he admired James's "masculine directness," his warmth and openness, and he joined in the general approbation of James's sensitivity and lively turn of mind. But he regarded him as naive for believing that individuals could control the path of history when clearly, greater forces did.[1]

But James did believe in the individual. He did not place his faith in Great Men who guide the destiny of nations, but rather in ordinary individuals, whom he did not find ordinary at all. He refused to treat people as abstractions. To him, Emilio Aguinaldo was not a "Little Brown Brother" but an actual person. The Filipino people should not be treated as a "painted picture" on a giant canvas of the march of man's progress but as flesh-and-blood individuals.[2] He abhorred sweeping theories of history that explained everything, big ideas that gave license to oppression of the human spirit. Highly suspicious of the civilizing mission of imperialism, he did not agree with Kipling, in his poem of the age, that the white man carried the burden of uplifting the "lesser races" ("the sullen, silent peoples/Half devil and half child"). He was typical of his era and class in his dress and mores, conventional in many of his attitudes. And yet he was refreshingly farsighted in at least one essential way: at a time when notions of racial superiority and the vogue of social Darwinism legitimized colonial domination, James stood out as a lonely voice for pluralism (a word, it seemed, only he could coin), for respect for the dignity and worth of each individual, no matter how foreign or "other." In this he was ahead of his time, embracing notions that would become clichés in the late twentieth century but were far from popular in 1898. It was as if James could peer into the global abyss of the next century, when "isms" would be used as an excuse to slaughter and oppress millions of people.

James loved America and understood her vibrant spirit, but he was wary of all orthodoxies, which he felt crushed the human spirit. In the spring of 1898 he had flirted with the seductions of war—he had believed, or half believed, that the war to liberate Cuba fell within the tradition of his nation's worthy struggles to advance the cause of freedom. But he feared that the subsequent (or at least what he assumed was subsequent) imperial impulse would lead America into blundering after other colonial possessions to annex foreign peoples she could not understand. Doing so would betray the ideals that had given Americans their own independence.[3]

James's strong feelings about the uniqueness of the human spirit were, as usual, shaped by his own experience. In late June and early July, while Roosevelt was reveling in his "crowded hour" and suffering with his men in the trenches on the San Juan Heights, James had experienced a kind of rapture on a mountaintop in upstate New York. Like Thoreau, James used nature as restorative and as inspiration. Late in June, exhausted by the year-end hurly-burly of exams and commencement, he had arrived at a woodsy refuge in northern New York. Sick with a bad cold, his mind was feverish, and not just with the grippe. He was reading the journals of George Fox, founder of the Quakers and a fellow seeker after "openings," or sudden illuminations.[4] His romantic side stirred as he watched the moonlight over

William James (Houghton Library, Harvard University)

the Adirondacks, and he'd written Pauline Goldmark, hoping to meet with her, her sister, and their Bryn Mawr friends on a mountaintop before the full moon set.[5]

The war was a real but distant worry. "No news from Santiago since last Friday here! What a suspense," William had written brother Henry on July 4. Then, after a "glorious day in the woods by myself," he wrote Alice to say that he had returned to his lodgings "to find Cervera's fleet destroyed." He also had found a telegram from "Miss Pauline" proposing a rendezvous on Mount Marcy the next day.[6] At 3:00 a.m. he set off with a guide to climb the tallest peak in New York, just over a mile high. In late afternoon, hearing the sound of a falling axe, he

Pauline Goldmark at twenty-two (Bryn Mawr Archives)

had ventured toward a campsite and found the Goldmark girls and their friends. The girls were dressed in boys' breeches and "cutaneously desecrated in the extreme," James later described them to Alice. (The girls had been camping for a few days and may have been a bit grubby and sunburned; they probably also glowed with good health.)

His senses exquisitely alert, he had stayed up all night while the young people slept. The night was still and moonlit, the sky swept clear. As James had stared heavenward, he was filled with spiritual and physical longing. He later described his feelings to his wife in stream-of-consciousness style: "The influences of Nature, the wholesomeness of the people around me, especially the good Pauline..." James, who was frank about his crushes with the all-patient Alice, may have caught himself, for he next wrote: "the thought of you and the children...all fermented within me." There, atop the mountain, he experienced what he called a "Walpurgis nacht." (This was not the most wholesome analogy he could muster writing his dear wife—in the half-pagan forests of northern Europe, Walpurgisnacht, the night of Saint Walburga, fell on the eve of May Day, when witches gathered in the mountains for a demonic orgy.) James wandered into the woods, where the "streaming moonlight lit up things in a magical checkered play, and it seemed as if the gods of all the nature mythologies were holding an indescribable meeting in my breast with the moral gods of the inner life." He knew he was experiencing something intensely "significant," but he was for once unable to articulate exactly what he was feeling, at least not in a letter to his wife. "Memory and sensation all whirled inexplicably together," he wrote—the best he could do, possibly because some of the feelings were unchaste. It was, in any case, "one of the happiest lonesome nights of my existence." The raw experience—the sensation of rapture—would stay with him, as a spur to his intellectual ponderings.

In the morning James, Pauline, and her friends set off on a hike. James, who had barely slept in two days, was gallant, perhaps overly so. He instructed his guide to carry some of the girls' possessions while he lugged his own pack, which weighed eighteen pounds. They walked and climbed for ten and a half hours, up and down steep mountain trails. "The girls kept up splendidly and were all fresher than I. It was true that they had slept like logs all night, whereas I was 'on my nerves.' I lost my Norfolk jacket," he wrote Alice, and he had staggered into camp that night "more fatigued than I have been after any walk."[7]

James did not know it right away, but he had strained his

heart. He sustained a "slight valvular lesion"; within a few weeks he was reporting that his heart was "kicking about terribly of late."[8] He never recovered. "The biggest tramp I ever took," as he described the hike after his ecstatic vigil, had done irreparable damage. Understandably, Alice was furious. Her husband had been a fool to carry his own pack out of chivalry. James's son Harry later wrote, "My mother, who was unable to find Pauline Goldmark sympathetic, could never forgive her."[9]

James's Walpurgisnacht may have been in part an older man's mooning, and Alice could hardly be blamed for seeing it that way. But as usual, James was able to divine greater meaning from his neuroses. While he had unwisely hiked in the Adirondacks and then traveled to California in the summer of 1898, he was turning over in his mind the importance and variety of the human spirit, and shaping a counterargument against the imperialists and social dogmatists. As he rattled westward on trains that summer, he closely read Tolstoy's *War and Peace*, Melville's *Typee*, and a study of Burmese culture — he was, as always, sampling the variety of the human condition and becoming increasingly convinced that ideology blinded man to the true worth and distinctiveness of the individual.

In August he arrived in northern California to deliver lectures at Berkeley and Stanford. He had been stunned by the Rockies, though the haze from forest fires rendered their peaks strangely opaque. The peaks were revelatory, almost monstrous in their incomprehensible grandeur. In San Francisco he was bored by dreary receptions with academics, and he resented having "thrust on him" a meeting with Phoebe Hearst — "the Mother of the editor of the N.Y. Journal (!)," he exclaimed to Alice, noting that Mrs. Hearst had donated millions to build Berkeley's campus.

But he was fascinated by the common folk he encountered on his travels and marveled at "the rugged and manly character of the population one is thrown with in the trains and in the stations — almost all men, but all brown & strong and manly to the last degree."[10] In his letters home he puzzled through what he had seen and absorbed in an alien land. "The good that this whole trip is doing me is of a queer sort," he wrote Alice. "It makes me see the world in such simple lines — the endless physical courage and energy of the common man at the basis of it, guided in certain channels by the enterprise of leading minds." The brave-hearted fraternity of the West drew in James, just as it had an earlier generation of neurasthenic easterners. To his brother Henry, James enthused about California, about the workingmen and soldiers he met there — "really a magnificent body of youths, such good firm serious & intelligent faces."[11] He wanted his children to experience the greatness and simplicity of the West and suggested that they attend Stanford and learn to ride horses just like those "in Frederic Remington's pictures."[12]

In October, back in Cambridge, James presented a "talk" (later published in the *Atlantic Monthly*) entitled "On a Certain Blindness in Human Beings." While he worshipped the steadfastness and courage of men, James declared, he rued their blindness toward others who were not like them, who were "blind and insensible to the inner feelings and the whole inner significance of lives that are different from our own." His address was a plea for tolerance, a manifesto of self-determinism. He sent a copy to Pauline Goldmark with a note: "I like to imagine that you care for it, or will care for it too. What most horrifies me in life is our brutal ignorance of one another."[13] James's slant in these talks was not geopolitical — he made no mention of imperialism. But privately, fulminating with his friends and colleagues, he was becoming more politicized.

By November he was in a state of rage against U.S. annexation of the Philippines. "Empire," he wrote his friend "Mack" Salter, "...means the killing of Aguinaldo and all who may resist us. It means the presumption to force our ideals on people to whom they are not native."[14] James had never been an activist, but as he watched his country embark on what was increasingly called its manifest destiny, he would become one of the leading voices warning against the unintended consequences of liberating a people by conquering them.

Roosevelt campaigned for governor surrounded by Rough Riders in their khaki uniforms. His events were heralded by a bugle call as if he were still storming Kettle Hill, and a traveling band repeatedly played "There'll Be a Hot Time in the Old Town Tonight."[15] Edith found the whole business exhausting. She wrote her sister Emily that Roosevelt was giving as many as sixteen stump speeches a day, and she sadly noted that little Ted had suffered a resurgence of his debilitating headaches. On election day, by a narrow 17,000-vote margin, Roosevelt was elected governor of New York. When he was inaugurated in Albany on New Year's Day 1899, Edith felt overwhelmed. "I could not look at Theodore or even listen closely to him or I should have broken down," she wrote Emily.[16]

"Theodore won a very great personal victory in New York," Lodge exulted to his friend George Lyman. "It was his own campaign and his personality which saved the state [Republican] ticket and the legislature." Lodge was engaged in his own campaign: to win Senate ratification of the peace treaty between the

United States and Spain, the document that formally awarded the Philippines to America. In mid-November, writing Cushman Davis, one of the peace commissioners appointed by McKinley to negotiate with Spain, Lodge breezily predicted that the Senate would ratify the treaty "without the slightest difficulty."[17]

His blithe optimism soon faded. "We are going to have trouble over the Treaty," Lodge warned Roosevelt on December 7.[18] A backlash was brewing, not just among mugwumps like James but among nativists who did not wish to see brown-faced Filipinos become Americans, or even the wards of America. "Are we to have a Mongolian state in this Union?" asked Representative John F. Fitzgerald of Massachusetts (John F. Kennedy's grandfather, the Irish politician who had mockingly chided Lodge about which boat his ancestors had taken). In New York businessmen and investors seemed to lose their enthusiasm for conquering new markets. "This huge materialistic community is at bottom either wrong or halfhearted on the Philippine question," Roosevelt grumbled in a letter to Lodge on January 26.[19]

Lodge labored mostly behind the scenes. Ever the political realist, he did not rely on patriotic speeches (he gave only one himself) but rather on the grease of legislation, arranging to have the White House hand out post office patronage and even a federal judgeship to one key vote.[20] Lodge and the treaty were saved by a perverse turn of events. In early February, two days before the Senate was scheduled to vote, fighting broke out between American soldiers and the Filipino rebels. It's not entirely clear how the shooting started, but a full-scale war quickly erupted. With American soldiers fighting and dying, senators rallied around the flag, closing ranks behind the president. The treaty passed by one vote.[21]

That day it had snowed in Washington—wet, heavy snow, depriving Lodge of his morning ride on horseback through Rock Creek Park. He was worn out, he confessed to Roosevelt. To his mother Lodge confided that the battle over the treaty was "the hardest, bitterest, closest fight."[22] Americans had been rabid to go to war in the spring of 1898. But the burdens of the empire they inherited—almost by accident, it sometimes seemed—weighed heavily, and most were eager to shrug them off. Hearst's headlines had been but a facade; Americans had gone to war not to save the Cuban people, but because they (rather like Roosevelt, if in less exuberant fashion) wanted a war—almost any war, but hopefully a conflict that was not too long or too painful. When the fighting in Cuba was finished and the troops came home (save for the ones being sent to the Philippines), most Americans were ready to pull back and live in prosperous and peaceful isolation, once more safely separated from the feuding nations of the Old World.

At the close of cabinet meetings, Lyman Gage, secretary of the treasury and a native of Mr. Dooley's Chicago, would amuse his fellow secretaries and the president by reading the satirical musings of Peter Finley Dunne. Dunne had his character Hennessey ponder the American dilemma in a vernacular that was both comic and grimly poignant: "I'm askin' mesilf will I annex Cubia or lave it to the Cubans? Will I take Porther Ricky [Puerto Rico] or put it by? An' what shud I do with the Ph'lippeens? Oh, what should I do with him? I can't annex thim because I don't know where they ar-re.... There are eight thousan' iv thim islands, with a popylation iv wan hundherd million naked savages; an' me bedroom's crowded with me an' th' bed." As Warren Zimmerman noted in his history of the period, *First Great*

Triumph, "It may not be too much to speculate that these genial satires on militarism, patriotism, and imperialism helped temper the extremes of America's expansionist policies."[23]

Americans had no desire to maintain a mighty military machine. The performance of the navy had been wonderful, thrilling, and yet... Congress did not want to pay to enlarge the fleet or even maintain it. Lodge fulminated on the Senate floor against the foolishness of "putting ships out of commission deliberately at such a time as this," and Roosevelt moaned "that we should find such difficulty in learning our lessons."[24]

But the two friends accepted political reality. The platform of the Republican Party was expansionist in the 1900 presidential election, but the Republicans soft-pedaled the issue. That included Lodge, who wrote an article in *Harper's Magazine* warning against the perils of electing William Jennings Bryan (the Democratic nominee again) but made no reference to imperialism or foreign policy.[25]

The Republicans' candidate for vice-president in the election of 1900 was Theodore Roosevelt. Roosevelt didn't want the job, or so he continually had insisted to Lodge. He would be bored and useless as McKinley's number two, he fretted. ("There is nothing to do as Vice-President," he wrote Bamie.) But Lodge knew better. As he had throughout Roosevelt's political career, Lodge played the role of consigliere and matchmaker. "The dear old goose actually regards me as a presidential possibility," Roosevelt disingenuously protested to Bamie.[26] In June Roosevelt made a late, dramatic appearance at the Republican convention in Philadelphia wearing a broad-brimmed cowboy hat, an emblem of his Cuban campaign. He was nominated unanimously. "Don't you realize," reportedly spluttered Roosevelt's old foe, Senator

Mark Hanna, "that there's only one life between this madman and the White House?"[27]

Shot by a mad anarchist, McKinley died of his wounds on September 14, 1901, and Roosevelt became president of the United States. He inherited a quagmire in the Philippines. American soldiers and Filipino rebels were engaged in a dirty war, with atrocities on both sides. The bodies of American soldiers were found with their genitals chopped off and stuffed in their mouths. The Americans began herding civilians into wretched camps to keep them away from the rebels — shades of Spain's *reconcentrado* policy in Cuba. Americans also borrowed from the Spanish a torture known as "the water cure" — holding a prisoner down and pouring water over his mouth to simulate the sensation of drowning. A general ordered that all males over the age of ten who ventured outside the internment camps should be shot on sight. Veterans of the Indian Wars of the West began burning native villages. One ordered that the island of Samar be turned into a "howling wilderness."

The anti-imperialist movement, which had been feckless during the election of 1900, took on new life. In October 1899, at the formation of the Anti-Imperialist League, William James had been installed as vice president, but, aside from writing letters to the newspapers, he does not appear to have done much in the way of agitating or organizing. James believed in the role of the public intellectual as an educator of the masses and as a check of reason on popular passion, but he entertained few illusions about his political influence. In his speeches he candidly admitted that mugwump anti-imperialists were seen as "priggish" and "bloodless bores."[28] He cringed as well at the self-defeating antipatriotic mood of the anti-imperialists. It became fashionable in highbrow circles, as the Philippine insurrection dragged on and became more sordid, to scorn the Stars and Stripes. In Cambridge, Sarah Shaw, mother of the martyred Robert Gould Shaw, frowned at a large American flag hanging in a window across the street from her house and exclaimed, "I wish I could pull that down!"[29] James was pained by such outbursts. He exulted in, as he put it, his country's "greenness, her plasticity, innocence, good intentions, friends, everything." But privately he railed. "God damn the U.S. for its vile conduct in the Philippine Isles," he wrote a friend in August 1902. To Henry Lee Higginson, he despaired that America could "puke up its ancient soul...in five minutes without a wink of squeamishness."[30]

By 1902 the anti-imperialist movement had outgrown its parochial, upper-crust origins in Boston. The movement was more broad based, numbering a major industrialist, Andrew Carnegie, and Mark Twain — a most effective polemicist who accused America of "debauching" her honor. Twain was able to acidly remind Americans why they were not, at heart, conquering oppressors. The press (though not Hearst's *Journal*, which remained pro-expansionist) increasingly questioned the cost and worth of America's far-flung empire. When newspapers began to publicize atrocities in 1902, public clamor generated calls in Congress for an investigation.

The burden fell on Lodge, who chaired a special committee on the Philippines but wished the subject of war crimes would quietly go away. Very grudgingly, Lodge had agreed to hearings, though only behind closed doors, and his temper was up. At one point Senator Teller of Colorado made some biting remarks about the military in the Philippines, and Lodge — with an uncharacteristic loss of control — rushed at the senator as if to strike him. A Boston newspaper described Lodge as "white to the lips."[31]

In May, Lodge's committee released a report that admitted to some "individual instances of wrong doing," but insisted that the abuses had been provoked by the rebels, who, according to Lodge, were guilty of far worse. The war lovers had exaggerated Spanish cruelty in order to get their war, and now they covered up the abuses of American troops. If morally dubious, there was at least a sort of symmetry.

President Roosevelt seems to have been puzzled and chagrined by the atrocities, although not quite believing in them. He privately wrote his friend Hermann Speck von Sternberg that "there have been some blots on the record," but he appears to have been more offended by the Americans' rough talk—calling the Filipinos "niggers," for instance—than by their rougher actions. He dismissed the water cure (also known as "waterboarding") as an "old Filipino method of minor torture" in which "nobody was seriously damaged." Roosevelt's solution to the problem was to grant an amnesty to the rebels—and declare victory. On July 4, 1902, the president announced an official end to hostilities, which he described with not a little hyperbole as the most glorious war in the nation's history. Despite his victory proclamation, the fighting sputtered on for more than a decade.

Over four thousand American soldiers would die in the Philippines. The Filipino rebels lost roughly five times as many, and perhaps two hundred thousand citizens perished from disease in the squalid relocation camps. As imperialists go the Americans were relatively benign once the fighting subsided. "Benevolent assimilation"—McKinley's term—proceeded in a paternalistic but not cruel way. (As historian and journalist Stanley Karnow has noted, Filipinos today "feel a closer affinity for America than, say, Indians do for Britain or Vietnamese do for France.") In

1907 America established a national legislature, the first in Asia, and nine years later pledged eventual freedom for the islands.[32] Still, it would take another thirty years before the islands were granted full independence. As early as 1907 President Roosevelt, for his part, was ready to let them go. He lamented to his friend and successor William Howard Taft that the islands were too far away to be of much use to the United States, and with eerie prescience he foresaw that they would make a tempting target for Japan.[33]

In April 1899, two months after the United States formally annexed the Philippines, Thomas Reed announced that he was stepping down as Speaker and would not run again for Congress. In his last days as Speaker, Reed had questioned why nativist congressmen worried about keeping out immigrants at a time when Washington was buying "10,000,000 Malays at $2 a head."[34] "Congress without Tom Reed!" exclaimed a New York *Herald* editorial. "Who can imagine it?" The *New York Times* declared his departure to be a "national loss" and wondered whether there was "something wrong" about politics that would drive Reed—a truly "public man"—into the private practice of law. Reed was still a popular figure. At a chamber of commerce banquet at Delmonico's in New York in late November, Reed was greeted with a roaring ovation. Governor Roosevelt also spoke, noted the *Times*, and received applause, but "the greeting accorded him was not comparable to that given Mr. Reed." Reed may have been privately gratified by this display of one-upmanship, but he was done with public life.[35]

Reed had occasionally kept a diary, and in 1900 he started it up again. On the first day of the new century he wrote, "I have

Reed in his New York law office (Library of Congress)

begun a new year away from politics." Quitting public life had been a "difficult decision," he wrote.[36] He had had no choice, he told his secretary, Asher Hinds. His conscience would not allow him to support the McKinley administration's policy of expansionism — or, as Reed called it, imperialism. Reed joined a New York law firm and made some money, and he found a new friendship with Mark Twain, who appreciated Reed's mordant and caustic sense of humor.

As the public cooled to foreign adventuring, Reed was content to see the jingoes squirm a bit. In mid-January 1902, when stories about atrocities in the Philippines were surfacing in the press, Reed and his wife were invited to a formal dinner at the

White House, now occupied by Reed's former ally Theodore Roosevelt. "Our welcome was very cordial," Reed recorded in his diary. "I think that this was the result of the change of administrations and of ideas regarding the war with Spain. People now begin to speak about Cuba and about the Philippines with much doubt." At the dinner, Reed noted, "Mrs. Reed thought Theodore was a bit nervous."[37]

At the very least, the president had been feeling anxious about Reed. It had come as a relief when, after long silence, Reed wrote Roosevelt a friendly letter in the summer of 1901. "Dear old fellow," Roosevelt wrote back, "I was much pleased—and in truth a little touched—to get your letter; and, after having shouted over it with delight I sent it over to Cabot."[38] But there was no going back to their old friendship.

Lodge had avoided Reed in the Speaker's last, angry days in Congress in the winter of 1899. "Reed is terribly bitter, saying all sorts of ugly things about the administration and its policy in private talks, so I keep out of his way, for I am fond of him, and I confess that his attitude is painful and disappointing to me beyond words," Lodge wrote Roosevelt. Lodge had been happy to run into Reed by accident in an old print shop in Paris in the summer of 1899—"We had a pleasant chat," Lodge wrote his mother. But the two old friends and fellow solons had fallen out of touch, and the split was not the sort that lent itself to mending with a single chance encounter.[39]

Reed missed power. "At the office, where I am very bored," he wrote in his diary on June 3, 1902. He lacked the "ambition," he felt, to become a "renowned lawyer." "I should go see the world, in which I have not much time to live," Reed mused. Though not yet sixty-five, he was feeling aged and poorly. "It seems to me that death is always in my view when I think of things that I want to do," he reflected later that month.

Reed did want to reconcile with Roosevelt and Lodge, but the effort was hard for such a proud man. At the end of August, when Roosevelt traveled to Portland, Maine, Reed somewhat stiffly noted, "My wife directed me to invite the President to stop by my house, and he responded that it would be a great pleasure." Roosevelt stayed for a half hour. "The President was the same young man as before," Reed recorded. The former Czar offered some desultory praise and advice to the president, but noted, "The war with Spain has upset our habitudes." A week later it was Lodge's turn to visit Reed. "I haven't seen him for three years," Reed wrote. "It seemed to me that Lodge, Roosevelt and all those men have given to the life of the Republic a rough shaking." The two men were at least cordial. "Lodge came and we had a good talk, as we used to," Reed wrote, trying to be dispassionate. "A very interesting man. After all it's necessary to separate our passions from our work. It seems to me that Mr. Lodge and his friends have inflicted much damage on the country, but they undoubtedly think otherwise."[40]

In December, as Reed walked through the Capitol revisiting his old haunts, he collapsed. He was mortally ill with kidney disease. In delirium, he began talking as if he were still Speaker, still sitting in the chair of the House or debating on the floor. He died in a Washington hotel room near midnight on December 6, 1902. "The country has not bred a nobler man," Mark Twain told reporters. President Roosevelt called on his widow the next day. She would not see him.[41]

The next day, "without ceremony," reported the Bangor, Maine, newspaper, Reed's casket was loaded into a hearse and carried to the train station for the long journey home. A bouquet of roses from Edith Roosevelt rested on the lid. A few Washingtonians gathered on the platform to see the body leave. One was Senator Henry Cabot Lodge.[42]

Earlier that year, when he had first begun to feel the twinges of mortality, Reed had tried to set down his thoughts about war. While Roosevelt extolled "the supreme triumphs of war" and yearned to unleash the "wolf in the heart" of overcivilized man, Reed prized civilization, by which he meant rationality and decency, above all things. In a letter to his old friend George Gifford, Reed expressed his sadness and anger over war's corrupting effects:

> *The worst thing about war is that it has practically to be fought on the basis of the most uncivilized and soon gets to be a mere matter of hatred. They were — these Filipinos — only a short time ago our wards to whom we owed sacred duties, duties we could not abandon in the face of a censorious world without soiling our Christian faith. Now they are "niggers" who must be punished for defending themselves. This is the history of the world with perhaps a stronger dash of hypocrisy than usual to soothe our feelings.*[43]

In Cuba, Roosevelt's onetime playmate and commanding officer, General Leonard Wood, was a benevolent despot. As military governor Wood improved the roads, built schools and hospitals, although he ruled with an indisputably iron hand. Roosevelt's sister Corinne visited Havana and, after a late-night tour with Wood, proclaimed that the streets were so clean she would be willing to eat her breakfast off them. There was good reason for this: Cubans who violated sanitary rules were horsewhipped.[44]

In the rush to war in April 1898, Congress had passed the Teller Amendment, guaranteeing Cuban independence after liberation from Spain. But in 1901 it passed the Platt Amendment, giving America the right to intervene in Cuba, in effect whenever it pleased. "There is, of course, little or no independence left in Cuba after the Platt Amendment," Wood privately confided to President Roosevelt in late 1901.

General Máximo Gómez had no illusions. "The Republic will surely come," he wrote a friend earlier that year, "but not with the absolute independence we had dreamed about."[45] Gómez, a decent and stoic figure, was struggling to adjust to reality in the age of Anglo-Saxon supremacy. In the first days after the Spanish defeat in July 1898, a scientist from America had visited him in his camp. The man produced a piece of string and asked whether he could measure the general's head; he was conducting a survey of skull size (and brain capacity) in nonwhite races. Gómez refused, angrily protesting that he was not to be mistaken for a monkey. But then he grudgingly acquiesced. It was all for science and civilization, he was reassured.[46]

The word "civilization" was a loaded term to the Cubans trying to build a republic. It meant not just cleaniness and order but, they now realized, denying the darker races the power to govern. Wood and Secretary of War Elihu Root (rewarded for getting Roosevelt around New York's tax requirements back when he ran for governor) wanted to reduce the Cuban voting roles by two thirds, to avoid the "black peril" that had seized Haiti and Santo Domingo when they were misruled by black men in the nineteenth century. At first the Cubans clung to José Martí's dream of a postracial society, a republic "with all and for all." In 1901 a constitutional convention voted for universal male suffrage.[47] But inevitably, a ruling class tied to U.S. commercial interests reemerged, and racism, always deeply rooted, worked its poison in Cuban society. Class and racial conflicts broke out; corruption thrived. American troops intervened twice, in 1902 and 1906. In 1908 disaffected black veterans of the revolution formed an independent political party. They were massacred by the thousands by the Cuban government, partly to forestall another U.S. intervention.*[48]

A profound misunderstanding occurred that would cripple Cuban-American relations for at least the next century. "Americans remembered 1898 as something done for Cubans; Cubans remembered 1898 as something done to them," writes historian Louis Pérez. Fidel Castro, whose father had been a soldier in the Spanish army, knew well the history of humiliation suffered by the Cuban rebels forbidden to enter Santiago for the Spanish surrender in 1898. On the second day of January 1959, when he marched into Santiago at the head of a rebel army, Castro played on long and bitter memories. "This time the revolution will not be thwarted!" he thundered. "This time, fortunately for Cuba, the revolution will be consummated. It will not be like the war of 1895, when the Americans arrived and made themselves masters of the country; then intervened at the last minute and later did not even allow Calixto García, who had been fighting for thirty years, to enter Santiago."[49] The memory of 1898 remains fresh and bitter in Cuba. On the old *camino real*, the

---

*Cuba's first nonwhite ruler was General Fulgencio Batista, a mulatto who took over the Cuban government in an army coup in 1933. He was embittered because he had been rejected by an all-white Havana tennis club. Thoroughly corrupt and tied to the American mafia, Batista would be ousted by Castro in 1959.

road from Siboney to Santiago marched by Roosevelt and his Rough Riders, Castro's government installed a giant billboard that shows General García's proud face and the words "*Liberdad y Dignidad*" — Liberty and Dignity. The Americans had helped Cubans achieve the former but robbed them of the latter at a critical moment in their history.

23

Never Ending

"And all the trumpets sounded..."

ILLIAM JAMES NEVER got over his scorn for Roosevelt's war lust. Nonetheless James could not help but admire, and perhaps envy, Roosevelt's brio and heartiness. "Roosevelt has some splendid qualities & instincts, and may do well," James wrote his brother Henry after Roosevelt ascended to the White House.[1] He respected the way Roosevelt stood up to business interests and hack politicians. In 1907, when President Eliot of Harvard neared retirement, James suggested that Roosevelt, who was approaching the end of his second term in the White House, succeed Eliot at his alma mater.[2]

James understood that it was useless to remind people of war's terrible cost. "Modern man inherits all the innate pugnacity and all the love of glory of his ancestors," he lectured students at Stanford in 1906.

Showing war's irrationality and horror is of no effect on him. The horrors make the fascination. War is the *strong* life; it is life *in extremis*.

Our ancestors have bred pugnacity into our bone and marrow, and thousands of years of peace won't breed it out of us. The popular imagination fairly fattens on the thought of wars. Let public opinion once reach a certain pitch, and no ruler can withstand it....In 1898 our people had read the word "war" in letters three inches high for three months in every newspaper.

And yet, just as James tried to make his peace with Roosevelt, he searched for a way to think about harnessing and redirecting the passions that made men worship war. What was needed, he told the Stanford students, was the *"moral equivalent of war."* He confessed to entertaining his own "utopia," in which "new energies and hardihoods continue the manliness to which the military mind so faithfully clings." The nation needed to find a way to celebrate and enshrine "martial virtues" without devoting them to the pursuit of violence. He proposed that young people be universally conscripted — to work at building roads and tunnels, on fishing boats and in mines, or constructing skyscrapers, "to get the childishness knocked out of them, and to come back into society with healthier sympathies and soberer ideas." Thus was born the idea of national service, later made real by the Depression-era Civilian Conservation Corps, the Peace Corps, VISTA, and other service organizations.[3]

James was not well, and though his heart, weakened by his overexertion on Mount Marcy, kicked up again, he continued to hike in the mountains and, in his experimental way, seek quack cures in Europe. He remained irrepressible. Ever curious, he sought out an eclectic mix of thinkers and writers, including Mark Twain and Admiral Mahan, to wrangle over life's questions. He regularly attended dinners celebrating his genius and scholarly accomplishments. "I enjoy being a lion," he confessed to Alice.[4]

Until the end of his life, James searched for its meaning. In September 1909 he attended a conference in Worcester, Massachusetts, "in order to see what Freud was like," he wrote. The Viennese psychoanalyst had come to America to discuss his revolutionary theories of the unconscious. James was not impressed. He thought Freud's dream theory far-fetched, and in any case found him "obsessed by fixed ideas"—a cardinal sin in the James church of pragmatic pluralism. Freud, on the other hand, was admiring of James. After two days together the two men walked to the train station. "James stopped suddenly," Freud recalled, "handed me a bag he was carrying and asked me to walk on, saying that he would catch up as soon as he had got through an attack of angina pectoris which was just coming on. I have always wished I could be as fearless as he was in the face of approaching death."[5]

As James lay dying of his heart condition less than a year later, he asked to be taken to the mountains, to his summer place in Chocorua, New Hampshire. Throughout his life his great and inspiring gift—as well as his unrelenting and often painful burden—had been acute self-consciousness. On August 26, 1910, his devoted and long-suffering wife, Alice, wrote in her diary, "William died just before 2.30 in my arms. I was coming in with milk and saw the change. No pain at the last and no consciousness."[6]

The woman who had helped introduce Theodore Roosevelt to the romantic mythology of war had changed her mind. Josephine Shaw Lowell still wore black to commemorate the death of her dashing husband, Charles Russell Lowell. But she had come to dislike monuments and battle flags that glorified war. In 1904 she asked Edward Emerson (son of Ralph Waldo) to go through her husband's war correspondence with an eye to weeding out letters that might enhance "the evil influence" of "military glamour." She had become an activist in the Anti-Imperialist League and in the fall of 1904 attended a Peace Congress in Boston. The Civil War, she still believed, had been a sacred struggle. But "I feel very differently about war since these more wicked modern wars," she wrote Emerson.[7]

She sent long, scolding letters to Roosevelt when she felt he was somehow trimming in his duty as a public servant. He replied patiently, if a bit condescendingly, usually at length. "Now my dear Mrs. Lowell, I am a little in a quandary how to answer you," he began one letter. "You are an old friend and you have been very dear to me. I cannot answer you as I would answer a man — or rather refuse absolutely to answer you as I should in the case of almost anyone else writing me as you have written."[8] Undaunted, she kept firing off letters, and Roosevelt did his best to respond, still respectful of the gently fierce Civil War widow who had come to his boyhood home, a living memorial to her brother's and her husband's sacrifice.

In October 1905, Lowell, ravaged by cancer, was visited by Jacob Riis, an old friend whom she shared with Roosevelt. Riis sat with her for a time and later recalled, "I think she knew eternity was just beyond.... She spoke of Roosevelt; and she sent the last message through me to him. It was a message of love and cheer. When I gave it to him, he said, 'She had a sweet, unworldly character; and never man or woman ever strove for loftier ideals.'"

Sitting by the fire as the shadows lengthened, "Effie" stroked Riis's hand and said, "Think of waiting for my husband for forty-one long years, forty-one years." When she died, her family buried her beside him.[9]

*   *   *

As president, Roosevelt was not particularly bellicose. At times he did huff and bluff; he "talked softly and carried a big stick." Using the threat of warships and a certain amount of deceit, he "took Panama," as he put it, and fulfilled Lodge's Large Policy with an ocean-to-ocean canal across the isthmus. To announce America as a global naval power, he sent the Great White Fleet around the world. But he did not get America into any wars—and even won a Nobel Peace Prize in 1906 for helping Russia and Japan end theirs.

After McKinley's assassination Mark Hanna had moaned, "I told McKinley it was a mistake to nominate that wild man in Philadelphia. I told him to think what would happen if he should die. Now look. That damned cowboy is president of the United States."[10] Hanna was not the first to misjudge Roosevelt. If he had been a "wild man" and a "damn cowboy" at times in his life, as president he was the man more familiar to Henry Cabot Lodge—neither a mugwump nor a machine pol, but a pragmatic idealist. He was an effective reformer, but only because he knew when to push and when to hedge. By a mixture of direct talk and clever machination, Roosevelt was able to handle the likes of Germany's Kaiser Wilhelm II and tycoons who had amassed vast fortunes by creating monopolistic business trusts. Mr. Dooley, Finley Peter Dunne's wise Chicago bartender, perfectly understood Roosevelt, concisely summarizing the president's approach to the trusts: "On wun hand I wud stamp them undher fut; on th' other hand, not so fast."[11]

Roosevelt showed remarkable emotional self-control as president, but a few people could enrage him—in particular, William Randolph Hearst. In 1906, after reading a scurrilous attack in one of Hearst's publications, Roosevelt inveighed against the "man with a muck rake." The image was from John Bunyan's *Pilgrim's Progress*, of a man who would not look up from the muck he was raking to reach for a heavenly crown. Roosevelt intended the analogy as a slam against Hearst's sensationalism, but investigative journalists quickly turned the term "muckraker" into a badge of honor.[12]

Hearst had continued to snipe at Roosevelt through the columns of his newspaper and with astringent cartoons. When he had gone on the Republican ticket as McKinley's running mate in 1900, the New York *Journal* pictured Roosevelt on a toy horse, waving a wooden sword as he bullied McKinley and made him cry. In truth, Hearst longed to *be* Roosevelt. With his high, almost girlish speaking voice, a limp handshake that was quickly withdrawn, and a known taste for chorus girls, Hearst was a most unlikely politician. Nevertheless he was elected to Congress in 1902, largely because he was able to spend freely to win votes. He bought a mansion on Lafayette Square across from the White House but only rarely showed up on the House floor to vote or debate. Already eyeing the presidency, Hearst made an expensive, unsuccessful run for the Democratic nomination in 1904. He tried and failed to win the race for mayor of New York in 1905 and ran for governor of New York in 1908.[13]

Roosevelt worried that he might actually win. "Hearst's nomination," he wrote Cabot Lodge in early October, "is a very very bad thing." Hearst was a clever populist, Roosevelt told Lodge, who knew how to excite the passions of the "have-nots." The intensity of Roosevelt's hatred of Hearst is indicated in a letter to an English editor, John Strachey. "Hearst's private life has been disreputable," Roosevelt wrote. "His wife [Hearst had married Millicent] was a chorus girl or something like that on the stage.... He preached the gospel of envy, hatred and unrest....

He is the most potent single influence for evil we have in our life."

Roosevelt fed rumors of Hearst's immorality to his Republican opponent for governor, Charles Evans Hughes, then administered the coup de grace in late October, on the eve of the election. The president dispatched Secretary of State Elihu Root, who was also Roosevelt's personal lawyer, to deliver a speech in which he announced, "with the President's authority, that he regards Mr. Hearst to be wholly unfit to be Governor, as an insincere, self-seeking demagogue." Root went on, again speaking "with the President's authority," to accuse Hearst of inciting the assassination of President McKinley by his "appeal to the dark and evil spirits of malice and greed, envy and sullen hatred." The next morning Hearst's newspapers caricatured "Root the Rat," but four days later Hearst lost by 60,000 votes out of 1.5 million cast.[14] Hearst's political career was over.

Curiously, if Hearst felt bitter about Roosevelt, he disguised his feelings. In the spring of 1916, only eight years after Hearst lost the governor's race, the two old foes began writing each other and occasionally dined together. Hearst asked Roosevelt to write articles for his publications, and though Roosevelt politely declined, he sent him his latest book. The two men shared a loathing for President Woodrow Wilson, but their bond clearly went deeper. Perhaps they understood that at some level the journalist and the politician needed each other. Roosevelt would never admit such a thing, but Hearst was in a way a kindred soul—a romantic, an adventurer, a self-promoter; for better and for worse, a profoundly American type.[15]

Roosevelt's bloodlust seemed to have been sated by his crowded hour in Cuba. But after he left the presidency in 1909 and relinquished power, the little boy who had worshipped the glorious victims of the Civil War was born again. "I have always been unhappy, most unhappy, that I was not severely wounded in Cuba in some striking and disfiguring way," he declared in his old age.[16] He abhorred weakness, in himself or anyone else. In 1912, as he was on his way to give a speech, Roosevelt was shot in the chest at point-blank range by a madman. The bullet's impact was diffused by Roosevelt's glasses case and the pages of the speech he was holding, but it left a dime-size hole in his rib cage. Roosevelt insisted on giving the speech nonetheless, and talked for over an hour, his teeth gritted, his face whitening as the bloodstain on his shirt spread.

Roosevelt craved dangerous adventure in an almost pathological way. On a recklessly daring expedition into the Amazon jungle in 1913 he cut his leg, and the wound became infected. Delirious at times, he asked to be left to die, and agreed to come along only when his son Kermit refused to leave him behind. With the advent of World War I, Roosevelt ranted that President Wilson was a coward for trying to keep the country out of war, and he attacked pacifists as less than men while demanding their persecution.[17] Though overweight and increasingly infirm, he proposed to Wilson that he be given command of a division to fight in France. Not wanting to make Roosevelt either a hero or a martyr, Wilson declined. "I don't understand," Roosevelt complained to Wilson's aide, Colonel E. M. House. "After all, I'm only asking to die." House, who was fed up with Roosevelt by this time, paused and replied, "Oh? Did you make that point quite clear to the President?"[18]

Roosevelt felt blessed to be able to send his sons to war. He would rather have his own children "die than have them grow up

TR in late 1918 (Theodore Roosevelt Collection, Houghton Library, Harvard University)

weaklings," he once said.[19] He need not have worried. The boys all saw combat, which in the Great War was vaster and grimmer than anything Roosevelt witnessed in Cuba. Archie recalled the sensation of shooting a German and then, in a rage, stomping on his face, staining his boot with blood up to the ankle. He felt, he later wrote, like a creature "of the Stone Age." When Archie was wounded by a German artillery barrage, there were toasts all around at Sagamore Hill. Roosevelt wrote Archie that "Mother, her eyes shining and her cheeks flushed...dashed her glass to the floor." The rest followed suit. Outsiders would have found this celebration perverse, and even Roosevelt's friends might have been put off, though they could not have been surprised. "Well, we know what it feels like to have a hero in the family!" Roosevelt exclaimed to his wounded son.[20] Quentin, the youngest boy, became a pilot and shot down a German. "The last of the lion's brood has been blooded!" Roosevelt exulted to son Kermit.

Then, on July 14, 1918, Quentin's plane was shot down in a dogfight. Quentin was killed, struck twice in the head by machine-gun bullets as he maneuvered. Someone recovered the axle of Quentin's downed plane and sent it to the Roosevelts. The family hung the bent, black piece of iron over the fireplace in the North Room, Sagamore Hill's trophy room. On the wall opposite hangs the head of an elk shot by the elder Roosevelt, and on its spreading antlers rests the sword Roosevelt carried (and tripped over) at Las Guasimas and the felt hat he wore as he charged up Kettle Hill. Roosevelt spent hours sitting in this room, staring blankly beyond the book in his lap, occasionally murmuring his youngest son's childhood nickname, "Quen-tee." The romance of war, at long last, gave way to heartbreak.

Not yet sixty, Roosevelt was blind in one eye from a boxing accident sustained in the White House. He suffered from anemia and recurring tropical fevers, from rheumatism and arthritis. He became dizzy when he walked. He was considerably overweight, weak and altogether physically done in, as well as emotionally devastated by his son's death. "It is no use pretending that Quentin's death is not very terrible," he wrote to his daughter-in-law Belle Willard Roosevelt from Dark Harbor, Maine, in August.[21] On Armistice Day, November 11, 1918, Roosevelt went into the hospital suffering from excruciating arthritis in his right leg and arm. He staggered home on Christmas Day, a sad affair in a household still grieving over the death of its youngest son. Less than two weeks later Roosevelt suffered a blood clot and died in his sleep. Archie cabled Ted and Kermit:

THE OLD LION IS DEAD.[22]

Henry Cabot Lodge delivered a eulogy for his oldest and dearest friend at a memorial service in the Capitol Rotunda. In 1895, when Lodge and Roosevelt were writing *Hero Tales*, Lodge ended his sketch of Robert Gould Shaw by drawing on *Pilgrim's Progress*, a staple of their youth: "When he fell, sword in hand, on the parapet at [Fort] Wagner, leading his black troops in a desperate assault, we can only say of him as Bunyan said of 'Valiant for Truth': 'And then he passed over, and all the trumpets sounded for him on the other side.'"[23]

Standing erect in the Rotunda, Lodge repeated: "And then he passed over, and the trumpets sounded for him on the other side." The ghosts of Civil War martyrs had never slipped from Lodge's and Roosevelt's consciousness. After Quentin died, responding to Lodge's letter of consolation, Roosevelt had compared his son to Shaw and Charles Russell Lowell.[24] As Lodge spoke, his voice broke, his New England reserve cracked, and he collapsed into a chair.[25]

The gloomy Henry Adams had predicted that Roosevelt's ascension to the White House would ruin his friendship with Lodge, but he had been wrong. Even after Roosevelt bolted the Republican Party in 1911 and split politically from Lodge, the two remained close, often riding together in the mornings.[26] "You cannot think what a joy it was for me to have those two talks with you," Lodge had written Roosevelt two days before Christmas 1918, in his last letter to his old friend.[27]

Lodge continued to grind away as a senator, a skillful parliamentarian who became his party's leader by the end of the First World War, but the work took its toll. Whenever the stress built up, as it did every year, he was plagued by stomach troubles and lost weight. He longed to rest and recover on Tuckernuck, but in the summer of 1909 his beloved son Bay had a heart attack while he was loafing with his father. Bay died in Lodge's arms. "You will never know the lonely agony of that moment for me," Lodge wrote his friend Sturgis Bigelow. Lodge never set foot on Tuckernuck again.[28]

In 1919, when Lodge outmaneuvered President Wilson and persuaded the Senate not to ratify membership in the League of Nations, he was portrayed as a bitter old man. Roosevelt was gone; Bay was gone; Nannie, too, of a stroke (it was said that she never recovered from Bay's death). Lodge had shared Roosevelt's visceral disdain for Wilson, and sitting in his library on Massachusetts Avenue, his right foot swinging like a metronome, he had plotted against Wilson's effort to create an international system that would, it was hoped, end future wars of aggression. One of his coconspirators was Roosevelt's sharp-tongued eldest daughter, Alice, who shared the animus of her father and "Uncle Cabot" for Wilson and worked the dinner-party circuit to kill the treaty. She later wrote in her reminiscences, *Crowded Hours* (again this phrase), that Lodge and another antitreaty senator had designated her "Colonel in the Battalion of Death."[29]

By 1924 Lodge was in eclipse, a lonely if still proud figure after nearly half a century of political struggle. At the Republican National Convention in Cleveland that summer he was essentially ignored; when the committees were picked, his name was not mentioned. Lodge's grandson, also named Henry Cabot Lodge, was indignant. Young Lodge (who would go on to become senator from Massachusetts and ambassador to South Vietnam) shared a hotel room with his grandfather. While the elder Lodge lay in bed reading from a volume of Shakespeare, the younger Lodge remonstrated against the shabby treatment. Years later the grandson recalled his grandfather: "I still remember him, lying calmly in his blue-and-white-striped pajamas, smiling, and turning back to his Shakespeare."

Later that summer young Lodge went to stay with his grandfather in Nahant. He and a friend, John Mason Brown, wrapped in towels for a dip in the sea, walked past the aged senator. "When he saw us his face took on the most angelic expression," recalled Brown. "He rose to his full height, and threw his arm out in our direction, in the pantomime of beginning a speech. He looked like an old Roman Senator standing there, beaming down at us with his smile. It seemed sort of like a hail and farewell."[30]

Lodge had not quite finished editing two volumes of his correspondence with Theodore Roosevelt when he died of a cerebral hemorrhage on November 9, 1924.[31] The funeral cortege proceeded from Harvard to Mount Auburn Cemetery, where Lodge's casket was placed in a brownstone mausoleum with an *L* carved above the black iron gate, alongside his wife, mother, and father. His resting place is not far from the graves of Effie and Charles Russell Lowell, in a sloping field of dead Brahmins spread across a green hillside by a bend in the Charles River.

At Groton, Theodore Roosevelt Jr., the little boy who had worshipped his father to the point of illness, wrote a poem called "The Norman Baron's Prayer":

Would God I might die sword in my hand
My gilded spur on my heel

Elder statesman Lodge (Library of Congress)

With my crested helmet on my head
And my body closed in steel....

Would God when the morning broke
I might by my friends be found
Stiff in my war worn harness
Ringed by dead foes all around.[32]

In the Great War, Theodore Junior fulfilled his father's aspirations by winning the Silver Star for daring raids into enemy trenches.[33] He went on to become a successful businessman and public servant—head of American Express and an executive at

Ted Jr. in World War II (Theodore Roosevelt Collection, Houghton Library, Harvard University)

Doubleday; assistant secretary of the navy; governor general of Puerto Rico and colonial governor of the Philippines.[34] But he missed his early calling. In April 1941 he persuaded General George C. Marshall, chief of staff of the army, to give him command of his old regiment. When he departed for training, his wife, Eleanor, wrote a friend, "Ted is very well and far happier than he has been for some years. He has got his teeth into something he knows he can do supremely well."[35]

Roosevelt had "Rough Rider" painted on his jeep. During the fierce fighting in Sicily in late 1943, he and his commander were relieved of their commands by General Omar Bradley for "wantonly" exposing themselves and their men to enemy fire. Bradley gave Roosevelt another chance on D-day. Roosevelt would be the only general officer landing in the first wave. At a conference of commanders before the invasion, Bradley told his officers they would have ringside seats at the greatest fight in history. "Ringside, hell!" Roosevelt whispered to the man next to him. "We'll be in the arena!"

Roosevelt's landing craft was the first to touch down on Utah Beach on June 6, 1944. Pushed by the current, the Higgins boat had arrived in Normandy about three-quarters of a mile off course. "Well, the war starts here," Roosevelt gamely announced to his men. Limping with a cane, the fifty-seven-year-old general led an assault on an enemy-held seawall, a feat that led Bradley to award Roosevelt the prize that had eluded his father—the Medal of Honor.[36] His life's work done, Roosevelt died of a heart attack a month later.

General George C. Patton would later write of Ted Junior, "Great courage, but he was no soldier." Like his father, the younger Theodore Roosevelt was not so much a soldier or a military man, or even a warrior. He was the pure expression of a spirit that beats in all men, the "wolf rising in the heart," the bloodlust that his father sought to summon in his own (subject, of course, to the laws of civilization and the rules of fair play). He was a rarity, but not unique in his time, or in any time. The Roosevelts, father and son, were war lovers. Because only the dead have known the end of war, they will not be the last.

The "gaudy pile" of a building that Roosevelt occupied as assistant secretary of the navy still stands. Renamed the Eisenhower Old Executive Office Building, it is now far too small to house the many departments it did during Roosevelt's time. Instead, it is home to senior White House staff. Roosevelt's old office is still there, still used. In recent years an occupant proudly hung a portrait of Roosevelt on the wall, to draw inspiration from it. As I. Lewis ("Scooter") Libby sat at his desk, toiling for his boss, Vice-President Richard Cheney, he had only to look at the wall to see the old war lover staring down on him.

Acknowledgments

I N 1899 THEODORE Roosevelt's wife, Edith, toured the battle-fields in Cuba where her husband had fought the year before. In later years she liked to tease her husband that San Juan Hill was not quite the steep ascent she had been led to believe. In the spring of 2007 I stood at the bottom of Kettle Hill (adjacent to San Juan Hill), where Roosevelt led his most famous charge. Kettle Hill is no taller than a building in downtown Washington—roughly a hundred feet high from its base. But the slope is in places as steep as forty-five degrees, and if you had to ride or run up it with men shooting at you, it must have looked high enough.

I had gone to Cuba to take a look at the battlefield, but I learned as much from the Cuban scholars there. Dr. Raul Izquierdo, president of the Cuban Institute of History in Havana, made me realize how recent the Spanish-American War seems to Cubans, who call it the War of 1895—a reminder that it was a war of liberation and that it began long before the Americans arrived in June 1898 to drive out the Spaniards. I learned more from Reynaldo Cruz Ruíz and Juan Manuel Reyes Cordero, history scholars in Santiago, and from Ricardo Alarcón, speaker of the National Assembly, a high-ranking Cuban official who was present at the creation of the revolution in 1959 and has somehow survived. My thanks as well to Mario Coyula and Dr. Eusebio

ACKNOWLEDGMENTS

Leal, historian of Havana, and to my lawyer, Steve Schwadron, for setting up the trip.

My greatest debt, once again, is to my researcher and friend Mike Hill. He is my trusted guide through the archival thickets and a genius at turning up the unexpected. He found, through Jeffrey Flannery of the Manuscript Division of the Library of Congress, the illuminating diary of Asher Hinds, chief aide to Speaker Thomas Reed. I am lucky to work with Mike's old friends Peter Drummey and Celeste Walker of the Massachusetts Historical Society—and lucky that Mike could read Henry Cabot Lodge's handwriting. At Harvard, Wallace Dailey of the Theodore Roosevelt Collection opened up the wonderful facilities of Houghton Library, where I spent many happy mornings reading Roosevelt's correspondence, written, I am glad to say, in a strong, clear hand. Charles Markis, chief of interpretation at the Sagamore Hill National Historic Site, gave us a memorable tour of TR's old home, and Carla Bailey at the University of Mary Washington secured microfilm of William Randolph Hearst's correspondence. Mike also had help from Richard H. F. Indemann, director of the George J. Mitchell Department of Special Collections and Archives at the library of Bowdoin College, Reed's alma mater and keeper of his papers.

In Cambridge I immensely enjoyed talking with Kathleen Dalton, Roosevelt's most insightful biographer, who shared some materials with me, and with Carol Bundy, biographer of Josephine Lowell's martyred husband, Charles Russell Lowell. At Princeton I benefited greatly from the advice and leads provided by Jeremy Adelman, chairman of the history department and scholar of Latin America.

I take the title of my book from John Hersey's wonderful World War II novel, *The War Lover*.

ACKNOWLEDGMENTS

My editor, Geoffrey Shandler, at Little, Brown, showed me why writers need editors, or at least editors as skillful as Geoff. My thanks to the whole team at Little, Brown—Geoff's assistant, Liese Mayer, and Carolyn O'Keefe, Heather Fain, Amanda Tobier, Peggy Freudenthal, copyeditor Chris Jerome, and proofreader Kathryn Blatt. My agent, Amanda Urban, was, as always, my pal and wise adviser, and I value more than I can say the friendship and shrewd insights of my boss at *Newsweek*, Jon Meacham.

My best editor, and a whole lot more than that, is my wife, Oscie. She and my daughters, Louisa and Mary, are the happiest stories in my life.

Notes

Abbreviations

HCL Henry Cabot Lodge
LOC Library of Congress, Washington, D.C.
MHS Massachusetts Historical Society, Boston
TR   Theodore Roosevelt

Introduction

1. Swanberg, *Citizen Hearst*, 514–15.
2. Nasaw, *The Chief,* 597.
3. See, generally, Nasaw, *The Chief,* 125–42; Swanberg, *Citizen Hearst,* 79–169.
4. Pizzitola, *Hearst Over Hollywood*, 82.
5. Swanberg, *Citizen Hearst*, 106.
6. Theodore Roosevelt, *Rough Riders*, 84.
7. Morison, *Letters of Theodore Roosevelt*, vol. 1, 417.
8. Ibid., 493.
9. Abbott, *Letters of Archie Butt*, 146.
10. Davis, *Cuban and Porto Rican Campaigns*, 217.
11. Leech, *In the Days of McKinley*, 232.
12. Garraty, *Henry Cabot Lodge*, 124.
13. HCL to Anna Lodge, June 26, 1898, MHS.
14. McCall, *Life of Thomas Brackett Reed*, 246.
15. Morgan, *William McKinley and His America*, 51.
16. Beisner, *Twelve Against Empire*, 43.
17. Cotkin, *William James*, 209.
18. Rejali, *Torture and Democracy*, 279–80.

1. Dreaming of Father

1. Goodwin, *Fitzgeralds and the Kennedys*, 65; Lodge, *Early Memories*, 104.
2. Lodge, *Early Memories*, 217.
3. Ibid., 30, 105.
4. Fisher, *House of Wits*, 201–2.

5. Goodwin, *Fitzgeralds and the Kennedys*, 52.
6. Adams, *Education of Henry Adams*, 41–42; Goodwin, *Fitzgeralds and the Kennedys*, 52.
7. Lodge, *Early Memories*, 19, 86.
8. Bundy, *Nature of Sacrifice*, 261.
9. Menand, *Metaphysical Club*, 32.
10. Lodge, *Early Memories*, 113.
11. Ibid., 27–28.
12. Ibid., 106.
13. Miller, *Henry Cabot Lodge*, 418.
14. Waugh, *Unsentimental Reformer*, 72; Lodge, *Early Memories*, 123.
15. Lodge, *Early Memories*, 118.
16. Dalton, *Theodore Roosevelt*, 31.
17. Sylvia Jukes Morris, *Edith Kermit Roosevelt*, 1–2.
18. Dalton, *Theodore Roosevelt*, 40.
19. Ibid., 26.
20. Dalton, "Theodore Roosevelt and the Idea of War," *Theodore Roosevelt Association Journal*, Fall 1981, 8–9; Teague, *Mrs. L*, 110.
21. Renehan, *Lion's Pride*, 17.
22. Morison, *Letters of Theodore Roosevelt*, vol. 8, 1425; Roosevelt and Lodge, *Selections from the Correspondence*, vol. 1, 284.
23. Waugh, *Unsentimental Reformer*, 29, 50, 55, 77.
24. Dalton, *Theodore Roosevelt*, 33; Bundy, *Nature of Sacrifice*, 262, 483–84; Waugh, *Unsentimental Reformer*, 85–87, 92, 129.
25. Morison, *Letters of Theodore Roosevelt*, vol. 1, 8–9.
26. Dalton, *Theodore Roosevelt*, 55.
27. Theodore Roosevelt, *An Autobiography*, 18, 23.
28. Dalton, *Theodore Roosevelt*, 67.
29. Morison, *Letters of Theodore Roosevelt*, vol. 1, 31; McCullough, *Mornings on Horseback*, 190.
30. Putnam, *Theodore Roosevelt*, 151, 169–70; Sylvia Jukes Morris, *Edith Kermit Roosevelt*, 53.
31. Edmund Morris, *Rise of Theodore Roosevelt*, 101.
32. Wister, *Roosevelt*, 6; Putnam, *Theodore Roosevelt*, 131.
33. Putnam, *Theodore Roosevelt*, 161; Morison, *Letters of Theodore Roosevelt*, vol. 1, 36.
34. Morison, *Letters of Theodore Roosevelt*, 42.
35. Zimmerman, *First Great Triumph*, 197.
36. Morison, *Letters of Theodore Roosevelt*, vol. 1, 45; Edmund Morris, *Rise of Theodore Roosevelt*, 125.
37. Theodore Roosevelt, *Autobiography*, 57.
38. Morison, *Letters of Theodore Roosevelt*, vol. 1, 55.

39. Dalton, *Theodore Roosevelt*, 81; McCullough, *Mornings on Horseback*, 256.
40. Edmund Morris, *Rise of Theodore Roosevelt*, 166.

2. The Noble Hacks

1. Lodge, *Early Memories*, 25.
2. Garraty, *Henry Cabot Lodge*, 63, 72.
3. HCL to Anna Lodge, April 18, 1880, MHS.
4. Edmund Morris, *Rise of Theodore Roosevelt*, 240–41.
5. Teague, *Mrs. L*, 3–4; Morison, *Letters of Theodore Roosevelt*, vol. 1, 68.
6. Roosevelt and Lodge, *Selections from the Correspondence*, vol. 1, 1, 3.
7. McCullough, *Mornings on Horseback*, 300; Garraty, *Henry Cabot Lodge*, 78.
8. Edmund Morris, *Rise of Theodore Roosevelt*, 262.
9. McCullough, *Mornings on Horseback*, 294.
10. Wister, *Roosevelt*, 27.
11. Garraty, *Henry Cabot Lodge*, 82.
12. Roosevelt and Lodge, *Selections from the Correspondence*, vol. 1, 5.
13. Edmund Morris, *Rise of Theodore Roosevelt*, 273.
14. Garraty, *Henry Cabot Lodge*, 126; Edmund Morris, *Rise of Theodore Roosevelt*, 259; Zimmerman, *First Great Triumph*, 149, 167, 176, 187.
15. Edmund Morris, *Rise of Theodore Roosevelt*, 262.
16. HCL to Anna Lodge, December 2, 1894, December 16, 1894, December 27, 1896, MHS.
17. Garraty, *Henry Cabot Lodge*, 123.
18. Miller, *Henry Cabot Lodge*, 419.
19. Morison, *Letters of Theodore Roosevelt*, vol. 1, 141.
20. Roosevelt and Lodge, *Selections from the Correspondence*, vol. 1, 25.
21. HCL to Anna Lodge, April 28, 1895, December 11, 1895, MHS.
22. Roosevelt and Lodge, *Selections from the Correspondence*, vol. 1, 142.
23. Lodge, *Early Memories*, 217.
24. Sylvia Jukes Morris, *Edith Kermit Roosevelt*, 107; Widenor, *Henry Cabot Lodge*, 2, 45, 56.
25. Goodwin, *Fitzgeralds and the Kennedys*, 46–66.
26. HCL to Anna Lodge, October 13, 1895, MHS.
27. Roosevelt and Lodge, *Selections from the Correspondence*, vol. 1, 58; Morison, *Letters of Theodore Roosevelt*, vol. 1, 483.
28. Roosevelt and Lodge, *Selections from the Correspondence*, vol. 1, 55.
29. Dalton, *Theodore Roosevelt*, 93; Roosevelt and Lodge, *Selections from the Correspondence*, vol. 1, 5.
30. HCL to Anna Lodge, June 29, 1890, MHS; Widenor, *Henry Cabot Lodge*, 78.

31. Morison, *Letters of Theodore Roosevelt*, vol. 1, 200.
32. Dalton, *Theodore Roosevelt*, 100.
33. Ibid., 93.
34. Roosevelt and Lodge, *Selections from the Correspondence*, vol. 1, 39–40.
35. Dalton, *Theodore Roosevelt*, 98, 103.
36. Townsend, *Manhood at Harvard*, 264.
37. Zimmerman, *First Great Triumph*, 219.
38. Edmund Morris, *Rise of Theodore Roosevelt*, 310.
39. Dalton, "Theodore Roosevelt and the Idea of War," *Theodore Roosevelt Association Journal*, Fall 1981, 7; Dyer, *Theodore Roosevelt*, 66–67; Dalton, *Theodore Roosevelt*, 39.
40. Dyer, *Theodore Roosevelt*, 57.
41. Widenor, *Henry Cabot Lodge*, 27.
42. Zimmerman, *First Great Triumph*, 458–59.
43. Garraty, *Henry Cabot Lodge*, 59.
44. Peter Collier, *The Roosevelts*, 77.
45. Lodge, "The Distribution of Ability in the United States," *Century Illustrated Magazine* 42, no. 5, September 1894.
46. Goodwin, *Fitzgeralds and the Kennedys*, 119.
47. Dyer, *Theodore Roosevelt*, 38.
48. Morison, *Letters of Theodore Roosevelt*, vol. 1, 282–83.
49. Josephson, *President Makers*, 54.
50. Zimmerman, *First Great Triumph*, 461; Wister, *Roosevelt*, 67–68.
51. HCL to Anna Lodge, January 18, 1891, March 17, 1890, MHS.
52. Garraty, *Henry Cabot Lodge*, 117.
53. Sylvia Jukes Morris, *Edith Kermit Roosevelt*, 21.
54. Ibid., 160.
55. Ibid., 4, 15–16, 78–81, 86, 91; Dalton, *Theodore Roosevelt*, 47, 85, 88–89, 104–16.
56. Garraty, *Henry Cabot Lodge*, 31.
57. Roosevelt and Lodge, *Selections from the Correspondence*, vol. 1, 55. Annotations made by Kathleen Dalton.
58. Garraty, *Henry Cabot Lodge*, 35.
59. Miller, *Henry Cabot Lodge*, 420.
60. Zimmerman, *First Great Triumph*, 157.

3. Manifest Destiny

1. Blight, *Race and Reunion*, 65; Rotundo, *American Manhood*, 233–34.
2. Sylvia Jukes Morris, *Edith Kermit Roosevelt*, 146.
3. Heather Cox Richardson, *West from Appomattox*, 276–77.
4. "Beauties of Wooded Island," *Current Literature* 14, October 1893.
5. "Boone and Crockett Club," *Forest and Stream* 30, no. 7, March 8, 1888.
6. *Forest and Stream* 31, no. 26, January 17, 1889.

7. Philippon, *Conserving Words*, 55–56.

8. McCullough, *Mornings on Horseback*, 316.

9. Wister, *Owen Wister Out West*, 164.

10. Chanler, ed., *Winthrop Chanler Letters*, 52.

11. Brands, *Reckless Decade*, 288.

12. Townsend, *Manhood at Harvard*, 32.

13. Werth, *Banquet at Delmonico's*, 69–72.

14. Hoganson, *Fighting for American Manhood*, 35.

15. Sylvia Jukes Morris, *Edith Kermit Roosevelt*, 155.

16. Bergin, *The Game*, 58.

17. Morison, *Letters of Theodore Roosevelt*, vol. 8, 1435.

18. Widenor, *Henry Cabot Lodge*, 24.

19. Slotkin, *Gunfighter Nation*, 41.

20. Heather Cox Richardson, *West from Appomattox*, 281.

21. Ibid., 281–82.

22. Morison, *Letters of Theodore Roosevelt*, vol. 1, 363.

23. Ibid., 156–57.

24. Sylvia Jukes Morris, *Edith Kermit Roosevelt*, 158.

25. Dalton, *Theodore Roosevelt*, 166.

26. Pérez, *The United States and Cuba*, 3–5.

27. Ibid., 7.

28. Musicant, *Empire by Default*, 29.

29. Morison, *Letters of Theodore Roosevelt*, vol. 1, 436.

4. The Large Policy

1. Baker, *Justice from Beacon Hill*, 152; Blight, *Race and Reunion*, 96, 392.

2. Roosevelt and Lodge, *Selections from the Correspondence*, vol. 1, 146.

3. Ibid., 148.

4. McCullough, *Mornings on Horseback*, 215.

5. Morison, *Letters of Theodore Roosevelt*, vol. 1, 464.

6. Chanler, ed., *Winthrop Chanler Letters*, vii.

7. Roosevelt and Lodge, *Selections from the Correspondence*, vol. 1, 82, 195.

8. Morison, *Letters of Theodore Roosevelt*, vol. 1, 493.

9. Ibid., 484.

10. Roosevelt and Lodge, *Hero Tales*, 23, 36, 221, 143–45, 123.

11. Ibid., 176–82.

12. Tuchman, *Proud Tower*, 137.

13. Zimmerman, *First Great Triumph*, 153.

14. Vorpahl, *My Dear Wister*, 217.

15. Musicant, *Empire by Default*, 33–34.

16. Roosevelt and Lodge, *Selections from the Correspondence*, vol. 1, 200.

17. Garraty, *Henry Cabot Lodge*, 161.

18. HCL to Anna Lodge, December 18, 1895, MHS.

19. HCL to Anna Lodge, February 17, 1896, MHS.
20. Widenor, *Henry Cabot Lodge*, 106; Musicant, *Empire by Default*, 32.
21. Morison, *Letters of Theodore Roosevelt*, vol. 1, 221; Edmund Morris, *Rise of Theodore Roosevelt*, 424; HCL to Anna Lodge, December 27, 1891, MHS; Seeger and Maguire, eds., *Letters and Papers of Alfred Thayer Mahan*, vol. 2, 11.
22. Tuchman, *Proud Tower*, 133.
23. Garraty, *Henry Cabot Lodge*, 152.
24. Ibid.
25. HCL to Anna Lodge, December 22, 1895, MHS.
26. Garraty, *Henry Cabot Lodge*, 163.
27. Levenson, ed., *Letters of Henry Adams*, vol. 4, 358; Townsend, *Manhood at Harvard*, 82.
28. Morison, *Letters of Theodore Roosevelt*, vol. 1, 509, 507.

5. The Individualist

1. Townsend, *Manhood at Harvard*, 37–38.
2. Skrupskelis and Berkeley, eds., *Correspondence of William James*, vol. 8, 108.
3. Ibid., vol. 2, 382–84.
4. Ibid., vol. 8, 114.
5. Ibid., vol. 2, 385.
6. Perry, *Thought and Character of William James*, vol. 2, 305; Cotkin, *William James*, 130, 145–46.
7. Morison, *Letters of Theodore Roosevelt*, vol. 1, 29.
8. Townsend, *Manhood at Harvard*, 244.
9. Dyer, *Theodore Roosevelt*, 4–5.
10. Townsend, *Manhood at Harvard*, 48.
11. Ibid., 27, 164; Menand, *Metaphysical Club*, 95; Robert Richardson, *William James*, 184–85.
12. Robert Richardson, *William James*, 25.
13. Skrupskelis and Berkeley, eds., *Correspondence of William James*, vol. 8, 109.
14. Perry, *Thought and Character of William James*, vol. 1, 365.
15. Robert Richardson, *William James*, 13, 20, 271–72, 327; Townsend, *Manhood at Harvard*, 13, 36, 167, 175; Fisher, *House of Wits*, 324.
16. Robert Richardson, *William James*, 23; Fisher, *House of Wits*, 478.
17. Myers, *William James*, 38.
18. Robert Richardson, *William James*, 349–52; Fisher, *House of Wits*, 528–32.
19. Robert Richardson, *William James*, 237.
20. Ibid., 317.
21. Menand, *Metaphysical Club*, 58, 77, 85; Lewis, *The Jameses*, 5. Also see Robert Richardson, *William James*, 305.

22. Townsend, *Manhood at Harvard*, 42, 164–65.
23. Robert Richardson, *William James*, 40–41, 54.
24. Ibid., 54–55; Bundy, *Nature of Sacrifice*, 279–80.
25. Lewis, *The Jameses*, 147–48.
26. Cotkin, *William James*, 32–33.
27. Lewis, *The Jameses*, 554.
28. Menand, *Metaphysical Club*, 218–19; Townsend, *Manhood at Harvard*, 44; Robert Richardson, *William James*, 83.
29. Townsend, *Manhood at Harvard*, 172–73.
30. Robert Richardson, *William James*, 65–74. But see Garrison and Madden, "William James: Warts and All," *American Quarterly* 29, no. 2 (Summer 1977), 215–16.
31. Menand, *Metaphysical Club*, 143.
32. Myers, *William James*, 13.
33. Menand, *Metaphysical Club*, 201, 216; Townsend, *Manhood at Harvard*, 59–60.
34. Menand, *Metaphysical Club*, 205; Robert Richardson, *William James*, 169–75, 267, 353; Fisher, *House of Wits*, 388.
35. Robert Richardson, *William James*, 306.
36. Lewis, *The Jameses*, 442–43.
37. Ibid., 459.
38. Skrupskelis and Berkeley, eds., *Correspondence of William James*, vol. 2, 384.
39. Fisher, *House of Wits*, 402.

6. Selling Papers

1. New York *Journal*, December 18, 19, 20, 1895.
2. Milton, *The Yellow Kids*, 193; Swanberg, *Citizen Hearst*, 3–6.
3. HCL to Anna Lodge, January 31, 1897, MHS.
4. Swanberg, *Citizen Hearst*, 8, 14; Phoebe Hearst to George Hearst, September 28, 1868, May 11, 1873, September 2, 1873; William Randolph Hearst to George Hearst, March 29, 1878; William Randolph Hearst to George Hearst, March 29, 1878, Bancroft Library, University of California, Berkeley.
5. Nasaw, *The Chief*, 32, 35. He is not listed in the Porcellian Club membership book, and John Lawrence, former graduate head of the club, denied that he had ever been a member.
6. Phoebe Hearst to George Hearst, October 22, 1885, November 12, 1885, August 1, 1888, Bancroft Library, University of California, Berkeley.
7. William Randolph Hearst to George Hearst, November 23, 1885, Bancroft Library, University of California, Berkeley.
8. Nasaw, *The Chief*, 75.
9. Swanberg, *Citizen Hearst*, 59–60.

10. Lundberg, *Imperial Hearst*, 51.
11. Pizzitola, *Hearst Over Hollywood*, 25.
12. Milton, *Yellow Kids*, xi, 28–29.
13. G. J. A. O'Toole, *Spanish War*, 68–69.
14. New York *Journal*, December 23, 1895, January 14, 1896.
15. New York *Journal*, December 8, 1895; G. J. A. O'Toole, *Spanish War*, 52–53.
16. G. J. A. O'Toole, *Spanish War*, 53.
17. Ferrer, *Insurgent Cuba*, 6–7, 121–26.
18. Milton, *Yellow Kids*, 53.
19. Musicant, *Empire by Default*, 50–56.
20. Millis, *Martial Spirit*, 41.
21. Milton, *Yellow Kids*, 47–49.
22. New York *Journal*, December 10, 16, 29, 1895.
23. Ibid., December 25, 1895, January 3, 1896.
24. G. J. A. O'Toole, *Spanish War*, 60.
25. New York *Journal*, December 17, 1895.
26. *Congressional Record*, 54th Cong., 1st sess., vol. 28, 1896, 2244–48.
27. Milton, *Yellow Kids*, 89–90.

7. The Czar

1. New York *Journal*, December 2, 1895.
2. Ibid., January 19, 1896.
3. Ibid., January 19, 24, February 7, 1896.
4. Diary of Asher Hinds, December 14, 17, 18, 19, 1895, LOC.
5. Robinson, *Thomas B. Reed*, 391; Tuchman, *Proud Tower*, 121.
6. Stevens, "Characteristics of Congressmen," *Leslie's Popular Monthly*, June 1894; *Philadelphia Times*, March 1897, in scrapbook in the Thomas B. Reed Collection, Special Collections, Bowdoin College, Brunswick, Maine.
7. Lodge, *Democracy of the Constitution*, 191.
8. Tuchman, *Proud Tower*, 123.
9. Robinson, *Thomas B. Reed*, 390.
10. Beisner, *Twelve Against Empire*, 205.
11. Robinson, *Thomas B. Reed*, 140–41.
12. Ibid., 1–19; Tuchman, *Proud Tower*, 120.
13. Lodge, *Democracy of the Constitution*, 195.
14. Tuchman, *Proud Tower*, 124–28.
15. Ibid., 129.
16. Ibid., 124, 129.
17. Leupp, "Personal Recollections of Thomas B. Reed," *Outlook*, September 3, 1910.

18. Diary of Thomas B. Reed, January 26, 31, 1889, March 28, 30, 1895, Thomas B. Reed Collection, Special Collections, Bowdoin College, Brunswick, Maine.
19. Roosevelt and Lodge, *Selections from the Correspondence*, vol. 1, 203–4.
20. HCL to Anna Lodge, November 30, 1893, MHS.
21. Lodge, *Democracy of the Constitution*, 200.
22. Ibid., 192.
23. HCL to Anna Lodge, November 24, December 21, 1889, MHS.
24. Roosevelt and Lodge, *Selections from the Correspondence*, vol. 1, 76.
25. Garraty, *Henry Cabot Lodge*, 104.
26. TR to Thomas B. Reed, August 7, 1895, Thomas B. Reed Collection, Special Collections, Bowdoin College, Brunswick, Maine.
27. TR to Thomas B. Reed, October 18, 1894, Thomas B. Reed Collection, Special Collections, Bowdoin College, Brunswick, Maine.
28. Robinson, *Thomas B. Reed*, 147.
29. Diary of Thomas B. Reed, January 16, 1893, Thomas B. Reed Collection, Special Collections, Bowdoin College, Brunswick, Maine; Beisner, *Twelve Against Empire*, 205.
30. Garraty, *Henry Cabot Lodge*, 109.
31. Robinson, *Thomas B. Reed*, 246.
32. HCL to Thomas B. Reed, November 10, 1894, Thomas B. Reed Collection, Special Collections, Bowdoin College, Brunswick, Maine.
33. Wister, *Roosevelt*, 44.
34. Dunn, *From Harrison to Harding*, vol. 1, 70.
35. Diary of Asher Hinds, February 2, 1896, LOC.
36. See, generally, Brands, *Reckless Decade*, 128–76.
37. Robinson, *Thomas B. Reed*, 356.
38. Ibid., 135.

8. The Pleasant Gang

1. Patricia O'Toole, *Five of Hearts*, 91, 283, 291.
2. Adams, *Education of Henry Adams*, 15–16.
3. Patricia O'Toole, *Five of Hearts*, 153.
4. Levenson, ed., *Letters of Henry Adams*, vol. 4, 332.
5. Ford, ed., *Letters of Henry Adams*, vol. 2, 91, 99; Adams, *Letters of Henry Adams*, vols. 4–6, 359, 342.
6. Ford, ed., *Letters of Henry Adams*, vol. 2, 91.
7. Adams, *Letters of Henry Adams*, vol. 2, 353.
8. Ford, ed., *Letters of Henry Adams*, vol. 2, 92.
9. Lodge, *Early Memories*, 238; Garraty, *Henry Cabot Lodge*, 41.
10. Ford, ed., *Letters of Henry Adams*, vol. 2, 95.
11. Edmund Morris, *Rise of Theodore Roosevelt*, 417.

12. Chanler, *Roman Spring*, 191, 195.
13. Adams, *Letters of Henry Adams*, vols. 4–6, 438.
14. Ibid., 344; Morison, *Letters of Theodore Roosevelt*, vol. 1, 433.
15. Patricia O'Toole, *Five of Hearts*, 91, 100.
16. Chanler, *Roman Spring*, 192–93.
17. Zimmerman, *First Great Triumph*, 183.
18. Patricia O'Toole, *Five of Hearts*, 217–20; Garraty, *Henry Cabot Lodge*, 122.
19. Josephson, *President Makers*, 22.
20. Morison, *Letters of Theodore Roosevelt*, vol. 1, 520.
21. Zimmerman, *First Great Triumph*, 161.
22. Roosevelt and Lodge, *Selections from the Correspondence*, vol. 1, 187.
23. Garraty, *Henry Cabot Lodge*, 181.
24. Adams, *Letters of Henry Adams*, vols. 4–6, 371, 368.
25. Patricia O'Toole, *Five of Hearts*, 285.
26. Adams, *Education of Henry Adams*, 349.
27. Millis, *Martial Spirit*, 46–49.
28. Adams, *Letters of Henry Adams*, vols. 4–6, 387.

9. *Aux Barricades!*

1. Morison, *Letters of Theodore Roosevelt*, vol. 1, 509.
2. Ibid., 519.
3. Ibid., 520–21.
4. Roosevelt and Lodge, *Selections from the Correspondence*, vol. 1, 215–16.
5. Adams, *Letters of Henry Adams*, vols. 4–6, 369, 433, 434.
6. Aldrich, *Old Money*, 3–28.
7. Robinson, *Thomas B. Reed*, 326.
8. Diary of Asher Hinds, March 8, 1896, LOC.
9. Robinson, *Thomas B. Reed*, 325, 334.
10. Roosevelt and Lodge, *Selections from the Correspondence*, vol. 1, 223.
11. Ibid., 214.
12. Morison, *Letters of Theodore Roosevelt*, vol. 1, 543.
13. Diary of Asher Hinds, June 8, 1897, LOC.
14. Morison, *Letters of Theodore Roosevelt*, vol. 1, 537.
15. Robinson, *Thomas B. Reed*, 338.
16. Leech, *In the Days of McKinley*, 7–8, 19, 23–26, 39.
17. Brands, *Reckless Decade*, 265–67; Gould, *Presidency of William McKinley*, 8–9, 51–52.
18. Roosevelt and Lodge, *Selections from the Correspondence*, vol. 1, 227.
19. Garraty, *Henry Cabot Lodge*, 169.
20. Ibid., 172; Townsend, *Manhood at Harvard*, 103.
21. Morison, *Letters of Theodore Roosevelt*, vol. 1, 546.
22. Garraty, *Henry Cabot Lodge*, 173.

23. Author's interview with Joseph Alsop.
24. Morison, *Letters of Theodore Roosevelt*, vol. 1, 554–55.
25. Roosevelt and Lodge, *Selections from the Correspondence*, vol. 1, 230.
26. Garraty, *Henry Cabot Lodge*, 174, 176.
27. Morison, *Letters of Theodore Roosevelt*, vol. 1, 565–66.
28. Zimmerman, *First Great Triumph*, 178.
29. Roosevelt and Lodge, *Selections from the Correspondence*, vol. 1, 240–43.
30. Ibid., 253; William Howard Taft to HCL, March 4, 8, 14, 1897, MHS.
31. George Lyman to HCL, March 23, 1897, MHS.
32. Morris, *Rise of Theodore Roosevelt*, 558.
33. Morison, *Letters of Theodore Roosevelt*, vol. 1, 573.
34. Morris, *Rise of Theodore Roosevelt*, 555.
35. Morison, *Letters of Theodore Roosevelt*, vol. 1, 584.
36. Leech, *In the Days of McKinley*, 106.
37. Roosevelt and Lodge, *Selections from the Correspondence*, vol. 1, 257.
38. Ibid., 253.
39. Ibid., 262.
40. Ibid., 263; Morris, *Rise of Theodore Roosevelt*, 560.
41. Metropolitan Club Records and "To the Board of Governors, the Metropolitan Club," June 16, 1897. Morison, *Letters of Theodore Roosevelt*, vol. 1, 626.
42. Roosevelt and Lodge, *Selections from the Correspondence*, vol. 1, 266.
43. Henry Adams, *Letters of Henry Adams*, vols. 4–6, 460.
44. Ibid., 437.
45. Millis, *Martial Spirit*, 67.
46. Josephson, *President Makers*, 66.
47. Gould, *Presidency of William McKinley*, 33.

10. Kinds of Courage

1. Swanberg, *Citizen Hearst*, 102.
2. New York *Journal*, January 12, 15, 16, February 12, 1896.
3. Morison, *Letters of Theodore Roosevelt*, vol. 1, 592.
4. Swanberg, *Citizen Hearst*, 85–87.
5. Brown, *Correspondents' War*, 104.
6. Swanberg, *Citizen Hearst*, 107; Milton, *Yellow Kids*, 194; Pizzitola, *Hearst Over Hollywood*, 14, 22.
7. Swanberg, *Citizen Hearst*, 107.
8. Paine, *Roads of Adventure*, 62–63.
9. Lubow, *Reporter Who Would Be King*, 1–5, 19, 130; Milton, *Yellow Kids*, 110–13.
10. Samuels, *Frederic Remington*, 26–27, 245–350.
11. Milton, *Yellow Kids*, 79.
12. New York *Journal*, January 31, February 13, 14, 1897.

13. Lubow, *Reporter Who Would Be King*, 190; Tone, *War and Genocide*, 10.
14. Tone, *War and Genocide*, 57–58, 99, 127, 136–47.
15. New York *Journal*, February 23, 1896; Swanberg, *Citizen Hearst*, 110–11.
16. Tone, *War and Genocide*, 8, 153–54, 164, 188, 218, 223.
17. Creelman, *On the Great Highway*, 177–78; Nasaw, *The Chief*, 127.
18. New York *Journal*, January 22, February 2, 28, 1897.
19. Ibid., February 12, 1897.
20. Lubow, *Reporter Who Would Be King*, 140–44.
21. Skrupskelis and Berkeley, eds., *Correspondence of William James*, vol. 2, 407.
22. Ibid., 406.
23. Cotkin, *William James*, 110.
24. Skrupskelis and Berkeley, eds., *Correspondence of William James*, vol. 2, 403.
25. Ibid., vol. 3, 5.
26. Lewis, *The Jameses*, 148.
27. Skrupskelis and Berkeley, eds., *Correspondence of William James*, vol. 3, 8–9.
28. Ibid., 9.
29. Ibid.

11. Romance

1. Morison, *Letters of Theodore Roosevelt*, vol. 1, 607.
2. Edmund Morris, *Rise of Theodore Roosevelt*, 456.
3. Morison, *Letters of Theodore Roosevelt*, vol. 1, 607–8.
4. Seeger and Maguire, eds., *Letters and Papers of Alfred Thayer Mahan*, vol. 2, 96, 100, 236, 281–82, 506; Hattendorf, ed., *Influence of History on Mahan*, 50–51.
5. Edmund Morris, *Rise of Theodore Roosevelt*, 569–71; *Boston Globe*; Providence (R.I.) *Bulletin*, June 2, 1897.
6. Edmund Morris, *Rise of Theodore Roosevelt*, 572.
7. Morison, *Letters of Theodore Roosevelt*, vol. 1, 637.
8. TR to HCL, June 17, 1897, TR to Secretary John Long, June 18, 1897; Morison, *Letters of Theodore Roosevelt*, vol. 1, 628; Edmund Morris, *Rise of Theodore Roosevelt*, 575–76.
9. Morison, *Letters of Theodore Roosevelt*, vol. 1, 642, 649, 651, 273, 655.
10. *New York Times*, September 8, 10, October 14, 1897; New York *Herald*, September 10, 1897; New York *Sun*, September 10, 1897.
11. Kathleen Dalton, *Theodore Roosevelt*, 167.
12. Roosevelt and Lodge, *Selections from the Correspondence*, vol. 1, 274.
13. Morison, *Letters of Theodore Roosevelt*, vol. 1, 680; Peggy and Harold Samuels, *Frederic Remington*, 259.
14. Morison, *Letters of Theodore Roosevelt*, 676, 685.
15. Leech, *In the Days of McKinley*, 163.

16. Spector, *Admiral of the New Empire*, 35–39; Leech, *In the Days of McKinley*, 159; Morison, *Letters of Theodore Roosevelt*, vol. 1, 691.

17. Morison, *Letters of Theodore Roosevelt*, vol. 1, 681; New York *Journal*, September 14, 16, 20, 1897; *New York Times*, September 18, 20, 1897.

18. New York *Journal*, August 17, 18, 29, 1897; Cross, "The Perils of Evangelina," *American Heritage* 19, no. 2, February 1968.

19. New York *Journal*, August 22, 23, 24, 1897.

20. Abbott, *Watching the World Go By*, 216.

21. New York *Journal*, October 8, 9, 10, 11, 1897.

22. Abbott, *Watching the World Go By*, 215–16; Whyte, *The Uncrowned King*, 334.

23. New York *Journal*, October 14, 1897.

24. New York *Journal*, October 17, 1897.

25. Swanberg, *Citizen Hearst*, 128.

26. HCL to Anna Lodge, August 4, 1892, MHS.

27. *Harper's*, July 1896.

28. Garraty, *Henry Cabot Lodge*, 193.

29. HCL to Anna Lodge, February 9, 1896, MHS; Garraty, *Henry Cabot Lodge*, 269.

30. HCL to Anna Roosevelt, June 9, 1897, MHS.

31. Morison, *Letters of Theodore Roosevelt*, vol. 1, 711.

32. Roosevelt and Lodge, *Selections from the Correspondence*, vol. 1, 272.

33. Schirmer, *Republic or Empire*, 29.

34. Garraty, *Henry Cabot Lodge*, 182.

35. HCL to Thomas B. Reed, August 20, 25, 1897; Thomas B. Reed to HCL, August 22, September 3, 1897, Thomas B. Reed Collection, Special Collections, Bowdoin College, Brunswick, Maine.

36. Reed, "The New Navy," *Illustrated American*, September 25, 1897.

12. The Stolen Letter

1. Garraty, *Henry Cabot Lodge*, 185.

2. Perry, *Thought and Character of William James*, vol. 2, 307.

3. Musicant, *Empire by Default*, 115.

4. Long, *Journal*, 213.

5. Morison, *Letters of Theodore Roosevelt*, vol. 1, 707.

6. Caroli, *Roosevelt Women*, 205.

7. Sylvia Jukes Morris, *Edith Kermit Roosevelt*, 167.

8. Morison, *Letters of Theodore Roosevelt*, vol. 1, 717–18.

9. HCL to Anna Roosevelt, November 28, 1897, MHS; Morison, *Letters of Theodore Roosevelt*, vol. 1, 723; Dalton, *Theodore Roosevelt*, 167.

10. Roosevelt, *Rough Riders*, 12–13.

11. Roosevelt and Lodge, *Selections from the Correspondence*, vol. 1, 285.

12. Morison, *Letters of Theodore Roosevelt*, vol. 1, 723.

13. Ibid., 748.
14. Ibid., 755.
15. Kerr, *Bully Father*, xx.
16. Morison, *Letters of Theodore Roosevelt*, vol. 1, 757.
17. Sylvia Jukes Morris, *Edith Kermit Roosevelt*, 119; Caroli, *Roosevelt Women*, 189.
18. Pérez, *War of 1898*, 7–9; Musicant, *Empire by Default*, 118–19; Offner, *An Unwanted War*, 68, 84–85.
19. New York *Journal*, January 13, 1898.
20. Long, *Journal*, January 13, 1898, MHS.
21. Morison, *Letters of Theodore Roosevelt*, vol. 1, 765; Dalton, *Theodore Roosevelt*, 168.
22. Morison, *Letters of Theodore Roosevelt*, vol. 1, 758, 765.
23. Collier, *Roosevelts*, 125.
24. Teague, *Mrs. L*, 42, 46.
25. Morison, *Letters of Theodore Roosevelt*, vol. 1, 234, vol. 8, 1430.
26. Kerr, *Bully Father*, 46.
27. Theodore Roosevelt, Jr., *All in the Family*, 183.
28. Theodore Roosevelt to Anna Roosevelt, March 16, 1895, April 26, 1891, Theodore Roosevelt Collection, Houghton Library, Harvard University, Cambridge, Massachusetts.
29. Collier, *Roosevelts*, 7.
30. Kerr, *Bully Father*, 12.
31. Dalton, *Theodore Roosevelt*, 168.
32. Morison, *Letters of Theodore Roosevelt*, vol. 1, 763–64.
33. G. J. A. O'Toole, *Spanish War*, 115–17.
34. Beer, *Hanna, Crane and the Mauve Decade*, 546.
35. HCL to Henry White, January 31, 1898, MHS.
36. Leech, *In the Days of McKinley*, 121–23.
37. Ibid., 121–23, 165.
38. Rubens, *Liberty*, 287–88; Milton, *Yellow Kids*, 214.
39. New York *Journal*, January 12, 19, 20, 1898.
40. New York *Journal*, January 26, 1898.
41. Hoganson, *Fighting for American Manhood*, 89.
42. New York *Journal*, January 25, February 9, 10, 11, 12, 1898.
43. Beer, *Hanna, Crane and the Mauve Decade*, 545–48.
44. Musicant, *Empire by Default*, 129–40; G. J. A. O'Toole, *Spanish War*, 26–30; Millis, *Martial Spirit*, 100–04.
45. Swanberg, *Citizen Hearst*, 136–37.

13. Remember the *Maine*

1. New York *Journal*, February 16, 17, 18, 1898.
2. Musicant, *Empire by Default*, 144.

NOTES

3. Rickover, *How the Battleship Maine Was Destroyed*, 46–47.
4. Nasaw, *The Chief*, 131.
5. New York *Journal*, February 21, 1898; Swanberg, *Citizen Hearst*, 138.
6. Swanberg, *Citizen Hearst*, 139–41.
7. Milton, *Yellow Kids*, 225–26.
8. Leech, *In the Days of McKinley*, 168.
9. Long, *Journal*, 215.
10. Morison, *Letters of Theodore Roosevelt*, vol. 1, 783–84.
11. Ibid., 775.
12. New York *Herald*, February 19, 1898.
13. Long, *Journal*, 215–16.
14. Morison, *Letters of Theodore Roosevelt*, vol. 1, 780.
15. New York *Herald*, February 19, 1898.
16. Morison, *Letters of Theodore Roosevelt*, vol. 1, 785–86.
17. Rickover, *How the Battleship Maine Was Destroyed*, 64–65.
18. Morison, *Letters of Theodore Roosevelt*, vol. 1, 783.
19. Edith Roosevelt to Emily Carow, February 1898, Theodore Roosevelt Collection, Houghton Library, Harvard University.
20. HCL to Anna Lodge, February 6, 1898, MHS.
21. HCL to Anna Lodge, February 12, 1898, MHS.
22. Morison, *Letters of Theodore Roosevelt*, vol. 1, 785.
23. HCL to Anna Lodge, February 26, 1898, MHS.
24. Edmund Morris, *Rise of Theodore Roosevelt*, 602.
25. Morison, *Letters of Theodore Roosevelt*, vol. 1, 784; Long, *Journal*, 217 and unpublished entry of February 26, 1898, MHS.
26. Sylvia Jukes Morris, *Edith Kermit Roosevelt*, 170.
27. Morison, *Letters of Theodore Roosevelt*, vol. 1, 786.
28. Ibid., 790.
29. Chanler, ed., *Winthrop Chanler Letters*, 65.
30. Morison, *Letters of Theodore Roosevelt*, vol. 1, 793, 795–96.
31. Ibid., 791, 796, 798, 801.
32. Edith Roosevelt to Emily Carow, March 7, 8, 1898, and undated letter in 1898, Theodore Roosevelt Collection, Houghton Library, Harvard University.
33. Morison, *Letters of Theodore Roosevelt*, vol. 1, 789.
34. Rickover, *How the Battleship Maine Was Destroyed*, 70, 91, 104, but see Trask, *War with Spain in 1898*, 35; Allen,"Remember the *Maine*?" *National Geographic* 193, no. 2, February 1998.
35. Tone, *War and Genocide in Cuba*, 242.
36. Leech, *In the Days of McKinley*, 174, 176.
37. Swanberg, *Citizen Hearst*, 142.
38. *New York Times*, March 27, 1898.
39. Dunn, *Gridiron Nights*, 66, 71–72.

40. Roosevelt, *Letters from Theodore Roosevelt to Anna Roosevelt Cowles*, 212.
41. Swanberg, *Citizen Hearst*, 141–42.
42. Ibid., 143.
43. Leech, *In the Days of McKinley*, 181; Musicant, *Empire by Default*, 144, 152, 157.
44. Brown, *The Correspondents' War*, 158.
45. Musicant, *Empire by Default*, 155; Long, *Journal*, April 2, 3, 4, 1898, MHS.
46. Leech, *In the Days of McKinley*, 169, 628.
47. Gould, *Presidency of William McKinley*, 78–90; Fry, "William McKinley and the Coming of the Spanish-American War," *Diplomatic History* 3, no. 1, Winter 1979.
48. Musicant, *Empire by Default*, 178; Trask, *War with Spain in 1898*, 14, 44.
49. Tone, *War and Genocide in Cuba*, 251.
50. Rubens, *Liberty*, 326–29; Tone, *War and Genocide in Cuba*, 236–38; Pérez, *War of 1898*, 17–18.
51. John D. Long to Mr. Nichols, April 15, 1898, MHS.
52. Trask, *War with Spain in 1898*, 42.
53. Musicant, *Empire by Default*, 168.
54. Kohlstaat, *From McKinley to Harding*, 66–67.
55. Hagedorn, *Leonard Wood*, vols. 1 and 2, 141.

14. The Trophies of Miltiades

1. Morison, *Letters of Theodore Roosevelt*, vol. 1, 745.
2. Millis, *Martial Spirit*, 112; Garraty, *Henry Cabot Lodge*, 186; Roosevelt, *An Autobiography*, 218.
3. Garraty, *Henry Cabot Lodge*, 188–90.
4. HCL to Anna Lodge, April 3, 1898, MHS.
5. HCL to Anna Lodge, April 22, 1898, MHS.
6. New York *Herald*, February 23, 1898.
7. Diary of Asher Hinds, February 28, 1898, LOC.
8. Leech, *In the Days of McKinley*, 169.
9. Diary of Asher Hinds, March 9, 1898, LOC.
10. New York *Journal*, January 21, 1898.
11. Robinson, *Thomas B. Reed*, 360.
12. Dunn, *From Harrison to Harding*, vols. 1 and 2, 234; Offner, *An Unwanted War*, 130.
13. Leech, *In the Days of McKinley*, 178–79; Offner, *An Unwanted War*, 151–52.
14. *New York Times*, April 7, 1898.
15. Offner, *An Unwanted War*, 182.
16. HCL to Anna Lodge, April 17, 1898, MHS.
17. Tone, *War and Genocide in Cuba*, 244.

18. Musicant, *Empire by Default*, 183.
19. London *Times*, *New York Times*, *Boston Globe*, New York *Journal*, April 14, 1898.
20. Asher Hinds Diary, April 13, 1898, LOC.
21. Roosevelt, *Pocket Diary, 1898*, April 16, 1898.
22. Morison, *Letters of Theodore Roosevelt*, vol. 2, 815.
23. *Boston Globe*, April 14, 1898.
24. Leech, *In the Days of McKinley*, 188.
25. Zimmerman, *First Great Triumph*, 264–65. See also Pérez, *War of 1898*, 19–20.
26. Musicant, *Empire by Default*, 189.
27. HCL to John Hay, April 21, 1898, MHS.
28. HCL to Anna Lodge, May 1, 1898, MHS.
29. Long, *Journal*, April 23, 1898, MHS.
30. Garraty, *Henry Cabot Lodge*, 193.
31. Long, *Journal*, April 22, 1898, MHS.
32. Garraty, *Henry Cabot Lodge*, 191; Chanler, ed., *Winthrop Chanler Letters*, 65.
33. Long, *Journal*, 224.
34. Ibid.
35. Adams, *Letters of Henry Adams*, vols. 4–6, 577.
36. Chanler, ed., *Winthrop Chanler Letters*, 68–70.
37. Patricia O'Toole, *Five of Hearts*, 296.
38. Morison, *Letters of Theodore Roosevelt*, vol. 2, 808.
39. Ibid., 817, 803.
40. Ibid., 817.
41. Dalton, *Theodore Roosevelt*, 171.
42. Morison, *Letters of Theodore Roosevelt*, vol. 2, 804.
43. Dalton, *Theodore Roosevelt*, 170.
44. Sylvia Jukes Morris, *Edith Kermit Roosevelt*, 172.
45. Morison, *Letters of Theodore Roosevelt*, vol. 2, 824.
46. Renehan, *Lion's Pride*, 27.
47. Abbott, *Letters of Archie Butt*, 146.

15. Hot Time

1. Lewis, *The Jameses*, 439–42.
2. Beisner, *Twelve Against Empire*, 37–39.
3. *New York Times*, May 1, 1898.
4. Skrupskelis and Berkeley, eds., *Correspondence of William James*, vol. 8, 354–55.
5. Santayana, *Middle Span*, vol. 2, 166.
6. Skrupskelis and Berkeley, eds., *Correspondence of William James*, vol. 3, 26.
7. Ibid., vol. 8, 358–59.

NOTES

8. Skrupskelis and Berkeley, eds., *Correspondence of William James*, vol. 2, 28–32.
9. Ibid., vol. 8, 361.
10. Spector, *Admiral of the New Empire*, 49.
11. Dewey, *Autobiography*, 171–73.
12. Spector, *Admiral of the New Empire*, 49–50.
13. G. J. A. O'Toole, *Spanish War*, 178–79.
14. Spector, *Admiral of the New Empire*, 56–57.
15. Musicant, *Empire by Default*, 219–30; G. J. A. O'Toole, *Spanish War*, 184–89; Spector, *Admiral of the New Empire*, 58–63; Dewey, *Autobiography*, 189–97.
16. New York *Journal*, May 2, 1898.
17. Leech, *In the Days of McKinley*, 205–6.
18. Millis, *Martial Spirit*, 162–63.
19. Spector, *Admiral of the New Empire*, 64–67; Leech, *In the Days of McKinley*, 208–9.
20. Leech, *In the Days of McKinley*, 207.
21. Spector, *Admiral of the New Empire*, 67.
22. Adams, *Letters of Henry Adams*, vols. 4–6, 589.
23. G. J. A. O'Toole, *Spanish War*, 191.
24. Zimmerman, *First Great Triumph*, 268.
25. Morison, *Letters of Theodore Roosevelt*, vol. 2, 822.
26. Roosevelt, *Rough Riders*, 14.
27. Roosevelt, *Pocket Diary, 1898*, May 6, 1898.
28. Roosevelt, *An Autobiography*, 224.
29. Roosevelt, *Pocket Diary, 1898*, April 16, 1898.
30. Roosevelt, *An Autobiography*, 220–21.
31. Long, *Journal*, May 4, 1898, MHS.
32. Roosevelt, *An Autobiography*, 225.
33. Hagedorn, *Leonard Wood*, vols. 1 and 2, 146; Roosevelt, *Rough Riders*, 15, 231.
34. Trask, *War with Spain in 1898*, 156.
35. Morison, *Letters of Theodore Roosevelt*, vol. 1, 108; Jones, *Roosevelt's Rough Riders*, 8.
36. Roosevelt, *Rough Riders*, 15; Samuels and Samuels, *Teddy Roosevelt at San Juan Hill*, 16.
37. Marshall and Outcault, *Story of the Rough Riders*, 29.
38. Morison, *Letters of Theodore Roosevelt*, vol. 2, 823.
39. Roosevelt, *Rough Riders*, 17.
40. Morison, *Letters of Theodore Roosevelt*, vol. 2, 824.
41. Marshall, *Story of the Rough Riders*, 33; Roosevelt, *Rough Riders*, 18–19.
42. Morison, *Letters of Theodore Roosevelt*, vol. 2, 829.
43. Samuels and Samuels, *Teddy Roosevelt*, 31.

44. Jones, *Roosevelt's Rough Riders*, 35.
45. Hagedorn, *Leonard Wood*, vol. 1, 151–52; Edmund Morris, *Rise of Theodore Roosevelt*, 620.
46. Morison, *Letters of Theodore Roosevelt*, vol. 2, 831.
47. Marshall, *Story of the Rough Riders*, 40–49; Jones, *Roosevelt's Rough Riders*, 32.
48. Roosevelt, *Rough Riders*, 34–35.
49. Hagedorn, *Leonard Wood*, vol. 1, 148–53; Morris, *Rise of Theodore Roosevelt*, 623.
50. Hagedorn, *Leonard Wood*, 154.
51. Jones, *Roosevelt's Rough Riders*, 42; Marshall, *Story of the Rough Riders*, 44; Westermeier, *Who Rush to Glory*, 81–82; Morris, *Rise of Theodore Roosevelt*, 624.
52. Morison, *Letters of Theodore Roosevelt*, vol. 2, 833.
53. Hagedorn, *Leonard Wood*, vol. 1, 155; Marshall, *Story of the Rough Riders*, 19, 47.

16. The Rocking-Chair Period

1. New York *Journal*, May 8, 1898.
2. Abbott, *Watching the World Go By*, 217.
3. Whyte, *Uncrowned King*, 413. See Creelman, *On the Great Highway*, 190, for unexpurgated text.
4. Nasaw, *The Chief*, 132; Gould, *The Presidency of William McKinley*, 62–63; Brown, *The Correspondents' War*, 141; Whyte, *Uncrowned King*, 393–99.
5. Brown, *Correspondents' War*, 130.
6. Abbott, *Watching the World Go By*, 228; Stevens, *Sensationalism and the New York Press*, 98.
7. Abbott, *Watching the World Go By*, 141; Milton, *Yellow Kids*, 296–98.
8. Nasaw, *The Chief*, 134.
9. New York *Journal*, May 10, 1898.
10. Nasaw, *The Chief*, 135.
11. Swanberg, *Citizen Hearst*, 146.
12. Milton, *Yellow Kids*, 292–93.
13. Nasaw, *The Chief*, 133–37; Pizzitola, *Hearst Over Hollywood*, 62–65; Brown, *Correspondents' War*, 135.
14. Nasaw, *The Chief*, 136; Milton, *Yellow Kids*, 297.
15. Roosevelt and Lodge, *Selections from the Correspondence*, vol. 1, 299.
16. Garraty, *Henry Cabot Lodge*, 194.
17. Roosevelt and Lodge, *Selections from the Correspondence*, vol. 1, 302.
18. George Lyman to HCL, June 9, 1898, MHS.
19. George Lyman to HCL, June 14, 1898, MHS.
20. Millis, *Martial Spirit*, 220.
21. HCL to Anna Lodge, May 22, 1898, MHS.

22. Roosevelt, *Pocket Diary, 1898*, May 30, 1898; Roosevelt, *Rough Riders*, 40–41.
23. Roosevelt, *Rough Riders*, 37.
24. Roosevelt, *Pocket Diary, 1898*, June 5, 1898.
25. Roosevelt, *Rough Riders*, 41.
26. Lubow, *Reporter Who Would Be King*, 163, 168.
27. Cosby, "A Roosevelt Rough Rider Looks Back," 49.
28. Davis, "The Rocking-Chair Period of the War," *Scribner's Magazine* 24, no. 2, August 1898.
29. Sylvia Jukes Morris, *Edith Kermit Roosevelt*, 177.
30. Lubow, *Reporter Who Would Be King*, 166–73.
31. Edith Roosevelt to TR, May 23, 1898, Theodore Roosevelt Collection, Houghton Library, Harvard University.
32. Edith Roosevelt to Emily Carow, June 3, 1898, Theodore Roosevelt Collection, Houghton Library, Harvard University.
33. Davis, "The Rocking-Chair Period of the War," *Scribner's Magazine* 24, no. 2, August 1898.
34. Roosevelt and Lodge, *Selections from the Correspondence*, vol. 1, 303.
35. Roosevelt, *Rough Riders*, 43.
36. Edmund Morris, *Rise of Theodore Roosevelt*, 626–27.
37. G. J. A. O'Toole, *Spanish War*, 172, 197–99, 201, 217, 220.
38. Edmund Morris, *Rise of Theodore Roosevelt*, 628.
39. Post, *Little War of Private Post*, 82–83.
40. Roosevelt, *An Autobiography*, 238; Roosevelt, *Rough Riders*, 45; Roosevelt and Lodge, *Selections from the Correspondence*, vol. 1, 304–7.
41. Lubow, *Reporter Who Would Be King*, 171.
42. Roosevelt and Lodge, *Selections from the Correspondence*, vol. 1, 304; Roosevelt, *Rough Riders*, 46.
43. Morison, *Letters of Theodore Roosevelt*, vol. 2, 839; Roosevelt and Lodge, *Selections from the Correspondence*, vol. 1, 305.
44. Davis, *Cuban and Porto Rican Campaigns*, 86.
45. Roosevelt, *Rough Riders*, 47.
46. Morison, *Letters of Theodore Roosevelt*, vol. 2, 843; Jones, *Roosevelt's Rough Riders*, 81.
47. Roosevelt, *Rough Riders*, 20, 33, 50.
48. Jones, *Roosevelt's Rough Riders*, 91–97.

17. Hurrying to Empire

1. Robinson, *Thomas B. Reed*, 358–64.
2. Leech, *In the Days of McKinley*, 213.
3. Beisner, *Twelve Against Empire*, 207.
4. Robinson, *Thomas B. Reed*, 365–66.
5. Tuchman, *Proud Tower*, 156.

6. Robinson, *Thomas B. Reed*, 362–67; Asher Hinds Diary, May 29, June 19, 1898, LOC.
7. James, *Letters of William James*, vol. 2, 74.
8. *Boston Globe*, June 16, 1898.
9. Beisner, *Twelve Against Empire*, 39, 73, 76.
10. Hemment, *Cannon and Camera*, 66–75; Swanberg, *Citizen Hearst*, 151.
11. Leech, *In the Days of McKinley*, 367.
12. Jones, *Roosevelt's Rough Riders*, 165.
13. Davis, *Cuban and Porto Rican Campaigns*, 116.
14. Roosevelt, *An Autobiography*, 238.
15. Roosevelt, *Rough Riders*, 52; Jones, *Roosevelt's Rough Riders*, 5; Gatewood, *"Smoked Yankees" and the Struggle for Empire*, 42–43.
16. Post, *Little War of Private Post*, 110–12; Morris, *Rise of Theodore Roosevelt*, 637.
17. Davis, *Cuban and Porto Rican Campaigns*, 119; Jones, *Roosevelt's Rough Riders*, 112.
18. Marshall and Outcault, *Story of the Rough Riders*, 78.
19. Roosevelt, *Rough Riders*, 55; Millis, *Martial Spirit*, 271; Hagedorn, *Leonard Wood*, vol. 1, 161–62; Marshall, *Story of the Rough Riders*, 89.
20. Davis, *Cuban and Porto Rican Campaigns*, 177.
21. Ferrer, *Insurgent Cuba*, 1–7, 121, 143–44, 146; Pérez, *War of 1898*, 83–90, 104–6.
22. Post, *Little War*, 126–29.
23. Pérez, *War of 1898*, 83.
24. Trask, *War with Spain in 1898*, 210.
25. Pérez, *War of 1898*, 86.
26. Trask, *War with Spain in 1898*, 206.
27. Roosevelt, *Rough Riders*, 57.
28. Hagedorn, *Leonard Wood*, vol. 1, 162.
29. Roosevelt, *Rough Riders*, 57.
30. Morison, *Letters of Theodore Roosevelt*, vol. 8, 646.

18. Ambush

1. Marshall and Outcault, *Story of the Rough Riders*, 91.
2. Roosevelt, *Rough Riders*, 60–61.
3. Marshall, *Story of the Rough Riders*, 95–100.
4. Ibid., 103, 111–12, 115, 119, 124.
5. Roosevelt, *Rough Riders*, 65.
6. Marshall and Outcault, *Story of the Rough Riders*, 104; Roosevelt, *Rough Riders*, 67.
7. Roosevelt, *An Autobiography*, 242.
8. Roosevelt, *Rough Riders*, 63.
9. Ibid., 67–68.

10. Millis, *Martial Spirit*, 274.
11. Hagedorn, *Leonard Wood*, vol. 1, 168–69; Jones, *Roosevelt's Rough Riders*, 134.
12. Morison, *Letters of Theodore Roosevelt*, vol. 1, 844.
13. Roosevelt, *An Autobiography*, 244–45.
14. Trask, *War with Spain in 1898*, 222.
15. Roosevelt, *Rough Riders*, 71.
16. Lubow, *Reporter Who Would Be King*, 178.
17. Morison, *Letters of Theodore Roosevelt*, vol. 2, 844–45.
18. Brown, *Correspondents' War*, 177.
19. Post, *Little War of Private Post*, 116.
20. Lubow, *Reporter Who Would Be King*, 180.
21. Davis, *Cuban and Porto Rican Campaigns*, 133–34.
22. Brown, *Correspondents' War*, 179.
23. See Roosevelt, *Rough Riders*, 199–200; Trask, *War with Spain in 1898*, 222. But see Edmund Morris, *Rise of Theodore Roosevelt*, footnote 48 on 847; Milton, *Yellow Kids*, 316–18; Samuels and Samuels, *Teddy Roosevelt at San Juan Hill*, 144–78.
24. Lubow, *Reporter Who Would Be King*, 179–80.
25. Davis, *Cuban and Porto Rican Campaigns*, 151–53.
26. Jones, *Roosevelt's Rough Riders*, 135, 138, 147.
27. Renehan, *Lion's Pride*, 30.
28. Morison, *Letters of Theodore Roosevelt*, vol. 2, 844–45.
29. Hemment, *Cannon and Camera*, 77–83; Rubens, *Liberty*, 300; Swanberg, *Citizen Hearst*, 153.
30. New York *Journal*, June 29, 1898.
31. Swanberg, *Citizen Hearst*, 183; Morison, *Letters of Theodore Roosevelt*, vol. 2, 845.
32. Davis, *Cuban and Porto Rican Campaigns*, 176.
33. Roosevelt, *Rough Riders*, 75.
34. Azoy, *Charge!*, 102.
35. Trask, *War with Spain in 1898*, 230–31; G. J. A. O'Toole, *Spanish War*, 293–94; Roosevelt, *An Autobiography*, 245; Davis, *Cuban and Porto Rican Campaigns*, 180.
36. Azoy, *Charge!*, 108.
37. Roosevelt, *Rough Riders*, 77–78.
38. Edmund Morris, *Rise of Theodore Roosevelt*, 650.
39. Roosevelt, *Rough Riders*, 79.

19. The Crowded Hour

1. Edith Roosevelt to TR, June 27, 1898, Theodore Roosevelt Collection, Houghton Library, Harvard University.

2. Sylvia Jukes Morris, *Edith Kermit Roosevelt*, 180.

3. Edith Roosevelt to Emily Carow, July 3, 1898, Theodore Roosevelt Collection, Houghton Library, Harvard University.

4. Sylvia Jukes Morris, *Edith Kermit Roosevelt*, 175, 181.

5. Edith Roosevelt to TR, July 1, 1898, Theodore Roosevelt Collection, Houghton Library, Harvard University.

6. Edith Roosevelt to Emily Carow, July 3, 1898, Theodore Roosevelt Collection, Houghton Library, Harvard University.

7. Sylvia Jukes Morris, *Edith Kermit Roosevelt*, 182; undated letters of Edith Roosevelt to Emily Carow, 1898, Theodore Roosevelt Collection, Houghton Library, Harvard University.

8. Collier, *Roosevelts*, 94.

9. G. J. A. O'Toole, *Spanish War*, 299, 302; Millis, *Martial Spirit*, 163.

10. Roosevelt, *Rough Riders*, 79–80; G. J. A. O'Toole, *Spanish War*, 303.

11. Roosevelt, *Rough Riders*, 80.

12. Ibid., 81; Trask, *War with Spain in 1898*, 239.

13. Davis, *Cuban and Porto Rican Campaigns*, 212.

14. Azoy, *Charge!*, 121–25.

15. Post, *Little War of Private Post*, 179.

16. Cosby, "A Roosevelt Rough Rider Looks Back," 103.

17. Roosevelt, *Rough Riders*, 82–83.

18. Samuels and Samuels, *Teddy Roosevelt at San Juan Hill*, 238.

19. Morison, *Letters of Theodore Roosevelt*, vol. 2, 853; Roosevelt, *Rough Riders*, 84.

20. Roosevelt, *Rough Riders*, 84–85.

21. Jones, *Roosevelt's Rough Riders*, 180.

22. Roosevelt, *Rough Riders*, 87–88; Jones, *Roosevelt's Rough Riders*, 181; author's tour of battle sites in Cuba.

23. Samuels and Samuels, *Teddy Roosevelt*, 248–62.

24. Jones, *Roosevelt's Rough Riders*, 181–82.

25. Davis, *Cuban and Porto Rican Campaigns*, 217–20.

26. Samuels and Samuels, *Teddy Roosevelt*, 254.

27. Jones, *Roosevelt's Rough Riders*, 182–84; Roosevelt, *An Autobiography*, 247.

28. Roosevelt, *Rough Riders*, 89–91.

29. Samuels and Samuels, *Teddy Roosevelt*, 269–70.

30. Ibid., 305.

31. Edmund Morris, *Rise of Theodore Roosevelt*, 654.

32. Post, *Little War of Private Post*, 192; Roosevelt, *Rough Riders*, 91.

33. Sylvia Jukes Morris, *Edith Kermit Roosevelt*, 181.

34. Post, *Little War of Private Post*, 163.

35. Milton, *Yellow Kids*, 331.

36. Creelman, *On the Great Highway*, 195.
37. Hemment, *Cannon and Camera*, 153; Creelman, *On the Great Highway*, 196.
38. Creelman, *On the Great Highway*, 203–12.
39. New York *Journal*, July 4, 1898.
40. Nasaw, *The Chief*, 141.

20. Matters of Honor

1. Roosevelt, *Rough Riders*, 95–96.
2. Gatewood, *Black Americans and the White Man's Burden*, 4–6, 75, 92–97.
3. Roosevelt, *Rough Riders*, 96; Gatewood, *"Smoked Yankees" and the Struggle for Empire*, 44–45, 78. See Morison, *Letters of Theodore Roosevelt*, vol. 2, 1304–6.
4. Gatewood, *"Smoked Yankees" and the Struggle for Empire*, 94.
5. Samuels and Samuels, *Teddy Roosevelt at San Juan Hill*, 265.
6. Roosevelt, *Pocket Diary, 1898*, July 1, 1898.
7. Roosevelt, *Rough Riders*, 98–101; Jones, *Roosevelt's Rough Riders*, 27, 61, 187, 193.
8. Roosevelt, *Rough Riders*, 101, 104. But see Roosevelt, *An Autobiography*, 265–67.
9. Morison, *Letters of Theodore Roosevelt*, vol. 2, 861.
10. Trask, *War with Spain in 1898*, 249–254; Musicant, *Empire by Default*, 428.
11. Roosevelt, *An Autobiography*, 249.
12. Davis, *Cuban and Porto Rican Campaigns*, 249; Lubow, *Reporter Who Would Be King*, 189.
13. Musicant, *Empire by Default*, 435–36.
14. G. J. A. O'Toole, *Spanish War*, 329–33.
15. Musicant, *Empire by Default*, 443–66.
16. Hemment, *Cannon and Camera*, 110–11, 206, 214–25; Nasaw, *The Chief*, 139–40.
17. Edmund Morris, *Rise of Theodore Roosevelt*, 657; Jones, *Roosevelt's Rough Riders*, 208, 228; Roosevelt, *Rough Riders*, 126.
18. Jones, *Roosevelt's Rough Riders*, 209; Trask, *War with Spain in 1898*, 335.
19. Roosevelt and Lodge, *Selections from the Correspondence*, vol. 1, 324–25.
20. Ibid., 316–20.
21. Lubow, *Reporter Who Would Be King*, 187; Samuels and Samuels, *Teddy Roosevelt at San Juan Hill*, 300–307.
22. Zimmerman, *First Great Triumph*, 297–98.
23. Azoy, *Charge!*, 157; Trask, *War with Spain in 1898*, 315.
24. G. J. A. O'Toole, *Spanish War*, 351; Jones, *Roosevelt's Rough Riders*, 238–44.
25. Ferrer, *Insurgent Cuba*, 190.
26. Milton, *Yellow Kids*, 348.

27. Whyte, *Uncrowned King*, 419.
28. Ferrer, *Insurgent Cuba*, 189.
29. Tone, *War and Genocide in Cuba*, 279–80.
30. Chanler, ed., *Winthrop Chanler Letters*, 89.
31. HCL to Henry White, August 12, 1898, MHS.
32. Morison, *Letters of Theodore Roosevelt*, vol. 2, 851–53.

21. Spoils of War

1. Edmund Morris, *Rise of Theodore Roosevelt*, 658.
2. Paine, *Roads of Adventure*, 269–70.
3. Roosevelt, *An Autobiography*, 252; Morison, *Letters of Theodore Roosevelt*, vol. 2, 864–65.
4. Long, *Journal*, August 7, 1898, MHS.
5. G. J. A. O'Toole, *Spanish War*, 362.
6. New York *Journal*, August 16, 1898.
7. Riis, "Mrs. Roosevelt and Her Children," *Ladies' Home Journal*, August 1902.
8. Sylvia Jukes Morris, *Edith Kermit Roosevelt*, 183.
9. Edith Roosevelt to Emily Carow, August 22, 1898, Theodore Roosevelt Collection, Houghton Library, Harvard University.
10. Morison, *Letters of Theodore Roosevelt*, vol. 2, 869.
11. Dalton, *Theodore Roosevelt*, 179; Sylvia Jukes Morris, *Edith Kermit Roosevelt*, 184–85.
12. Morison, *Letters of Theodore Roosevelt*, vol. 2, 873.
13. HCL to Winthrop Chanler, August 26, 1898, MHS.
14. Dalton, *Theodore Roosevelt*, 6.
15. Morris, *Rise of Theodore Roosevelt*, 672–74; Riis, *Theodore Roosevelt*, 199–200.
16. Morison, *Letters of Theodore Roosevelt*, vol. 2, 880.
17. Morris, *Rise of Theodore Roosevelt*, 678.
18. Swanberg, *Citizen Hearst*, 165–66; Brisbane, "Great Problems in Organization: The Modern Newspaper in War Time," *Cosmopolitan*, September 1898.
19. Swanberg, *Citizen Hearst*, 164.
20. Nasaw, *The Chief*, 145; Musicant, *Empire by Default*, 635–36; New York *Journal*, September 22, October 15, 28, 1898.
21. Nasaw, *The Chief*, 147–48.
22. HCL to John Hay, August 17, 1898, MHS.
23. Thayer, *John Hay*, vol. 2, 337.
24. Adams, *Education of Henry Adams*, 360.
25. Samuels, ed., *Henry Adams*, 346; Adams, *Letters of Henry Adams*, vols. 4–6, 589.
26. John Hay to HCL, April 5, 1898, MHS.
27. Patricia O'Toole, *Five of Hearts*, 300.

28. Ibid., 302–3.
29. HCL to George Lyman, June 8, 1898; HCL to Brooke Adams, June 20, 1898; HCL to George Lyman, June 15, 1898; George Lyman to HCL, June 21, 1898; all MHS.
30. HCL to Anna Lodge, June 26, 1898, MHS.
31. HCL to Josephine Shaw Lowell, July 23, 1898, MHS.
32. Garraty, *Henry Cabot Lodge*, 195–96.
33. Roosevelt and Lodge, *Selections from the Correspondence*, vol. 1, 323.
34. Zimmerman, *First Great Triumph*, 312.
35. Karnow, *In Our Image*, 67, 74–75.
36. Zimmerman, *First Great Triumph*, 304–8.
37. Widenor, *Henry Cabot Lodge*, 111; Samuels, ed., *Henry Adams*, 345.
38. HCL to John Hay, April 21, 1898, MHS.
39. Widenor, *Henry Cabot Lodge*, 113.
40. Zimmerman, *First Great Triumph*, 312, 319–20.
41. Leech, *In the Days of McKinley*, 342.

22. A Certain Blindness

1. Santayana, *Middle Span*, vol. 2, 166–67.
2. Beisner, *Twelve Against Empire*, 46.
3. See, generally, ibid., 38–52.
4. Skrupskelis and Berkeley, eds., *Correspondence of William James*, vol. 8, 379–83; Robert Richardson, *William James*, 375.
5. Ibid., 384.
6. Skrupskelis and Berkeley, eds., *Correspondence of William James*, vol. 3, 38, and vol. 8, 388.
7. Ibid., vol. 8, 390–91.
8. Robert Richardson, *William James*, 382.
9. Ibid., 375–76.
10. Ibid., 403.
11. Skrupskelis and Berkeley, eds., *Correspondence of William James*, vol. 2, 42.
12. Ibid., vol. 8, 418.
13. Robert Richardson, *William James*, 381, 385.
14. Skrupskelis and Berkeley, eds., *Correspondence of William James*, vol. 8, 454.
15. Dalton, *Theodore Roosevelt*, 179–80.
16. Edith Roosevelt to Emily Carow, September 23, October 19, 1898; January 3, 1899, Theodore Roosevelt Collection, Houghton Library, Harvard University.
17. HCL to Cushman Davis, November 18, 1898, MHS.
18. Roosevelt and Lodge, *Selections from the Correspondence*, vol. 1, 368.
19. Morison, *Letters of Theodore Roosevelt*, vol. 2, 924.
20. Garraty, *Henry Cabot Lodge*, 201–2.

21. Zimmerman, *First Great Triumph*, 325.
22. HCL to Anna Lodge, February 5, 12, 1899, MHS.
23. Zimmerman, *First Great Triumph*, 354–56.
24. Widenor, *Henry Cabot Lodge*, 117; Roosevelt and Lodge, *Selections from the Correspondence*, vol. 1, 393.
25. Widenor, *Henry Cabot Lodge*, 120.
26. Morison, *Letters of Theodore Roosevelt*, vol. 2, 1112, 1119, 1138, 1159, 1267–68.
27. Ibid., 1337–38.
28. Beisner, *Twelve Against Empire*, 39.
29. Santayana, *Middle Span*, 168.
30. Beisner, *Twelve Against Empire*, 40, 44, 48.
31. Schirmer, *Republic or Empire*, 236.
32. Karnow, *In Our Image*, 12–14.
33. Zimmerman, *First Great Triumph*, 412–15; Garraty, *Henry Cabot Lodge*, 210.
34. Robinson, *Thomas B. Reed*, 369, 378–81.
35. *New York Times*, April 19, November 22, 1899.
36. Diary of Thomas Reed, January 1, 1900, Thomas Reed Collection, Bowdoin College, Brunswick, Maine.
37. Ibid., January 15, 1902.
38. TR to Thomas Reed, June 14, 1891, Thomas Reed Collection, Bowdoin College, Brunswick, Maine.
39. Roosevelt and Lodge, *Selections from the Correspondence*, vol. 1, 370; HCL to Anna Lodge, June 4, 1899, MHS.
40. Diary of Thomas Reed, June 3, July 23, August 26, September 3, 4, 6, 1902, Thomas Reed Collection, Bowdoin College, Brunswick, Maine.
41. Robinson, *Thomas B. Reed*, 384; Bangor (Maine) *Daily News*, December 8, 1902; Boston *Herald*, December 8, 1902.
42. Bangor *Daily News*, December 8, 1902.
43. Thomas Reed to George Gifford, April 17, 1902, Thomas Reed Collection, Bowdoin College, Brunswick, Maine.
44. Zimmerman, *First Great Triumph*, 374–75.
45. Pérez, *War of 1898*, 35.
46. Ferrer, *Insurgent Cuba*, 201.
47. Scott, *Degrees of Freedom*, 186–87, 201–14.
48. Ibid., 214, 223, 242–44.
49. Pérez, *War of 1898*, 125–27.

23. Never Ending

1. Skrupskelis and Berkeley, eds., *William and Henry James*, 409.
2. Garrison and Madden, "William James: Warts and All," *American Quarterly* 29, no. 2 (Summer 1977), 212.

3. Robert Richardson, *William James*, 515.
4. Ibid., 388, 400, 492.
5. Ibid., 515.
6. Lewis, *The Jameses*, 583.
7. Josephine Shaw Lowell to Edward Emerson, August 24, October 3, 1904, MHS.
8. Morison, *Letters of Theodore Roosevelt*, vol. 2, 1193.
9. Jacob Riis, "In Memoriam: Josephine Shaw Lowell," 43–101.
10. Heather Cox Richardson, *West from Appomattox*, 334.
11. Garraty, *Henry Cabot Lodge*, 225.
12. Patricia O'Toole, *When Trumpets Call*, 30.
13. Swanberg, *Citizen Hearst*, 175–230.
14. Nasaw, *The Chief*, 208–12.
15. Ibid., 249.
16. Dalton, "Theodore Roosevelt and the Idea of War," *Theodore Roosevelt Association Journal*, Fall 1981, 10.
17. Patricia O'Toole, *When Trumpets Call*, 252–57, 283, 285.
18. Collier, *Roosevelts*, 194.
19. Dalton, "Theodore Roosevelt and the Idea of War," 10.
20. Patricia O'Toole, *When Trumpets Call*, 360, 350.
21. Morison, *Letters of Theodore Roosevelt*, vol. 8, 1359.
22. See, generally, Patricia O'Toole, *When Trumpets Call*, 386–404; author's tour of Sagamore Hill.
23. Roosevelt and Lodge, *Hero Tales*, 182.
24. Roosevelt and Lodge, *Selections from the Correspondence*, vol. 2, 535.
25. Patricia O'Toole, *When Trumpets Call*, 404.
26. Garraty, *Henry Cabot Lodge*, 220–21, 292.
27. Roosevelt and Lodge, *Selections from the Correspondence*, vol. 2, 550.
28. Garraty, *Henry Cabot Lodge*, 246, 270–72.
29. Daniels, *Time Between the Wars*, 16–59.
30. Miller, *Henry Cabot Lodge*, 65.
31. Garraty, *Henry Cabot Lodge*, 421.
32. Collier, *Roosevelts*, 126.
33. Patricia O'Toole, *When Trumpets Call*, 369–73.
34. Renehan, *Lion's Pride*, 226.
35. Collier, *Roosevelts*, 399.
36. Renehan, *Lion's Pride*, 34, 236–37.

Bibliography

Manuscript Collections

Asher Hinds Diary, Manuscript Division, Library of Congress, Washington, D.C.

Papers of Henry Cabot Lodge, Massachusetts Historical Society, Boston

Theodore Roosevelt Collection, Houghton Library, Harvard University, Cambridge, Massachusetts

Thomas B. Reed Collection, Bowdoin College, Brunswick, Maine

Books and Articles

Abbott, Lawrence. *The Letters of Archie Butt.* Garden City, NY: Doubleday, 1924.

Abbott, Willis J. *Watching the World Go By.* Boston: Little, Brown and Company, 1933.

Adams, Henry. *The Letters of Henry Adams.* Vols. 4–6. Cambridge, MA: Harvard University Press, 1989.

———. *Education of Henry Adams.* Boston: Mariner Books, 2000.

Aldrich, Nelson. *Old Money: The Mythology of America's Upper Class.* New York: Knopf, 1988.

Allen, Thomas. "Remember the Maine?" *National Geographic* 193, no. 2 February 1998.

Azoy, A. C. M. *Charge! The Story of the Battle of San Juan Hill.* New York: Longmans, Green, 1961.

Baker, Liva. *Justice from Beacon Hill: The Life and Times of Oliver Wendell Holmes.* New York: HarperCollins, 1991.

"Beauties of Wooded Island." *Current Literature* 14, October 1893.

Beer, Thomas. *Hanna, Crane and the Mauve Decade.* New York: Knopf, 1941.

Beisner, Robert L. *Twelve Against Empire: The Anti-Imperialists, 1898–1900.* New York: McGraw-Hill, 1968.

Bergin, Thomas G. *The Game: The Harvard-Yale Football Rivalry, 1875–1983.* New Haven, CT: Yale University Press, 1984.

Blight, David. *Race and Reunion: The Civil War in American History.* Cambridge, MA: Belknap Press of Harvard University Press, 2001.

BIBLIOGRAPHY

"Boone and Crockett Club." *Forest and Stream* 30, no. 7, March 8, 1888.

Brands, H. W. *The Reckless Decade: America in the 1890's.* New York: St. Martin's, 1995.

Brisbane, Arthur. "Great Problems in Organization: The Modern Newspaper in War Time." *Cosmopolitan*, September 1898.

Brown, Charles H. *The Correspondents' War: Journalists in the Spanish-American War.* New York: Charles Scribner's Sons, 1967.

Bundy, Carol. *The Nature of Sacrifice: A Biography of Charles Russell Lowell, Jr. 1835–1864.* New York: Farrar, Straus and Giroux, 2005.

Caroli, Betty Boyd. *The Roosevelt Women.* New York: Basic Books, 1998.

Chanler, Margaret. *Roman Spring: Memoirs.* Boston: Little, Brown and Company, 1934.

Chanler, Mary, ed. *Winthrop Chanler Letters.* New York: Privately printed, 1951.

Collier, Peter. *The Roosevelts: An American Saga.* New York: Simon and Schuster, 1995.

Cosby, Arthur F. "A Roosevelt Rough Rider Looks Back." Unpublished manuscript in Theodore Roosevelt Collection, Houghton Library, Harvard University.

Cotkin, George. *William James: Public Philosopher.* Urbana: University of Illinois Press, 1994.

Creelman, James. *On the Great Highway: The Wanderings and Adventures of a Special Correspondent.* Boston: Lothrop, 1901.

Cross, Wilbur. "The Perils of Evangelina." *American Heritage* 19, no. 2, February 1968.

Dalton, Kathleen. "Theodore Roosevelt and the Idea of War." *Theodore Roosevelt Association Journal*, Fall 1981.

———. *Theodore Roosevelt: A Strenuous Life.* New York: Vintage Books, 2002.

Daniels, Jonathan. *The Time Between the Wars.* Garden City, NY: Doubleday, 1966.

Davis, Richard Harding. *Cuban and Porto Rican Campaigns.* New York: Charles Scribner's, 1898.

———. "The Rocking-Chair Period of the War." *Scribner's Magazine* 24, no. 2, August 1898.

Dewey, George. *Autobiography of George Dewey: Admiral of the Navy.* New York: Charles Scribner's, 1913.

Dunn, Arthur Wallace. *Gridiron Nights.* New York: Frederick Stokes, 1915.

———. *From Harrison to Harding: A Personal Narrative.* Vols. 1 and 2. New York: G. P. Putnam's Sons, 1922.

Dyer, Thomas G. *Theodore Roosevelt and the Idea of Race.* Baton Rouge: Louisiana State University Press, 1980.

Ferrer, Ada. *Insurgent Cuba: Race, Nation and Revolution, 1868–1898.* Chapel Hill: University of North Carolina Press, 1999.

BIBLIOGRAPHY

Fisher, Paul. *House of Wits: An Intimate Portrait of the James Family.* New York: Henry Holt, 2008.

Ford, Worthington Chauncey, ed. *Letters of Henry Adams.* Vol. 2. Boston: Houghton Mifflin, 1938.

Fry, Joseph A. "William McKinley and the Coming of the Spanish-American War: A Study of the Besmirching and Redemption of an Historical Image." *Diplomatic History* 3, no. 1, Winter 1979.

Garraty, John A. *Henry Cabot Lodge: A Biography.* New York: Knopf, 1953.

Garrison, George R., and Edward H. Madden. "William James: Warts and All." *American Quarterly* 29, no. 2, Summer 1977.

Gatewood, Willard B., Jr. "Negro Troops in Florida, 1898." *Florida Historical Quarterly* 49, no. 1, July 1970.

———."*Smoked Yankees*" *and the Struggle for Empire.* Urbana: University of Illinois Press, 1971.

———. *Black Americans and the White Man's Burden.* Urbana: University of Illinois Press, 1975.

Goodwin, Doris Kearns. *The Fitzgeralds and the Kennedys.* New York: St. Martin's, 1987.

Gould, Lewis L. *The Presidency of William McKinley.* Lawrence, KS: Regents Press of Kansas, 1980.

Hagedorn, Hermann. *Leonard Wood: A Biography.* Vols. 1 and 2. New York: Harper's and Brothers, 1931.

Hattendorf, John B., ed. *The Influence of History on Mahan.* Newport, RI: Naval War College Press, 1991.

Hemment, John C. *Cannon and Camera.* New York: D. Appleton, 1898.

Hoganson, Kristin L. *Fighting for American Manhood: How Gender Politics Provoked the Spanish-American and Philippine-American Wars.* New Haven, CT: Yale University Press, 1998.

James, William. *Letters of William James.* Henry James, ed. Vol. 2. Boston: Atlantic Monthly Press, 1920.

Jones, Virgil Carrington. *Roosevelt's Rough Riders.* Garden City, NY: Doubleday, 1971.

Josephson, Matthew. *The President Makers: The Culture of Politics and Leadership in an Age of Enlightenment, 1896–1919.* New York: G. P. Putnam's Sons, 1968.

Karnow, Stanley. *In Our Image: America's Empire in the Philippines.* New York: Random House, 1989.

Kerr, Joan Paterson. *A Bully Father: Theodore Roosevelt's Letters to His Children.* New York: Random House, 1995.

Kohlstaat, Herman. *From McKinley to Harding: Personal Recollections of Our Past Presidents.* New York: Charles Scribner's, 1923.

Leech, Margaret. *In the Days of McKinley.* New York: Harper and Brothers, 1959.

BIBLIOGRAPHY

Leupp, Francis. "Personal Recollections of Thomas B. Reed." *Outlook*, September 3, 1910.

Levenson, J. C., ed. *Letters of Henry Adams*. Vol. 4. 1892–1899. Cambridge: Belknap Press of Harvard University Press, 1988.

Lewis, R. W. B. *The Jameses: A Family Narrative*. New York: Farrar, Straus and Giroux, 1991.

Lodge, Henry Cabot. "The Distribution of Ability in the United States." *Century Illustrated Magazine* 42, no. 5, September 1894.

———. *Early Memories*. New York: Charles Scribner's Sons, 1913.

———. *The Democracy of the Constitution*. Freeport, NY: Books for Libraries Press, 1966.

Long, John Davis. *Journal*. Rindge, NH: R. R. Smith, 1956.

Lubow, Arthur. *The Reporter Who Would Be King: A Biography of Richard Harding Davis*. New York: Charles Scribner's Sons, 1992.

Lundberg, Ferdinand. *Imperial Hearst: A Social History*. New York: Equinox Press, 1936.

Marshall, Edward, and Richard F. Outcault. *The Story of the Rough Riders*. New York: G. W. Dillingham, 1899.

McCall, Samuel. *The Life of Thomas Brackett Reed*. Boston: Houghton Mifflin, 1914.

McCullough, David. *Mornings on Horseback*. New York: Simon and Schuster, 1981.

Menand, Louis. *The Metaphysical Club*. New York: Farrar, Straus and Giroux, 2001.

Michelson, Charles. *The Ghost Talks*. New York: G. P. Putnam's Sons, 1944.

Miller, Stuart Creighton. *"Benevolent Assimilation": The American Conquest of the Philippines, 1899–1903*. New Haven, CT: Yale University Press, 1982.

Miller, William. *Henry Cabot Lodge: A Biography*. New York: James H. Heineman, 1967.

Millis, Walter. *The Martial Spirit*. Cambridge, MA: Riverside Press, 1931.

Milton, Joyce. *The Yellow Kids: Foreign Correspondents in the Heyday of Yellow Journalism*. New York: Harper & Row, 1989.

Morgan, Howard. *William McKinley and His America*. Kent, OH: Kent State University Press, 2003.

Morison, Elting E. *The Letters of Theodore Roosevelt*. Vols. 1, 2, and 8. Cambridge, MA: Harvard University Press, 1951, 1954.

Morris, Edmund. *The Rise of Theodore Roosevelt*. New York: Ballantine, 1979.

Morris, Sylvia Jukes. *Edith Kermit Roosevelt: Portrait of a First Lady*. New York: Coward, McCann and Geoghegan, 1980.

Musicant, Ivan. *Empire by Default: The Spanish-American War and the Dawn of the American Century*. New York: Henry Holt, 1998.

BIBLIOGRAPHY

Myers, Gerald E. *William James: His Life and Thought.* New Haven, CT: Yale University Press, 1986.

Nasaw, David. *The Chief: The Life of William Randolph Hearst.* Boston: Houghton Mifflin, 2000.

Offner, John L. *An Unwanted War: The Diplomacy of the United States and Spain Over Cuba, 1895–1898.* Chapel Hill: University of North Carolina Press, 1992.

O'Toole, G. J. A. *The Spanish War: An American Epic, 1898.* New York: W. W. Norton, 1984.

O'Toole, Patricia. *When Trumpets Call: Theodore Roosevelt After the White House.* New York: Simon and Schuster, 2005.

———. *The Five of Hearts: An Intimate Portrait of Henry Adams and His Friends, 1880–1918.* New York: Simon and Schuster, 2006.

Paine, Ralph D. *Roads of Adventure.* Boston: Houghton Mifflin, 1922.

Pascal, Janet B. *Jacob Riis: Reporter and Reformer.* Oxford: Oxford University Press, 2005.

Pérez, Louis A., Jr. *Lords of the Mountain: Social Banditry and Peasant Protest in Cuba, 1878–1918.* Pittsburgh, PA: University of Pittsburgh Press, 1989.

———. *The War of 1898: The United States and Cuba in History and Historiography.* Chapel Hill: University of North Carolina Press, 1998.

Perry, Ralph Barton. *The Thought and Character of William James.* Vols. 1 and 2. Boston: Little, Brown and Company, 1935.

Philippon, Daniel J. *Conserving Words: How American Nature Writers Shaped the Environmental Movement.* Athens: University of Georgia Press, 2002.

Pizzitola, Louis. *Hearst Over Hollywood: Power, Passion and Propaganda in the Movies.* New York: Columbia University Press, 2002.

Post, Charles. *The Little War of Private Post: The Spanish-American War Seen Up Close.* Lincoln: University of Nebraska Press, 1999.

Putnam, Carleton. *Theodore Roosevelt: A Biography.* New York: Scribner's, 1958.

Reed, Thomas B. "The New Navy." *Illustrated American.* September 25, 1897.

Rejali, Darius. *Torture and Democracy.* Princeton, NJ: Princeton University Press, 2007.

Renehan, Edward J., Jr. *The Lion's Pride: Theodore Roosevelt and His Family in Peace and War.* New York: Oxford University Press, 1998.

Richardson, Heather Cox. *West from Appomattox: The Reconstruction of America After the Civil War.* New Haven, CT: Yale University Press, 2007.

Richardson, Robert. *William James: In the Maelstrom of American Modernism.* Boston: Houghton Mifflin, 2006.

Rickover, H. G. *How the Battleship Maine Was Destroyed.* Washington, D.C.: Naval History Division, Department of the Navy, 1976.

BIBLIOGRAPHY

Riis, Jacob. "In Memoriam: Josephine Shaw Lowell." New York: Charity Organization of New York.

———. "Mrs. Roosevelt and Her Children." *Ladies' Home Journal*, August 1902.

———. *Theodore Roosevelt: The Citizen*. New York: Outlook Company, 1904.

Robinson, William A. *Thomas B. Reed: Parliamentarian*. New York: Dodd, Mead, 1930.

Roosevelt, Theodore. *Letters from Theodore Roosevelt to Anna Roosevelt Cowles, 1870–1910*. New York: Charles Scribner's, 1924.

———. *Selections from the Correspondence of Theodore Roosevelt and Henry Cabot Lodge, 1884–1918*. Vols. 1 and 2. New York: Scribner's, 1925.

———. *The Rough Riders*. New York: Signet, 1961.

———. *An Autobiography*. New York: DaCapo, 1985.

———. *Pocket Diary, 1898: Theodore Roosevelt's Private Account of the War with Spain*. Wallace Finley Daily, ed. Cambridge, MA: Harvard University Press, 1998.

Roosevelt, Theodore, and Henry Cabot Lodge. *Hero Tales*. Nashville: Cumberland House, 2000.

Roosevelt, Theodore, Jr. *All in the Family*. New York: G. P. Putnam's Sons, 1929.

Rotundo, E. Anthony. *American Manhood: Transformations in Masculinity from the Revolution to the Modern Era*. New York: Basic Books, 1993.

Rubens, Horatio S. *Liberty: The Story of Cuba*. New York: AMS, 1970.

Samuels, Ernest, ed. *Henry Adams: Selected Letters*. Cambridge, MA: Belknap Press of Harvard University Press, 1992.

Samuels, Peggy, and Harold Samuels. *Frederic Remington*. Austin: University of Texas Press, 1985.

———. *Teddy Roosevelt at San Juan Hill: The Making of a President*. College Station: Texas A&M Press, 1997.

Santayana, George. *The Middle Span: Persons and Places*. Vol. 2. New York: Charles Scribner's Sons, 1945.

Schirmer, Daniel B. *Republic or Empire: American Resistance to the Philippine War*. Cambridge, MA: Schenkman Publishing, 1972.

Scott, Rebecca. *Degrees of Freedom: Louisiana and Cuba After Slavery*. Cambridge, MA: Harvard University Press, 2005.

Seeger, Robert, and Doris D. Maguire, eds. *Letters and Papers of Alfred Thayer Mahan*. Vol. 2, 1890–1901. Annapolis, MD: Naval Institute Press, 1975.

Skrupskelis, Ignas K., and Elizabeth M. Berkeley, eds. *Correspondence of William James*. Vols. 2 and 3. Charlottesville: University of Virginia Press, 1993, 1994.

———. *William and Henry James: Selected Letters*. Charlottesville: University of Virginia Press, 1997.

BIBLIOGRAPHY

————. *Correspondence of William James.* Vol. 8. Charlottesville: University of Virginia Press, 2000.

Slotkin, Richard. *Gunfighter Nation: The Myth of the Frontier in Twentieth-Century America.* New York: Atheneum, 1992.

Spector, Ronald. *Admiral of the New Empire: The Life and Career of George Dewey.* Columbia: University of South Carolina Press, 1974.

Stevens, John D. *Sensationalism and the New York Press.* New York: Columbia University Press, 1991.

Stevens, Walter B. "Characteristics of Congressmen." *Leslie's Popular Monthly,* June 1894.

Swanberg, W. A. *Citizen Hearst.* New York: Charles Scribner's Sons, 1961.

Teague, Michael. *Mrs. L: Conversations with Alice Roosevelt Longworth.* Garden City, NY: Doubleday, 1972.

Thayer, William Roscoe. *John Hay.* Vol. 2. Boston: Houghton Mifflin, 1916.

Tone, John Lawrence. *War and Genocide in Cuba, 1895–1898.* Chapel Hill: University of North Carolina Press, 2006.

Townsend, Kim. *Manhood at Harvard: William James and Others.* New York: W. W. Norton, 1996.

Trask, David F. *The War with Spain in 1898.* Lincoln: University of Nebraska Press, 1981.

Tuchman, Barbara. *The Proud Tower.* New York: Macmillan, 1966.

Vorpahl, Ben. *My Dear Wister: The Frederic Remington–Owen Wister Letters.* Palo Alto, CA: American West Publishing, 1972.

Waugh, John. *Unsentimental Reformer: The Life of Josephine Shaw Lowell.* Cambridge, MA: Harvard University Press, 1997.

Werth, Barry. *Banquet at Delmonico's: Great Minds, the Gilded Age, and the Triumph of Evolution in America.* New York: Random House, 2009.

Westermeier, Clifford. *Who Rush to Glory: The Cowboy Volunteers of 1898.* Caldwell, ID: Caxton, 1958.

Whyte, Kenneth. *The Uncrowned King.* Berkeley, CA: Counterpoint, 2009.

Widenor, William. *Henry Cabot Lodge and the Search for an American Foreign Policy.* Berkeley: University of California Press, 1980.

Wilkinson, Burke. *Uncommon Clay: The Life and Works of Augustus Saint Gaudens.* New York: Harcourt, Brace, Jovanovich, 1985.

Wister, Owen. *Roosevelt: The Story of a Friendship, 1880–1919.* New York: Macmillan, 1930.

————. *Owen Wister Out West: His Journals and Letters.* Fanny Kemble Wister, ed. Chicago: University of Chicago Press, 1958.

Zimmerman, Warren. *First Great Triumph: How Five Americans Made Their Country a World Power.* New York: Farrar, Straus and Giroux, 2002.

Index

INDEX

INDEX

INDEX

INDEX

INDEX

INDEX

INDEX

INDEX